The United States Marine Corps in the Civil War— The First Year

by
David M. Sullivan

 White Mane Publishing Company, Inc.

This White Mane Publishing Company, Inc. publication
was printed by
Beidel Printing House, Inc.
63 West Burd Street
Shippensburg, PA 17257-0152 USA

In respect for the scholarship contained herein, the acid-free paper used in this book meets the guidelines for permanence and durability of the Committee on Production Guidelines for Book Longevity of the Council on Library Resources.

For a complete list of available publications
please write
White Mane Publishing Company, Inc.
P.O. Box 152
Shippensburg, PA 17257-0152 USA

Library of Congress Cataloging-in-Publication Data

Sullivan, David M., 1942-
The United States Marine Corps in the Civil War / by David M. Sullivan.
p. cm.
Includes bibliographical references and index.
Contents: v. 1. The first year
ISBN 1-57249-040-3 (v. 1 : acid-free paper)
1. United States. Marine Corps--History--Civil War, 1861-1865.
2. United States--History--Civil War, 1861-1865--Campaigns.
I. Title.
E591.S94 1997
973.7'41--dc21 97-19798
CIP

PRINTED IN THE UNITED STATES OF AMERICA

To my wife, Peg,
for being with me
throughout the entire journey

Table of Contents

List of Illustrations

All National Archives photographs in the text with the prefix 127, followed by the letters G or N, were accumulated by, and formerly under the custody of the Marine Corps Historical Center. Those marked below with an asterisk are published for the first time.

Chapter 1

Chapter 2

Chapter 3

Chapter 4

Chapter 5

Chapter 6

Chapter 7

Chapter 8

Foreword

In 1775 this fledgling nation established a navy and authorized a Corps of Marines. This small corps of soldiers-from-the-sea initially served on board men of war as ship's police, and, when engaged in battle, boarded the enemy or prevented him from doing the same. When ashore they served as security forces at naval ship yards.

Some eighty-five years later, as the dark storm clouds of the Civil War swept over the United States, the role of Marines had changed very little. Sixty-three officers, and some 1,800 enlisted men were carried on the rolls of the Corps, primarily at sea. It was a Corps which knew only the rudiments of battalion drill. Operations above the company level were but a distant memory from the Mexican War.

After the first shots of the Civil War thundered at Fort Sumter, the nation's Corps of Marines would dramatically change and expand. Beginning with the first battle of Manassas, Marine battalions saw active service in the field. Their naval role would expand far beyond the vision of our founding forefathers, and in doing so, prepare the Marine Corps for the expeditionary missions it would provide the United States during the 20th and into the 21st century.

Over the past four decades, three major histories of the Marine Corps have been published. The Marine tradition has benefited greatly from these excellent works. However, relatively few pages in each of these works is devoted to the Civil War. This perpetuates the image that the Corps contributed little, and did nothing to distinguish itself. That notion will now be forever dispatched. David Sullivan has turned his long and diverse research into a full-length history of the Corps in the Civil War. And he does it masterfully. In weaving an expanding role for Marines to serve their nation, Sullivan observes how they begin to ingrain themselves with the virtues of moral leadership and personal ethical standards which all Marines, past, present, and future, aspire to live by.

Sullivan has captured the personal struggles of this unique time in history when Marines and shipmates separated by ideology, a love for their home states and families, had to eventually fight against one another. The national schism is reflected among the officers of the United States Marine Corps. Twenty officers severed the bonds of brotherhood to follow the fortunes of the South. Nineteen formed the nucleus of the Confederate States Marine Corps, and faced their former comrades in arms in battle throughout the war.

The reader meets Col. Robert E. Lee and a young J.E.B. Stuart of the U.S. Army, and 1st Lt. Israel Greene, commander of the Marines, as the incident at Harpers Ferry is related in vivid detail. He feels the emotion of the Marines as they avenge the death of a shipmate, Pvt. Luke Quinn, first Marine fatality in what was to become the Civil War.

From Harpers Ferry, the Marines fight valiantly through the pages of his work, participating in every major and most minor naval engagements of the war. The author's meticulous research explodes many myths, and corrects injustices that have existed for over a century. Among the fallacies which have persisted is the misconception that the Marines at Bull Run gave a poor accounting of themselves. In the words of a Confederate officer who witnessed their actions, nothing could be further from the truth. It has now been revealed that after being bloodied and beaten back, Marines rallied and advanced further into the Confederate lines than any other Union force during the battle. In spite of their lack of experience and limited training, the spirit of Semper Fidelis (not yet the official motto of the Marine Corps) prevailed. Marines of all ages owe a great deal of debt to Mr. Sullivan for uncovering the details of this valiant incident, and adding it to the annals of our Corps.

Marines were unjustly given the blame for the debacle of the Naval Column at the Second Battle of Fort Fisher (January 15, 1865). Sullivan provides evidence that the failure was due to improper planning and leadership on the part of Rear Adm. David D. Porter, and the ineptitude of Lt. Cdr. K. Randolph Breese, who was totally inexperienced in operations ashore. The Marines went where they were told to go, and did what they were trained to do. Many died gallantly. The blame for the repulse of the naval force had to be put somewhere, and Porter was reluctant to accept it. The Marines served a purpose, totally unfair and unjustified.

It is a revealing history, a walk through history so to speak, as we note the Corps' expansion. As early as 1861, when Northern forces blockaded the South Atlantic Coast, the mission of shipboard Marines began to evolve into an expeditionary role. When combat missions arose ashore, all Marines went over the side. Most often, these were hastily assembled ship's detachments sent to capture prisoners, seize small islands, or conduct riverine operations. On occasion, however, large numbers of Marines served as components in brigade-sized combat operations ashore. Viewed from the perspective of history, it is possible to equate these primitive maneuvers from-the-sea to the modern Marine Corps in its role as the nation's Force-in-Readiness, capable of projecting naval power ashore anywhere in the world.

The depth of Sullivan's research is astounding, for he has truly compiled the most complete documentation of the Civil War Corps. Discovering numerous, never before referenced original source materials, Sullivan interweaves his biographic history with a blending of official correspondence, personal papers, and letters of young Marines, recording moments of heroism, personal hardship, trials of small unit leadership, and the horrors of war. It was not the intent of the author to simply glorify the Marine Corps. The austere living conditions, the fear, the greed, the tremendous obstacles put in the way by the system of the times, and the political maneuvering of officers who could have better served their Corps by putting ambition and personal desires aside are part of this chronicle.

A history of the United States Marines in the Civil War is long overdue. David M. Sullivan has devoted nearly a decade in compiling *The United States Marine Corps in the Civil War.* It will become a classic. This fast moving, all encompassing account will be fascinating reading for all U.S. Marines, as will as Civil War scholars, and anyone simply interested in learning the true details of the Marines' participation in the War Between the States. These volumes are rich with incidents where the heroic actions of individual Marines in the Civil War could well serve as role models for Marines entering the 21st century.

It has always been a distinct honor to serve in the nation's Corps of Marines. However, it has never been easy, nor is it intended to be! Only special people who have gone through the "Rites of Passage"—the tough training, education, discipline, and demanding experience of recruit training at locations like Philadelphia, Quantico, Parris Island, and San Diego—earn the title United States Marine. They keep the title, and the pride they have in being a Marine, through dedicated, selfless service to our great nation in peace, war, or other conflicts and dangerous situations. Always faithful in combat and in life—hence, "Once a Marine, Always a Marine." Our Civil War brothers, neglected by history, bypassed for over a century, have truly earned and retained the title Marine.

We Marines owe David M. Sullivan a special debt of gratitude for his authoritatively researched effort of our Civil War Warriors. Henceforth, when we gaze upon the Marine Corps Battle Color at a parade or ceremony, the blue and grey Civil War battle streamer displayed with all the other honors bestowed upon our Corps will have a special meaning for us. The gallant Warriors of that era will share rightfully in the love and respect we harbor in our hearts for all Marines.

Marines, past, present, and future should read and re-read this account to insure that the important lessons of this tragic period in American and Marine Corps History are learned—never again to be repeated or forgotten. Clearly, this book is a prime candidate for our Commandant to consider for his Reading List.

Semper Fidelis,
Al Gray, Marine
29th Commandant

Acknowledgments

All historical works are constructed upon a foundation of contributions made by persons who were willing to give of themselves beyond what was expected. These volumes are no different. Throughout the course of the research, a select group of friends sustained my efforts, providing assistance from their special fields of endeavor. Without them, this work would never have come to fruition. Alphabetically listed, a debt of gratitude is owed Alice S. Creighton, Head, Special Collections Branch, Nimitz Library, United States Naval Academy; Lt. Col. Charles H. Cureton, USMCR, Chief, Museums and Historical Services, Fort Monroe, Virginia; Charles R. Haberlein, Jr., Curator, Photographs Section, Naval Historical Center; the late Prof. Edward Haggeman, University of Louisville; Prof. Jay S. Hoar, University of Maine; Becky Livingston, Military Reference Branch, National Archives; Richard T. Long, Oral Histories Branch, Marine Corps Historical Center; Michael J. McAfee, Curator, West Point Museum; George Menegaux, former GySgt., USMC; J. Michael Miller, Senior Archivist, Marine Corps University Archives; Lt. Col. Edward S. Milligan, USA (Ret.); James Nicholson, Philadelphia *Daily News;* Col. F. Brooke Nihart, USMC (Ret.); Harry Roach, Publisher and Editor of *Military Images;* Charles R. Smith, Historical Writer, Marine Corps Historical Center; Kenneth L. Smith-Christmas, Curator of Material History, Marine Corps History and Museums Branch; Maj. Richard T. Spooner, USMC (Ret.); and A. Kerry Strong, Director, Marine Corps University Archives.

The generosity of the Marine Corps Historical Foundation in providing a grant to finance the research for this endeavor is acknowledged with grateful appreciation.

Special thanks are also due Dr. Martin Gordon, for his insightful editorial comments and criticisms, and to Harold E. Collier, for his skillful course corrections in navigating this work toward publication.

The expert camera work of Robert Vaugh resurrected many faded Marine images and made it possible to include them in this work.

During the course of my research, it was my good fortune to locate several descendants of Marine officers and enlisted men who allowed me full access to family collections. The letters of 2d Lt. Robert E. Hitchcock written during his brief service as an officer of Marines were located, and, through the courtesy of Mrs. Robert McKey Grinnell, made available. These were subsequently donated to the Marine Corps Historical Center. The generosity of Mr. Theodore Haviland, III, allowed the personal papers of his great-grandfather, Bvt. Brig. Gen. Robert L. Meade, USMC, to be extensively consulted. This collection was subsequently donated to the Marine Corps University Archives. Cynthia R. Howe, Louise Russell, and Barbara R. Williams, great-granddaughters of Bvt. Brig. Gen. Robert L. Meade, USMC, furnished copies of photographs from the Elizabeth Meade Russell Collection; Mr. John D. Reynolds provided copies of the letters written by his great-great-grandfather, Lt. Col. John George Reynolds, USMC, and two images of his ancestor. Permission to use the Civil War diaries of Marine officer John Campbell Harris was graciously given by his granddaughter, Mrs. Henry M. Watts, and made available by her son, Mr. Benjamin F. Pepper. Mrs. Jo Clemons, great-granddaughter of Col. John Lloyd Broome, USMC, granted permission to use several personal letters written by her ancestor and had a copy of his oil portrait made especially for this work. Mrs. Frances Rich Hartswick, a collateral descendant of 2d Lt. John C. Morgan, USMC, furnished copies of his correspondence and official papers. The diary and other papers of O. Sgt. Charles T. Young were made available by his great-great-great-grandson Michael Talbot. Material relative to the service of Marine Musicians James, Richard, and William Baxter, was contributed by Hugh Baxter. Mr. Jeffrey M. Ketterer provided copies of the letters written by his Civil War Marine ancestor, Pvt. Richard S. Dalbey, and a wartime image.

Contacts with descendants of the families of other Civil War Marine officers and enlisted men yielded substantial information. For their cooperation with this project, a major debt of gratitude is owed Mrs. Mary B. Moulding, great-grandniece of Capt. Joseph F. Baker; Maesimund Banning Panos, daughter of 2d Lt. Edward P. Banning; Mrs. Nicholas Benton, collateral descendant of 2d Lt. Horatio R. Bigelow; C. Carter Smith, descendant of Pvt. Charles Brother; William

C. Holland, great-grandson of Capt. William H. Cartter; Mrs. Betty Van Church, whose late husband was a direct descendant of 1st Lt. Frank L. Church; Mrs. Harry Megson, collateral descendant of 2d Lt. George W. Cummins, Jr.; Dr. Elizabeth Wood, great-granddaughter of 2d Lt. Charles H. Daniels. Chris Truitt, great-grandson of Maj. Lucien L. Dawson; Beverly Denig Jones, compiler of the Denig Family history for material relative to Sgt. John H. Denig; Col. Bill G. Fendall, USAF (Ret.), historian of the Fendall Family, Lady Antonia Dalrymple, great-granddaughter, and Lord Henry George Reginald Molyneux Herbert, Carnavon, great-grandson of Maj. Philip R. Fendall, Jr.; Edward J. Freyburg, great-grandson of Capt. Philip H. W. Fontané; Mrs. Caspar P. Kramer and Mrs. Dorothy J. C. Sampson, collateral descendants of Maj. George R. Graham; MacDonald Greene, grandson of 1st Lt. Israel Greene; Edward O. Parry, descendant of 1st Lt. John C. Harris; Mrs. Charles M. Carson, collateral descendant of 2d Lt. Henry L. Ingraham; Mrs. Caroline S. Chastain, great-grandniece of 1st Lt. William S. Kidd; F. H. McElrath, historian of the McElrath Family for information regarding 1st Lt. Thomas L. McElrath; Marshall A. Hudson, great-great-grandson of Capt. William A. T. Maddox; Mrs. Manly L. Curry, great-granddaughter of Lt. Col. Ward Marston; Miss Louise Russell, great-granddaughter of Bvt. Brig. Gen. Robert L. Meade; William W. Smyth, grandnephew of Bvt. 1st Lt. Edward R. Miller; W. B. Carnochan, great-grandnephew of 2d Lt. Gouverneur Morris; Fr. William C. Winlock, Major, USA (Ret.), for material concerning Capt. Frank Munroe; Duffield Ashmead, III, great-grandson of 1st Lt. Richard R. Neill; Cdr. Leonard L. Nicholson, III, USCG (Ret.), grandnephew of Lt. Col. Augustus S. Nicholson; Mrs. George Wheaton, granddaughter of Capt. Norval L. Nokes; John Connor, grandson of Pvt. Daniel O'Connor, USMC; Mrs. Mary P. Livingston, great-granddaughter of Sgt. Miles Oviatt; Mrs. Adelaide Trigg, granddaughter of 2d Lt. John L. Rapier, CSMC; Mrs. Claire Frew for material relative to 1st Lt. Jacob Read; Charles Brewer, great-grandson of Maj. William W. Russell; Mrs. Carole Pennock, collateral descendant of 1st Lt. Charles L. Sherman; former Marine William L. Shuttleworth IV, great-grandson of Col. William L. Shuttleworth; Miss Mary Caroline Rogers, great-granddaughter of 2d Lt. Alexander D. Sparks; Jane W. Hogan, and her husband, "Red," a former Marine, for information regarding her grandfather, 1st Lt. Eugene B. Sturgeon; Mrs. Shirley Stanton, a collateral descendant of Capt. Archibald S. Taylor; Mrs. Helen Ignace, great-granddaughter of Sgt. Andrew J. Tomlin; Ted Williams, grandson, and Col. Thomas E. Watson, USA (Ret.), and John E. Watson, great-grandsons of Col. Charles F. Williams; and Mrs. Thomas C. Dendy, great-granddaughter of 2d Lt. Erasmus Youngblood.

Many private collectors, historians, and writers made their Marine Corps material available for this work. Through their generous assistance, numerous images and documents appear in publication for the first time. Grateful appreciation is due Paul Loane; MGySgt. Jack D. McCord, USMC (Ret.); former Marine Sergeant Howard A. Hoffman; Andrew Parker, Jr.; Donald Wisnoski; Sal Alberti; Robert Ball; Marty Bertern; Howard Brandes; Richard A. Bruhn; B. Richard Burg; Peter Buxton; Jimmer Carden; Caxton Printers and Paul B. Evans; Donald L. Collins; Henry Deeks, former Marine John De Leeuw; Col. John A. Driscoll, USMC (Ret.); Dr. Ray Giron; Howard Gosdorfer; Emerick Hanzl; Thomas Harris; Samuel Howell, IV; Rance Hulshart; Mrs. David Jaehnig; Charles H. James; Phil Katcher; Paul Kallina; Michael Kane; John W. Kuhl; former Marine Sergeant William D. Langlois; Tom MacDonald; Robert Marcotte; John McCormack; David Murdoch; Richard Newey; former Marine Russell Parks; Barry Pipino; Jerry Rinker; Martin Schoenfeld; Dr. William Schultz; Dale S. Snair; Bryce Suderou; Steven Sullivan; Ken Turner; Dale West; Michael Kauffman; and Robert Wadsworth.

The staff of the Marine Corps Historical Center at the Washington Navy Yard extended full cooperation and encouragement throughout the research-gathering process. Special thanks to Maj. John T. Dyer, USMCR (Ret.), Art Curator, Benis Frank, Chief Historian, and D. J. Crawford, Head, Historical Reference Branch.

A particular debt of gratitude is owed Lt. Col. Michael V. Maloney, USMC (Ret.), Executive Director, Marine Corps Command and Staff College Foundation, Inc., for granting permission to use the painting "At All Times Ready" as cover art.

Thanks, also, to MGySgt. Mike Ressler, Chief Librarian, United States Marine Band, who lent his expertise in the realm of Marine Music, along with several excellent prints and photographs to this effort.

The courtesy of National Archives personnel, despite the volume of requests I made, was unwavering. The assistance of William E. Lind, Barry L. Zerby, and Richard W. Peuser of the Military Reference Branch, Rita Connolly, Still Picture Branch, Lu Lathan, Publication Sales Branch, and the Center for Legislative Archives is gratefully acknowledged.

Personnel at the Naval Historical Center furnished a substantial amount of material to the project. The Operational Archives Branch provided generous access to the files of Marine Corps officers and enlisted personnel. Particular appreciation is due Edward Finney of the Photographs Section for fulfilling the many requests made of that department.

All with whom I came into contact at the Library of Congress, Manuscripts Division, Photographs Division, and Photoduplication Services, were courteous in fulfilling the many requests I made of them, and generous in guiding me to other sources of information.

The photographic archives of the Special Collections Branch, United States Army Military History Institute, were the source of many images used in this work. Special thanks to Randy Hackenburg for his skillful navigation through the thousands of photographs in the custody of that organization, while directing me to those most pertinent to my research. Thanks also to Col. James Enos, USAF (Ret.), for his excellent work in making copy prints from the negative files of the Special Collections Branch.

Scores of public and private repositories, local and state historical societies, and university and college libraries were queried in the course of my research. Those that were instrumental in the collection of material used in this effort, and persons associated with certain organizations who took a special interest in my work are gratefully acknowledged. Connecticut: the Connecticut Historical Society and the Connecticut State Library of Hartford. Delaware: Dr. Constance Cooper of the Historical Society of Delaware and Marjorie McNinch of the Hagley Museum and Library at Wilmington. Florida: Tom Hambright of the Monroe County, May Hill Russell Library of Key West, and Sandra Johnson of the Pensacola Historical Society. Illinois: Ralph Pugh of the Chicago Historical Society. Iowa: the Iowa State Historical Society. Kansas: the Kansas State Historical Society. Massachusetts: The Boston Public Library; Noah Dennen, Curator, Medford Historical Society; the Peabody and Essex Museum of Salem; the Rutland Public Library; the American Antiquarian Society of Worcester; and the Worcester Public Library. Missouri: The St. Louis Mercantile Library. New York: the New York State Archives; Tom Duclose, Curator, Military Museum, New York State Division of Military and Naval Affairs; the Allegany Area Historical Association; the Buffalo and Erie County Historical Society; the Cattaraugus County Historical Museum of Olean; Susan Robey of the DeWitt Historical Society of Tompkins County and the Special Collections Library at Cornell University, Ithaca; the Franklin D. Roosevelt Presidential Library at Hyde Park; the University of Rochester; and the Union College Library at Schenectady. Ohio: John Grabowski of the Western Reserve Historical Society at Cleveland. Pennsylvania: Louise T. Jones of the Historical Society of Pennsylvania; J. B. Post of the Philadelphia Free Library; Steven Wright of the Civil War Library; Sarah Weatherwax of the Library Company of Philadelphia; Lila Fourhman-Shaull of the Historical Society of York County, and Jonathan Stayer of the Pennsylvania State Library. South Dakota: James

C. Hunt of the Mitchell Area Historical Society, and Jeannette Allard Fiskum of the Sioux Valley Genealogical Society. Vermont: the Chittendon County Historical Society at Burlington. Virginia: the Virginia State Library, the Museum of the Confederacy, Richmond; Irene Roughton, Associate Registrar, Chrysler Museum, and the Mariner's Museum at Newport News, Virginia. Wisconsin: the State Historical Society of Wisconsin. To those who assisted, and whose names I have inadvertently omitted, my apologies and sincere gratitude.

This work is respectfully dedicated to all Marines, past, present and future, but in particular to those members of my family who proudly wore the Eagle, Globe, and Anchor. My son, L/Cpl. Andrew W. Sullivan, and daughter, Cpl. Charla E. Sullivan; my uncle, Pvt. Arthur J. Pearson, a "China Marine," who served with the old 4th Regiment at Shanghai during 1927–1929; Cpl. James J. McFadden, Jr., my cousin, who, while serving with the 3rd Battalion, 29th Regiment, 6th Marine Division, was wounded during the Battle of Okinawa; and Cpl. Alfred A. Pearson, another cousin, who saw a year of combat in Korea with F Battery, 2d Battalion, 11th Regiment, 1st Marine Division.

INTRODUCTION

Two ambrotypes of 1st Sgt. James Buckner, U.S. Marines, was the genesis of this work. These unusual images brought about an interest in Buckner's career as a Marine. Research revealed that he began his twenty-six-year career in the Corps as a Music Boy in 1839, and served ashore and afloat during the Mexican and Civil Wars. His long service with the Corps was related in an article published in the January–February 1988 issue of *Military Images.* Harry Roach, publisher of that journal, prompted me to compose another Marine Corps article covering the post-Civil War period. While researching illustrations for this work, I discovered that 19th-century images of Marines were extremely difficult to locate, particularly those who served during the Civil War. Published material contained fewer than a dozen images of Marine officers who took part in that conflict. Further, the personal histories of many of the Marine officers of the period were limited. After discussions with staff members of the Marine Corps and Naval Historical Centers as to the feasibility of a brief work covering the United States Marine officers of the Civil War, the idea of an illustrated, biographical dictionary took root.

During the course of my efforts to locate an image of every Marine officer who served between 1861 and 1865, contact was made with the late Edward R. Haggeman, Professor of English and Humanities, University of Louisville. Professor Haggeman, a former Marine officer who served in the Pacific during World War II, took a keen interest in my effort. Maintaining that published material dealing with the experience of the Corps during this critical period of our nation's history was largely cursory in nature, Haggeman, in terms reflective of his years as a Marine officer, strongly suggested

I turn the biographical dictionary into a full-length history of the Corps in the Civil War.

Maj. Richard S. Collum, USMC, a veteran of the Civil War, was responsible for two histories of the Corps. The first was published in 1875 under the title *History of the United States Marine Corps.* M. Almy Aldrich was author, but Collum provided all of the material upon which the book was based. The second bears the title *The History of the United States Marine Corps,* but was published under his own name in 1890, and reprinted in 1903. Collum devoted a significant portion of his work to the Civil War experience of his Corps, but relied almost exclusively on official reports. Since Collum certainly had access to the personal experiences of many of his fellow officers who took part in the conflict, it is disappointing that he chose not to inspire his writing with their reminiscences.

Following World War I, John W. Leonard and Fred F. Chitty wrote *The Story of the United States' Marines.* Their account of the services of the Marines during the Civil War covers some thirty-seven pages, and appears to have been based primarily upon Collum's works. However, for the first time, the personal observations of a Civil War Marine are included in the text. Although Leonard and Chitty's work suffers from more than a few errors of fact in the text, the overall impact of their work was much enhanced by the inclusion of Cpl. Henry Hallowell's description of the part the Marines took in the December 24–25, 1864, and January 13–15, 1865, Battles of Fort Fisher.

Col. Clyde H. Metcalf, USMC, published *A History of the United States Marine Corps* in 1939. Although 130 pages of the 555 in his work were devoted to the Civil War period, Metcalf, following Collum's example, used material primarily from official records.

Over the course of the last thirty-five years, three major histories of the Marine Corps have been published. The Marine tradition has benefited handsomely by these excellent works, all of which incorporated the recollections of those who were "on the ground" into the text. Regrettably for the Civil War reader, the focus of *Soldiers of the Sea,* Col. Robert D. Heinl, Jr., USMC, 1962; *The Marine Corps Story,* J. Robert Moskin, 1977; and *Semper Fidelis: The History of the United States Marine Corps,* Col. Allan R. Millett, USMCR, 1980, is the Marine Corps in the 20th century. The relatively small number of pages in each of these works devoted to the Civil War Marines unfortunately does little to challenge the verdict of most period historians; that the Corps did little to distinguish itself.

The predilection that the Marine Corps did little to enhance its reputation during the Civil War is not confined to the pages of historical works. The Corps itself seems to perpetuate the notion.

Interviews with dozens of former Marines, including my son and daughter, reveal that instructors assigned the task of teaching the history of the Corps to recruits at Parris Island and San Diego seldom spend more than a few minutes discussing the Civil War. A highlight of each annual Marine Corps Birthday Ball is the recitation of battles in which Marines took part. Omitted is any mention of engagements fought during the Civil War. The same holds true for mess nights. During a Command Visit to Parris Island in 1989, I found that no one from the Public Affairs Office was remotely aware of the significance of the surrounding area to the history of the Corps. All were surprised to learn that Marines landed at Hilton Head Island on November 7, 1861, and that Bay Point was used as a staging area for Marine operations throughout the war. Both of these sites are within a few miles from the Recruit Depot.

This unfortunate situation is not confined solely to enlisted Marines. The customs, traditions, and history of the Corps taught to young Marine officers in basic school, largely omit references to the Civil War period. Moreover, discussions with officers who entered the Corps from the Naval Academy show they brought with them the history of the Civil War as taught from the perspective of the Navy, which is, to say the least, less than conducive to the reputation of the Marines. The 1864 observations of 2d Lt. Ruffin Thomson, an officer of Confederate States Marines, might well reflect the view of his counterparts on the other side. Writing to his father, Thomson stated:

> Our Corps has been represented in many fights with the Yanks, but what they did was always appropriated by the Navy proper with whom they were acting . . . in fact in almost every action the Marines have played their part. But being Subordinate to the Navy, we got but little credit.

Little has been done since to rectify that situation. In the years following the Civil War, no Marine officer penned his wartime memoirs or wrote an account of hostilities of 1861–1865 from the perspective of the Corps. However, scores of naval officers published their reminiscences, while others turned their literary efforts to the maritime history of the conflict. The experiences of the Marine Corps, beyond reproducing a few official after-action reports, were largely omitted from these works. Based upon these many factors, a conclusion was reached that there was need for an extensive chronicle of the Civil War Marine Corps.

The amount of Civil War related Marine Corps material, given the small numbers of officers and men who served between 1861 and 1865, is limited. Nevertheless, a significant amount of material has come to light since the research for this work was undertaken. The personal papers, letters, and journals of both officers and enlisted Marines uncovered during the past several years comprise the mainstream of this work. In order to preserve the character and integrity of their view of the Corps and the war, the letters written by Civil War Marines reproduced in the text of these volumes appear as they were written. No corrections have been made with regard to spelling or grammar. Because many were written without punctuation, spaces have been inserted at the end of sentences for the convenience of the reader. Whether authored by a well-educated officer or untutored enlisted man, these writings give evidence of a pride in Corps and Country that is unsurpassed by Marines of any generation.

Melding the human element of this new material with official correspondence and records of the period raises the history of the Corps in the Civil War to a new level of understanding; one that surmounts the long accepted consensus that the Marine Corps' participation in the conflict was an embarrassment to its proud and venerable history.

David M. Sullivan
Rutland, Massachusetts
January 1996

List of Abbreviations

CSA	Confederate States Army; the regular army
CSMC	Confederate States Marine Corps
CSN	Confederate States Navy; the regular navy
CWL	Civil War Library and Museum, Philadelphia, Pennsylvania
LC	Library of Congress
LN	Louisiana State Navy
MCHC	Marine Corps Historical Center, Washington, D.C.
NA	National Archives of the United States, Washington, D.C.
NHC	Naval Historical Center, Washington, D.C.
NHF	Naval Historical Foundation, Washington, D.C.
PACS	Provisional Army of the Confederate States; the volunteer forces
PNCS	Provisional Navy of the Confederate States; the naval force authorized to exist only for the duration of the war
USA	United States Army; the regular army
USAF	United States Air Force
USAMHI	United States Army Military History Institute, Carlisle Barracks, Pennsylvania
USCG	United States Coast Guard
USMC	United States Marine Corps
USMCR	United States Marine Corps Reserve
USN	United States Navy
USV	United States Volunteers; the volunteer force

VMC	Virginia Marine Corps
VN	Virginia Navy; the naval force of the Commonwealth of Virginia

Marine Corps, army, and naval ranks

Pvt.	private
Cpl.	corporal
L/Cpl.	lance, or acting corporal
L/Sgt.	lance, or acting sergeant
Sgt.	sergeant
O. Sgt.	orderly sergeant
Gy Sgt.	gunnery sergeant
MGy Sgt.	master gunnery sergeant
1st Sgt.	first sergeant
QM Sgt.	quartermaster sergeant
Sgt. Maj.	sergeant major
2d Lt.	second lieutenant
1st Lt.	first lieutenant
Capt.	captain
Maj.	major
Lt. Col.	lieutenant colonel
Col.	colonel
Brig. Gen.	brigadier general
Maj. Gen.	major general
Lt. Gen.	lieutenant general
Bvt.	brevet

Ld.	landsman, the equivalent of the modern seaman recruit
Sea.	seaman
O. Sea.	ordinary seaman
Boats.	boatswain
QM	quartermaster
Midn.	midshipman
Ens.	ensign
Lt. Cdr.	lieutenant commander
Cdr.	commander
Commo.	commodore
Rear Adm.	rear admiral

1

Prelude to the Storm: United States Marines at Harpers Ferry

In the late evening hours of October 17, 1859, a solitary engine and tender came to a halt with a rush of steam and squeal of brakes at the Sandy Hook, Maryland station of the Baltimore and Ohio Rail Road. 1st Lt. Israel Greene, USMC, who, with eighty-six Marines, had been sent to put down a "riotous outbreak" at Harpers Ferry, Virginia, earlier that day, made his way through the militiamen crowding the station platform to report to Bvt. Col. Robert E. Lee, USA. Greene and his Marine detachment had been at the Sandy Hook station since 9:30 P.M. While he waited for Lee to arrive, the Marine officer used his time profitably. Circulating among the militia units, and listening to their officers, Greene learned what had brought them all to this place. As he jostled his way toward the engine, 1st Lt. James E. B. Stuart, followed by Lee, both men exhibiting the signs of a most uncomfortable sixty-mile journey made at breakneck speed, stepped down from the cab. Stuart, Greene noted, wore the uniform coat of the United States Army and a wide-brimmed hat. Lee, his dark moustache and gray hair flecked with ashes accumulated during the trip, was in civilian dress.[1] Greene stepped forward and reported. Wiping the soot from his face and coat, Lee listened intently as Greene presented the situation as he knew it. Late Sunday night, October 16, an armed band of abolitionists led by a man calling himself Smith but thought to be John Brown of Kansas,[2] had seized the Armory and taken several of the workers prisoner. The insurrectionists had also ventured into the countryside and taken a number of prominent citizens as hostages, among them Col. Lewis W. Washington, the grandnephew of George Washington. Armed men had taken control of the railroad bridges over the Potomac and Shenandoah Rivers, killing Shepard Heyward, a free negro, in the process. By morning, a number of townsmen had taken up arms and exchanged shots with the brigands. Later, the first units of the Jefferson County Militia filtered into the town and after several sharp exchanges of gunfire, drove the mysterious strangers into the fire engine house within the Armory grounds. Two assaults on the engine house, one by the Jefferson County volunteers and another by a hastily organized company from Martinsburg, had been repulsed with heavy casualties. Since then, the raiders and militia had been exchanging occasional shots. The rioters had killed the Mayor of Harpers Ferry, Fontaine Beckham, during the sporadic sniping, and William Thompson, one of Brown's men captured earlier by the militia, had been slain in retaliation. A few other raiders had been killed trying to escape. From all accounts, including the number of breakfasts served to those in the engine house by the owner of the Wager Hotel that morning, Greene calculated there were less than two dozen rioters, but they were armed with Sharps breech-loading rifles.

Greene's assessment of the situation, while sufficient for Lee to formulate a plan to put down the insurrection, hardly lent itself to the excitement of the day's events.

Contemporary view of Harpers Ferry

The town's soon to be most famous building, the fire engine house, can be seen below and slightly to the left of center.

MOLLUS Collection, USAMHI

Shortly after 7:00 A.M. that morning, the B&O Through Express Passenger Train pulled into the station at Monocacy, Maryland. Barely waiting for the train to come to a halt, Conductor A. J. Phelps vaulted from the cars, bounded across the platform and burst into the dispatch office. Without pausing for breath, much less explain why his train was five hours behind schedule, Phelps ordered Dispatcher F. Mantz to telegraph the Transportation Master at Baltimore. Within the hour, an incredulous telegrapher at the Camden Station in Baltimore handed W. P. Smith, the equally disbelieving B&O Master of Transportation, the first news of an attack upon the United States Armory at Harpers Ferry, Virginia.

Monocacy, 7.05 A.M., October 17, 1859

W. P. Smith,

Baltimore.

Express train bound east under my charge was stopped this morning at Harpers Ferry by abolitionists. They have possession of the bridge and the arms and armory of the United States. Myself and Baggage Master have been fired on and Hayward, the colored porter, is wounded very severely, being shot through the body, the ball entering the body below the left shoulder blade and coming out the left side. The Doctor says he cannot survive. They are headed by a man who calls himself Anderson, and number about one hundred and fifty strong. They say they have come to free the slaves and intend to do it at all hazards.

The leader of those men requested me to say to you that this is the last train that shall pass the bridge either East or West. If it is attempted, it will be at the peril of the lives of those having them in charge. When daylight appeared we were finally permitted to pass, after being detained from half-past one o'clock to half-past six. It has been suggested you had better notify the Secretary of War at once. The telegraph wires are cut East and West of Harper's Ferry, and this is the first station that I could send a dispatch from.

A. J. PHELPS.[3]

A much agitated Smith directed an immediate reply to Ellicott's Mills, the next stop on Phelps' journey to Baltimore. He accused the conductor of exaggerating the situation. Why would abolitionists stop B&O trains? Further, how did Phelps know they were abolitionists? Was he sure there were more than one hundred? Were their objectives made known to him? Smith wanted concrete assurances of the situation before he made the decision to "proceed to extremities."[4]

Despite his misgivings as to the accuracy of Conductor Phelps' message, Smith notified B&O President John W. Garrett of the alarming telegram received from Monocacy. Garrett quickly organized his office at the Camden Station as an impromptu command center to better control the situation, but events had already progressed much further than he or Smith anticipated.

At 10:00 A.M., Smith received a telegram from John T. Quynn, B&O Agent at Frederick, Maryland. Word of the Harpers Ferry incident had reached Frederick, and militiamen were already assembling there. Quynn wanted to know if he should forward the new volunteers to Harpers Ferry.[5] Shortly thereafter, Agent Diffey of the Martinsburg, Virginia, Station wired his version of what had happened at Harpers Ferry. He heard that the armed men at Harpers Ferry had planted guns on the railroad bridge. Moreover, a group of locals were arming themselves in preparation to attack the insurrectionists.[6] A telegram had been sent to the Baltimore Newspaper Press from Frederick reporting of "a formidable negro insurrection at Harper's Ferry," and "an armed band of abolitionists" in "full possession of Harper's Ferry and the United States Arsenal." "They are led by about two hundred and fifty whites and a gang of negroes fighting for their freedom," and "were determined to have liberty, or die in the attempt."[7] It was a certainty that the news had been passed along to the press in other major cities.

Faced with the prospect of incendiary newspaper accounts reaching the public, coupled with unauthorized and unorganized armed bands ready to descend upon Harpers Ferry, Garrett realized that controlling the situation was beyond his means. He quickly fired off a succession of telegrams. He told Secretary of War John B. Floyd that the "United States Armory and our bridges are in full possession of large bands of armed men said to be abolitionists."[8] After relating what he knew of the situation at Harpers Ferry, Garrett continued, "Can you authorize the government officers and military from Washington to go on our train at 3:20 this afternoon to the scene?"[9] Garrett next told President James Buchanan pointedly that "The presence of United States troops is indispensable," and that "the rioters are more than two hundred strong."[10] Maj. Gen. George H. Steuart, commander of the First Light Division, Maryland Volunteer Militia, and Governor Henry A. Wise of Virginia were also informed of the conditions at Harpers Ferry.[11] Steuart responded that five companies of the First Light Division would be on the 4:00 P.M. train for Harpers Ferry from Baltimore.[12] Wise issued orders through Garrett to Col. John T. Gibson at Charlestown, commander of the 55th Regiment

(Jefferson County), Virginia Militia, authorizing him to call out as many of his troops as he needed to suppress the disturbance.[13]

Anticipating the requirements of the Federal Government in forwarding troops to Harpers Ferry, Garrett ordered Smith to wire the B&O Agent at Washington to place whatever rail transport was needed at the disposal of the War Department. If arrangements were speedily completed, a special train would be made up to depart Washington at 1:00 P.M. In case of delay, the regular 3:20 P.M. Express from Washington would also be available.[14]

In Washington, confusion prevailed. Buchanan, not fully trusting Garrett's report, wired the Postmaster of Baltimore to make inquiries. At noon, a telegraphic confirmation arrived at the White House. The Armory at Harpers Ferry had indeed been seized and the railroad bridges obstructed. The mail train had been fired upon and all telegraphic communication with the town severed by the rioters. Curiously, Postmaster John Morris informed the President that it was widely believed that those responsible for the outbreak of violence were not free negroes and abolitionists but disaffected "operatives" at Harpers Ferry.[15] Whoever was responsible, the outbreak had to be put down, and quickly. Not entirely comfortable with the thoughts of emotionally charged militiamen performing the task, Buchanan wanted his Federal troops to resolve the matter. From the time that the first report of trouble reached the President, responsibility for the suppression of the riot was in the hands of his Secretary of War.

Floyd's first action was to find U.S. Regulars to send to Harpers Ferry. The 3rd Artillery Regiment, commanded by Col. William Gates, USA, was stationed at Fort Monroe, at the tip of the James Peninsula in Virginia. Despite being nearly a two-day journey from the trouble spot, the 3rd Artillery would have to be sent. No other substantial body of soldiers were closer. Floyd dictated a brief telegram to the commanding officer, ordering him to put three full companies of troops aboard that evening's boat to Baltimore for service at Harpers Ferry.[16] Floyd handed the dispatch to a messenger and sent him off to the War Department telegrapher.

Floyd next sought someone to command the operation. Lt. Col. Robert E. Lee had recently reported to the Department after finishing court-martial duty at New York. Lee was spending a few days at home before returning to his post with the 2d U.S. Cavalry in Texas. His residence was just across the Potomac River in Arlington, Virginia. Floyd took his pencil and hastily wrote a note to Chief Clerk of the War Department, Col. William R. Drinkard.

Monday morning
October 17, 1859

Col. Drinkard/

Send a special messenger to Col. Robert Lee to report here immediately.[17]

Floyd sealed the note in an envelope and handed it to an office messenger who dashed off to find Drinkard.

As the messenger hurried out of Floyd's office in search of Drinkard, he passed a young cavalry officer named James E. B. Stuart in the Secretary's anteroom. Stuart, waiting to see the Secretary of War on personal business that morning, immediately became distracted from the purpose of his visit. The whisperings, comings and goings of some very intense-looking clerks outside the Secretary's anteroom had piqued his interest. Stuart listened intently, trying to determine what was going on.[18]

What *was* going on that morning was definitely cause for the Chief Clerk Drinkard to dismiss Stuart and tell him to make an appointment for another day. Fate, however, intervened in the form of the messenger from the Secretary's office. Drinkard opened the envelope, read the contents, remembered the waiting Stuart and gauged the man to be the "special messenger" he needed. He quickly penned an order to Lee, directing him to report to the Secretary as quickly as possible, sealed it in an envelope and stepped outside his office door. Stuart was asked if he would deliver a very important message to Lee at his home in Arlington. In an instant, Stuart forgot his entrepreneurial errand, took the order, and was quickly on his way.

Floyd now had his expedition commander and the troops for the expedition but there was a problem. While the former was within minutes of his office, the latter would not get under way until that evening. A Federal military presence was required at Harpers Ferry at the earliest possible moment. The only other Regular forces that would be able to join Lee any sooner than the artillerists from Fort Monroe were the Marines stationed at Marine Barracks, Washington, and, being subject to the orders of the Secretary of the Navy, were beyond his authority.

The Secretary of War was ordinarily territorial in matters of jurisdictional prerogative. But Floyd was a Virginian, and as a young lawyer had been horrified by Nat Turner's bloody revolt of 1831. The specter of another slave rising but on a much larger scale was more than enough to sweep away any reservations he may have had in asking another member of the cabinet for help. Floyd went to the Navy Department to brief Secretary of the Navy Isaac Toucey of the situation at Harpers Ferry.[19] He presented the time factor involved with the Fort Monroe contingent as the case for sending Marines to Harpers Ferry as quickly as possible. Toucey agreed to make the necessary arrangements at once.

Toucey immediately dictated an order to Col. John Harris, Commandant of the Marine Corps. The message was entrusted to Chief Clerk of the Navy Department Charles W. Welsh, who wasted no time in getting to the Marine Barracks in southeast Washington. He passed through the gates on Eighth Street just before noon and was directed to the Officer of the Day, 1st Lt. Israel Greene. How many Marines were available for immediate duty? the Chief Clerk wanted to know.[20] Checking his duty roster, Greene saw that there were twelve non-commissioned officers and ninety privates, more or less, at the barracks and on duty in the immediate vicinity.[21] Informing Welsh that he could not give an exact number, Greene wondered what sort of trouble was afoot that brought the Chief Clerk on such an errand.[22] Welsh then left Greene and went to Harris' office to present him with Toucey's message.

Col. John Harris

Commandant of the United States Marine Corps, 1859-1864, shown here with the single star rank insignia of a brigadier general, indicative of his position as head of the Corps.

NA Photograph 111-B-4419

When Welsh was shown into the Commandant's office, Harris instantly knew something critical had occurred. John Harris had been Commandant of the Marine Corps for slightly over ten months and this was the first time the Chief Clerk had personally delivered a dispatch from the Navy Department. The contents of the dispatch confirmed Harris' suspicion.

Navy Department
Oct. 17, 1859

Sir:

Send all the available marines at Head Quarters, under charge of suitable officers, by this evening's train of cars to Harpers Ferry, to protect the public property at that place, which is endangered by riotous outbreak.

The men will be furnished with a proper number of ball cartridges, ammunition and rations, and will take two howitzers and schrapnel.

The Commanding officer on his arrival at Harper's Ferry, will report to the Senior Army Officer who may be there in command. Otherwise he will take such measures as in his judgment may be necessary to protect the Arsenal and other property of the United States.

I am respect'y
Y'r obt. servt.
(signed) Isaac Toucey

Colonel
John Harris
Commandt. Marine Corps
Head Quarters[23]

As Welsh waited for Harris' response, the Commandant examined his records. Toucey said he wanted "suitable officers" sent with the detachment. Harris saw that Bvt. Maj. George H. Terrett, commanding Marine Barracks, Washington, was still on leave of absence. Greene was next in seniority. He would have to command the expedition. That left two officers available; 1st Lts. Charles A. Henderson and Edward Jones. One should accompany Greene, leaving the other behind in charge of the barracks. However, Henderson had been reporting himself sick lately, and was simply not up to performing either assignment. Jones would remain in charge at the barracks and Greene would take the detachment by himself. Harris would send along O. Sgt. James McDonough to assist Greene. Under the circumstances, it was the best he could do. Harris looked up from his papers and told Welsh that he would issue the necessary orders to ready a Marine detachment for Harpers Ferry and that Israel Greene would be in command.

1st Lt. Israel Greene
Mitchell (S.D.) Area Historical Society

Welsh, having filled Harris in on Secretaries Floyd and Toucey's plans regarding time of departure, rendezvous with the army officer who would command at the scene, and other details of the expedition, then took his leave. Harris then drafted orders for Lieutenant Greene.

Head Quarters, Marine Corps
October 17th, 1859

Sir;

You will take command of a detachment of Marines and proceed by the 3:20 PM train to Weverton, Maryland. On your arrival there, you will communicate with the senior officer of the Army, who will either be there or in its vicinity with such instructions as he may have to give you in carrying out his orders from the President of the United States.

You will take with you two 12 pound howitzers with such ammunition as may be necessary to serve them efficiently in case of them being required for use.

Very Respectfully Yours
(Signed) Jno Harris
Col., Comdt.

Lt. I. Greene
Com'g. Detachment
Head Quarters[24]

Harris sent Orderly Sergeant McDonough to summon Greene to his office. When Greene arrived, he and the Commandant discussed what was known of the situation at Harpers Ferry, the coming expedition, and how it would be made up. Orderly Sergeant McDonough would go, as would O. Sgt. Joseph Mundell from the barracks. The rest of the detachment would be made up of four sergeants, three corporals, two drummers, one fifer, and seventy-four privates.[25] A few noncommissioned officers, musicians, and privates too sick to travel or just enlisted would stay behind. It was regrettable that a detachment of thirty-nine Marines had left the barracks for Brooklyn[26] before news of the Harpers Ferry trouble arrived.

After his discussion with the Commandant, Greene immediately began to organize his detachment. Sergeants cleared the barracks of Marines and sent for the daily duty men at the kitchen, stables, and elsewhere. After falling the men in, Greene told them to prepare for an expedition. Telling them as much as they needed to know, Greene dismissed them to secure weapons, ammunition and rations. Surprisingly, the organization went well. The detachment

William W. Russell, Major and Paymaster, United States Marine Corps

Courtesy of Charles A. Brewer

marched to the Washington depot of the Baltimore and Ohio in plenty of time to board the 3:20 P.M. train for the Relay House.

Just before Greene marched his men out of Marine Barracks, Washington, another officer joined the expedition. Toucey, aware that Harris was caught short-handed of officers, sent orders for Maj. William W. Russell, paymaster of the Marine Corps, to accompany Greene in an advisory capacity. Russell, a staff officer, could not, by law, exercise command, but his presence might steady the younger officer.[27]

Just after Greene arrived at the depot, a messenger came from the Navy Department with sealed orders from Toucey. Worried that Harris did not have time to fully explain the situation and what was expected of Greene, the Secretary sent a copy of the Department's orders to Harris for Greene's guidance.[28] With Russell standing at his elbow, Greene read the orders, pocketed the papers, and ordered his detachment to form up. The Marines boarded the train and departed Washington on schedule. Years later, Greene would recall, "It was a beautiful clear autumn day and the men were exhilarated by the excitement of the occasion, which came after a long, dull season of confinement in the barracks, and enjoyed the trip exceedingly."[29]

The Marine detachment arrived at Relay House, detrained and settled down to wait for the Express to Harpers Ferry. In due time, a train of sixteen cars steamed into Relay from Baltimore. On board were Brig. Gen. Charles C. Egerton, Jr., Maryland Volunteer Militia, the four companies of the Baltimore militia that made up the 2d Light Brigade and the erstwhile Transportation Master, W. P. Smith, who, under direct orders from Garrett, was personally responsible for ensuring and reporting the safe passage of the troops to Harpers Ferry.[30]

When the train carrying the Marines reached Frederick, Maryland, a dispatch was brought on board and handed to Greene. It contained orders and Greene's first knowledge of the army officer who was in command of the operation. The Marines were instructed to

The Relay House

Frank Leslie's Magazine

proceed only as far as Sandy Hook, a village about one mile east of Harpers Ferry, and there await the arrival of Lt. Col. Robert E. Lee.[31]

As the train rumbled its way westward, Russell and Egerton discussed what might transpire once they reached Sandy Hook. Egerton said his orders were not to cross into Virginia. Russell assured him that any orders that Lee received from the Secretary of War would take precedence.[32] Egerton replied that as soon as he and Lee met, the services of the 2d Light Brigade would be tendered for any duty the commander desired.

After delivering Lee's orders to him at his Arlington home, Stuart offered his services to Lee as Aide-de-Camp. Lee accepted and the two men were quickly on their way to Washington. Lee reported at the War Department, and, with Stuart, was quickly taken under escort by Floyd. The President was expecting them at the White House.

After a brief exchange of formalities at the Executive Mansion, Buchanan explained the events of the last few hours to Lee as he knew them. Floyd offered information regarding the contingent from Fort Monroe and the detachment from Marine Barracks, Washington. Buchanan did not know what Lee would find when he arrived at Harpers Ferry but the President had prepared for the worst. A proclamation of martial law was handed to Lee.[33] Taking leave of the

President and Secretary of War, Lee and Stuart headed for the Washington depot of the B&O. Stuart took a short detour to borrow a uniform coat and a saber, but Lee still wore the civilian clothes Stuart found him attired in that morning.[34]

By the time the two reached the Relay House, the Express to Harpers Ferry had already left, taking the Marines with it. While he waited for a special train to be brought up, Lee wired ahead to Frederick, ordering the Marines to wait for him before entering Harpers Ferry. He also wrote to Floyd, reporting on his current status and the latest rumors. The insurrectionists now numbered five hundred, Lee wrote, and the 2:00 P.M. train from the west had yet to

Robert E. Lee

Battles & Leaders

James Ewell Brown Stuart

Museum of the Confederacy

arrive. No reliable information was to be had for the telegraph lines from Harpers Ferry were still dead.[35]

Lee and Stuart waited impatiently at Relay for the special train that was promised by B&O officials. Soon, Engine 22 and its tender pulled into the station. Engineer G. F. Gilbert called down to Lee and Stuart, summoning them to join him in the cab.[36] Was this the special train to bring the commander of the operation to his destination? Lee and his aide climbed aboard, with, one has to believe, smiles of resignation. The engine swiftly departed Relay, and, with throttle wide open, sped off toward the west. Six hours later, Engine 22 braked to a stop at Sandy Hook. Moments after alighting from the engine,

Lee received his first reliable information regarding the conditions at Harpers Ferry from Greene.

After Greene completed his report, Lee ordered him to form his men and accompany him across the railroad bridge. As the detachment made its way through the darkness, behind the Wager Hotel and into the Armory grounds through a back gate, Lee took careful note of the layout of the buildings. Once all were safely inside the compound, the militiamen were relieved and the Marines took over the task of securing the area around the engine house.[37]

As Lee made his reconnaissance, his first impulse was to immediately storm the engine house with the Marines and put and end to the affair. But there was the matter of the hostages. In the darkness, the Marines would not know friend from foe. In the certain tumult of the action, the lives of the hostages would be in danger. He decided to wait for daylight.[38]

During the sleepless night that followed, Lee decided to keep the President's proclamation in his pocket. The situation at Harpers Ferry, in his judgment, did not require martial law. He then wrote out a message for the Secretary of War stating that he had halted the troops from Fort Monroe at Fort McHenry to await further instructions. At Harpers Ferry, he reported, the insurgents were barricaded in the engine house and held some of the areas most prominent

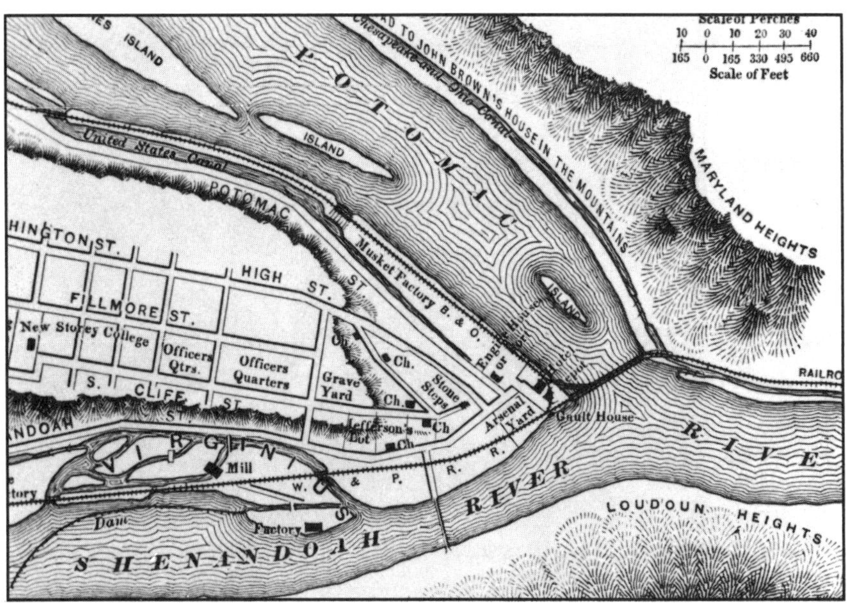

Map of Harpers Ferry

From John Brown, 1800–1859: A Biography fifty Years After

citizens as hostages. Marines had been posted around the Armory while the militia from Virginia and Maryland were stationed in the village. He ended his dispatch by saying, "I . . . shall endeavor to secure and protect the rioters; they have killed several citizens and several of them have been killed."[39] He also wrote out his surrender demand to the leader of the insurgents.

The Marines around the engine house spent a quiet, although damp and uncomfortable night. The rain fell in a steady drizzle. They had not brought their camp equipage, and they sorely missed the shelter of tents.[40] Those fortunate enough to be stationed near trees hunkered down under the protection of overhanging boughs. Perhaps a few Marines dozed off but the excitement of the situation and the anticipation of the morning's work kept sleep at a distance.

At dawn, Monday, October 18, Lee, with Stuart at his side, came down to the Armory grounds. The militia from Maryland and Virginia were quickly formed around the outskirts of the compound and waited for orders. The Marines, led by Greene and Russell, marched smartly into the grounds and, in stark contrast to the militiamen, formed ranks with a precision that made the Maryland and Virginia officers envious. Townspeople began drifting toward the Armory. The drift became a wave and soon the entire town was turned out with everyone jockeying for a better vantage point to observe the impending action.[41]

Harpers Ferry as seen from Maryland Heights

Baltimore and Ohio Railroad

The engine house at Harpers Ferry

NA Photograph 127-N-525271

Lee called Col. Edward Shriver, commander of the Frederick militiamen and senior officer of the Maryland Volunteer Militia present, to his side. Indicating that the affair was more a state than Federal matter, Lee offered the honor of attacking the insurgents to the Marylanders. Colonel Shriver backed away. "These men of mine have wives and children at home. I will not expose them to such risks," Shriver said to Lee. "You are paid for doing this kind of work."[42]

Momentarily taken aback by Shriver's remarks, Lee quickly regained his composure and called Col. Robert W. Baylor, senior officer of the Virginia Militia, forward. Since Maryland declined the honor, would Virginia take it? Baylor, to Lee's chagrin, also declined, saying the Marines, whom he referred to as "mercenaries," should have the job.[43]

Lee then turned to Greene and asked if the Marines would accept the honor of "taking those men out." The lieutenant accepted with pride and sincere thanks, sweeping his cap from his head as he did so.[44]

Greene prepared his storming party according to Lee's instructions. One sergeant, one corporal, and ten privates were selected and brought forward. Twelve more were selected as a reserve. Two of Greene's huskiest Marines were chosen to wield sledge hammers on the engine house door. Once the assault detachment had been

Col. Robert W. Baylor
Virginia State Library

formed, Lee told the Marines what he wanted done. Once the door was battered down, they were to force their way into the engine house. There was to be no shooting. Bayonets were to be used against anyone, including Blacks, who offered resistance. Greatest care was to be taken that the hostages were not harmed. Turning to Greene, Lee explained that Stuart was going to take a surrender demand to the engine house. If it was accepted, the Marines were to take charge of the insurrectionists and see that no harm came to them. If it was declined, Stuart would take cover and make a signal. Stuart and Greene agreed that a wave of Stuart's hat would indicate a rejection by the insurgents. Lee and Stuart then retired; Lee to a vantage point about forty feet away from the engine house, and Stuart to the center of the yard.[45]

About 7:00 A.M., Lee signaled Stuart forward. Flag of truce in hand, the cavalryman advanced to one of the doors and shouted that he had a communication for Smith. The door opened about four inches and revealed a face that Stuart knew from his tour of duty during the fighting between free-staters and pro-slavery forces in Kansas. There was no mistaking the hawk-like visage; the leader of the raiders was indeed John Brown.[46] Equally menacing was a cocked Sharps carbine aimed directly at him. Unfazed by the threat, Stuart presented Brown with Lee's demand for surrender.

Headquarters Harper's Ferry
October 18, 1859

Colonel Lee, United States Army, commanding the troops sent by the President of the United States to suppress the insurrection at this place, demands the surrender of the persons in the armory buildings.

If they will peaceably surrender themselves and restore the pillaged property, they shall be kept in safety to await the orders of the President. Colonel Lee represents to them, in all frankness, that it is impossible for them to escape; that the armory is surrounded on all sides by troops; and that if he is compelled to take them by force he cannot answer for their safety.

R. E. Lee
Colonel Commanding
United States Troops[47]

Brown heard the demand and immediately began to make counterproposals and presentations of his own, all of them ultimately ending with Brown's insistence that he be allowed to leave with his men and the hostages. From within the engine house, the cries of the hostages rang out, imploring Lee to negotiate with Brown. All were momentarily silenced when Colonel Washington called out, in what Lee remarked was a splendid example of "the old revolutionary blood" of his forebears, "Never mind us. Fire!"

But Washington's ardor was not shared by his fellow hostages. Their cries for mediation grew louder at the thought of Washington's bold statement being acted upon. Brown picked up the pace of his rambling commentary, trying to be heard above the lamentations of his captives. Finally, Stuart had enough. Stepping away from the opened door, he waved his hat.

At Stuart's signal, Greene ordered his brawny sledgehammer men to the door of the engine house. In an instant, the two Marines were flailing in rhythmic succession. Heavy blows thundered upon the door but to no avail. The suspension apparatus by which the doors were operated absorbed all the pounding. Seeing that their exertions were gaining nothing, Greene ordered the two Marines away from the door. Just then, he spotted a sturdy ladder lying on the ground a few feet away. Calling out to the reserve squad to ground arms and take hold of the ladder in battering ram fashion, Greene prepared a second assault.

John Brown
Kansas State Historical Society

With a good running start and five Marines on each side, the ladder turned battering ram made a

"At All Times Ready."

Marines prepare to batter down the door of the engine house.

Artist: Don Stivers. Courtesy Marine Corps Command and Staff College Foundation

Marines force their way into the engine house over the body of mortally wounded Private Luke Quinn

From the Harpers Ferry Diorama, Marine Corps Museum "Time Tunnel"

slight breach in the engine house door on the first try. Retreating several yards, a second rush was made. With a loud crack, the door gave way and a hole at the bottom appeared. Greene was quickly through the opening, followed by Russell wielding a rattan switch and the rest of the Marines, who went "rushing in like tigers."[48]

Gunfire erupted, followed by groans of pain. Clambering over the fire engine that Brown's men had jammed against the door as their protection, Greene made his way into the room.

Recalling the scene several years later, Greene said, "I found the room so full of smoke that it at first was hard to distinguish anything. One of the first men I bumped into proved to be Col. Lewis Washington, one of Brown's hostages. Col. Washington stepped up to me and shouted in my ear. 'That's Ossawatamie Brown!' at the same time indicating one of the figures kneeling and facing the hole in the door with his gun ready. . . . I had my sword raised in the air ready to strike and as Col. Washington gave me the above information, I struck down John Brown, the blow being of sufficient force to render him unconscious for a time."[49]

The blow struck Brown on the back of his neck. As he slumped forward, Greene thrust his sword at the old man's chest. Had Greene been carrying his regulation sword, Brown would have been killed on the spot.[50] However, in his haste to form his detachment back at the barracks, Greene had buckled on his "light dress sword." The blade was not intended for this sort of work, and, as Greene made his lunge, bent double when it struck the breast plate of Brown's cartridge box belt.[51]

After subduing Brown, Greene turned his attention to what was happening elsewhere in the engine house. Just beyond the hole in the door lay Pvt. Luke Quinn, his lifeblood spilling from an abdominal wound which would prove fatal.[52] Close by was Pvt. Matthew Ruppert trying to staunch the blood from a gunshot wound to his face. Greene reckoned that Brown had shot Quinn but his comrades thought otherwise. Sure that raider Jeremiah G. Anderson had laid their friend low, several Marines took special interest in dealing with him. Anderson was pinned to the rear wall by bayonet thrusts, then dragged from the engine house to die.[53] Another of Brown's men,

Col. Lewis Washington points out "Ossawatamie"

From the Harpers Ferry Diorama, Marine Corps Museum "Time Tunnel"

Jeremiah G. Anderson
Kansas State Historical Society

Dauphin Thompson
Kansas State Historical Society

Dauphin Thompson, was trapped underneath one of the fire engines. He died, weapon in hand, under the bayonets of the Marines. Two others were spared when Greene called a halt to the action. The affair was over in less than three minutes.

Brown's prisoners were escorted from the engine house by their rescuers, and great shouts of joy and approval went up from the crowd. Greene then ordered his men to take Brown and the surviving insurgents outside and to post a guard around them.[54] As Brown and his companions were taken out, the cheers of the crowd turned to ominous threats of dealing with them on the spot. The yard of the engine house quickly filled, and the Marines were, for a moment, hard pressed to keep the mob at bay.[55] Those who called for a rope were soon pushed back by musket-brandishing Marines and order was restored. Lee made his way through the crowd and, reaching the wounded, called for blankets to cover them and physicians to attend their wounds. Sensing that the press of the crowd, eager to see the leader of the abolitionist force in his misery, would give no room for doctors to attend the wounded man, Lee ordered Brown to be moved to the paymaster's office. Luke Quinn was carried into the building by his comrades and placed in the next room. A priest was sent for to administer the last rites of the Roman Catholic Church to the dying Marine.

When those who had brought the wounded men to the haven of the paymaster's office departed, Congressman A. R. Boteler paid a visit

Scene in the engine house courtyard after Marines ended the drama at Harpers Ferry

Oil painting by Charles Waterhouse.
Marine Corps Historical Center 29-4-500

to Brown. A short conversation took place marked by Brown's admission of disappointment that like-thinking whites as well as slaves did not rally to him, and a violent display of anger when the priest who had been attending to Private Quinn came into the room to see if he could be of assistance. As Boteler departed, he passed Russell in the entry. Russell had his own conversation with Brown and later told Boteler that when he entered Brown's room, the old man was standing, his clothes undone, and examining a wound on his side. As soon as he realized Russell was in the room, he quickly returned to his bedding.[56]

After the activity in the Armory yard quieted somewhat, Lee sent a message to the Secretary of War, stating that he had accomplished his mission. The rioters were either captured, dead, or mortally wounded. Lee, thinking that Brown's head wounds were mortal, included "Ossawatamie" among the latter.[57] The message was received at Washington at 10:30 A.M., and a much relieved John B. Floyd wasted no time in spreading the news throughout the government. Transportation Master Smith sent off hurried messages; the first to an anxious Garrett saying that the outbreak had been subdued, praising the Marines and particularly Maryland's native son, William Russell. Smith said he had never before seen "so thrilling a scene."[58] Smith's second telegram was to newspaper offices at Cincinnati and points west, stating, "Harper's Ferry insurrection entirely suppressed; all the outlaws killed or arrested by United States Marines."[59]

A local farmer, John Unseld, somewhat miffed that no one paid attention to him when he reported that two of Brown's gang were at the schoolhouse across the river, went to Lee. Lee listened patiently and, believing the farmer's story, ordered the Baltimore Greys and a detachment from the 53rd Maryland Regiment to investigate the schoolhouse. They found no raiders when they arrived; the two posted there by John Brown had long ago departed, abandoning their comrades at Harpers Ferry to their fate. They did find several crates full of Sharps carbines, and each member of the Greys and the 53rd took one as a souvenir. The leftovers were brought back to the arsenal and turned in.

When Unseld returned from the schoolhouse, he made one more request of Lee. Would the Colonel send another company to search the farmhouse that the insurgents were living in before the attack on the Armory? Sensing that important evidence might be found at the raiders' lair, Lee sent Greene and a squad of Marines to make a search.

After a six-mile march, the party came upon a frantic scene at the Kennedy Farm. The locals, aware of what had happened at Harpers Ferry, were ransacking the place for usable items and souvenirs. At the approach of the Marines, they all scattered, leaving the house empty for Greene and Unseld to search. There were no firearms to be found in the house, just boxes of clothing, trunks of miscellaneous material, and a carpet bag full of letters and papers.[60] The trunks and the carpet bag were loaded on a wagon for delivery to the authorities.

Then there was the matter of the pikes. Greene found hundreds of them stored in the farmhouse. The pikes presented a logistics problem. The wagon would not hold all of them. Greene then got the idea that the former looters might be turned to good purpose. Telling those who remained nearby that they could each have five of the pikes, he ordered Unseld to break open a window and throw the pikes to the waiting recipients. Giving away only five to each willing farmer (or entrepreneur who saw a ready made souvenir he could sell) hardly made a dent in the load he would have to bring back to Harpers Ferry, so Greene upped the spoils to ten and then to fifty per person. Finally, he told them to take as many as they wished. As his Marines threw the pikes out of the window, Greene watched as those below scrambled for their prizes and perhaps thought about the difference a few hours made. The same men who had faced death at the engine house were now gleefully pitching the pikes through the window and laughing at the antics of the locals. Soon enough the lust for the free goods had been satiated. What remained was loaded on the wagon and the party returned to Harpers Ferry.[61]

The Kennedy farm house; John Brown's Maryland lair while he plotted the attack on Harpers Ferry

Hundreds of pikes, weapons for the slaves Brown intended to liberate, were thrown from the upper windows by Marines to a crowd below as souvenirs.

Kansas State Historical Society

While Greene was clearing out Brown's headquarters, the old man was holding court in the paymaster's office at Harpers Ferry. Several dignitaries had arrived by train and Lee granted them permission to see Brown. Governor Henry A. Wise led a delegation which included Senator James M. Mason of Virginia, and Congressmen Clement Vallandigham of Ohio and Charles Faulkner of Virginia. Lee joined the group, along with Stuart and Brown's former hostage, Colonel Washington. Several reporters, including a representative of the *New York Herald* were also present.[62]

For more than three hours, the bloodied abolitionist lay on a makeshift bed on the floor and answered questions from all sides. He explained and justified his reasons for coming to Harpers Ferry, made false claims that he and his men had surrendered when the Marines broke into the engine house (vehemently denied by those who were at the scene), and that he and his men fired only because the Marines fired first (also vigorously denied). He then went on to discuss philosophy, theology, and even medicine. Finally, Brown concluded his discourse and his audience departed.[63]

During the afternoon, the unfortunate Quinn breathed his last. A grave was dug in the cemetery across the street from the Armory grounds and his body was laid to rest with full military honors. He would be followed to the grave by hundreds of thousands who gave their lives to determine whether John Brown's mission was fantasy or prophecy.

Russell, his advisory role to Greene completed, returned to Washington in the early afternoon accompanied by Transportation Master W. P. Smith.[64]

The next day, Lee made arrangements to transfer his prisoners to Charlestown, Virginia. Greene and his detachment formed a close guard around a strange procession of prisoners and notables as they made their way to the cars. Brown and Aaron Stevens, another wounded raider, were carried to the depot in a wagon. Following them and on foot were Governor Wise and his party of Congressional inquisitors of the previous day. Next in line were the three uninjured members of Brown's band, Shields "Emperor" Green, Edwin Coppoc, and John Copeland. Marines marched under arms on all four sides of the cortege.[65] Behind them came a mob, howling "Lynch them! Lynch them!" They retreated only when Governor Wise turned to them and called them cowards for demanding the rope for the prisoners.[66] At the depot, the prisoners were handed over to the marshal of Virginia's western district and the sheriff of Jefferson County. Greene and a squad of Marines escorted them to Charlestown.[67]

Later that day, Lee received a report that the village of Pleasant Valley was under attack by supporters of Brown's cause. Although such an event was highly unlikely, Lee decided to investigate. Greene had just returned from Charlestown with his Marines when Lee took them and Stuart to Pleasant Valley. As he suspected, Lee found nothing but tranquillity in the area. The little command then returned to Harpers Ferry.[68]

Waiting for Greene at Harpers Ferry were telegraphic orders from the Navy Department to return to Headquarters, Marine Corps with his detachment.[69] Having been without sleep for nearly forty hours, Greene could not imagine more welcome news. Lee told him to prepare to depart on the 1:15 A.M. train to Baltimore. Lee and Stuart would accompany him.[70] It is reasonable to assume that all slept soundly during the entire journey.

Greene and his Marines reported in at Headquarters during the morning of October 20, and resumed the normal routine of barracks duty. Pvt. Matthew Ruppert soon recovered from his facial wound and returned to duty.[71]

Toward the end of the month, Greene was summoned to Charlestown as a witness for the Commonwealth of Virginia at the trial of John Brown, remained two weeks but was never called to testify.[72] During his absence, the Secretary of War forwarded copies of Lee's official report of the Harpers Ferry disturbance to his counterpart at the Navy Department. Lee was generous in his praise for the Marines and their officers, stating, "I must also express my thanks to . . . Major Russell, and Lieutenant Green [*sic*], for the aid they afforded me, and my entire commendation of the conduct of the detachment of marines who were at all times ready and prompt in the execution of any duty."[73] Toucey sent transmittal letters to both Russell and Greene on November 5, 1859, expressing his pleasure for the official mention of their gallant services.[74]

Harris was well-pleased with the performance of his Corps during the trouble at Harpers Ferry. The rapid deployment of the detachment, the efficient manner in which the siege of the engine house was ended, and the hostages freed brought praise from his military colleagues, the government and from civilians as well. A letter from Lee bore testimony.

Arlington, near Washington
24 Decr, 1859

Col. Harris
Commd., U.S. Marines
Washington City, D.C.

Colonel;

Your Corps has captivated so many hearts in Virginia, that you must not be surprised at the desire of her sons to enter its ranks.

As one evidence, I enclose you the petition of a "young & hearty" scion, whose military enthusiasm must make amends for his orthography. I have informed him that his letter has been referred to you.

With sincere wishes for a Merry Xmas & Happy New Year to you & Mrs. Harris, I remain very truly yours

R. E. Lee

Enclosure.

Hedgesville Berkley Co Va
December 21st/59

Colonel Lee. Dear Sir it is with pleasure that i take my Seat to Address you Having a desire to join the Service i concluded that i would Address you on the Subject as i am young and hearty. i would like to join the marines at Washington if you will rite and let me know the terms there will be several come with me. i am 20 years old i have an order from my parents given before and witnessed by a Justice of the peace in my District please write Soon and i will come

George W..Miller
Hedgesville Berkley
County Virginia[75]

Soon enough, the excitement of the suppression of John Brown's insurrection died out and the Marines of the Harpers Ferry detachment went on to other assignments. Although no Marines were present at Charlestown, Virginia, when Brown was hanged, word filtered back of a message he left with one of the guards that escorted him to the gallows. Northern abolitionists made a rallying cry of the words, while Southern fire-eaters pointed to them as the creed of all above the Mason-Dixon Line. Others dismissed them as the ravings of a doomed madman. To the Marines who had seen John Brown at the engine house or in his sick bed in the paymaster's office at Harpers Ferry, they were something else. Those who had caught a glimpse of the passion that burned in his eyes could not help but feel a sense of foreboding when they read, or listened as others read aloud, Brown's last testament. "I, John Brown, am now quite certain that the crimes of this guilty land will never be purged away but with blood."[76]

2

Secession and Separation

The presidential election campaign of the summer of 1860 was the most intense in the short history of the United States. Upon its outcome hinged the future direction of the nation. Four major presidential tickets with widely divergent views on the focal point of the campaign were offered to the voters. The Republican Party, presenting Abraham Lincoln and Hannibal Hamlin as its nominees, espoused a platform of not interfering with but containing slavery where it already legally existed. The Democratic Party was split into sectional factions. The Northern entity chose Stephen A. Douglas and Herschel V. Johnson as its standard bearers and ran on a vague campaign of deciding the slavery issue in Federal Territories by popular sovereignty. The Southern version put forth John C. Breckenridge and Joseph Lane as its candidates and hung its fortunes for expanding the "peculiar institution" to the Territories by way of a Federally enacted Slave Code. The Constitutional Union Party nominated John Bell and Edward Everett, representing preservation of the status quo and offering no platform at all. No city, town or village in the country was without active political organizations. No voter was without a strong opinion.

There were no organized "Lincoln Wide-Awakes," or "Bell Ringer" clubs within the military services, but strong political opinions were held nonetheless. Among the officers of the services, politics based upon sectionalism strained and broke friendships of a lifetime. Southern-born officers wrestled with choices they might be faced with if Abraham Lincoln won the fall election. It was no secret that a Republican victory in November might lead to the break-up of the Union. While some firebrands welcomed the thought of dismembering the country or putting arrogant, slave-owning Southerners in their place, most hoped that a candidate of moderation would prevail.

The Marine Corps was not without its share of problems generated by the politics of 1860. The Corps was deeply embarrassed by a report which appeared in the November 2, 1860, issue of the New York *Times*.

Perversion of Military Authority to Party Ends

To the Editor of the New-York Times,

Yesterday afternoon, while standing on the porch of the Marine Barracks at the Brooklyn Navy Yard, I saw one of the Marines come forward, and ask permission from the officer of the day (Lieut. JACOB READE) to go out and register his name as a voter, in view of the approaching election. The officer inquired whom he intended to vote for

"For honest old ABE LINCOLN," replied the man. "For LINCOLN! Then go back; you can't go out sir," said the officer, turning on his heel, while the soldier went back to his quarters.

This occurrence interested me somewhat inasmuch as I had seen the same officer approached by one of the Corps not five minutes previous to make the same request with an entirely different result. Among the inquiries, the man was asked how he intended to vote.

"I shall probably vote for BELL & EVERETT," was the answer.

Thereupon the officer ordered: "Sergeant, send for a Corporal to accompany this man out that he may register his name," adding as he gaily swung his sabretache, "If you are going to vote for Lincoln, by G-d, you should not stir a step."

I need not add this impertinent meddling with the rights of citizenship on the part of a United States Officer meets with the severest reprobation among the Corps, there being an impression in many minds that such conduct comports neither with official station nor the common instincts of a gentleman. To be sure, this is but an individual instance of interference with civil duty by military force, and the parties immediately interested will be left to form what opinions they choose; but how far military authority is to be prostituted to the uses of political trickery is a matter which touches the honor & good name of the entire Corps d'armee, and challenges the attention of every candid & fair minded citizen.

Respectfully &c
Vindex

Brooklyn, Nov., 2, 1860[1]

As soon as Capt. Abraham N. Brevoort, commanding officer of Marine Barracks, Brooklyn, saw the newspaper item in the *Times,* he immediately sent a disclaimer to the Editor.

The Marine Corps and the Election

Marine Barracks, Brooklyn, N. Y.
Nov. 3, 1860

To the Editor of the New York Times:

In justice to the Marine Corps, I have to request that you will publish my disapproval of the conduct of Lieut. Jacob Read, referred to in a communication to your paper of the 3rd Inst., and further, that his conduct has been by me reported to the Commandant of the Corps.

A. N. BREVOORT
Capt., Commanding [2]

That same day, Brevoort wrote to Harris enclosing copies of the *Times* with the embarrassing report and his response, further stating that he had investigated the matter and found it to be true. Additionally, Read had disobeyed strict orders that recruits on drill were not to leave the compound. The lieutenant's conduct in the matter was, wrote Brevoort, "calculated to bring discredit on the service."[3]

Read was not slow to defend his actions. As soon as he learned of Brevoort's official report, he took up his pen in defense and reported the facts to Harris as he saw them. The recruit who left the barracks area was not on *liberty,* but under the charge of a non-commissioned officer and was brought back in under ten minutes. Read admitted expressing himself "thoughtlessly and carelessly," and complained that "the affair is made to wear a different appearance by a reporter permitted to hang around the Barracks and pick up for use the unguarded words which sometimes very naturally and excusably escape the lips, even of older and more habitually discreet persons than myself."[4]

After posting his explanatory communication, Read saw Brevoort's letter to the editor of the *Times,* and wrote his second letter of the day to the Commandant, requesting the matter be brought to the attention of the Secretary of the Navy. Harris did so on November 10.[5]

The Secretary's response was not what Brevoort anticipated. Expecting orders to prepare charges against Read, Brevoort was stung by the reply from Washington.

> . . . the Department does not deem the offense of Lieut. Read of sufficient importance to demand a Court-Martial.

> You will reprimand him for his disobedience of orders and will also inform Captain Brevoort that the Department disapproves of his course in the matter in giving publicity through the newspapers.[6]

The political situation was not confined to the barracks, yards, and other military establishments within the borders of the United States. The importance of the election was felt aboard the naval vessels on foreign stations as well. Writing to his brother in Delaware, 1st Lt. James H. Jones, commander of the Marine Guard of USS *Susquehanna* then visiting Spezia, Italy, commented, "We are all very anxious to hear the result of the election. I cannot bring myself to believe that Lincoln will be successful. If he is, I am fearful that the South will begin to put her threats into execution, However, In a week or so, I suppose we shall get the news out here."[7]

Even as Jones wrote the letter, his worst fears had already been realized. Lincoln had won the election and throughout the South, despite protestations from the President-elect that he intended no interference with their institutions, leaders began to bring the threat of secession into reality. 1st Lt. Andrew J. Hays, an Alabamian by birth, arrived at New York aboard the U.S. Sloop *Savannah* shortly after the election. He wrote his mother that he was attempting to see which way the political winds were blowing, "I may go South soon but cannot tell yet about my movements. It is quite cold here at present, the climate of Alabama I would much rather prefer." [8] One does not know whether Hays was referring to the weather or the political atmosphere of the time. Perhaps both.

On December 20, 1860, South Carolina issued an ordinance dissolving the union between itself and the United States. The lower tier of Southern states followed South Carolina out of the Union during the course of the next few weeks: Mississippi, on January 9, 1861; Florida, on January 10; Alabama, on January 11; Georgia, on January 19; Louisiana, on January 26; and Texas, on February 1. Up to this time, no Marine officer had made any move to resign his commission. All seemed to be waiting for cooler heads to prevail. Sen. John J. Crittendon of Kentucky offered what appeared to be the solution to the dilemma in the form of six constitutional amendments: the prohibition of slavery north of the Missouri Compromise line, but granting Federal protection to the institution below that demarcation; popular sovereignty on the issue of slavery in all future states; prohibition of Congressional action relative to constraints upon slavery in any of the territories; slavery in the City of Washington could not be ended by Federal action, but only by a majority vote of the Capital's citizens; protection of interstate transportation of slaves; Federal compensation for the recovery of escaped slaves; and that no future amendments to the constitution could overrule these six.[9] President-elect Lincoln intimated considering part of what became known as the Crittendon Compromise, but would never accept expansion of slavery to the Territories, regardless of how the residents of those Territories felt on the subject. Lincoln's support in committee managed to kill the compromise measures, but Crittendon remained undaunted. Proposing a national referendum to decide the subject, he managed to force a full Senate vote on January 16, 1861. The measure lost by two votes.

The national crisis was also a matter of concern to Pvt. Daniel L. Boyer, and his comrades at Marine Barracks, Washington. Barracks rumor reflected a simple solution to the problem. All expected to be sent to Charleston, and were confident in their ability to "bring them smart fellows to terms."[10]

Throughout the post-election period, rumblings were heard in Washington that the first move of the Southern states, should they decide to secede from the Union, would be to seize Federal property within their borders. Telegrams and letters were sent to installation commanders to be especially vigilant to this possibility. Of particular importance to the Federal Government were two military posts situated on critical routes of communications; Fort McHenry at Baltimore Harbor, and Fort Washington, a few miles below the Capitol on the Maryland side of the Potomac River. To prevent Maryland secessionists from seizing these strategic positions, the usually lethargic Buchanan Administration sprang into action.

On January 5, 1861, Secretary of the Navy Isaac Toucey ordered Harris to dispatch forty Marines, fully equipped for fifteen days, to Fort Washington to guard against any hostile moves toward that place.[11] Accordingly, Harris issued orders to Bvt. Maj. George H. Terrett to take charge of a detachment of two officers, three sergeants, three corporals, two musicians, and forty privates and proceed without delay to Fort Washington.[12] Provisions for fifty men for fifteen days were picked up at the Washington Navy Yard.[13]

Three days later, Toucey ordered Harris to send a detachment to Fort McHenry for a similar tour of duty.[14] 1st Lt. Andrew J. Hays, who was still pondering the climate, political and otherwise, was ordered to take another officer, three sergeants, four corporals, two musicians and thirty privates on the 4 P.M. train to Fort McHenry that afternoon. They were to garrison the fort until relieved by the army.[15] Hays arrived at Fort McHenry the next day, reported that all was quiet, and that he was sending out frequent patrols to guard against arson.[16] A day later, an incendiary device did strike Fort McHenry but it was not the kind Hays was guarding against.

Fort Washington on the Potomac River
NA Photograph 428-N-1156428

On January 10, 1861, Bvt. Col. Harvey Brown, U.S. Artillery, arrived at Fort McHenry and, under orders from Lt. Gen. Winfield Scott, took command of the post, three companies of artillery due to arrive from Fort Leavenworth, and the Marine detachment.[17] Harris learned of the order the next day and promptly exploded in a blaze of temper. He dashed off a letter to Toucey, pointing out that Lieutenant General Scott's order placing Colonel Brown of the army in command of Marines was in direct violation of the Act of 1834, Section 2. Marines were only to be placed under army orders at the direction of the President. Harris sarcastically mentioned that Scott "might, with the same propriety, order an officer to assume command of the Head Quarters of the Corps." Further, Harris went on, General Scott's assuming command of a Marine officer without authority, despite being illegal, was completely lacking in good taste.[18] Toucey immediately issued orders for Lieutenant Hays to return to Headquarters as soon as the artillerists from Fort Leavenworth arrived. Harris' temper had completely cooled when he reported to Toucey that Hays had returned from Fort McHenry. In fact, the Commandant went out of his way to praise a detachment which had done less than four days detached duty. Wrote Harris, ". . . it affords me pleasure to add that he (Lieutenant Hays) reports the detachment as having behaved remarkably well, obeying all orders promptly and cheerfully; which is saying a great deal for recruits in this inclement weather."[19]

Things were not going well at Fort Washington, either. On January 16, Capt. Algernon S. Taylor reported that it was the professional opinion of 1st Lt. George W. C. Lee of the engineers, "that 150 tolerably organized men could enter this place against the force now here. As I do not wish to be placed in a position to detract from the high character of my Corps, I feel myself bound to make this report."[20] Harris sent what reinforcements he could to Fort Washington under the command of 2d Lt. George P. Houston on January 18. A week later, Taylor's detachment was relieved.

The problems at Forts McHenry and Washington were merely annoyances when compared to the news from Pensacola, Florida.

Harris was well aware that Florida was leaning towards secession. For several days in late December and early January, he scanned his messages for news from Florida. An early intimation that the Marine Barracks at Pensacola was in jeopardy came when a letter from the contractor for rations was delivered to Capt. Josiah Watson.

Fort McHenry

Medford Historical Society

Pensacola, December 29, 1860.

Dear Sir:

I will furnish rations under my contract [for] 1861 till I give you notice.

Yours, most respectfully, etc.
C. P. Knapp,
Per Ira Smith.

Captain Watson,
Commanding Marine Barracks, Warrington

P. S. My object in addressing as above is this, if Florida goes out of the Union I will not furnish afterwards.

Yours, etc.,
C. P. Knapp,
Per Ira Smith.[21]

Watson promptly sent Maj. William B. Slack, Quartermaster of the Corps, this discomfiting news, asking for specie to purchase rations since government credit was nil. The message was received on January 5, 1861, and Slack immediately sent it to Harris. There was nothing Harris could do but forward the reports to the Navy Department. All Toucey could do was to tell Harris to write Watson, informing the Captain that he could get his rations from the commandant of the Navy Yard.[22] Before Slack's reply with the Naval Secretary's instructions reached Watson, the entire situation at Pensacola had turned upside down.

Between 8:00 and 9:00 A.M., January 12, 1861, Watson received a summons from Capt. James Armstrong, USN, commandant of the Pensacola Navy Yard.[23] The messenger told Watson that the Commodore wanted the Marines formed up, ready for immediate service, fully armed and equipped. Before Watson left to see Armstrong, he turned the detachment out and placed them under the charge of O. Sgt. Samuel F. Reynolds.

Capt. Josiah Watson, USMC, shown here as a second lieutenant wearing the undress uniform of the 1839 regulations
Dr. William Schultz Collection

Armstrong told Watson that a body of armed men was said to be marching on the navy yard. If this was true, he wanted the Marines ready to go into action at a moment's notice. Returning to the barracks, Watson stopped to check on the Marines guarding the gates to the yard and make sure they understood their orders regarding any attempt by unauthorized persons to enter the yard. All understood that they were to fire a shot into the air as a warning to the command. The Captain then hurried on to the barracks to brief his noncommissioned officers on the situation.

Elevation of Marine Barracks, Pensacola, Florida

Marine Corps Museum, Quantico, Virginia

After Watson left Commodore Armstrong, a message was delivered to the yard commandant from 1st Lt. Adam J. Slemmer, USA.[24] Slemmer, with an under strength Battery G, 1st U.S. Artillery, had occupied Fort Pickens on Santa Rosa Island in Pensacola Harbor on January 10. Understanding the dilemma he faced if forced to oppose an assault from the mainland with only his forty-six men, Slemmer asked Armstrong for help. In the event that Armstrong was contemplating surrender, would he send the Marines to Fort Pickens to bolster his meager force? Slemmer never received a reply.[25]

At 1:30 P.M., Armstrong again sent for Watson. Expecting orders to bring his Marines into action, Watson was shocked to hear Armstrong state the installation had been surrendered and that he and his detachment were prisoners of the State of Florida. Caught completely by surprise, Watson wondered why his men had not fired the warning shots to alert the garrison that strangers were attempting to gain entry. He later learned that secessionist officers from the yard had greeted Alabama and Florida troops at the gate, ordering the Marines to let them pass.

Shortly thereafter, Col. Tennent Lomax, acting under the aegis of state authorities, took possession of the barracks, with all the arms, accouterments, and equipment belonging to the Marines.[26] Watson gave the order to form up and stack arms but some of the men, laboring under great emotional strain, cursed and swore, saying they would rather die than suffer the humiliation of surrendering without a fight. In the end, though, the Marines did stack their arms. Adding insult to injury, Lomax ordered the Marines out of their spacious accommodations and into two small rooms so that the rest of the barracks could be occupied by three hundred Alabama troops. Under orders from Lomax not to leave the rooms, the Marines were spared the sight of the United States Flag being lowered from its staff in the navy yard.

There was no formal ceremony at the main part of the yard where the flag staff was situated. The secessionist troops moved as a mob to the center of the yard, no order or discipline evident in either officers or rank and file. Lt. Francis B. Renshaw, a naval officer of some thirty-three years of service had gone over to the secessionists and ordered Quartermaster William Conway, a weather-beaten old tar, to lower the flag.[27]

As he approached the flag staff, a worker from the ordinary quarters, an Englishman named James Ivey, rushed up to him and said, "Conway, you old ——. Do not haul that flag down, for, if you do, I hope your arm may be paralyzed!" Conway replied, "My boy, you little know what you are talking about. I am complying with an order

James Ivey
Courtesy of Mrs. Helen Little

from my superior officer and things are now changed within a few short hours."[28] But Ivey's tongue-lashing gave Conway second thoughts about the task, and he stepped away, refusing to lower the flag.[29] Renshaw quickly found other hands to do the job and the Stars and Stripes came down, replaced by what Ivey called, " . . . a piece of dirty yellow bunting with one single star in the middle."[30]

Cdr. Henry Walke, commander of the steamer *Supply,* had been engaged in transporting munitions and supplies from the Pensacola Navy Yard to Fort Pickens on Santa Rosa Island.[31] As soon as he saw the flag being struck, he signaled USS *Wyandotte* to bring off the Marines as a reinforcement to Fort Pickens. It was too

Marine Barracks, Pensacola, after occupation by rebel forces
Miller's Photographic History of the Civil War

late. The Marines had laid down their arms and were now prisoners. With great frustration, he signaled *Wyandotte* to disregard his order.[32]

The next morning, Captain Watson received information from Commodore Armstrong that the Marines, and any officers who wished to, could depart from Pensacola aboard *Supply.* Watson formed his men, marched them to the dock and turned them over to Commander Walke for passage north. He left the next day for Mobile and took the land route to New York.[33]

After the loyal forces were evacuated from the Pensacola Navy Yard, an uneasy stalemate prevailed. On January 18 and 20, Thomas Hamilton and the Marine Guard of USS *Wyandotte* volunteered to go to Fort Pickens and assist in mounting guns.[34] The Florida troops made preparations to attack Fort Pickens where Slemmer and his artillerists were quite ready to take them on. Reinforcements on board USS *Brooklyn,* including her Marine Guard under the command of 1st Lt. George R. Graham, were ready to land and support the meager garrison of Fort Pickens. USS *Macedonian* was standing by to land her Marines as well. In order to prevent a clash of arms, Capt. Samuel Barron, USN, suggested both sides draw back. If preparations for the attack on Fort Pickens were suspended, perhaps the Navy Department would not land reinforcements and thereby provoke hostilities. Both sides agreed to the truce and a friendly atmosphere prevailed with regular mails and supplies being sent to

The Navy Yard at Pensacola under rebel control as viewed from Fort Pickens
Naval Historical Center Photograph NH 59122

Fort Pickens from the secessionist mainland.[35] It would last for more than two months.

Captain Watson arrived in Brooklyn on January 28, 1861, a week before his detachment. Reporting his arrival to Harris, he enclosed a parole handed to him by a Mr. Shipley, clerk to Victor Randolph.[36] Formerly a captain in the U.S. Navy, Randolph resigned his commission on January 10, and was now working with the secessionist forces.

Pensacola Navy Yard
January 16, 1861

> Captain Josiah Watson of the U.S. Marine Corps, having given his parole of honor not to bear arms against the State of Florida, has permission to leave this place with his family and private property without hindrance or molestation.
>
> *(signed) V. M. Randolph,*
> *Captain, Commanding Navy Yard.*[37]

Watson had never used the parole, and claimed he had never even read the paper until he arrived in New York. Further, he denied ever giving his parole; that Colonel Lomax had told him he was on parole, and he had kept silent on being so informed.[38] Watson's protestations found little sympathy with Harris. January had been a most hectic month for his office—the hurried occupations of Forts Washington and McHenry, the surrender of the Pensacola Navy Yard, and the January 22 call to put all the Marines at Marine Barracks, Brooklyn, under arms to counter a rumored assault on the Brooklyn Navy Yard.[39] These exigencies had frayed his nerves. His patience was stretched to the limit and he was in no mood to deal with Watson. Harris forwarded the letter and the parole to Toucey for his actions, commenting, "I enclose to the Department a copy of a letter from Captain Watson, reporting his arrival in Brooklyn, and enclosing a copy of his parole of honor. As I am not aware of the United States being at war with Florida, I report the facts for the action of the Department."[40] For several days thereafter, Watson had to weather the icy disapproval of his Commandant. It was something of a relief when Harris ordered Watson to appear before the Court of Inquiry that was meeting in Washington as a witness in the matter of the surrender of the Pensacola Navy Yard. Whatever resentment Harris may have felt toward Watson was quickly forgotten when Harris received another irritating order from Lt. Gen. Winfield Scott.

In the early days of February 1861, Congress suddenly awoke to the uncomfortable fact that it was situated in a city that was Southern in every facet of its existence. Congress learned there was no plan to counter mob violence should there be an attempt by the residents of the city to seize the capital. Scott was charged with rectifying the oversight.

On February 12, 1861, Secretary of War Joseph Holt received Scott's plan to counter street riots.[41] The various infantry and artillery units of the Regular Army were to rendezvous at predesignated places in the capital and follow established procedures for putting down any civil insurrection. Shortly after presenting his plan to the Secretary, Scott had an afterthought and sent a second communication to the War Office.

Hon. Secretary of War
Dear Sir;

In the order which you read, just now, you may remember that nothing was said of the Marines. No doubt that Colonel Harris, chief of the corps, would comply with any call that I might make on him, but to make everything regular, I will ask that the Secretary of the Navy be requested to issue his order to Colonel Harris,

Marines marching outside Marine Barracks, Washington, 1861
Harper's Weekly, Courtesy of George Menegaux

directing him to report to me for temporary duty in the District of Columbia with as large a part of his corps as can be spared from guarding his own barracks and at the Washington Navy Yards.

I wish to insert in the order (alluded to above) a paragraph to this effect:- In the event of an act of mob violence in the City of Washington, that all the Marines that can be spared for the purpose will hasten to Capitol Square.

I await further orders

Very truly yours,
(Signed) Winfield Scott
Feb. 12, 1861.[42]

In view of the official indignation Harris had registered when Scott placed an army officer in command of the Marines at Fort McHenry a month previous, Scott could not have been more wrong in assuming that the chief of the Marine Corps would cheerfully submit to a second helping of that particular affront. When presented with Scott's plan of action to prevent mob control of the capital and official orders to comply with that part which affected the Marine Corps, Harris seethed with ire. Exhibiting remarkable control, Harris sent off a communication to Toucey pointing out Scott's second violation of The Act of 1834, Section 2, in as many months. Harris wrote, "On reflection, it occurs to me that the necessary order from the President, assigning the Marines to duty with the army has not been promulgated . . ."[43] The next day, Toucey replied that Harris was correct; the Marines had not been detached for service with the army by order of the President.

It is clear that Harris was not trying to avoid sending his Marines into the thick of civil unrest. He had done so at a moment's notice when ordered to send a detachment to quell the insurrection at Harpers Ferry. Nor was he playing the bureaucrat, or twisting Scott's dignity like some malapert lawyer. It had been a long and often bitter struggle for Harris' predecessor at the head of the Corps, Bvt. Brig. Gen. Archibald Henderson, to establish by law the relationship between the Marine Corps and the army.[44] Harris was not about to permit the slightest variance from the Act of 1834.[45]

By mid-February, it was quite apparent that the seven seceding States had no intention of returning to the Union. In an age when loyalty to one's native state mattered more than allegiance to the central government, military officers from the seven began to submit their resignations and offer their services to the governors of their native states. A total of fifty-one naval officers had resigned in the preceding two months, a situation with ripple effects spreading out as far as the Pacific Squadron.[46] The second officer of the Marine Guard attached to the flagship of the Pacific Squadron, appalled at the flight from the service, penned his testament of loyalty to the Navy Department.

2d Lt. J. Howard Rathbone, USMC
Howard Gosdorffer Collection

U S Ship Lancaster
off Panama
February 6, 1861

Hon. Isaac Toucey
Secretary of the Navy
Sir:

At a time like the present when almost daily officers of the Navy are resigning instead of doing their utmost to preserve the Union and the honor of the Flag, it seems to me no more than proper for those officers who remain loyal to express to you their devotion to the Union and their readiness to assist in enforcing the laws. I therefore take this opportunity of addressing you and declaring my willingness to undertake in my comparatively humble position any duty the Government may assign me.

I have the honor to be
Very Respectfully
Your Obt. Serv't.
J. Howard Rathbone
2d Lieutenant
U.S. Marines[47]

Rathbone's testimonial notwithstanding, it was only a matter of time before Southern-born officers of the Marine Corps would do likewise.

The first Marine officer to submit his resignation was 2d Lt. Calvin L. Sayre, an Alabamian who had been commissioned on June 3, 1858. Sayre returned from his first cruise aboard USS *St. Marys* on January 12, and found the country in political chaos. His native state had seceded the day before he arrived at the Brooklyn Navy Yard. Wishing desperately to return home and discuss his future with family and friends, Sayre applied to the Navy Department for a leave of absence. It was denied.[48] After reporting to Marine Barracks, Washington, Sayre again applied for leave. It was again denied.[49] Unable to learn the state of affairs in Alabama or to discuss what course he should take with his family, Sayre submitted his resignation to the Department on February 14, 1861. It was promptly accepted.[50]

After Sayre's resignation was officially accepted, he went to the various offices of the Marine Corps Staff to settle his accounts and to take his leave. Although he had only been in the Corps for two and a half years, he made a distinctly favorable impression with his seniors. Paymaster Russell bid farewell and handed Sayre a letter expressing his personal feelings. Writing that Sayre's departure from the Corps would be a source of regret to his brother officers but to none more than himself, Russell continued, ". . . your course has been alike creditable to you as an officer and a gentleman, and I feel sure that in saying good bye with a 'God speed you,' I express the united sentiment of your brother officers of the Corps."[51] The farewell of the Adjutant and Inspector was no less sincere. Maj. Henry B. Tyler, Sr., clearly understanding the circumstances of Sayre's departure, gave him a parting letter, writing, "I hope in whatever situation you may hereafter be placed that your days be peaceful and happy and should your lot be cast in military life that you will rise to eminence in the estimation of your countrymen."[52]

Sayre's last good-bye was to Harris. The Commandant had only known Sayre for the brief few weeks he had served at Marine Barracks, Washington, since returning from sea duty. However, he had made such a favorable impression with Harris that he was compelled to write a letter of recommendation, closing with, ". . . his bearing as an officer and gentleman has met with my entire approbation. I regret that the unsettled state of the Country makes it, in his opinion, necessary he should resign."[53] Within a month of his emotional leave-taking at Washington, Sayre had tendered his services to Confederate President Jefferson Davis at Montgomery and had been detailed to Texas as an acting assistant general and mustering officer. On March 29, 1861, Sayre was appointed a first lieutenant of Confederate States Marines.[54]

Over the next eleven months, nineteen of Sayre's brother officers would follow him out of the Corps. When certain officers left the Corps, genuine regret was felt by those they bade farewell. The departure of others was a source of relief within the Corps. At least one resulted in a scramble to fill his position even before he left it.

1st Lt. Jacob Read wrote his letter of resignation on February 27, stating that Georgia, his native state, had called for his services.[55] No emotional farewells accompanied Read's departure from

New York. His commanding officer, Capt. Abraham N. Brevoort, still smarting from the official rebuke he had received from the Navy Department over his handling of the pre-election business with Read, was gratified to see him go. In less than a week, Read had accepted the position of captain, Company D, 1st Georgia Regulars. He also held a commission as captain of Confederate States Marines dating from May 21, 1861, but there is no record of his ever having served with the Corps at any time.[56]

That same day, 2d Lt. Becket K. Howell finally received his parchment commission from the Navy Department, something he had been waiting for since he was appointed to the Corps on August 1, 1860. He promptly telegraphed Montgomery, Alabama, and asked Jefferson Davis, his brother-in-law[57] and mentor, for counsel.

Capt. Jacob Read, 1st Georgia Regulars
Miller's Photographic History of the Civil War

2d Lt. Becket K. Howell
NHC Photograph NRL (O) 36

"Shall I resign or not?"[58] He received Davis' affirmative reply the next day. Howell wrote the Navy Department, acknowledging receipt of his commission and returning it with his resignation.

On leaving Marine Barracks, Washington, Howell received a letter of recommendation from Harris, ending with the personal comment, " . . . he has my sincere wishes for his prosperity in whatever walks of life his future may lead him."[59] Howell traveled to Montgomery after his resignation and was commissioned first lieutenant of Confederate States Marines on March 29.

Joining Howell in resigning their commissions were 1st Lt. George Holmes (February 28), 2d Lt. Henry L. Ingraham (late February), and 1st Lt. Andrew J. Hays (March 1). Both Hays and Holmes received letters of recommendation from Harris. Hays was lauded as "a high-toned gentleman." Further, "Should he decide to enter any other military corps, I take pleasure in recommending him as a gentleman to be relied upon at all times." Harris concluded his letter by saying, "With many good wishes for his future prosperity and success in whatever field of duty that awaits him, I am very sincerely his friend."[60] A letter in almost identical terms was handed to Holmes. If Ingraham, then aboard USS *St. Louis* off Pensacola, had been in Washington, it is very likely that he would have received a similar recommendation. All three were made commissioned officers of the Confederate States Marine Corps dating from March 29, 1861, Hays and Holmes captains, and Ingraham a first lieutenant.[61]

In light of what was happening in the South, the Harris letters appear out of place. Written at a time when Southern authorities had taken over several Federal installations, with reports from the secessionist government in Montgomery that more such seizures were in the offing, and in full knowledge that the incoming administration

1st Lt. George Holmes
Courtesy of John J. B. Cooper

2d Lt. Henry L. Ingraham as he appeared when a midshipman at the United States Naval Academy
Courtesy of Mrs. Charles M. Carson

of Abraham Lincoln made no secret of the fact that it intended to recover the property of the government, the very officers that Harris was recommending for future military employ might use their skills to oppose the Federal recovery. There is no evidence that Harris was a supporter of secession, nor was he ever called to account for the sentiments expressed in the letters, although his clerks had every opportunity to divulge their contents to interested parties. The letters were probably nothing more than representations of a genuine bond between the officers of the Marine Corps, the understanding of their Commandant when these young officers followed the dictates of their consciences and severed that bond, and the unstated hope that they might never be called to bear arms against each other.

Congress looked upon the resignations from the military services in a different light. Recognizing that those who left the service did so with a full understanding that they might soon bear arms against the United States, a Special Committee of the House of Representatives was convened to investigate the matter. Citing the fact that Toucey accepted the resignations of naval and Marine officers without hesitation or inquiry, thereby committing "a grave error, highly prejudicial to the discipline of the service, and injurious to the honor and efficiency of the Navy," a resolution of censure was passed on March 2.[62]

In the waning hours of the Buchanan Administration, Harris gathered his staff officers and the officers and men stationed at Marine Barracks, Washington, and paid a final tribute to the departing President. Marching to the White House, the Marines saluted Buchanan with great gusto.[63] The Washington *Evening Star* covered the ceremony and gave the following account to its readers:

> The battalion of United States Marines, four companies strong, paraded today under command of Maj. Terrett, with Lieut. Nicholson as acting adjutant. The Marines marched from their barracks to the Executive Mansion by way of Pennsylvania avenue and paid their respects to President Buchanan. They were accompanied by the Marine Band in full strength under Prof. Scala. with the drum corps conducted by Drum Maj. Roche.
>
> The day was warm and the dust blinding to the eyes, yet the battalion made a fine appearance, marching well and paying strict attention to dressing each platoon by its guides, so that at no time were the men out of line. Marching into the grounds of the Presidential Mansion by the West Gate, the battalion halted in the carriageway until President Buchanan appeared and took position on the pavement which approaches the portico from the west. The battalion was again formed in column of platoons, guides right, and marched in review before the President, who stood

> uncovered until the column had passed. Meantime, the band played, 'Hail to the Chief.'
>
> The Marines then moved into line and marched by the flank to Madison place, where they halted for a rest. They marched back to their barracks by the same route, attracting favorable attention from the thousands of Washingtonians on the streets and the inaugural visitors, who have already begun to arrive in large numbers.[64]

Such a display must have cheered the Chief Executive, whose weary spirit bore the bruises from a legion of critics who blamed his lack of decisive action for the entire secession difficulty.

The Marines at the Washington Barracks were aware of the potential for trouble. Private Boyer's letters of early 1861 reflect the view of the young men who would be called out to defend the capital.

> Everything here is on a war footing. There is, at present, about 1500 U.S. Army soldiers here, including the Marine Corps which for the time being act as U.S. soldiers for land duty. . . . We expect to be ordered out the 4th of March to guard the capitol as them southern Fire Eaters are talking about taking it about that time. . . . They are getting ready here for troublesome times. The Marines from all the Norther Rendivous are concentrating here and if the south attempts to take the capitol I'm thinking they will find troublesome times. . . . Well I enlisted for service and I am thinking that my wishes will be gratified before long.[65]

Inauguration Day, Monday, March 4, 1861, saw Washington awaken to a grim overcast sky, and the promise of rain. The heaviness of the clouds was seen by many as an omen of what the new administration brought to the nation. Throughout Washington, signs of a military presence were everywhere. Cavalry detachments and squads of soldiers were posted along the streets, while sharpshooters took positions on the rooftops of government buildings. Cannon were deployed at strategic locations and, to the keen observer, not just to fire salutes to the incoming President. Anchored off the Washington Navy Yard was the steamer USS *Pawnee.* Her Marine Guard, under the command of 1st Lt. Edward McD. Reynolds, was under arms, ready to land at a moment's notice to quell any disturbance or to assist in the inauguration of the President-elect.[66] Rumors of assassination plots abounded in Washington.[67] There was genuine concern for the safety of Lincoln, and Scott was taking no chances.

There was also concern, however, that the day be marked with the usual and expected festivities. The Marine Band, under orders from the departing Toucey, had reported to the Commissioner of Public Buildings (but today acting in his capacity as Chief Parade Marshal) Benjamin B. French at City Hall at 9:00 A.M.[68] Forming up in the inaugural parade, the band marched from City Hall to the White House where the procession picked up the carriage carrying the former and next occupant. The stirring martial music helped dispel some of the gloom brought on by the weather as the parade made its way to the Capitol Building.

After Lincoln's swearing in as the 16th President of the United States and his inaugural address, in which he made entreaties to those alienated by his election, promising not to interfere with their way of life and saying that the national forces would never fire the first shot to bring about war, the cannon boomed out in salute. The Marine Band struck up martial airs as well-wishers surrounded and congratulated the President. James Buchanan, whose countenance had measurably improved now that the heavy burden of the office was in Lincoln's hands, wished his successor well and left the platform. This was the signal for the second duty of the day for the Marine Band.

Toucey, in a gesture of respect toward his departing leader, had made arrangements for a military escort to accompany Buchanan as he left the White House for the last time. The First Battalion of the District Militia would form an honor guard for the former President and shepherd him from the Executive Mansion to the Washington Depot for his journey home to Lancaster, Pennsylvania. The Marine Band would join the escort and provide appropriate music for the occasion.[69] The Marine Band had started the day playing one President into history and now brought it to a close, playing another into retirement.

On March 7, the incoming administration took charge in Washington. As Secretary of the Navy Gideon Welles took office, there was no immediate change in Navy Department policy regarding resignations nor would there be until after Fort Sumter had been attacked. During this entire period, the Special Committee of the House railed against the practice of letting those who submitted resignations go with impunity. Although the incident took place after the Navy Department took a more stern attitude toward officers who tendered their resignations, the actions of former Marine officer Hays were a clear example to the Committee of why departing Southerners should not have been allowed to go their way unfettered.

On April 15, O. Sgt. James Thompson, noncommissioned officer in charge of the Marine Guard aboard the Receiving Ship

Princeton at the Philadelphia Navy Yard, went to the office of the assistant quartermaster of the Marine Corps, Capt. William A. T. Maddox, on Spruce Street to make a requisition. Much to his surprise, Hays was in the office. Seeing Sergeant Thompson enter, Hays went to him, shook his hand and told him how happy he was to see him. The two exchanged pleasantries and then Hays got down to business. Did Sergeant Thompson know any sergeants or other good Marines who wanted to better themselves? Hays would guarantee them a good position in the Confederate service. Thompson replied that he did not and further, he himself, a native Pennsylvanian with thirty years of service to the Corps, would never consider leaving his country in such a time of peril. Hays said he didn't think Thompson would leave the Corps but there was the possibility that he knew some who would. The two men then parted and Thompson completed his business at the office.[70]

When Thompson returned to the Receiving Ship, he made a written report of the entire affair and handed it to Capt. Henry K. Hoff, USN, commanding officer of *Princeton*.[71] Hoff forwarded the report to the Secretary of the Navy, who passed it down to Harris. The Commandant was thoroughly embarrassed to learn that the "high toned gentlemen" he had so fondly bid farewell to six weeks earlier was attempting to seduce enlisted men of the Marine Corps to desert to the Confederacy.

Maddox was also drawn into the imbroglio. The Secretary of the Navy demanded to know what Hays was doing in his office and why hadn't Maddox reported the conversation between Hays and Sergeant Thompson? Maddox claimed he knew nothing of the matter and did not hear the conversation. Since all three of the office clerks working for Maddox came to his defense, no charges were filed against him. However, Maddox, a native of Maryland, was viewed with suspicion by Welles for a long time after the incident.

No Marine officers resigned their commissions for the first month and a half of the Lincoln Administration, although there was much discussion among the Virginia-born as to what they would do if their native state withdrew from the Union. While a guest at the Washington residence of Maj. Henry B. Tyler, Emily Thorn, was privy to a conversation which she immediately reported to the Navy Department. Tyler, she wrote, had made no secret of the fact that he would not fire a shot against his brothers of the South. Further, if Virginia left the Union, he would resign and follow her. He was sure he would not go alone, that every officer of the Corps from his state would join him.[72]

Virginia withdrew from the Union on April 17, five days after the first shells fell upon Fort Sumter. The secession of Virginia led to a second round of resignations from the Corps, not beginning with Tyler, nor by Virginians but by two Marine officers who had no apparent connection with the Southern Cause at all. By the time Welles ordered the destruction of the Navy Yard at Norfolk, Virginia on the night of April 20, the resignations of Capt. Jabez C. Rich of Maine, and 1st Lt. Adam N. Baker of New Hampshire, had been submitted. Both would shortly turn up in Richmond, Virginia to accept commissions in the Virginia Marine Corps.[73] Baker, after a rocky start, had been shaping up as a fine officer. He would be missed. Upon the consolidation of Virginia forces with those of the Confederacy, Baker accepted a first lieutenant's commission in the Confederate States Marines, ranking from June 6, 1861.[74] Rich, however, was another matter. His mental state had long been in doubt. He was likely to disobey an order and then report himself for doing so just to provoke his commanding officer. His post aboard the Receiving Ship *Pennsylvania* had been one where he would cause the least amount of trouble. His departure caused no concern at Headquarters, Marine Corps, or in the Navy Department. He was commissioned captain of Virginia Marines on May 20, 1861, was dismissed from that service for inefficiency on August 21, 1861, accepted a commission as captain of Confederate States Marines on October 26, 1861, and was dropped from that Corps as of October 10, 1862.[75]

Capt. Jabez C. Rich, USMC
NA Photograph 127-G-525995

Maj. Henry Ball Tyler, Adjutant and Inspector, USMC, in the full dress uniform of the 1852 regulations
Courtesy of the Chrysler Museum, Norfolk, Virginia

Tyler's prediction that all of Virginia's sons serving as officers of the Marine Corps would follow

Bvt. Maj. George H. Terrett, USMC
NA Photograph 127-G-521522

her fortunes was somewhat off the mark There were eleven Marine officers on duty in April 1861 who had been appointed from Virginia. Only seven tendered their resignations.[76] However, there was now a decidedly different attitude at the Navy Department regarding resignations. After the fall of Fort Sumter, Welles took a narrow view of those who would leave their country in its hour of need. Very few resignations were accepted by the Navy Department after Fort Sumter, none from officers of the Marine Corps.

Bvt. Maj. George H. Terrett, the hero of the Battle for Mexico City during the War with Mexico, submitted his resignation on April 22.[77] It was declined and he was dismissed by order of the President on May 6. Terrett accepted a commission as a colonel in the Provisional Army of Virginia, which he held until August 22, 1861. He was, in the meantime, commissioned major of Confederate States Marines to rank from June 20, 1861, and commanded the Confederate States Marine Battalion at Drewry's Bluff for most of the war.[78] Capt. Algernon S. Taylor forwarded his resignation on April 25. It, too, was declined and he was dismissed on May 6. Taylor would accept the commission of lieutenant colonel in the Provisional Army of Virginia before entering the Confederate States Marine Corps as major and quartermaster. Major Tyler submitted his resignation on May 2, but was dismissed as of May 6. He accepted a commission as lieutenant colonel of Confederate States Marines on June 18, 1861, and commanded the 3rd Brigade under Brig. Gen. Braxton Bragg at Pensacola for a time during the summer of 1861.[79]

Tyler's attempted resignation brought about a flurry of applications from other Marine officers anxious to assume the office of Adjutant and Inspector of the Corps. No fewer than seven officers were suggested for the post; Harris recommending either Capt. Addison Garland or Capt. John Grayson to the Navy Department.[80] Political influence prevailed in the final selection, length of service notwithstanding, and 1st Lt. Augustus S. Nicholson was appointed to the office much to the outrage of Harris.[81]

The remaining Virginians who "went South" were on sea duty when their state left the Union. Capt. Robert Tansill, commanding the Marine Guard aboard USS *Congress,* forwarded his resignation when word of secession reached the Southern Hemisphere. Upon the return of *Congress* from duty off the coast of Brazil on August 23, 1861, Tansill was notified that his resignation had been declined, that he had been dismissed, and further, that he was under arrest. He was soon confined at Fort Warren in Boston Harbor as a prisoner of war. Tansill was held until January 10, 1862. After his release, he went to Richmond and accepted a commission as captain of Confederate States Marines to rank from January 22, 1862, which he held until February 15, 1862. He then resigned to become colonel of the 2d Virginia Artillery Battalion.[82]

Capt. Robert Tansill, USMC, shown here in the uniform of a colonel, Provisional Army of the Confederate States

MCHC Photograph

Tyler's son, 1st Lt. Henry B. Tyler, Jr., arrived at New York aboard the captured slave ship *Nightingale* on June 15. His subsequent misadventures were reported in the *New York Times.*

> Lieut. TYLER, it seems, is a Virginian, and being a Virginian and of the F(rench) F(orrest) type, he could be no more nor less than a Secessionist of the first water. Like a true Secessionist, no sooner had he set foot on land from his long cruise, than he made a rush for the nearest bar-room, where he commenced imbibing strong potations, and giving vent to strong secession sentiments. Gen. SCOTT, he did not hesitate to say was a "d-d old s-n of a b-h." President LINCOLN was a "babboon," and the Government of the United States was a "d-d humbug that ought to be upset and replaced by a monarchy." This and much more of similar secession logic did Lieut. TYLER inflict upon his astonished hearers.

1st Lt. George P. Turner, USMC, shown here as a second lieutenant wearing the pre-1859 undress uniform

Ralph W. Donnelly Papers, MCHC

During his peregrinations about the City, he chanced on Sunday morning to drop into the headquarters of the Harbor Police, which he mistook for a hotel, and called for a drink. Not getting his drink, he commenced to damn the place, and by a natural gradation of logic, he fell to damning the country, the Government and the people that would support such a place. His conversation finally became so interesting that one of the policemen present invited him to walk up Broadway. During the promenade the policeman, by dint of professing to be a simon pure Secessionist himself, drew from the lieutenant. . . . other interesting items.

The news article went on to say . . . that he, Tyler, confessed to having feigned his illness while aboard USS *Saratoga* so that he could use it as a reason for getting back to this country; that he would use the illness as a reason for submitting his resignation and if that tact failed, he would strip off his uniform and make his way to the Confederacy incognito. Tyler and the policeman parted company and the former was not seen for a few days. He was spotted and arrested by a detective who brought him to the Brooklyn Navy Yard and placed him in the custody of Commodore Breese. The reporter hoped that now that "the patient" had been handed over to the ministrations of the Government authorities, the treatment for his "disease" would be what Tyler deserved.[83] Tyler was kept under close confinement aboard the Receiving Ship *North Carolina.* While under arrest, he tendered his resignation, but it was rejected and he was dismissed on June 21.[84] He would shortly follow his father into the Confederate States Marines, accepting the position of first lieutenant.

1st Lt. George P. Turner, sent home from USS *Cyane* on a sick ticket, arrived in New York and mailed his resignation to Washington on June 24. He was notified of his dismissal the next day. Turner was confirmed as a second lieutenant in the Marine Corps of Virginia on May 2, 1861, but never served. He was commissioned first lieutenant of Confederate States Marines to rank from July 2, 1861, and promoted to captain on December 5, 1861.[85]

Bvt. Capt. John D. Simms arrived aboard USS *Richmond* from the Mediterranean on July 3, and submitted his resignation two days later. It was declined and he was dismissed on July 8. Simms entered the Confederate States Marine Corps with the rank of captain on July 15, 1861, and compiled an admirable record as a company and battalion commander.[86]

Two of the seven letters of resignation submitted by Marine officers from Virginia are in sharp contrast. Capt. Robert Tansill's letter is a lengthy discourse on the right of a person who took the oath of office to protect and defend the Constitution to interpret it. As he interpreted the Constitution, any state had the right to secede and he would not take up arms to force it back into the Union. Such action on the part of the government was tantamount to despotism. He would have no part in the destruction of liberty in his country.[87] Capt. Algernon S. Taylor, on the other hand, did not resort to moral or philosophical discussions of his reasons for tendering his resignation. He simply stated, "I cannot consent to serve a Black Republican Government any longer."[88]

The last Virginian to tender his resignation was 1st Lt. Alexander W. Stark. Serving aboard USS *St. Marys* off the California coast, Stark did not receive news of the outbreak of the war until long after it happened. Once he did learn of Fort Sumter and the secession of his native state, he wrote to the Navy Department on June 4, tendering his resignation. That letter apparently never reached the Navy Department and after waiting several weeks for a reply, Stark again submitted his resignation. This second letter, dated September 23, 1861, reached the Navy Department on October 17. On that day, Welles wrote Stark, informing him that he had been dismissed from the service from the moment he received the notification in hand. The letter was given to 1st Lt. Jehu A. Burrough, who was scheduled to ship for the Pacific Squadron in November for duty aboard USS *Cyane*. Burrough's

Bvt. Capt. John D. Simms, USMC, photographed when a second lieutenant, wearing the 1839 undress uniform

Courtesy of Edith S. Bingham

departure was delayed and by the time he joined *Cyane* and that ship made San Francisco, Stark had been agonizing for more than three months. On January 9, 1862, Burrough delivered Welles' letter to Stark. It was the most unusual dismissal from any service during the war. Stark was the only one of the twenty U.S. Marine Corps officers who resigned or were dismissed not to be commissioned in the Confederate States Marine Corps.[89]

The attempted resignation of 1st Lt. J. Ernest Meiere was an embarrassment to none other than President Abraham Lincoln. On April 3, 1861, Meiere was joined in marriage with Nannie Buchanan, the daughter of Capt. Franklin Buchanan USN.[90] Among the guests were President Lincoln, Senator Stephen A. Douglas, and several members of the Cabinet. A grand party was held at the Buchanan's residence at the Washington Navy Yard. At the height of the celebration, the President reportedly cut the wedding cake.[91] The President was mightily chagrined when he learned that Meiere, after being ordered to duty aboard USS *Anacostia* on April 20, had a change of commitment and submitted his resignation dated April 24. He was subsequently dismissed from the service but not before Harris had written another of his sterling letters of recommendation.[92] It is certain that Lincoln did not share Harris' sentiments. Meiere accepted a commission as first lieutenant of Confederate States Marines to date from May 8, 1861. He was promoted captain on December 5, 1861, and gained a reputation as one of the best officers of that Corps.[93]

1st Lt. J. Ernest Meiere, USMC
NA Photograph 127-G-516403

Israel Greene, the captor of John Brown at Harpers Ferry, was a New Yorker by birth, a citizen of Wisconsin, but was married to a Virginia belle. On April 25, Greene arrived at Boston aboard USS *Niagara,* returning from a cruise that brought the Japanese diplomatic delegation back to their native land in 1860. Before anyone went ashore, the officers of the ship, crew, and Marines were informed that an oath of allegiance was required of all. Officers who refused were to be expelled from the ship; enlisted personnel would be confined.

Greene, fellow Marine 2d Lt. George Butler, Navy Lts. Isaac N. Brown, David P. McCorkle, Chief Eng. William P. Williamson, 1st Eng. H. Ashton Ramsey, and Midn. Edmund G. Read declined to take the oath. All were ordered from the ship without orders to report to the commandant of the navy yard or the Department. The day after these officers refused to take the so-called "iron-clad oath," the citizens of Boston demanded that Gov. John Andrew arrest them all. Some were roughed up on the streets of Boston and all were arrested when they tried to leave the city. Capt. Silas Stringham, USN, took them from the hands of the authorities and confined them aboard the Receiving Ship *Ohio* at the Boston Navy Yard, where they were detained for ten days. Orders finally came from Navy Department for their release.[94] Lieutenant Butler, once he had been thoroughly apprised of the reasons for the required oath, did swear it and was restored to duty. Greene returned to his home in Berryville, Virginia, and sent a letter of resignation to the Navy Department on May 17.[95] It was received and rejected that same day and Greene was dismissed from the Marine Corps. Greene soon accepted a commission as a captain in the Virginia Provisional Army but resigned on June 19, 1861, to accept a commission as captain of Confederate States Marines. He was promoted Adjutant and Inspector with the rank of major, on August 24, 1861.[96]

Also arriving aboard *Niagara* were Pvt. George W. Miller, the enthusiastic young Virginian who petitioned Robert E. Lee for assistance in joining the Marine Corps after being captivated by their performance at Harpers Ferry, and the three friends who enlisted with him. They declined to take the oath of allegiance and were promptly put under guard, sent ashore, and confined at Marine Barracks, Brooklyn. Captain Brevoort, commanding officer of Marine Barracks, Brooklyn, wrote Harris for instructions. He, in turn, informed the Secretary of the Navy of the situation, suggesting the four be given disgraceful discharges from the Marine Corps. Welles agreed.

1st Lt. Israel Greene, shown here in the uniform of the Confederate States Marine Corps
MCHC Collection

On May 16, Pvts. George W. Miller, William W. Fox, John R. McNealea, and Richard H. Wiley were ejected from the Corps.[97] They were among the very few enlisted men who turned their backs on their Flag and Corps.[98]

1st Lt. John R. F. Tattnall took longer than all of his fellow Southerners in deciding which course to follow. While he was serving aboard USS *Constellation* of the African Squadron, Georgia, his home state, placed him tenth on the list of twenty captains in the Regular Georgia Army in February 1861. He offered his services to Georgia's governor on February 28, 1861, but took no action toward resigning his commission. At thirty-two years of age, almost half his life had been spent as Marine officer. Tattnall seemed reluctant to sever the ties he had forged with fellow officers who had welcomed him into the service as a raw seventeen-year-old second lieutenant. On October 7, after being transferred to the Marine Guard of USS *San Jacinto,* his decision was made. He wrote out his resignation[99] and announced his intention to resign to Capt. Charles Wilkes, USN, his commanding officer.[100] Wilkes demanded his sword but Tattnall threw it over the side. Wilkes promptly had him arrested and placed in irons.[101] When *San Jacinto* arrived at New York on November 22, Tattnall was informed of his dismissal from the Marine Corps and sent to Fort Warren as a prisoner of war. He was held until January 13, 1862. Upon his release he went immediately to Richmond, where he was commissioned captain of Confederate States Marines to rank from January 22, 1862.[102]

1st Lt. Thomas S. Wilson, USMC
Courtesy of Dr. Cecil Auner

1st Lt. Thomas Smith Wilson, second officer of the Marine Guard of USS *Congress*, submitted his resignation dated August 21, 1861, when his ship returned from cruising the waters off the coast of Brazil. He, like his commanding officer Capt. Robert Tansill, was dismissed as of August 24, arrested and sent to Fort Warren as a prisoner of war. He would be held until January 19, 1862. After his release and repatriation, Wilson accepted a commission as captain of Confederate States Marines to rank from January 24, 1862. His record as a company commander and combat leader during the war was unsurpassed in either Corps of Marines.[103]

Had the case of 2d Lt. Lucien L. Dawson been known to the Navy Department in 1861, he would have had some explaining to do. While he was serving as second officer of the Marine Guard of USS *Hartford,* and far removed from the problems at home, it seems that one of his Texas relatives tendered his services to the Confederate States. In due course, he was nominated by President Jefferson Davis and, on May 21, 1861, unanimously confirmed by the Provisional Congress as a first lieutenant of Confederate States Marines.[104] Dawson was the only man to have the distinction of being listed as an officer in both the United States and Confederate States Marines at the same time.[105]

Marine officer Lucien L. Dawson
Courtesy of Chris Truitt

The last Marine officer who was dismissed as a result of the turmoil of 1861 was 1st Lt. Charles A. Henderson, son of Bvt. Brig. Gen. Archibald Henderson, Commandant of the Corps 1820–1859. It did not happen until 1863, however. At the start of the war, Henderson was on sick leave from the Corps. Suffering from heart disease, Henderson had not performed any duty since October 30, 1859, and had been placed on official leave because of his illness on July 10, 1860. He had been living at Alexandria, Virginia, but, when war came, the excitement of the times proved to be too much for him.[106] He subsequently moved to Fauquier County, Virginia, and later to Marianna, Florida, to escape the war. Henderson was placed on the Retired List as the result of his illness on December 11, 1861.

While Welles was perusing the list of Marine officers in July 1863, he noticed that Henderson's name was carried as a retired officer of Marines. Although Lincoln had approved Henderson's name being placed on the Retired List, Welles, aware that his brother Richard was a serving officer of Confederate States Marines and another brother, Octavius, was a captain in the First Virginia Battalion, assumed that Charles was as disloyal as they were. Consequently, he ordered that Henderson's name be stricken from the rolls as of January 1, 1863.[107]

Years later, Col. Charles G. McCawley, then Commandant of the Marine Corps, attempted to right the wrong done to his old comrade. He stated that shortly after the end of the war, Henderson learned of his dismissal from the Corps, and informed the Department that he had submitted his resignation in May 1861. Further, he had taken no part in the war.[108] It was, however, too late for Henderson to realize any comfort from this friendly gesture. He died at Marianna, Florida, on July 22, 1865, and the record of his dismissal remained on the books of the Navy Department. The eldest son of the Fifth Commandant of the Marine Corps deserved a better fate.

1st Lt. George Richard Graham, descended from a old and prominent Virginia family, but born in Washington, D.C., was also faced with a dilemma when confronted with a test of his loyalty. Graham had expressed his willingness to take the oath of allegiance, but when it was thrust upon him by Capt. William W. McKean, USN, he declined.[109] McKean refused to listen to Graham's explanation and ordered him from the ship and to take passage to Washington and explain himself to the Navy Department.[110]

Graham returned to his ship and explained the situation to his commanding officer, Cdr. Charles H. Poor, USN.[111] Graham was perfectly willing to take the oath but did not want to violate the wishes of his mother. He had written her requesting her counsel and awaited her reply. Recognizing Graham to be as loyal as any officer on his ship, Poor kept him on duty. In due time, the ship that was to take Graham to Washington arrived and on it was the letter he had been waiting for. With his mother's blessing, Graham took the oath and saved himself a mortifying appearance before the Secretary of the Navy.[112]

1st Lt. John Lloyd Broome was also a victim of Captain McKean's high-handed actions regarding the oath of allegiance. On May 25, 1861, Broome heard rumors about all officers being required to take a new oath. He immediately wrote one out and had it witnessed by his commanding officer aboard USS *Powhatan,* Lt. David D. Porter, USN, and forwarded it to the Navy Department.[113] On June 6, McKean came aboard the ship and told all the officers that they would have to sign an oath drawn up by McKean's staff. The simple thing would have been for Broome to shrug his shoulders and sign this oath. However, Broome was not a simple man. He was obstinately proud and being forced to sign an oath that he had no hand in formulating was an assault upon his dignity. He refused to sign it. Instead, he presented another oath of his own making, saying it was more valid than the one being forced upon him.[114] McKean was not satisfied and ordered Broome to report to Washington and explain his actions.[115]

Porter tried to intercede with McKean, but McKean was adamant that Broome must be detached from the ship. But Broome was also adamant. He would not sign McKean's oath. Being entirely consistent, Broome drew up another oath, had it witnessed by Porter and sent it off to Washington. He also sent off a letter to his brother George, explaining the situation and asking him to send a letter attesting to the oath. Secretary Welles sent a reassuring letter to George Broome stating that the Department had no doubts regarding Broome's loyalty.[116] The reassurance was unfortunately directed to the wrong brother.

Broome was allowed to remain aboard ship while the matter was being settled in Washington. As he waited on *Powhatan,* Broome fell into a state of deep depression worrying over what the Department was going to do to him. He felt sure that the Secretary disapproved of his actions and no one could persuade him otherwise. No word came from Washington. Over the next few weeks, his depression became worse. He finally suffered a nervous breakdown and had to be ordered from *Powhatan.*[117] Broome was hospitalized and after several weeks of treatment, and the understanding that his loyalty was not at issue, made a complete recovery. A hearing before a Retiring Board in November 1861 ended any doubt regarding his restoration to duty, and Broome was ordered to the command of the guard of USS *Hartford* on December 27.

William A. T. Maddox, Captain and Assistant Quartermaster, U.S. Marine Corps
Courtesy of Marshall Hudson

The last act to play out in the loyalty issue featured Capt. William A. T. Maddox, the assistant quartermaster who had run afoul of Welles over the incident concerning former Lieutenant Hays and his conversation with Sergeant Thompson in April. Welles received word from a supposedly reliable source that Maddox was making secessionist statements at his club in Philadelphia. Welles demanded an explanation.[118]

Maddox was thunderstruck when he read in Welles' letter the words he was supposed to have said, "The day Maryland secedes, I will resign." In a long explanatory letter, he pointed out to Welles that secessionist ideas were completely foreign to him; there was no officer more loyal than he. As far as making such statements at his club, with the press of work in getting the materiel necessary for the large increase in the Marine Corps, he hardly had time to socialize. Furthermore, since the death of his wife, he had only gone to his club to pick up his messages. It was clear to Maddox that a personal enemy had planted these fabrications in an attempt to discredit him.[119] Welles was satisfied with the explanation submitted by Maddox and no more was heard about his alleged disloyalty.

The defection of one-third of the officers of the Marine Corps had left it badly bruised and shaken.[120] However, there was every chance for recovery. Newly promoted officers held forth the promise of admirably filling the places of their departed seniors. But they would have to be quick studies. Until the new appointees were ready to assume their duties, sergeants would be handling guards that formerly were commanded by lieutenants, lieutenants taking over detachments that formerly were the exclusive province of captains. The Corps would adapt to the situation. Charged with responsibilities previously unheard of in the Corps, the young officers of the Corps looked at maps of the Confederate coastline and saw 3,000 miles of opportunities to distinguish themselves.

Marine Barracks, Washington, 1861

Artist: Theodore R. Davis, American Heritage Picture Collection

3

THE SWORDS ARE DRAWN

The Marine Corps was a small organization when the opening gun of the Civil War was fired at Fort Sumter on April 12, 1861. The Commandant and his military family, the Adjutant and Inspector, Paymaster, Quartermaster, and Assistant Quartermaster, were at the top of its hierarchy. The Line consisted of: 1 lieutenant colonel, 4 majors, 13 captains, 20 first lieutenants, and 20 second lieutenants. There were 1,694 enlisted men: 101 sergeants, 137 corporals, 28 members of the Marine Band, 11 boys learning music, 70 musicians, and 1,347 privates. Just over one-third of the enlisted men were stationed at one or another of the Marine Barracks at Washington, D.C.; Brooklyn, New York; Boston, Massachusetts; Norfolk, Virginia; Philadelphia, Pennsylvania; Portsmouth, New Hampshire; and the Washington Navy Yard. The remaining two-thirds were serving aboard five receiving ships at the navy yards and thirty-four warships protecting American interests in the Far East, the Mediterranean, the Gulf of Mexico, the western Pacific or patrolling the waters off West Africa.[1]

In his November 1860 report to the Secretary of the Navy, Colonel Harris urgently pleaded for an increase in the numbers of officers and enlisted men in the Marine Corps. Emphasizing his belief that the Corps was stretched beyond its ability to provide even adequate training in artillery and infantry drill, or to supply sufficient manpower to protect government property at the navy yards and fill the Marine Guards required for the fleet, Harris wanted Secretary of the Navy Isaac Toucey to ask Congress for 7 more captains, 14 more first lieutenants, 6 more second lieutenants, and an additional 932 privates.[2] Congress, with only an eye on the Federal purse strings and blind to the future, despite the discordant rumblings from the South after the election of Abraham Lincoln, ignored the request. No increase was made in the rank and file or in the number of officers.

Marine Barracks, Washington Marine Band and Headquarters Detachment

NA Photograph 127-N-514952

On December 26, 1860, Maj. Robert Anderson, sensing the danger that his exposed garrison at Fort Moultrie in Charleston Harbor faced should the secessionists of South Carolina make good their threats of seizing Federal installations within the borders of their state, quietly moved his command, Batteries E and H, 1st U.S. Artillery, to Fort Sumter under the cover of darkness.[3] The outraged South Carolinians demanded that Anderson's force be returned to Fort Moultrie; the move having been made without the permission of their "independent nation." The demand was ignored. Instead, President James Buchanan ordered Fort Sumter supplied and reinforced.

On January 5, 1861, the steamer *Star of the West* left New York, Capt. John McGowan of the Revenue Marine, at her helm. Aboard was a detachment of two hundred army troops from the Governor's Island Depot, commanded by 1st Lt. Charles R. Woods, USA, for the relief of Fort Sumter.[4] Four days later, the unarmed vessel tried to enter Charleston Harbor, but was driven off when South Carolina forces fired on her from Fort Moultrie and Morris Island. Anderson's garrison was stranded with only six weeks' rations. Buchanan suddenly realized that the fire-eaters of South Carolina were serious about defending their newly independent realm. He took the firm position that his administration would not be responsible for shedding the first fratricidal blood and left the matter to the incoming President to resolve.

When the Lincoln administration took office in March, the Fort Sumter issue was at the head of a list of priorities. Lincoln received advice from every quarter. Patriotic citizens sent schemes to effect the relief; some bizarre, some worthy of merit. Faint-hearted Congressmen beseeched Lincoln to evacuate Anderson's force. Secretary of State William H. Seward, who thought that maintaining the Fort Sumter garrison would provide the excuse for bringing on war, also advised evacuation.[5] Word from the Army was that maintaining the flag over Fort Sumter would take 20,000 troops. The Navy thought otherwise. If the President would authorize a relief expedition, there would be no lack of naval officers willing to lead it.

Lincoln was being pulled from all directions. He was undecided and needed information from the scene and an unemotional evaluation as to the success of a relief operation. The President ordered Secretary of War Simon Cameron to find a person with the knowledge to assess the situation.[6] The order was passed to Lt. Gen. Winfield Scott, commander in chief of the Army.[7] He chose Gustavus V. Fox, a former naval officer who had resigned in 1856 after eighteen years service to manage a complex of woolen mills in Massachusetts.[8]

Fox was among the many private citizens who offered plans for the relief of Fort Sumter, his being the most feasible. He was also a no nonsense individual who could be completely relied upon. His plan had been approved by Scott during a series of meetings in February and had been presented to then Secretary of War Joseph Holt. Buchanan initially expressed some interest in Fox and his proposal, but lack of commitment from the White House indicated the President's desire for the new administration to handle the matter. Now that Lincoln might be leaning toward a relief expedition to Fort Sumter, the plan submitted by Fox was resurrected.

Gustavus Vasa Fox
Battles and Leaders

Fox left for Charleston the day he received the orders from Scott and arrived in that city on March 21. He visited Fort Sumter and discussed the supply situation with Major Anderson. Anderson told him his supplies would run out on April 15. The two men then discussed various possibilities of bringing supplies and reinforcements to the fort without arousing the suspicions of the South Carolinians. Fox thought it could be done, but Anderson was skeptical. Nevertheless, Fox continued formulating a relief plan.

When Fox returned to Washington, his recommendation was that the fort should be supplied. Moreover, he immodestly pressed acceptance of his plan as the most feasible and put forth his claim to command the expedition. As the Administration mulled over the Fort Sumter situation, Lincoln and the Cabinet frequently called upon him to explain various parts of his plan, which, in essence, was quite simple. Since the bar at Charleston was particularly shallow, rebel authorities knew the warships of the U.S. Navy could only pass it at high tide. High tide came during the daylight hours. At night, it would be impossible. But Fox countered that it was not impossible. He would cross the bar with shallow draft tugboats; not the frail type that worked the harbors of the South but powerful New York tugs that could carry both supplies and men to Fort Sumter. The answers Fox supplied were Lincoln's key in winning the Cabinet to his way of thinking. On March 30, Lincoln gave Fox preliminary approval to fit out a relief force. On April 4, full approval was granted, and Fox immediately went to New York to charter the tugs *Freeborn, Uncle Ben, Yankee*, and the transport steamer *Baltic*.[9]

Orders were sent to the Navy Department to have the commanding officers of USS *Pawnee, Pocahontas,* and *Harriet Lane* prepare for sea at the earliest possible moment. To the War Department went an order to box up a year's worth of supplies and have 200 men ready to transport. The Secretary of the Navy ordered USS *Powhatan* readied for sea service, forgetting that the Department had approved the landing of her stores and placing the ship out of commission a few days earlier. Apprised of his error, Welles quickly revoked his order and demanded the ship be readied for duty.[10] Officers who had gone on leave were tracked down and ordered to return to New York. Those officers not immediately found were replaced by others. Enlisted men presented a different problem. There were not enough crew members to work the ship. Consequently, the draft of 300 sailors that was intended to reinforce the threatened Norfolk Navy Yard had to be broken up to fill up the crew of *Powhatan.* In contrast to the difficulties the navy was having with its personnel, the Marines that would be part of the relief expedition were already in place. The Marine Guard of USS *Pawnee* was under the charge of O. Sgt. Timothy O'Brien, while that of USS *Pocahontas* was headed by O. Sgt. Edward Dunn. 1st Lt. John L. Broome commanded the Marines aboard USS *Powhatan.*[11] Overall command of the expedition was given to Fox. He would oversee the operation from the *Baltic.*

From the first, things went wrong. President Lincoln gave orders to Lt. David D. Porter to take *Powhatan* to the relief of Fort Pickens, unaware that Fox had counted her in his plans. *Powhatan* left New York on April 6. Her sea-going launches and heavy battery were an integral part of the operation. Failure to communicate between the Chief Executive and his Naval Secretary cost Fox one-third of the fire power he might need if the expedition had to defend itself.

The expedition got off to a bad start. Instead of departing in unison or at least on the same day, the ships left in a staggered fashion between April 7–10. Command, communications, and control were forfeited from the start. A violent gale battered the ships as they rounded Sandy Hook, New Jersey, making a concerted arrival off Charleston on the morning of April 11 an impossibility. A whole day was lost to the storm. When *Baltic* arrived at the rendezvous point at 3:00 A.M. on the morning of April 12, only *Harriet Lane* was on station. *Pawnee* did not appear until 6:00 A.M. *Pocahontas* would not arrive until the next day. The tug *Freeborn* never left New York and the *Uncle Ben* was captured off Wilmington, North Carolina. *Yankee* arrived after Fort Sumter had surrendered.

Despite the handicap the mission labored under, Fox was determined to proceed. His report said the fort could be relieved and he was going to make every possible effort to fulfill his obligation. Orders to get under way were issued within the hour.

As *Baltic* and *Harriet Lane* moved toward the harbor, the flashes from the shore batteries were clearly seen in the distance, followed seconds later by the dull roar of shells exploding on and about Fort Sumter. For an instant, Fox was transfixed by the magnitude of what he was witnessing—but for an instant only. Fox quickly refocused his attention to the mission. The plan he submitted had a provision for the relief expedition to fight its way to Fort Sumter but USS *Powhatan* was the linchpin of that option. Without *Powhatan*, Fox was unwilling to make the run in. He ordered the ships to reverse course. Another strategy had to be worked out. As the two vessels steamed back to their starting point, they met *Pawnee* coming up to engage the Charleston batteries. Fox ordered her commander, Capt. Stephen Rowan, USN, to come about. Proceeding into Charleston Harbor was an heroic gesture but would result only in the loss of the ship. Other alternatives had to be explored.

The relief flotilla withdrew to the periphery of Charleston Harbor hoping to see signs of the remaining vessels attached to the operation. The horizon was empty. During the day, the steamer *Nashville* and other merchant shipping arrived off the bar but the

Rebel batteries fire on Fort Sumter while the Federal relief flotilla in the outer harbor watches in frustration

Harper's Weekly

USS *Pocahontas*, Marines standing in front of the poop deck
Massachusetts Commandery, MOLLUS Collection, USAMHI

relief force remained fragmented. None of the tugs was there to run in the relief supplies. Neither *Powhatan* nor *Pocahontas* had yet arrived. Simply stated, Fox had neither the carrying capacity to bring the reinforcements in safely, nor the fire power to force a passage to Fort Sumter. There were no realistic alternatives; Fox had to wait until the two warships came up.

Throughout the day, the men of the relief expedition watched impotently as Fort Sumter absorbed the incessant fire of the shore batteries. Scarcely a minute went by without a shot registering on the fort. Hour after hour the bombardment continued. All day and through the night. The dawn of April 13 broke with clouds and rain. Fox scanned the horizon. There was still no sign of the missing warships. Desperate to send even token supplies to Fort Sumter, Fox considered sending in small boats. *Pawnee*'s launch was hoisted out loaded with a howitzer and ammunition boxes, crew, and Marines under arms for an expedition, but Fox quickly rejected the idea because the sea was too rough.[12] A frustrated Fox searched for signs of *Powhatan*. Her launches were big enough to handle the rough surf. He had factored that into his calculations. But where was the ship?[13]

Although his plan was coming apart, Fox was still determined to make an effort to get to Fort Sumter. A schooner tried to run into Charleston that morning and was seized by the *Pawnee*. She looked strong enough to make the effort. Fox ordered the supplies transferred to the schooner as quickly as possible. The men plunged into the work, but just after 8:00 A.M., a huge column of black smoke began to rise from the fort. All eyes were turned to the spectacle and the supply transfer ground to a halt. By noon flames were seen rising into the sky. When USS *Pocahontas* came up just after 2:00 P.M., the fort was answering the bombardment only sporadically. Thirty minutes later, the flag staff at Fort Sumter was shot away. Fox observed no responding fire from Sumter's guns and canceled plans to send in the supplies. All thoughts now turned to saving Major Anderson and his men.[14]

On the morning of April 14, Cdr. John P. Gillis, USN, commanding officer of USS *Pocahontas*, personally took a boat in and offered Anderson whatever assistance he needed in evacuating his men.[15] Gillis remained until the next day, surveying the damage to the fort, the still smoldering interior, and wondered how the heroic little band survived the conflagration. The victorious South Carolinians were generous to the vanquished. They allowed the National Flag to be hoisted again and honors paid to it. After firing a fifty-gun salute to the flag, the tattered ensign was lowered. The Fort Sumter garrison, with side arms and personal property, was brought to Charleston and transferred to the *Baltic* for passage to New York.

The Confederate flag flies over Fort Sumter
Massachusetts Commandery, MOLLUS Collection, USAMHI

As the *Baltic* made its way up the channel and came among her companions, the spirits of the begrimed and exhausted combatants of Fort Sumter were raised as they heard cheers from the flotilla roll across the waves. Again the cheers came, and a third time. As the cheers faded, *Pawnee, Harriet Lane, Pocahontas,* and *Yankee* fell in with *Baltic* as a nautical guard of honor.[16] When the ships turned north, a Marine from the guard of *Pocahontas* pondered the events of the past two days. He had only seen the very end of the bombardment of Fort Sumter, but that was enough to bring back memories of a day in the Fall of 1859. Pvt. Augustus Greenhaugh was there when John Brown was dragged from the engine house at Harpers Ferry. He heard about the old man's final message about washing away the sin of slavery with blood. Up to now, it seemed to be nothing more than the ravings of a fanatic who was about to pass into eternity. In the smoke and flames of Fort Sumter, Brown's prophecy transfigured into current events.

Poor planning and faulty execution, not to mention the intrusion of foul weather into the mix, prevented the Fort Sumter expedition from accomplishing its mission. However, even if all the pieces of the plan had been in place, running the gauntlet of hostile fire to deliver the reinforcements and supplies would likely have done nothing more than to increase the number of targets for the rebels to shoot at. Realistically, Fort Sumter was untenable. Fort Pickens, on the other hand, was another matter. While Sumter stood at the center of Charleston Harbor with all of her approaches covered by land batteries, Fort Pickens was easily reached from the sea. Only the unofficial truce that had been in effect since January prevented Federal troops from reinforcing Fort Pickens.

When viewed from the perspective of significance to the Union naval effort, Fort Pickens was far more important to the Federal Government. Fort Sumter only controlled the approach to Charleston. Control of Fort Pickens was the key to not only Pensacola, but the entire Gulf Coast of the Confederacy. President Lincoln recognized that fact early on; thus, his personal intervention in the Fort Pickens relief expedition. On April 1, Lincoln wrote orders placing Lt. David D. Porter, USN, in command of USS *Powhatan*, and directing him "at any cost or risk (to) prevent any expedition from the mainland reaching Fort Pickens or Santa Rosa Island."[17] He was also to escort the chartered steamer *Atlantic* with Col. Harvey Brown, USA, and four companies of troops to reinforce the beleaguered defenders of the fort.[18] Further orders were issued preventing news of Porter's mission from leaking out. Even the Navy Department was not to be informed that the ship was being readied for sea.

Atlantic left New York an hour before *Powhatan* cast off her mooring lines. As Porter prepared to take *Powhatan* to sea, Cdr. Andrew H. Foote, USN, telegraphed the Navy Department that Porter had taken out *Powhatan* on the direct orders of the President.[19] This was in direct contradiction of Welles' order assigning the ship to the Fort Sumter relief operation.[20] Welles immediately went to the President. Confronted by an exasperated Welles, Lincoln told Secretary of State Seward to inform Porter to relinquish his command and turn the ship over to the Sumter operation.

Lt. Francis A. Roe, USN, was sent on a chartered steamer to catch *Powhatan* and inform Porter of the change.[21] Roe succeeded in overtaking Porter but returned to New York without changing *Powhatan*'s course. Porter declined to obey the order turning him back to New York. The unarmed *Atlantic* was ten miles out and dependent upon *Powhatan* for protection to Fort Pickens. Porter chose to obey the initial set of orders he received from the President and headed *Powhatan* south.

The situation at Pensacola had remained, from the Federal side, unchanged. No reinforcements had been landed and 1st Lt. Adam J. Slemmer still held Fort Pickens with Battery G, 1st U.S. Artillery. On the shore, however, matters had progressed to the point that the Lincoln government questioned its blind obedience to the arrangement of "no preparations for attack, no reinforcements" made during the waning days of the Buchanan administration. The rebels had erected a series of heavy artillery emplacements on the mainland opposite Fort Pickens. Troops from the Gulf States were constantly arriving and, in the opinion of Federal naval officers observing the buildup, would soon have a force large enough to make an assault on Fort Pickens with a good chance of success. This information was instrumental in Lincoln's decision to violate the agreement made by his predecessor.

On March 12, 1861, Lieutenant General Scott sent an order to go ashore the seventy-five men of Battery A, 1st U. S. Artillery commanded by Capt. Israel Vogdes, USA.[22] They had been aboard ship off Fort Pickens waiting to land since February 9.[23] He did so with the complete approval of the Navy Department and the President. However, when Capt. Henry A. Adams, USN, senior naval officer on the Pensacola station, received the order, he refused to obey it. To do so would violate the established agreement and, in his judgment, bring about the opening of armed hostilities.[24] Welles replied to Adams' vacillation in the strongest terms. The troops would be landed, previous arrangements notwithstanding.[25]

On April 12, 1861, Adams received Welles' sternly worded order and immediately complied. At the request of Captain Vogdes, the Marine Guards of all the ships at Pensacola were to be landed to augment the garrison of Fort Pickens that night.[26] 1st Lt. George R. Graham and forty enlisted Marines were USS *Brooklyn*'s compliment. 1st Lt. John C. Cash and forty-nine enlisted Marines came from USS *Sabine*. USS *Wyandotte* sent off O. Sgt. Thomas Hamilton and ten enlisted Marines, while USS *St. Louis* embarked twenty-four under the charge of O. Sgt. Thomas Bowe. The Marines from the various ships were sent to USS *Brooklyn*, and placed under Graham's command.

Vogdes and his men were embarked in *Brooklyn*'s boats and towed by *Wyandotte* to within one mile of Santa Rosa Island. The

Marines, sailors, and artillerists reinforce Fort Pickens, April 12, 1861
NA Photograph 127-N-526608

Landing the reinforcements for Fort Pickens on Santa Rosa Island, April 12, 1861
NHC Photograph NH 73741

1st Lt. George R. Graham, USMC, commander of Marine reinforcements to Fort Pickens
Author's Collection

boats were then cast off and the artillerists were rowed the rest of the way in. After landing Vogdes' detachment, the boats were rowed back and the Marines sent in the same fashion. It was close to dawn when the boats neared Santa Rosa Island. The Marines were to land near the mouth of a small river on the island, some distance from the fort. In his haste to be the first Marine ashore, Musician George Gardner gathered up his drum, rushed to the front of his boat and jumped over the side. Much to his surprise, the water was over his head. Redeeming the embarrassing situation, Gardner used his drum as a buoy and with rapid kicks of his feet, struck out for the shore. The water-logged Marine drummer reached the shore at the same time as the boats.

Because the landing was in full view of the rebel batteries no one chose to remain in such an exposed position for long. Musician Gardner recalled:

> Lieut. Graham stepped a shore and started off on a run for the Fort about 600 yards distance and I after him. We passed all the rest so the race here was to be in the Fort. 1st was (between) Graham and my self. he capt. the lead till we come to the Ditch between us and the Casemates and there Graham run into the ditch into the mud and water up to his neas so I passed him . . . and entered the Salyport of the Fort being the 1st Marine to enter out of the three Guards and I was the drummer of the Sabine Guard.[27]

Captain Adams reported the immediate execution of the orders from the Navy Department and the successful landing of the artillerists and the Marines to the total ignorance of the rebels until the reinforcement had been completed.[28]

Continuing Musician Gardner's narrative:

> I don't think the Rebles was awar of the Fort being Reenenforced til they heard us all give 3 Tremendious Cheers on histen a New Stares and Stripes over the Fort after halling the other down that was in Rags. Slimmer had a Barral of Whiskey Broken oppen and ever man got a good gill. We wure in the Fort 5 days nothing to eat but

Marines inside Fort Pickens

Harper's Weekly

> Pork & Beans and the sun being So hot and the land all being Sandy and how our Eyes all becum Sore. The 5th day brought Harvey Brown with Reenforcements from the North. on there landing we marched to the beach and Embarked again each Guard to his Respective Ship.[29]

USS *Powhatan* arrived off Fort Pickens at 1:30 P.M., April 17. With her came the transport *Atlantic* with Colonel Brown and Battery M, 2d U.S. Artillery. Now that the Army was in force at Fort Pickens, the Marines were ordered to their ships. The *Sabine*'s guard returned on the eighteenth, and those of the other ships on the twentieth.

A reporter for the *New York Times* sent a dispatch north concerning the landing of the Marines and the esteem in which he held them.

> Important from the Gulf Fleet
>
> The Marine Guard of the *Wyandotte* gunboat has been sent ashore on Rosas Island to do picket guard for the tired-out garrison there, Let me here name one bright spot in the Navy. It is the Marine corps. Extra loyalty in trying times seems to be a characteristic—I had nearly said peculiarity—of Marines everywhere. . . . America should call them

> 'National,' because when every other branch of the country's service has black spots in it, the Marines loom out in moral grandeur—true, unreproachable and brave. I am delighted to see by the papers, and to learn from private letters that the corps at home is just as its representatives are here. Oh, that we had ten thousand Marines![30]

Three days later, Colonel Brown probably wished the same.

On the morning of April 23, movements of rebel vessels off Pensacola gave Brown the impression that they were attempting to launch an operation against Fort Pickens. Two steamers and several boats were reported as attempting to make a landing on Santa Rosa Island. Brown hurriedly sent a request to the fleet for the return of the Marines. The guards, which had hardly settled back into their duties aboard ship, were sent ashore on April 23, joined by Lieutenant Broome and 43 enlisted Marines from USS *Powhatan*.[31] This time the Marines were kept ashore for over a month while Brown attempted to fathom the intentions of the enemy. As he pondered rebel Maj. Gen. Braxton Bragg's movements ashore, Brown kept everyone extremely busy. Drummer Gardner concluded his commentary with a few words about how the time was spent . . . "old Brown commenced to fortifyen the Fort. Each man had to carry 40 Sand Bags a day for 3 months before he finish and before we wure returned to the ship a gain."[32]

When Brown was satisfied there was no immediate threat from the mainland, the Marines were allowed to return to their ships. By May 27, all the Marines had departed from Santa Rosa Island with the thanks of Colonel Brown.

Head Quarters, Fort Pickens, Fla.
May 26, 1861

Orders
No. 46

The services of the Marines being no longer indispensably necessary, they are relieved from duty at this post.

The colonel commanding takes pleasure in publishing his entire approval of the conduct and appreciation of the services of Lieutenant Cash and his command, which have been of great value and always cheerfully rendered, and the conduct of the troops uniformly correct and soldierly.

By order of Colonel Brown,
(Signed) G. D. Bailey
2nd Lieut. 2nd Arty.
Adjutant.[33]

Fort Pickens remained in Union hands throughout the entire war. Only once did Southern troops land on Santa Rosa Island, and that amounted to nothing more than an harassing raid on October 9, 1861. The camp of the 6th New York was overrun but the Confederate forces withdrew, having accomplished their purpose. Among the raiders was former Marine officer Calvin L. Sayre. Sayre acted as aide-de-camp to expedition commander Brig. Gen. Richard H. Anderson, PACS. During the withdrawal of the rebels to their boats, Sayre, "while fearlessly using his revolver with effect, had his thigh bone shattered just above the right knee by a musket-ball, and, being left upon the ground, fell into the hands of the enemy."[34]

On April 15, 1861, Lincoln issued a proclamation declaring the turmoil in the seven seceded states "too powerful to be suppressed by the ordinary course of judicial proceedings," and called for seventy-five thousand militia to suppress the illegal actions of the secessionists, and retake the forts and other public property seized from the Federal Government.

Throughout the North, the President's message caused great excitement and a burst of genuine patriotism. People in every city, town, and village took to the streets to give strong vocal approval to the President's course. Men of all ages rallied to the colors. The voices of moderation were drowned in a sea of revenge for Fort Sumter. Lincoln was well-pleased by the response, but such was almost expected from the states north of the Mason-Dixon Line. What was more important to the President was the response from the slave-holding states that still remained in the Union. What would Missouri, North Carolina, Tennessee, Arkansas, Kentucky, Maryland, and Virginia do? Were there enough Union men in those states to hold them in loyalty to the National Government? Within forty-eight hours, Lincoln began to receive answers.

The Commonwealth of Virginia had long been a force for reconciliation between the fire-eaters of the Deep South and Washington, calling for peace conventions to amicably settle the disputes that threatened to tear the nation apart. While acting as a voice of moderation, Virginia also kept its options open, electing delegates to a secession convention that met at Richmond on February 13, 1861. An initial vote of this convention had registered 60 to 53 in favor of Union. These delegates were called back into session as soon as the President's call for troops reached the office of Governor John Letcher.[35]

In a telegram dated April 15, 1861, the Secretary of War requested 2,340 men from Governor Letcher under the provisions of the militia act of 1795. Letcher fired back his reply, "Your object is to subjugate the Southern States, and a requisition made upon me for such an object . . . will not be complied with."[36] Two days later, the secession convention adopted an ordinance dissolving thc Union between Virginia and the United States.[37]

Virginia forces moved quickly to capture Federal property within the Commonwealth. Harpers Ferry was seized by Virginia troops on April 18. That same day, Maj. Gen. William B. Taliaferro was charged with the task of capturing the United States Navy Yard at Norfolk.[38] Taliaferro arrived on the morning of the nineteenth to find the military preparations woefully inadequate to the task of seizing the yard. Accordingly, he chose to try and keep reinforcements from reaching the besieged yard while accumulating sufficient strength to make a demand for the surrender of the facility. Taliaferro feared the heavy batteries of the ships anchored in the Elizabeth River. He felt it would have been an easy matter to overpower the Marines attached to the navy yard, but was not at all anxious to see if his men would stand naval gunfire.[39]

On the day that Virginia broke away from the Union, Capt. Charles S. McCauley, USN, held the post of Commandant of the Norfolk Navy Yard.[40] Under his charge were the following vessels:

Columbia. Frigate laid up in ordinary since 1855.

Columbus. Ship-of-the-Line laid up in ordinary since 1848.

Cumberland. Frigate brought in for overhaul on March 23, 1861.

Delaware. Ship-of-the-Line laid up in ordinary since 1844.

Dolphin. Brig in ordinary since December 22, 1860.

Germantown. Sloop of War ready for crew since March 25, 1861.

Merrimack. Screw Frigate in ordinary undergoing repairs since February 16, 1860.

New York. Ship-of-the-Line. Unfinished and on the stocks since 1820.

Pennsylvania. Ship-of-the-Line and Receiving Ship at Norfolk since 1842.

Plymouth. Sloop of War and training ship at Norfolk since 1855.

Raritan. Frigate laid up in ordinary since 1853.

United States. Frigate laid up in ordinary since 1849.

To protect these ships and the yard, the Navy Department had at its disposal Lt. Col. James N. Edelin, 1st Lt. Adam N. Baker and sixty-six enlisted men at the Marine Barracks. If needed, Capt. Jabez C. Rich and thirty-five enlisted men of the Marine Guard aboard the Receiving Ship *Pennsylvania* could be called upon. The Marine Guard of Cumberland was still aboard ship. In the event of trouble, Capt. Matthew R. Kintzing, 2d Lt. Charles Heywood and forty-four enlisted men were available for service. A few hundred seamen of all ratings from the Receiving Ship and *Cumberland* could also be pressed into action.

Welles, despite administration hopes that Virginia would remain loyal to the Union, anticipated problems at Norfolk. As a precaution, he had ordered 300 naval personnel with officers and supplies sent from New York on March 31, but the Fort Sumter relief expedition took the better part of that effort. Faced with a critical shortage of manpower, Welles had to choose between sending reinforcements to defend the yard or providing crews to take the ships out of harm's way. On April 10, Captain McCauley was ordered to exercise great vigilance in protecting the public property at Norfolk and to remove the ships and stores should the area be threatened by rebels. The next day, McCauley was told that no time should be lost in getting the Plymouth and the Merrimack ready for sea. Commo. Samuel L. Breese, USN, received instructions to send 200 sailors from New York for the *Merrimack*.[41]

The bombardment and surrender of Fort Sumter threw the plans to safeguard the materiel and vessels at Norfolk into confusion. Welles had learned that there were only sixty-three sailors available at New York on April 15, hardly sufficient to crew the *Merrimack*. If Virginia decided for secession, all that the Department wished to save could not be rescued. There was simply not enough manpower.[42] Welles apprised McCauley that conditions warranted saving only *Plymouth, Dolphin, Germantown,* and *Merrimack*. These ships should be loaded with as much government property as possible. However, McCauley was cautioned not to take precipitate action. These extreme measures should only be taken if the yard was in immediate danger and, at that point, defending the vessels and stores at all hazards was his responsibility.[43]

The orders from the Navy Department should have galvanized McCauley into action. They did not. McCauley was simply too old to accept the responsibility. He chose to focus on those sections of his orders that demanded action on his part if *immediate danger threatened*. Consequently, the Herculean efforts of Chief Engineer Benjamin F. Isherwood, USN, in getting *Merrimack* ready for sea went for nothing.[44] Convinced the rebels had blocked the channel,

McCauley ordered her engines shut down. No efforts were made to evacuate the valuable naval stores. Reports of heavy batteries being erected to menace the yard weakened what little resolve the old officer had mustered. Instead of making preparations to defend the vessels and property in his charge, McCauley, according to Isherwood, was overwhelmed by the crisis, immobilized by the responsibility, and numbed into inaction by liquor.[45]

After learning that McCauley was incapable of handling the situation at Norfolk, Welles fired off a flurry of orders by telegraph on April 18, trying to make the best of a very bad situation. He ordered Commo. Hiram Paulding, USN, to Norfolk to relieve McCauley and to make every effort to move the ships out of the yard.[46] If circumstances warranted, Paulding was authorized to destroy what he could not carry away. Capt. Samuel F. DuPont, USN, was ordered to send all the available men and arms under his charge at the Philadelphia Navy Yard to Norfolk.[47] Commodore Breese received instructions to send the sailors from New York to Norfolk immediately, even if it meant chartering a civilian vessel. Cdr. William W. Hunter, USN, was directed to send fifty recruits from the Receiving Ship *Allegheny* at Baltimore.[48]

The next day, Welles sent out orders to Commo. Franklin Buchanan, USN, at the Washington Navy Yard to load explosives aboard USS *Anacostia* for passage to Norfolk to be used to blow up the yard if the rebels seemed likely to overrun it. Marine Barracks, Brooklyn, received orders to send all available Marines to Washington aboard USS *Pocahontas* at once. Colonel Harris was ordered to prepare 100 Marines ready for immediate service and to have them board USS *Pawnee* without delay.[49] Pvt. Daniel Boyer reported he did not know whether he was standing on his head or his heels when he told his sister of the preparations for the expedition.

> We were ordered out on the Parade Ground, . . . and had to pack knapsacks, sling them, put on our belts, and fall out under arms in about 15 minutes time. I did not get skeered but as a fellow says, I felt "nervously agitated."[50]

Welles began to receive replies to his telegraphic orders on the nineteenth, as well. Captain DuPont notified the Department that the chartered steamer *Keystone State* would leave Philadelphia that night with fifty Marines, fifty sailors, and four 12-pounder howitzers.[51] Breese reported that at least 173 recruits, and possibly as many as 225, were being readied for transport to Norfolk and would leave at 3:00 P.M. on the twentieth. The report from Baltimore, however, was decidedly negative. Commander Hunter reported that the Baltimore Steam Packet Company had positively refused to transport the recruits from the Receiving Ship. Despite the loss of the men from Baltimore, on balance the operation seemed to be progressing very well, at least at his end. Events at Norfolk were completely different.

The situation at Norfolk was almost totally out of control. McCauley had been abandoned by thirteen of the twenty-one officers of the yard, including Marine officers Rich and Baker, and seemed incapable of making any firm decisions. The mechanics failed to report to work. The yard watchmen walked off their jobs, while citizens came into and left the yard at will, carrying with them large amounts of arms and ammunition. Marines were used to fill the places of the watchmen in addition to their normal duties but there were not enough of them to handle the situation. Virginia troops were reported erecting batteries and training their heavy guns on the yard. The Elizabeth River channel was thought to be completely obstructed. As many as three thousand Virginia troops were said to have surrounded the yard.[52] Overcome with despair, McCauley gave orders to scuttle all of the warships in his charge. Pvt. Daniel O'Connor, one of *Cumberland*'s Marines, wrote his sister an account of the process from his vantage point.[53]

> We were in a bad positian then expecting to be attacked that night On the morning of 20th the secionists had 3 batterys around us we spiked the guns in the navy yard and were employed in breaking the arms all that day & sinking the ships we sent a leutinant with a flag of truce to the authorothys to know on what conditions we could go out but they gave us no satisfaction so we intended to fight our way out or die in the attempt we intended to burn up the navy yard & shipping for there was not water enough to sink the ships & blow down portsmouth Gosport & norfolk the river was blocked & if we could not get out burn the ship & go on board the yankee of New York a little steemer that came to our assistance they tried to take the yankee about 11 oclock that day but they were (illegible) of our long tom on the forecastle which is 11 inches boer they ceased her but they let her go very quick when we pointed our pivot gun at her they spoke of masacreeing the whole of us & taking the navy yard & shipping that night but we intended to sell our lives as dear as possible[54]

As McCauley's orders were being carried out, Welles' hurriedly organized expedition was steaming toward Norfolk with all possible speed. In addition to the Marine detachment commanded by 1st

Lt. Augustus S. Nicholson, thirteen naval officers and 140 seamen had joined *Pawnee* under orders to bring off *Merrimack*, *Germantown*, *Plymouth*, and *Dolphin*. The explosives and combustibles originally loaded aboard USS *Anacostia* were transferred aboard.[55] Paulding stopped at Fortress Monroe to squeeze 360 men of the 3rd Massachusetts Volunteers and their commanding officer Col. David W. Wardrop aboard ship before making his final run to Norfolk.

Pawnee arrived at the navy yard at 8:00 P.M., and Private O'Connor described the scene as being very tense.

> i was posted on the first gangway. i reported a steamer & the quarter master said she was an enemys ship. the long roll was beat every man to his quarters the leutenant was going to fire at her all the sentinals were ordered in off the boats and gangways for battle & there was a dead silence our leutenant hailed her what steamer is that She answered U. S. ship Pawney at that word the air rung with cheers[56]

Within minutes of pulling up to the wharf, an officer from *Pennsylvania* had come aboard to give a situation report. The naval officers sent from Washington to take out those ships deemed worth saving were shocked to learn they had all been scuttled at 4:00 P.M. and were now settling on the bottom of the harbor. A frantic mission to see if they could be saved proved fruitless. Commodore Paulding ordered them all prepared for the torch. Parties were dispatched to the various parts of the yard to destroy what could not be easily salvaged, The Marines from *Pawnee* relieved their brothers in arms from the barracks, some being sent to the yard gates to deny entrance to those who might interfere with the work.[57] Other Marines patrolled the yard. Private O'Connor reported that a party from USS *Cumberland* assisted in the destructive work.[58] Sailors with heavy sledge hammers smashed the trunnions from scores of guns and pounded away at every bit of machinery that came into view. Heavy guns were spiked and small arms broken, twisted and thrown from the wharf into the harbor. Turpentine and other combustibles were landed from *Pawnee* and liberally spread about those structures and ships slated for burning. Powder trails were laid to the ship houses, storehouses, the dry dock, and all of the vessels.

Such work, especially done under the pressure that hung over the wrecking crews, brought about a great thirst. Water sufficed until some enterprising tar discovered a sutler's canteen. The locks were quickly forced and barrels of ale and other spirits were rapidly distributed. Of course, once the alcohol had worked its way with those engaged in the demolition, carelessness invaded their tasks and not all of what might have been was destroyed. The work "finally degenerated into a grand hurrah."[59]

Lt. Col. James N. Edelin
NA Photograph 127-N-520482

While the demolition parties were about their work throughout the yard, Private Boyer was part of a detachment sent to prevent the locals from interfering with the destruction of the yard.

> We went ashore and stood Guard at No. 1 Gate. They were about 2000 seccesionists outside and were fully expected every moment to heave the gates opened. They called us all sorts of names. Attempted to force the gate But word was sent to the ship and about 50 sailors, armed to the teeth and dragging with them a pair of Howitzers came to our rescue. We stood Guard for about six hours when all of a sudden a rocket flashed in the air and we faced to the Right About, and went off in Double Quick time to the Pawnee.[60]

Boyer's detachment and the other Marines on guard were recalled to the ship with the demolition parties about 1:45 A.M. *Pennsylvania*'s Marine Guard was taken aboard *Pawnee*; those from the Norfolk Barracks were sent to *Cumberland*.[61]

As the Marines from the Norfolk Barracks formed up and prepared to board ship, O. Sgt. John H. Myers slipped out of the ranks and ran back into the yard. Lieutenant Colonel Edelin felt sure that Myers had not deserted, but supposed the man, who had been on constant duty for several days, was desperate to send a message to his family before leaving. When he failed to return, Edelin assumed the sergeant had been seized by the mob from the city that was then swarming through the gates. Edelin later reported that, with the exception of Capt. Jabez C. Rich and 1st Lt. Adam N. Baker who absented themselves to join the rebels, the entire command had remained loyal.[62]

In the confusion of the night's work, Marines from the Receiving Ship and the barracks became intermingled. Consequently, Edelin did not notice that Pvt. Julius Heilman of the *Pennsylvania*'s Guard was missing. He had earlier been ejected from his ship by order of Lt. Edward Donaldson, USN, for refusing to defend her.[63] Edelin also failed to see that Sgt. Thomas Grogan and Pvt. Joshua Charlesworth were not present.[64] Also forgotten in the pandemonium of the night were five Marines who were patients at the Naval Hospital in Portsmouth, Virginia.[65]

At 2:00 A.M., the Marine Barracks broke out in flames. Capt. Charles Wilkes, USN, who had been sent to take command of *Merrimack* but instead saw to her firing, thought the blaze had started by accident but a correspondent to the *Petersburg Express* reported a different cause of the fire. He stated that the plan of the government was to leave everything at Norfolk in a state of ruination and would have succeeded but for the act of one man.

> A sergeant of the marines named Myers, knowing what was to take place and not wanting to be carried off with his company, set fire to the barracks before the appointed time, and endeavored to escape in the confusion. He succeeded but was shot at several times while scaling the walls. This circumstance in creating a lack of confidence

Destruction of the Norfolk Navy Yard

NHC Photograph NH 59179

> in their own men and fearing an attack from without, they discontinued the plans for firing the buildings but marched their men aboard the ships and waited for the tide.[66]

By 3:30 A.M., all was in readiness. *Pawnee* hauled off from the navy yard wharf and took *Cumberland* under tow. At 4:20, a signal rocket was fired and the navy yard was set ablaze. Anticipating hostile action from Portsmouth and Norfolk, the crew was beat to quarters and the starboard battery cast loose. All of the Marines formed on the deck under arms. The leaping flames from the navy yard made the ships ideal targets but they passed down river without incident. Boyer watched in awe as the conflagration consumed the yard.

> The commenced one of the most sublime and terrible sights I ever witnessed. 2 large Ship Houses, in one of which the Line of Battle Ship New York was on the stocks and everything appretaining to one of the largest Navy Yards in the United States was fired in a hundred different places. Besides the ship of the line Pennsylvania, one of the largest vessels in the service, the Frigate Merrimac, sloop of war Germantown and 2 other vessels. Aminition Balls, and everything in the yard were thrown over board. About 1000 cannon of the largest calibre were spiked and everything in the yard was totally destroyed to keep them out of the hands of the seccesionists. The scene was perfectly awful. The flames reach to an height of about 500 feet. While the Guns on the Pennsylvania which were doubled shotted and pointed at the yard, they became heated going off all combined to render the scene one of the most terrible I ever witnessed.[67]

The yard at Norfolk was severely damaged by the fires but was not completely destroyed. The dry dock passed into the hands of Virginia naval forces without any harm done to it; the powder charges set to destroy it failed to ignite. It stood ready to receive another prize of the rebels, the remains of USS *Merrimack*. Raised from the bottom of the harbor, *Merrimack* was towed to the dock and emerged eleven months later as the ironclad CSS *Virginia* to wreak havoc at Hampton Roads. Also passing into the hands of the Virginians were several hundred heavy guns that ultimately reached the fortifications at Pensacola, Mobile, Vicksburg, New Orleans, and many other places. In terms of eventual lives lost, this failed attempt to reclaim those guns made Norfolk a military disaster of the first order.

Their job done, the Marines were sent back to Marine Barracks, Washington. *Keystone State* took on board the guard from

Pennsylvania and those from Marine Barracks, Norfolk for passage to the Washington Navy Yard, reporting at Headquarters on April 23.[68] *Pawnee* followed with Lieutenant Nicholson's detachment two days later. Those Marines were retained at the Navy Yard for several days, bolstering the forces protecting it against possible attack by Southern sympathizers in the District of Columbia.[69] Boyer found himself detached from *Pawnee*, and performing guard duty at the Long Bridge over the Potomac River, "Bivoucing in the open air with a soft plank for a couch, a knapsack for a pillow and a U. S. M. blanket for a coverlid," sure that "if there is any virtue in hard usage," he "got enough of it."[70]

In the days and weeks that followed the opening of armed hostilities between the North and South, Marines saw active service on the newly established blockade. Several vessels were seized as they attempted to exit or make Southern ports. The first such seizure took place when USS *Cumberland* captured the rebel tug *Young America* and the arms laden schooner *George M. Smith* in Hampton Roads on April 24, 1861. Marines generally formed part of the boarding parties and prize crews. Marines fortunate enough to serve on vessels that made captures of ships violating the blockade and condemned by Prize Courts shared in the money brought by the sale of these prizes and their cargo. The Marine Guard of *Cumberland* shared in the $13,280.28 brought by the capture of *Young America*.[71] The prize money was a welcome addition to the meager monthly pay the enlisted Marines earned, and would later play a major role in the dispute regarding the eligibility of Marine recruits for enlistment bounties. For the present, the excitement of running down blockade runners was a welcome change from the normal routine of barracks duty. Sea duty, not surprisingly, was much sought after by enlisted Marines, and the Commandant was not above receiving letters from lowly privates requesting that posting.

There were other reasons for requesting sea duty apart from the lure of prize money. On April 24, 1861, 2d Lt. Philip R. Fendall wrote the Commandant, requesting a posting to any ship headed for a foreign station. By obtaining such duty, wrote Fendall, "my father will be much gratified."[72] Fendall's father, Philip R. Fendall, Sr., well-known District of Columbia attorney and intimate of President Lincoln, did not make the request from a desire to keep his son out of harm's way.

The elder Fendall's first cousin was Robert E. Lee. His brother-in-law, former U.S. Senator from Mississippi Albert Gallatin Brown, was a company commander in the 18th Mississippi Infantry. In that

Marine officer
Philip Richard Fendall, Jr.
NHC Photograph NH 16108

unit was his nephew Robert Y. Brown, and more importantly, his own son James R. Y. Fendall. It was not beyond the realm of possibility that one member of his family would fight another on the battlefield. The prospect was too terrible to contemplate.[73]

Marines also saw action on the Potomac River in the early days of the war. Four Marines were detached from the Washington Navy Yard on April 23 to augment the crew of USS *Mount Vernon* when that ship was dispatched on a reconnaissance down river. No signs of enemy batteries were seen but a boatload of men was observed leaving the Lower Cedar Point Lightship. Ten rounds from the muskets of the Marines and a shell from the deck gun failed to bring the boat to, and it escaped. When rail transport was blocked from Baltimore, USS *Anacostia*, *Pawnee*, and *Pocahontas* were assigned convoy duty, escorting troopships to the capital. Marine Guards of all three vessels were kept under arms and alert to any attempt by hostile forces to impede passage up river.

The situation at the Washington Navy Yard was difficult at best. Since the recall to Headquarters of the Marine detachment that had been on duty at the yard after its return from Norfolk, only a forty-man guard and three companies of District militia remained on duty. The militia refused to perform any functions that took them out of the City of Washington, and, as a group, were not reliable.[74]

On May 24, Federal forces made the first offensive move against Virginia. Arlington Heights, the site of Robert E. Lee's residence, and the City of Alexandria were the objectives. Several regiments of infantry, accompanied by cavalry and artillery led by Brig. Gen. Samuel P. Heintzelman, USV, marched to Alexandria by way of the Aqueduct and the Long Bridge.[75] The New York "Fire Zouaves" under the command of Col. Elmer E. Ellsworth were transported from the Washington Navy Yard aboard the steamer *Baltimore* and USS *Mount Vernon*.[76] USS *Pawnee* arrived off Alexandria before either Heintzelman's column or the Zouaves.[77] Cdr. Stephen C. Rowan decided to score a coup for the Navy and sent Lt. Reigert B. Lowry,

USN, ashore to demand the surrender of the city.[78] Col. George H. Terrett, former brevet major of U.S. Marines, commanded the Virginia troops garrisoning Alexandria. Terrett did not surrender, but agreed to evacuate the city so as not to place the women and children in danger. Lowry agreed.[79]

The transports carrying Ellsworth and his Zouaves came up shortly before the departure of Terrett's troops, and a few desultory shots were exchanged between the New Yorkers and the rear guard of the Virginia troops. Ellsworth was then told by Commander Rowan of the arrangement between Lowry and Terrett. The Zouaves landed, expecting only a peaceful occupation of Alexandria. Sailors and Marines debarked from *Pawnee*, and seized some railroad cars. They also raised the American flag on the Alexandria Customs House, leaving a small guard of Marines to secure the building. The occupation of the city went without incident until Ellsworth saw a Confederate flag fluttering in the breeze from a staff atop the Marshall House, a well-known Alexandria inn. Dashing inside with four men, Ellsworth went to the roof and cut down the offending banner. Descending the stairs with his trophy, Ellsworth was confronted by shotgun-wielding James Jackson, the innkeeper. Jackson fired and Ellsworth fell dead, the flag tangling around his body as he collapsed. Jackson turned his shotgun at Cpl. Francis E. Brownell, who leveled his musket on the assailant. Both fired at the same time. Jackson's slug missed its mark but Brownell's shot struck Jackson in the face, killing him instantly. In a matter of seconds, the North and South had their first martyrs. The unknown Jackson was vaulted into fame throughout the South, an instant hero. The dapper little Ellsworth, on

Potomac Flotilla firing on rebel batteries at Aquia Creek
NHC Photograph NH 73736

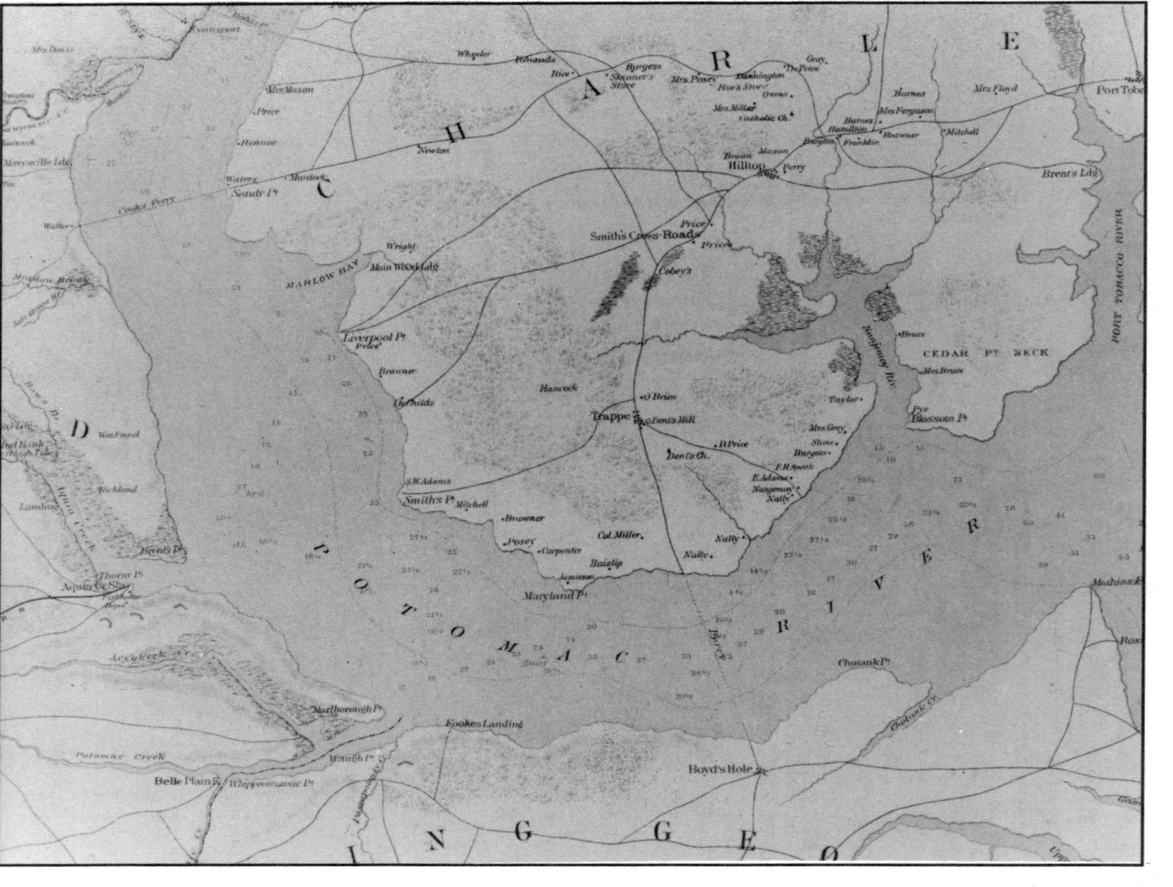

Area of operations, Potomac River, Virginia, Spring 1861

RG 94, Civil War Atlas, plate VIII

the other hand, was well-known for his pre-war exhibitions with his Zouave Company. He was also an intimate friend of the Lincoln Family. Marines from *Pawnee* formed part of the honor guard that escorted Ellsworth's body back to Washington to lie in state at the White House.

A week after the occupation of Alexandria, Marines, led by O. Sgt. George McConnell aboard USS *Anacostia,* participated in the first serious engagement of the war on the Potomac. *Anacostia, Thomas Freeborn,* and *Resolute* took the rebel batteries at Aquia Creek under fire on the morning of June 1. After a spirited exchange of two hours' duration, the enemy guns were silenced. The contest reopened when the rebel gunners commenced firing from a second tier of batteries on an elevation to the rear of those put out of action. After an hour, the guns of the warships not being able to gain the range of the enemy, flotilla chief Cdr. James H. Ward, USN, ordered a withdrawal.[80]

The next day, Commander Ward's flying squadron returned to the enemy batteries at Aquia Creek accompanied by USS *Pawnee.* A furious five-hour battle ensued with the shore batteries. *Thomas Freeborn* was struck several times during the fight and at the conclusion of the day's work was taking in water through her hull. *Pawnee* was hit by nine enemy shells, none causing serious damage. Ward reported nearly 1,000 enemy shells were fired during the battle, while his ship fired 300, and the enemy batteries were twice silenced, the result of the accurate fire from his ship.[81] Another version, perhaps closer to the truth of the engagement, was reported by Capt. William F. Lynch, VN, commanding the naval batteries at Aquia Creek.[82] Keeping a close count of the number of shots fired by his guns and those of his opponents, Lynch tallied 207 from *Thomas Freeborn,* and 392 from *Pawnee.* In return, the Virginia naval guns sent only 56 shots at the ships, firing only when they came in range.[83]

Despite the disparity in numbers of shots fired and received, the reporters were in agreement that the contest had been fought well on both sides. They had used up most of their ammunition and powder.[84] That, coupled with the fatigue of the gunners ashore and afloat, brought an end to the battle. It had been a thrilling fight. Both sides experienced the fear and exhilaration of being under fire. It had been the best sort of a clash, a battle with all the noise, smoke, sweating, and swearing of war, but minus the blood of shipmates or comrades. For all the shot and powder expended, only one minor injury was reported on either side, a facial scratch suffered by Commander Rowan of *Pawnee.*

The June 1–2, 1861, battles at Aquia Creek were the first serious engagements of the Civil War in which Marines burned powder. To some, it was long overdue. *Pawnee*'s Marines had witnessed the Stars and Stripes hauled down in humiliation at Fort Sumter and

Norfolk. Aquia Creek allowed them to vent weeks of anger and frustration by returning the favors of the enemy with interest.[85]

Pawnee transported survey parties to the Mathias Point area on June 5 and 6, landing them under the protection of O. Sgt. Timothy O'Brien and the Marine Guard, the operations being under the command of naval lieutenants Henry M. Blue (June 5), and James C. Chaplin (June 6).[86] The survey parties spent the two days unhindered by the rebels and returned to the ship.[87]

Three weeks later, June 25, 1861, *Pawnee* returned to Mathias Point, and made a reconnaissance of the area, suspecting the rebels were preparing to erect a battery. At 5:30 A.M., a landing party, consisting of sixty sailors and Marines, was put ashore to flush out a suspected Confederate force lying in ambush. After advancing into the brush, the Federal force came under fire and had to fall back, but the Southerners were quickly driven off by a few well-placed shells from *Pawnee*'s guns. The engineers sent ashore with the landing party completed their survey of the enemy ground and returned to the ship with news that a large camp was located beyond some small hills. Rowan opened fire, dispersing the enemy, but he felt sure they would reoccupy the area as soon as the ship left.[88]

The next day, Ward decided to level the enemy camp at Mathias Point and to burn down the foliage along the shore that might camouflage a battery. Rowan was ordered to send two boats of men armed with muskets and bayonets or cutlasses. In addition to the men, Rowan was to send quantities of tar and other inflammables, with all the axes and hatchets he had on board.[89] Ward was going to make certain the ground was scourged.

Just after noon, the flotilla arrived off Mathias Point. The rebel pickets were driven off and a landing party from *Pawnee* was sent ashore. All felt confident that *Freeborn*'s guns would keep the Southerners at bay, just as those of *Pawnee* had protected them the previous day. Unfortunately, the threat of naval gunfire did not have the same effect on the enemy as it had twenty four hours earlier. Confederate infantry let loose a fusillade of musketry from the woods, sending the landing party flying back to its boats. *Freeborn* quickly opened fire, setting off a vigorous and prolonged duel between heavy ordnance and small arms. Swept up by the heat of battle, Ward left the bridge and joined in the action, taking command of *Freeborn*'s bow gun. While sighting the gun, Ward was struck in the abdomen by a musket ball, and mortally wounded. With night approaching, the contest was broken off and the flotilla withdrew.

This little affair was entirely different from the noisy but injury-free exchange of June 1–2. *Pawnee*'s landing party brought off two badly wounded seamen. Aboard *Freeborn*, two sailors were severely wounded. Commander Ward was dead and the war was real.[90]

4

A Rocky Road to Readiness: The Corps Stumbles to a War Footing

When President Abraham Lincoln announced his intention to suppress the rebellion and blockade the Southern ports, the Marine Corps found itself woefully unprepared for the tasks that lay ahead. The authorized strength of the Corps at 1,568 privates, with appropriate numbers of noncommissioned officers and musicians, was not adequate to cover the anticipated requirements of the naval service. However, when the Navy Department mulled the acquisition of fifteen suitable vessels for conversion to blockade enforcers, Harris seized the moment. His November 1860 request to increase the strength of the Corps by 27 line officers and 932 privates was resurrected and sent to Welles.

The Secretary of the Navy recognized the need for additional Marines in the expanded role for which the Navy was preparing. Under ordinary circumstances, the proposed increases of officers and enlisted men required Congressional action. Congress was not then in session. However, there was a way to increase the number of privates without the approval of Congress. The Act of March 3, 1849, provided that the President could substitute Marines for landsmen in the Navy when he deemed it necessary for the efficiency of the Corps.[1] On April 22, 1861, Welles notified Harris that the President had approved the enlistment of an additional five hundred privates under the terms of the 1849 law. To accommodate the increase in privates, new positions would be created for forty sergeants, forty corporals, fifteen drummers, and fifteen fifers.[2] It was not all that Harris wished, but it was a start and an indication that Welles might be receptive to the needs of the Corps.

Within a week of the President's approval, Harris changed his previous guidance on recruiting. Formerly, he wanted only men with prior service; "no new or green hands."[3] Now, Harris told the commanding officers of the several Marine Posts to "enlist all the good looking young, effective American citizens that may offer that are not less than 5 feet, 5 inches in height."[4] Each commanding officer was to enlist up to one hundred men and train them as quickly as possible.

The ink on the orders was hardly dry when Bvt. Maj. John George Reynolds, commanding Marine Barracks, Boston, reported a recruiting success of sorts, but it was not his. The 14th Massachusetts Infantry, one of the regiments forming the "Irish Brigade," had "recruited" nine Marines of Irish heritage. One, Sgt. William Baker, falsely presented himself to Massachusetts Governor John Andrew as being honorably separated from the Corps and was commissioned a first lieutenant in the 14th.[5] He induced the other eight to follow him in desertion. Major Reynolds, by way of barracks rumor, had learned of their actions and sent his son, 1st Lt. Edward McD. Reynolds, USMC, to Governor Andrew with a request for assistance in recovering the men.[6] None was forthcoming from the Governor or from the State Adjutant General. Even the Boston Police declined to help. The reputation of the Irishmen of the regiment was so much feared that even their kinsmen of the police force would not go among them.[7] Major Reynolds had to write them off his books as deserters.

The recruiting efforts for the first two and a half weeks of May, with the exception of Philadelphia, were hardly spectacular. By May 18, Brooklyn had brought in twenty-one recruits, Boston, thirty-eight, and Headquarters, four. The Philadelphia Rendezvous, however, signed ninety-three recruits into the Corps.[8] Those figures encouraged Harris to press Welles for permission to further increase the numbers of the Corps. The increase authorized by the President on April 22, although gratifying to Harris, was not sufficient to meet the growing demands for Marine Guards to send aboard ships fitting out and the security force at the Washington Navy Yard. The Corps needed the additional 432 privates over and above the 500 granted by Lincoln in April.[9]

Welles apparently did not accede to Harris' request as readily as he had anticipated. There was considerable doubt as to whether the Corps was in a position to accept the additional recruits. Welles confronted Harris with some disturbing news. The Quartermaster's Department of the Marine Corps had been unable to fill requisitions made upon it for replacing worn out gear, or for outfitting recruits entering the service.[10] That office was so far behind in acquiring new uniforms and accouterments from its contractors, it was unlikely the President would approve the additional 432 men. In fact, Lincoln was rethinking his April 22 approval of 500

Maj. William B. Slack, Quartermaster, USMC
Civil War Library

recruits.[11] An embarrassed Commandant immediately demanded an explanation from the Quartermaster, Maj. William B. Slack.

The Quartermaster's office was indeed in a quandary. The outbreak of hostilities had confronted Major Slack with a situation of unprecedented magnitude. Previously, when asked to submit a statement of expenditures for the period February 1 to the expiration of the current Congressional Session, Slack reported a figure of $41,172.56.[12] Although events proved that sum to be woefully inadequate, Slack, in all fairness, was compelled to submit estimates based upon the force at hand, not for the requirements of an expanded, wartime Corps. Further, until April 1861, the Quartermaster had been following the time-honored practice of his office which emphasized a slow, methodical approach to procurement procedures. Notices were placed in the newspapers when goods were required. Bids were received, and contracts awarded and signed. Because the specifications were so exacting, time consuming manufacture was the rule, and not the exception. Once the goods were finished, Assistant Quartermaster, Capt. William A. T. Maddox, examined every part of the product. Variances from the high standards of the Corps usually resulted in the goods being rejected. Contractual obligations compelled the manufacturer to remake any product that did not meet the specifications established by the Quartermaster's Department. While this practice might have been acceptable in peacetime, it was impractical, not to mention unworkable, in war.

On April 20, Slack asked Maddox to reconsider his rejection of a supply of fabric furnished by the Washington Mills Company of Massachusetts. Slack told Maddox that his recent trip through the North had revealed a shortage of quality fabric. If, upon re-examination of the fabric, Maddox found it "not equal to the standard pattern, at least sufficiently near it to warrant accepting them for the public service," the Assistant Quartermaster was to overlook the quality of the material and receive it.[13] Less than a week later, Maddox was again instructed to re-examine a shipment of fabric he had condemned as not meeting the standards of the Corps. While the goods being received may not have been perfect in every respect, at least those contractors were attempting to make good on their deliveries. Far too many others were not.

Another Marine Corps contractor was Isaac C. Noe & Co. of New York City. On December 29, 1860, Noe accepted a contract to produce 1,000 yards of dark blue flannel, one and one-half yards wide, and 2,000 yards of dark blue flannel, three quarters of a yard wide. The contract had the usual penalty clause which stated that if the goods were not received in sixty days, the Quartermaster reserved the right to purchase on the open market any portion of the order not delivered. The contractor was liable for the difference between the contract price and the open market price. The date that Noe's flannel was due, March 29, 1861, came and went with no delivery. Slack, being a mild-mannered sort, did not press Noe. He would not until Assistant Quartermaster Maddox noticed the outstanding contract while reviewing unfilled orders at the end of April.

Noe's tardiness in delivering the flannel had the potential for serious difficulties. Without the yard goods, the tailors who had contracted to cut, make, and trim the finished product were idle. More importantly, the new recruits authorized by the President could not be properly uniformed. What was taking Noe so long? Since the President's call for volunteers, prices for flannel had soared. Was Noe taking advantage of the higher prices by delivering the flannel contracted for at a lower, peacetime price by the Corps to volunteer regiments and collecting a tidy profit? Slack dashed off a letter to Noe demanding some explanation of the delay. Suspicions laid aside for the moment, he also enclosed an order for additional flannel, making a total of 5,000 yards from this contractor.[14]

By the middle of May, Noe was still delinquent in his deliveries. Major Slack wrote him, saying that although 1,300 yards of the much needed blue flannel had been delivered, Noe had to do better. Slack went on to say that it was his nature to give contractors as much time as he could, but there was a limit to his patience. Even though Noe had not lived up to the terms of his contract and was behind in delivery of some 3,700 yards of flannel, Slack told him that yet another order for flannel would be forthcoming.[15] The next day, Slack sent an order for 3,000 more yards of dark blue flannel plus 1,000 yards of linen to Noe.

On May 21, Slack being far behind in his inventory, notified the Department of the problem with Noe, requesting authority to make purchases on the open market of items that were still undelivered. Welles approved the request. But Slack, rather than take steps to remedy the inexcusable situation with Noe, merely sent him another letter of warning.[16] A telegram followed on May 24, urging delivery of the flannel. Finally, on June 1, Slack invoked the penalty clause of the Noe contract and bought the flannel by purchase on the open market. The difference between the contract price and the market price was deducted from money owed Noe for items delivered under other contracts.[17]

Noe continued to be a problem for Slack. He defaulted on deliveries of the linen ordered May 18, 1861, and Slack had to again invoke the penalty clause of the contract. But Noe was not alone in failing to comply with the terms of a contract with the Marine Corps. James Smith & Sons of New York failed to make good on a promised delivery of cartridge boxes. W. Matthews & Co. of New York did not deliver the cap pouches contracted for on the agreed date. John Mast & Co. of Philadelphia could not deliver a promised order of fatigue caps and cap pouches.[18] William Lang & Co. of Boston was berated by Slack for failing to deliver the fine cloth necessary for the enlisted Marine dress coat when promised. The list went on and on, but Slack seemed powerless to force compliance in contractually agreed upon delivery dates. The mills of the North were inundated with orders for military cloth. Even those contractors with the best of intentions fell victim to the glut of orders and promised more than they could deliver. Others, grown wealthy on the high prices the outbreak of the war had brought with it, did not worry about contractual penalty clauses. They were but a trifling business expense when compared to the enormous profits to be made.

As a consequence of the breakdown in the procurement system, the elimination of the Napoleonic-style uniforms prescribed by the 1839 Uniform Regulations did not proceed so rapidly as planned. The new style uniform, authorized in the regulations approved January 24, 1859, had been in the process of being gradually phased in over the course of the two years before the outbreak of the war. In the summer of 1859, guards being formed for sea duty were the first Marines to be issued the new pattern dress coat, shako, and fatigue cap. Their dress trousers and fatigue uniforms remained old pattern. These would be replaced upon returning from their cruises when the Quartermaster's Department had built up an ample stock. As contractors made deliveries of the new pattern uniforms and the old style clothing was worn out, replacements would be made.

By early April 1861, the changeover was near completion. Most of the enlisted Marines had now been uniformed in the fashion prescribed by the 1859 Uniform Regulations. The changeover was proceeding so smoothly that Slack sent Brevet Major Reynolds at Boston

Detachment on parade at Marine Barracks, Philadelphia, illustrating the uniforms worn during the period following the adoption of the 1859 Regulations

The sergeant, *front row, left*, is attired in the proper fatigue uniform. The second, sixth, seventh, and ninth Marines from the left have the 1859 dress uniforms as do the second, third, and fourth in the rear row from the right. The first Marine in the rear row has the 1859 dress uniform, but wears the Mexican War-style forage cap. The rest of the Marines are wearing 1839 dress uniforms. The lack of uniformity shown in this image was in total disregard of instructions from the Commandant to have all Marines performing duty ashore to be dressed alike. The new pattern uniform was to be issued only to Marines slated for sea duty until ample supplies were on hand.

Photograph Courtesy of Emerick Hanzl

A Marine sergeant and five privates, attired in the dress uniform of the 1859 regulations, pose for a Brady photograph at Marine Barracks, Washington in April 1862

Courtesy of Randy McNally

instructions to dispose of the old pattern uniforms at public auction.[19] Then came war, the expansion of the Corps, and the failure of the contractors to provide goods on a timely basis. By the beginning of May, Slack became quite careful in regard to disposing of the old pattern uniforms. Four music boys were sent to their permanent duty stations by way of Philadelphia and were told to stop at the office of the Assistant Quartermaster to take delivery of their uniform caps. Maddox was ordered to issue them new pattern caps *if possible*.[20] By the end of the month, with the bottleneck caused by the lack of contractor deliveries choking the supply system, Slack instructed Capt. Abraham N. Brevoort at New York to dispose of old pattern uniforms only if they were no longer serviceable and *condemned by survey*.[21] It was not until July 6 that Slack felt sufficiently comfortable with the delivery of the new uniforms to authorize Maddox to sell all the remaining old pattern clothing in his stock.[22]

Ultimately, rigid enforcement of contracts enabled the Quartermaster's Department to meet the demands of the expanding Corps. Slack became less and less willing to listen to excuses for non-delivery of contracted goods. When a delay was reported, Slack was quickly out of his Washington office and en route to the scene to investigate the circumstances for himself. Open market purchases replaced goods not provided by contractors, and new contractors replaced those whose performance was found wanting.

Uniforms were but one of Slack's headaches. A requisition for spare parts for the M1855 Springfield rifled musket forwarded to the Secretary of War on April 19, 1861, was returned unfilled due to the occupation of the arsenal at Harpers Ferry by Virginia forces. The order was subsequently sent to the armory at Springfield, Massachusetts.[23]

The hostile actions of the secessionists of Baltimore also contributed to the Corps' supply problems in the early days of the war. When soldiers of the 6th Massachusetts crossed the city while making railroad connections on April 19, 1861, a mob gathered. The troops were jostled, insulted, and finally stoned. A pistol shot rang out, followed by the report of musket fire. Wounded citizens fell to the pavement and a full-fledged riot broke out in which three soldiers and twelve civilians were killed. The Baltimore Police finally intervened and escorted the soldiers to the safety of Camden Station where they boarded cars for the rest of the journey to Washington.

Secessionist fever gripped the city and spread beyond Baltimore. To prevent further passage of Northern troops through the city, all the bridges connecting Maryland with the North were burned. Washington's land communication with the North was severed.

The Quartermaster of the Marine Corps was also cut off from the North. Arms ordered by the posts at Boston and Portsmouth could not be sent because of the blockade in Maryland. Slack became deeply concerned over a case of muskets he had sent to Boston by Adams Express on April 19, the day of the Baltimore troubles. On May 1, there was still no sign of it at Boston.[24] The lack of muskets at Boston was seriously hampering Major Reynolds' efforts to perform his duties at the Boston Navy Yard. He could not drill his new recruits nor provide instruction on the shooting range without them. That shortage was so bad that Reynolds took rifles from other Marines so that the guards at the navy yard gates could be armed.[25] The missing muskets were finally located by the shipping company and brought through the Maryland obstructions on May 3. Meanwhile, Slack sent another case of muskets to Reynolds via Adams Express, but, as far as subsequent deliveries of arms to Marine posts in the North, the Quartermaster rethought the security of the overland route and decided against it. Until Maryland was pacified, he would ship arms by water.[26]

The rapid pace of events and the sudden calls upon the quartermaster for arms found his store of modern weapons at Washington insufficient to meet the remand. The outbreak of hostilities caught the Corps in a transitional period when the old M1842 .69 caliber, smoothbore musket was being replaced by the .58 caliber rifled musket. As was the case with the old and new uniforms, the various posts and detachments of the Corps were found with a mixture of the two weapons, but Slack was doing his best to meet the exigencies of the times. For example, he sent requisition for 1,000 M1855 Springfield rifled muskets "wanted for immediate use" to the War Department on May 9.

While Slack waited for the War Department to fill his request, some shuffling of weapons was required. When Reynolds complained that the increase in the number of sentinels required at the Boston Navy Yard compelled him to post untrained recruits armed with muskets taken from others, Slack had to countenance the practice. Explaining the difficulties in the procurement process, Slack wrote Reynolds regarding the dearth of the M1855 Springfield:

> Recent requisitions upon the Navy Department for other supply of this arm have not been complied with and am informed that no more can be received for many months to come. Under these circumstances, it will be necessary to re-introduce at the several posts, the arm used by the Corps pervious to the recent change.

Slack also said that new muskets then being used for duty ashore should be exchanged for the old pattern M1842 musket whenever possible:

> It is desirable to arm guards detailed for sea service with the new musket (cal .58) so long as the number of

> that arm on hand at the several stations will enable us to do so, but after that supply is exhausted guards for sea service will have to be armed with muskets, caliber .69.[27]

Further compounding Slack's difficulties was the War Department's reply to his May 9 request for 1,000 new pattern rifled muskets. The Army simply could not comply with the requisition. The amount requested was, at the time, not on hand. Further, the requisitions of the Army would take preference over those of the Marine Corps. However, the War Department communication stated, "The Marine Corps can be furnished immediately with new percussion muskets, smoothbore, calibre .69, and that is the best this Department can do under existing circumstances."[28] Resigning himself to the fact that the Corps was, for the present, relegated to the bottom of the pecking order at the War Department, Slack forwarded his order for the old pattern weapons, ending his requisition with the plea, "New muskets, if you please, not the altered ones."[29]

While Harris nervously awaited Lincoln's decision on his request for more Marines, the recruiting numbers for the last two weeks of May, again with the exception of Philadelphia, fell off slightly. Nevertheless, Harris remained confident that some added effort by the commanding officers of his Marine Barracks would bring forth the desired results.[30] Harris based Philadelphia's noteworthy success on its recruiting rendezvous. Separate and considerably distant from the barracks, the commanding officer of the Philadelphia Rendezvous had but one responsibility and that was to produce recruits for the Corps. He felt sure that duplicating the example of Philadelphia would bring comparable results at the other posts. Accordingly, Harris urged Brevoort to open a rendezvous in New York City. But Brevoort had his hands full with personnel turnover at Marine Barracks, Brooklyn. His command turned over just about every month. As fast as guards were being sent aboard ship, others were being transferred to the barracks. Marines were being sent to other stations, being discharged, and were being sent to and returned from the Brooklyn Naval Hospital. The new barracks had just been completed on May 4 and problems were cropping up with all that movement. Further, Brevoort, at age 72, was the oldest serving officer in the Corps. The years had taken their toll and he just did not have the stamina to take on more responsibility.[31] Harris' suggestion to open a rendezvous was politely rebuffed.[32]

Satisfied that the Quartermaster of the Corps was doing his best to eliminate the causes for the backlog of unfilled requisitions, Lincoln finally approved the additional 432 privates on May 30. By that time, the Department had directed Harris to furnish more than 500 enlisted Marines for ships going into commission.[33] Complicating that equation was the disturbing fact that only 287 recruits had been enlisted since Harris first gave instructions to his post commanders at the end of April. When the 32 discharges, 15 re-enlistments, and 11 desertions reported in May were factored in, the result showed the Corps 241 men short of the required 500. In the months and years that followed, demand for Marines consistently exceeded the number of men available for duty. It was a problem that Headquarters, Marine Corps, was unable to resolve until the war was nearly over.

Another part of Harris' conundrum was trying to fill an ever increasing number of vacant and new billets with a decreasing number of officers. The six officers who resigned in February and March were quickly replaced by Congressional appointees, but those who were dismissed in April and May were not replaced until June.[34] The seven who had their names stricken from the rolls of the Corps in June were not replaced until August. Those positions had to be filled so he could release seasoned officers to satisfy the immediate need for commanding officers of Marine Guards for the new warships going into commission.

The eight young gentlemen who were appointed as second lieutenants of Marines in early June were a disparate group. Their ages ranged from nineteen to thirty. The youngest, Frank Munroe, had strong political connections, being the protégé of Montgomery Blair, the Postmaster General of the new administration. Joseph F. Baker inherited the political support his elder brother John had gathered when the latter withdrew his application to the Corps in favor of an appointment to the Regular Army. Robert W. Huntington, a hell-raising college boy, made his professors at Trinity College sigh with relief when he dropped out of school on April 22, 1861, to enlist in Company A, 1st Connecticut Volunteers. John H. Grimes was certain of an appointment. His uncle was James W. Grimes, Senator from Iowa and chairman of the Senate Naval Affairs Committee. Jehu A. Burrough had only a widowed mother who supported herself and her son by running a boarding house to back him, but his honest plea for a position in the service won the support of Pennsylvania Senator Charles Ten Eyck. William H. Parker, the oldest of the group, was a married man with a family, and looking for a chance to better himself. William H. Hale had something of a dark side. When Mexico erupted into Civil War in 1857, Hale deserted his wife and two young sons to join the Liberal Army of Benito Juarez. He served as a lieutenant colonel of artillery from 1857-1860. Having seen the elephant, Hale was anxious to continue his profession under his own flag. He compiled an impressive list of sponsors, being recommended by President Lincoln, Vice President Hamlin, Postmaster

General Blair, New Hampshire Senator John P. Hale, and former Massachusetts Governor Nathaniel P. Banks. The last of the eight was Robert E. Hitchcock, perhaps the only one of the group whose appointment to the Corps satisfied a long-term desire to become a Marine. Hitchcock's application to become an officer of Marines had been on file with the Navy Department since January 7, 1861, months before those of any other of his fellow appointees.

The eight candidates were all appointed with dates of rank from June 5, 1861. Their places on the seniority list, however, were not to everyone's satisfaction. Complaints were made and Hitchcock related what transpired to his father in a letter home.

> I stand *six* instead of *two.* Baker, we find, made a great fuss about his standing last and the Secy. of the Navy put our names in a hat and drew them out, and I came out six, Hale, eight, Grimes, seven. A fuss will be made I think. Well, I have got my commission and ought to be satisfied, and I am satisfied. (Baker rose from last of the eight positions to number three.)[35]

2d Lt. John H. Grimes
Andrew Parker Collection

2d Lt. Jehu A. Burrough
Ken Turner Collection

2d Lt. William H. Parker
NA Photograph 127-N-517102

2d Lt. William H. Hale
Andrew Parker Collection

2d Lt. Frank Munroe
Courtesy of Fr. William S. Winslet

2d Lt. Robert E. Hitchcock, in the uniform of the Norwich University Corps of Cadets
Norwich University, 1819-1911. Her History, Her Graduates, her Roll of Honor

Advancement in rank being worth the turmoil might have been the viewpoint of those who benefited by the departure of the officers who aligned themselves with the South. Before the Secession Crisis, spending years at the same rank was the rule, not the exception. Remaining a second lieutenant for six to ten years was not uncommon. The average time a first lieutenant spent in grade before being promoted to captain was fourteen years. A captain could expect to remain at that rank for at least nineteen years. The following comparative seniority lists for the months of January and June 1861 show the significant changes caused by the resignations and dismissals.

January 1861		June 1861	
Name	Date of Lineal Rank	Name	Date of Lineal Rank
Colonel, Commandant		*Colonel, Commandant*	
John Harris	January 7, 1859	John Harris	January 7, 1859
General Staff		*General Staff*	
Henry B. Tyler, Adj. & Insp.		Augustus S. Nicholson, Adj. & Insp.	
Wm. W. Russell, Paymaster		Wm. W. Russell, Paymaster	
Wm. B. Slack, Quartermaster		Wm. B. Slack, Quartermaster	
Wm. A. T. Maddox, Asst. QM.		Wm. A. T. Maddox, Asst. QM.	
Lieutenant Colonel		*Lieutenant Colonel*	
James Edelin	January 7, 1859	James Edelin	January 7, 1859
Majors		*Majors*	
William Dulany	November 17, 1847	William Dulany	November 17, 1847
Thomas S. English	February 18, 1853	Thomas S. English	February 18, 1853
Ward Marston	December 10, 1855	Ward Marston	December 10, 1855
Benjamin Macomber*	January 7, 1859	John George Reynolds	May 30, 1861
Captains		*Captains*	
Abraham N. Brevoort	March 6, 1838	Abraham N. Brevoort	March 6, 1838
John G. Reynolds	March 3, 1847	Jacob Zeilen	September 14, 1847
George H. Terrett	March 16, 1847	Addison Garland	October 15, 1854
Jacob Zeilen	September 14, 1847	Josiah Watson	December 10, 1855
Jabez C. Rich	November 27, 1853	Isaac T. Doughty	March 14, 1856
Addison Garland	October 15, 1854	Wm. L. Shuttleworth	September 28, 1857
Josiah Watson	December 10, 1855	Robert Tansill	November 19, 1858
Isaac T. Doughty	March 14, 1856	John C. Grayson	January 7, 1859
Algernon S. Taylor	July 17, 1857	Matthew R. Kintzing	August 1, 1860
Wm. L. Shuttleworth	September 28, 1857	John D. Simms	May 7, 1861
Robert Tansill	November 29, 1858	John C. Cash	May 7, 1861
John C. Grayson	January 7, 1859	James H. Jones	May 24, 1861
Matthew R. Kintzing	August 1, 1860	Edward McD. Reynolds	May 30, 1861
First Lieutenants		*First Lieutenants*	
John D. Simms	September 14, 1847	Thomas Y. Field	October 15, 1854
John C. Cash	September 21, 1852	Charles G. McCawley	January 2, 1855
James H. Jones	September 1, 1853	Charles A. Henderson	December 10, 1855
Edward McD. Reynolds	November 27, 1853	James Wiley	September 27, 1856
Thomas Y. Field	October 15, 1854	George R. Graham	October 22, 1856
Charles G. McCawley	January 2, 1855	John R. F. Tattnall	February 22, 1857
Israel Greene	July 19, 1855	John L. Broome	September 28, 1857
Jacob Read	August 19, 1855	Wm. Stokes Boyd	December 13, 1857

Charles A. Henderson December 10, 1855
Augustus S. Nicholson March 14, 1856
James Wiley September 27, 1856
George R. Graham October 22, 1856
John R. F. Tattnall February 22, 1857
Andrew J. Hays July 17, 1857
John L. Broome September 28, 1857
Wm. Stokes Boyd December 13, 1857
George Holmes April 5, 1858
Robert L. Browning* November 29, 1858
Adam N. Baker August 1, 1860
Henry B. Tyler, Jr. October 23, 1860

Second Lieutenants
Julius E. Meiere April 16, 1855
Alexander W. Stark July 19, 1855
David M. Cohen August 19, 1855
James Lewis September 25, 1855
Clement D. Hebb March 14, 1856
George P. Turner September 27, 1856
Philip H. W. Fontané February 22, 1857
Alan Ramsay March 1, 1857
Philip R. Fendall, Jr. October 17, 1857
Thomas S. Wilson December 13, 1857
John Schermerhorn January 10, 1858
Charles Heywood April 5, 1858
Calvin L. Sayre June 3, 1858
Henry L. Ingraham July 1, 1858
J. Howard Rathbone October 25, 1858
Lucien L. Dawson January 13, 1859
George Butler February 11, 1859
Becket K. Howell August 1, 1860
George W. Collier September 5, 1860
George P. Houston October 25, 1860[36]

* Died

Alexander W. Stark March 1, 1861
David M. Cohen March 2, 1861
James Lewis May 6, 1861
Clement D. Hebb May 7, 1861
Philip H. W. Fontané May 7, 1861
Alan Ramsay May 7, 1861
Philip R. Fendall, Jr. May 18, 1861
Thomas S. Wilson May 24, 1861
John Schermerhorn May 30, 1861
Charles Heywood May 30, 1861
J. Howard Rathbone June 26, 1861
Lucien L. Dawson July 1, 1861

Second Lieutenants
George Butler February 11, 1859
George W. Collier September 5, 1860
George P. Houston October 25, 1860
Philip C. Kennedy February 14, 1861
James Forney March 1, 1861
Louis M. Goldsborough, Jr. March 1, 1861
William H. Cartter March 2, 1861
McLane Tilton March 2, 1861
John H. Higbee March 9, 1861
Frank Munroe June 5, 1861
Robert W. Huntington June 5, 1861
Joseph F. Baker June 5, 1861
Jehu A. Burrough June 5, 1861
William H. Parker June 5, 1861
Robert E. Hitchcock June 5, 1861
William H. Hale June 5, 1861
John H. Grimes June 5, 1861

Harris made the best arrangements he could with the officers he had. However, the best intentions are often thwarted by unforeseen obstacles. When USS *Minnesota* was released from the yard mechanics at Boston and designated flagship of the Home Squadron in early April, Harris ordered Capt. Algernon S. Taylor to prepare for sea duty as commander of her Marine Guard. But Taylor's attempted resignation and subsequent dismissal forced Harris to select another officer, Bvt. Lt. Col. William A. Dulany, commander of Marine Barracks, Portsmouth. Stating that "The large force of the Home Squadron calls for the services of a field officer," Harris ordered Dulany to the *Minnesota.*[37] Dulany apparently prevailed upon the Secretary of the Navy to allow him to remain at Portsmouth because Capt. William L. Shuttleworth received orders dated May 2, 1861, directing him to report to *Minnesota* as Senior Marine Officer of the Home Squadron.

2d Lt. Philip H. W. Fontané
Author's Collection

USS *Mississippi* was scheduled to take on her crew and Marines at Boston on May 13. 1st Lt. Augustus S. Nicholson was ordered to that ship as commander of her Marine Guard on May 3. However, Nicholson was appointed Adjutant and Inspector of the Corps on May 6. Consequently, Harris had to select 2d Lt. Philip H. W. Fontané for the position. Fontané had two years and three months sea duty under the tutelage of Capt. Josiah Watson aboard USS *Roanoke*. The Commandant was comfortable with the match of officer and warship.

When 1st Lt. Israel Greene refused to take the oath of allegiance aboard USS *Niagara* on May 2, Capt. William W. McKean, USN, ordered him from the ship. Harris chose 2d Lt. Clement D. Hebb to replace Greene and ordered him to Boston. Hebb had over two years sea duty aboard the Sloop of War *Falmouth* and seemed a good choice for *Niagara*'s Marine Guard. However, Hebb was soon relieved by Capt. Josiah Watson, and, on May 18, ordered to command the guard of USS *Colorado*. His stay aboard this warship was also of short duration, being relieved by 1st Lt. Edward McD. Reynolds on June 7.[38]

Marine officer Clement D. Hebb
Michael J. McAfee Collection

1st Lt. James Wiley had been granted a month's leave of absence on April 15, but volunteered to return to duty should his services be required.[39] Harris accepted Wiley's offer and posted him to the command of the guard of USS *Wabash* on May 8.

When the Navy Department ordered a Marine Guard for USS *Savannah* on May 21, there were no experienced officers available for duty. Consequently, 2d Lt. Philip C. Kennedy, with only three months of instruction was dispatched to that ship. Guards were ordered for *Jamestown* and *Roanoke* the next day, causing Harris to send two more inexperienced officers to those ships. 2d Lt. George P. Houston was detached to *Jamestown* and 2d Lt. James Forney, who had just turned seventeen years of age in January, and had but ten weeks of drill under his belt, was sent to *Roanoke.* 2d Lt. John H. Higbee joined for duty at Headquarters on April 5. On June 18, he was ordered to command the Marines aboard USS *Vincennes.* Harris was sorely distressed at having to send the young officers to sea with so much responsibility and so little training. Assigning good sergeants to each ship was the most he could do to help them, and that led to additional problems.

When Brevet Major Reynolds requested an experienced sergeant to help him at Marine Barracks, Boston, Harris had to turn him down. All the experienced sergeants were required for sea duty. Reynolds would have to make do with what he had. Harris was so pressed for Marines who knew their drill and duty to fill up the guards of all the vessels now fitting out, that he had to tell Reynolds that two of the four Marines slated for disgraceful discharges at his post would be reprieved and put to duty.[40]

The recruiting situation improved in June when 314 recruits were accepted into the Corps and sixteen old hands re-enlisted when their terms expired. Harris sent Sgt. Samuel F. Reynolds to Pittsburgh, Pennsylvania, to open a recruiting rendezvous on June 1. He had told Reynolds to have all the prospective Marines examined by a physician and board them at not more than 75 cents per day. Thirty fatigue uniforms were sent along with Reynolds in hope that they would be filled with good men. Harris was delighted with Reynolds' efforts. Between June 3-25, forty-three men were enlisted.[41] He was, however, perplexed when one of the recruits turned out to be someone he recognized.

Recruit Lawrence Keslar had seen service with the Corps before. In May 1859, he had deserted his post at the Boston Navy Yard and, when caught, disgracefully discharged from the service, not to be re-enlisted. Harris questioned Keslar closely. The young man was very sorry about his past and anxious to retrieve his good name. All he wanted was another chance. Impressed with Keslar's sincerity, Harris agreed to petition the Secretary of the Navy on his behalf.[42] Upon Harris' recommendation, the Navy Department approved Keslar's re-enlistment. The Commandant was much chagrined, however, when Keslar deserted on July 3.[43]

The special session of Congress called by President Lincoln was due to reconvene on July 4, 1861. This presented an opportunity for

Harris to reap for his Corps some of the benefits the rest of the military establishment was enjoying. His November 1860 proposal to increase the Corps had been partially acted upon; the rank and file being increased by two-thirds. However, the number of officers remained unchanged. In mid-June, Harris presented Welles with a proposal to significantly change the organization of the Marine Corps.

> Abstract for the better organization of the Marine Corps
>
> Section One:
>
> Be it enacted, etc., that from and after the passage of this Act, the United States Marine Corps shall consist of the officers, non-commissioned officers, musicians and privates, viz:

One Brigadier General, Commandant
Two Colonels
Two Lieutenant Colonels
Four Majors
One Adjutant and Inspector
One Paymaster
One Quartermaster
Two Assistant Quartermasters
Thirty Captains
Forty First Lieutenants
Thirty Second Lieutenants
Two Sergeant Majors
Two Quartermaster Sergeants
Two Drum Majors
Two Principal Musicians
240 Sergeants
270 Corporals
50 Musicians for the Band
90 Drummers
90 Fifers
3,000 Privates

> Provided that the officers composing the Staff of the Corps shall, after ten years service as such in they shall hold rank assigned to them by the Act of March 2d, 1847, be promoted. The Adjutant and Inspector, the Paymaster and the Quartermaster, respectfully to the rank of Lieutenant Colonel, and the Assistant Quartermasters, respectively, to the rank of Major.
>
> Section Two:
>
> And be it further enacted that the President of the United States shall, by and with the advice and consent of the Senate, appoint, first by promotion of the officers now in the Marine Corps and then by selection of the officers hereby authorized.

> Section Three:
>
> And be it enacted that all acts, or parts of acts relating to the officers or enlisted men of the Marine Corps not inconsistent with the provisions of this act, be and the same are hereby continued in full force and effect.[44]

Welles agreed that some increase in the number of Marine officers was required. However, his July 4, 1861, report to Congress was deliberately vague as to what the increase should entail. Pointing out that the strength of the Corps had been increased to 2,500 privates while the officers remained the same as when the Corps numbered 1,100 rank and file, Welles wrote, "This number is altogether insufficient, and it is therefore recommended that there be an additional number created, and if the session is sufficiently prolonged, and entire reorganization of the Corps may be expedient."[45] Any change in the structure of the Corps was bound to instigate controversy. The Navy Department would be happy to have this political battle fought in the halls of Congress.

On July 6, an order from the Navy Department arrived at Headquarters, Marine Corps, directing Harris to detail 100 Marines to the Gulf Squadron. The Commandant took this opportunity to reverse Brevet Lieutenant Colonel Dulany's success of May in keeping his comfortable post as commander of Marine Barracks, Portsmouth. The 100 Marines being prepared for Gulf Squadron duty would be Dulany's responsibility. Upon his arrival in the Gulf, he would report aboard USS *Colorado* and assume the duties of Senior Marine Officer. Harris made sure that Dulany would be kept busy by telling him to make frequent visits to all of the ships of the Gulf Squadron with Marines aboard, reporting his inspection visits to the Adjutant on a regular basis.[46]

Dulany, with forty-four years of experience as a "sea lawyer" in Marine Corps politics did not accept his orders as a matter of routine. He cleverly crafted a letter to the Secretary of the Navy, accepting his orders but, at the same time, raising certain points that were sure to create a furor when he arrived in the Gulf. Dulany posed questions to the Secretary that were bound to confuse the issue. In order to avoid misunderstandings when he reached the *Colorado*, what quarters would he occupy and where would he mess? This being the first time a brevet lieutenant colonel received orders to squadron duty, there was no established precedent. With that question "innocently" inserted, Dulany went directly to the heart of the matter, stating:

> My assimilated rank in the Navy is above that of the oldest Commander in the Navy and with this relative rank, I presume I am entitled to have quarters in an appropriate part of the ship. I therefore would most respectfully ask that a written order be given pointing out my proper position on the Flagship.[47]

Dulany knew full well that Welles would not give the requested order. It would have caused an outrage among the naval officers aboard the flagship. Insisting that they take less comfortable quarters to accommodate a Marine officer was a precedent that Welles was not going to establish. Dulany's orders to the Gulf were revoked.[48]

5

"Their Backs to the Enemy": The Marine Battalion at Bull Run

The early days of July 1861 found Marine Barracks, Washington, a beehive of constant activity. Recruits by the score had joined from the Rendezvous at Philadelphia during June and forty-four more would arrive on July 10, all of them as green as shamrocks in May. So many had arrived that the post stable had been appropriated as a temporary barracks, forcing the officers to make other arrangements for their horses. 2d Lt. Robert E. Hitchcock described the scene from his vantage point in a letter to his parents. Responding to their query as to why he did not write more often, Hitchcock wrote:

> I must tell you why I do not and cannot write oftener. 1st. I am acting Adjutant and take my regular duty as officer of the day with the rest of the Corp. 2nd. We have 377 raw recruits and they have to be drilled four hours a day and I have a part of them to drill We are short of drill Sergts., having only four at the post at present, this you see puts extra duty on to me. 3rd. We have to study Tactics and Military generally and recite to Maj. Reynolds, who is a graduate of West Point, and very sharp upon <u>every</u> point of a military character and the result is that the recitation is three hours long sometimes.[1] Now take all these duties, then consider that we have to rise at 3:30 AM, and you can easily imagine that by night or when an opportunity is offered for rest that we are glad to take advantage of the opportunity.[2]

He went on to say that he very much enjoyed what he was doing, particularly the authority his new position held. He liked having his orders obeyed.

Another viewpoint was expressed by one of the recruits Lieutenant Hitchcock enjoyed exercising command over. Pvt. John E. Reily enlisted at Philadelphia on June 22, 1861. An Irishman by birth and a laborer by trade, Reily had joined Marine Barracks, Washington, with a draft of forty-eight recruits from Philadelphia on June 29. To his parents, the young recruit wrote:

> I send you these few lines to let you know that I am in good health and well satisfied with the life of a Marine   I never had work since I was able to work that I like as well as this We only have three hours drill a day   We raise at half past 3 Oclock in the Morning and drill one hour and a half before Breakfast and the same in the evening   I do not think I will be here over four Months at furthest before I be sent on board some ship   They are sending them as soon as They are drilled to Philadelphia Brooklyn Boston and Portsmoth N. H.   as long as we stay about Navy Yards we cannot save over Nine Dollars per Month   We have to pay 75 cents a month for washing and 20 Cs for to support the Naval Asylum and we get out on liberty every four days for about five hours   I was on liberty Monday afternoon and I went to Col. Smalls Camp and seen a few I was acquainted with   If I be here in the beginning of October I will try to send you some money and my likeness for we get paid every three Months while We are here   The first of the month was pay day so that the next pay day will be on the first of October   I feel better here than I have for the last four years   We have nothing to do but lay about the barricks from six Oclock in the morning unto five Oclock in the evening and then we have to drill for one and a half and then go to bunk at nine Oclock   We will be drilled better in one Month here than the Volunteers would in six Months We get pretty good living here   good wheat flour every Meal fresh beef every other day with soup   Any body that wants to go church can go every Sunday to any they want to   We go to swim once a week.[3]

All too soon, the life that Reily described as idyllic to his parents came to an end. His boast of Marines being better drilled in one month than volunteer regiments were in six was going to be put to the test.

1st Lt. Alan Ramsay USMC, was just ending a week's leave in Washington when he heard that a battalion of Marines was going to be ordered to duty with the Army and would be attached to the command of Col. Andrew H. Porter, USA.[4] If the reports were true, he wanted to be part of the expedition. When he got back to his post aboard USS *Richmond* at New York, Ramsay asked Harris for assignment to active service with the battalion.[5] Harris received Ramsay's letter on the thirteenth and immediately replied:

> I have received your letter of the 11th instant, asking to be attached to a Battalion of Marines that is about to join the Army to which I reply that I have no knowledge of such a Battalion but if such an order be given, I will command it myself and will be glad to have you with me although I fear your services cannot be dispensed with on the "Richmond."[6]

Soon enough, the Commandant of the Corps was made aware that a battalion of Marines was going to take part in an offensive into Virginia. There are no surviving records concerning any meeting between Harris and Welles regarding the Marines serving with the Army. What is known is that on the same day as Harris sent his letter to Ramsay, professing ignorance regarding the battalion being formed for duty with the Army, a telegram was sent to Ramsay from the Secretary of the Navy ordering him back from New York and directing him to report to the Commandant.[7] It is very likely that after posting his letter to Ramsay, Harris pondered the matter. There were rumblings about a push into Virginia all over Washington. It is probable that Harris went to see Welles, presented Ramsay's letter, and asked if there was any truth to the matter. Welles undoubtedly showed him the previous day's request from the War Department for a battalion of Marines to serve temporarily in the field under Brig. Gen. Irvin McDowell, USV.[8] Wrote Secretary of War Simon Cameron, "I have the honor to request that the disposable effective marines now here may be organized into a battalion, and held in readiness to march on field service . . ."[9]

Given Harris' temperament and the great pride he had in himself and his office, it is likely that he was outraged and humiliated at being kept in the dark while plans for his Corps were being made. He surely demanded explanations as to why he was not consulted in the matter, and why a first lieutenant had precise information on the subject before the Commandant of his Corps did. Welles was similarly proud and equally jealous of his prerogatives. Given that the orders summoning Maj. John G. Reynolds from Boston and Bvt. Maj. Jacob Zeilen from Philadelphia to duty with the Marine Battalion originated not with the Commandant, but the Secretary of the Navy, a clear departure from established protocol, it is likely that Welles and Harris did not part on the best of terms.[10] Harris' humiliation was complete when he learned that he would not command the Marines in the field as he had informed Ramsay.

The actual orders from the Department to the Commandant to form the Marine Battalion were not issued until July 15. They read:

> You will be pleased to detail from the barracks four companies of eighty men each, the whole under the command of Major Reynolds, with the necessary officers, non-commissioned officers and musicians, for temporary field service under Brig. General McDowell, to whom Major Reynolds will report. General McDowell will furnish the Battalion with camp equipage, provisions, etc.[11]

Welles then notified the War Department that the Marine Battalion requested on the twelfth would be ready for duty in the field as soon as it was needed.

Before the orders were made known to the troops, rumor and barracks gossip had alerted all at Marine Barracks, Washington, that they were taking the field against the rebels. The news was quickly relayed to those at home. 2d Lt. William H. Cartter, by virtue of his being the senior second lieutenant, would be commanding one of the four companies. It was a matter of expediency, there being no other officers readily available for the position. Cartter, nevertheless, was quite pleased with his elevation and wrote his mother:

> I am agoing to leave for the seat of the war (Richmond, Va.) where I expect we will have a fight now. I am well and expect to be a Captin or a Seignior 1st Lieut. before. . . . Now do not fret yourself about me, for all is for the best whatever may hapen.[12]

Lieutenant Hitchcock wrote home with a sense of foreboding. Things were not going the way he would have liked and he did not hesitate to speak his mind.

Marine Barracks
Washington, D.C.
July 14th, 1861

Dear Parents:

Your letter came to hand yesterday. I was very happy to hear from you at this time in particular. Last night after I passed down the line to receive the reports of the companies, I was met by Captain Jones, who said to me, Mr. Hitchcock, "prepare to take the field on Monday morning." So tomorrow morning will see me and five other Lieuts. with 300 Marines (raw recruits in every sense of the term) on our way to Fairfax Court House to take part in a bloody battle which is to take place, it is thought, about Wednesday. This is unexpected to us, and the Marines are not fit to go into the field, for every man of them is as raw as you please, not more than a hundred of them have been here over three weeks. We have no camp equipage of any kind, not even tents, and after all this, we are expected to take the brunt of the battle. We are to be commanded by Maj. Reynolds I suppose. We shall do as well as we can under the circumstances: just think of it, 300 raw men in the field! We shall drill all day, and work hard. I have been very busy all the day thus far, but have taken a little time to write you. I have left my things with Lieut. Wm. H. Parker, and my watch also, he has my address and will take good care of my clothes, watch, etc. By writing to him you can find out about my matters. In case anything happens to me, he will send my things to you, and you can do as you like with them. Lieuts. Baker, Burroughs and Parker will be left here at the Barracks, and any of them would be pleased to give you information in regard to me or my matters. I hope the God of Battles will give me strength and wisdom to act wisely, and do my duty well. I am not prepared to die, but I am prepared to serve my Country, and stand by the Stars and Stripes till the last. I am well and in good spirits. May God bless you all, is the wish of your

Affectionate son,
Robt.

My love to all, and best regards to all my friends. I am just informed we leave tomorrow evening. Robt.[13]

Hitchcock was not alone in thinking that the battalion was not ready for field service. Reynolds felt similarly. They were in good company. McDowell knew the entire force he was taking into Virginia was not ready for battle. But the enlistments of the three months volunteers were running out. If he did not meet the rebels now, the entire recruiting process, the training and everything else would have to be repeated with new organizations. The President knew his fears but assured him that he would meet the enemy on equal terms. Lincoln told him, "You are green, it is true but they are green, also. You are green alike."[14] The public demanded battle; so did the Congress. And so McDowell put aside his misgivings and prepared to meet the enemy.

On July 15, McDowell sent Harris a list of equipment that he wanted the Marines to carry into the field.

Memo for Col. Harris

The battalion of Marines to be equipped as follows.
Arms.
Accoutrements.
Ammunition - (boxes full)
Haversacks. (with three days rations)
Canteens + cups
Blanket - in a roll with the ends tied and worn from the right shoulder to the left side; a pair of stockings to be rolled up in the blanket.

No knapsacks - no tents. Two wagons to come over for the camp kettles + mess pans, and mess kits.

The battalion to start for the other side in time to pass the long bridge by 3:00 P.M. tomorrow. They will follow up the Columbia Turnpike as far as the New Fort and Toll Gate where they will receive further orders.

McD.[15]

Major Slack found his department unable to fill the requirements. Recruits undergoing drill at Marine Barracks, Washington, were not issued haversacks or canteens. Consequently, McDowell's orders placed the Quartermaster's Department in a difficult situation. Slack quickly sent a telegram to Captain Maddox at Philadelphia:

> 300 watchcoats and 350 haversacks and canteens wanted here for immediate use. If you have not all the number required, send all you have at once and telegraph Barnum (the contractor for haversacks and canteens) to send you immediately all he has on hand and employ extra force in making up the balance. If you can get any coats from barracks, do so.[16]

Maddox replied by telegraph that the haversacks and canteens were on hand. A much relieved Slack telegraphed back, directing Maddox to send them to Washington by Express. They had to be on hand by tomorrow morning, July 16.

The night before the march found the young Marine officers musing about what the expedition into Virginia would bring. Those who had been selected to stay behind were grousing over their bad fortune. Those who were designated for company assignments were relieving pre-battle jitters by chatting about how the Union forces were going to give the Confederates what they deserved. There was much good-natured bantering over the morning's march into enemy country. Hitchcock did not join in the fun. Giving his watch and other belongings to Parker along with his father's address just in case he did not return, Hitchcock was conspicuous by his sober attitude. Those who were making light of the expedition, suffered a rebuke from Hitchcock, who chided them for talking about it in such a trifling manner.[17]

Harris issued supplementary orders for the expedition on the morning of July 16. Major Nicholson, the Staff Adjutant and Inspector was assigned as Adjutant of the battalion. Major Slack would accompany the battalion as Quartermaster until he was relieved by an assistant quartermaster from the Army. The battalion would leave Marine Barracks, Washington, at 2:00 P.M.

Before the battalion left, Harris had a conversation with Pvt. Joseph Pennypacker who reported himself sick that morning. The tenor of that exchange was sent to the Navy Department. It lent a little humor to the hours of feverish preparations.

> Private Joseph Pennypacker of this Post is on the sick list and says he is satisfied that soldiering does not agree with him and therefore wishes to obtain his discharge.
>
> I think his wish not to accompany the Battalion today is proof that he lacks the material to make a good soldier and that it would be for the best interests of the service to discharge him on the settlement of his accounts.[18]

Major Reynolds formed the Marine Battalion on the parade ground shortly before the 2:00 P.M. departure time. His staff consisted of Nicholson, Slack, a sergeant-major, and QM Sgt. Smith Maxwell. Company A was commanded by Bvt. Maj. Jacob Zeilen with 2d Lts. Frank Munroe and John H. Grimes as subalterns. Company B was commanded by Capt. James H. Jones with 2d Lt. Robert W. Huntington. Company C was led by 1st Lt. Alan Ramsay, 2d Lt. Robert E. Hitchcock joining him. Company D was in charge of 2d Lt. William H. Cartter. His second officer was 2d Lt. William H. Hale. In terms of combat experience,

Maj. John G. Reynolds, USMC, commanding Marine Battalion
Courtesy of John D. Reynolds

Bvt. Maj. Jacob Zeilen, commanding Company A
George Menegaux Collection

Capt. James H. Jones, commanding Company B
George Menegaux Collection

1st Lt. Alan Ramsay, commanding Company C
Massachusetts Commandery, MOLLUS Collection, USAMHI

2d Lt. William H. Cartter, commanding Company D
MCHC Collection

only Reynolds, Nicholson, Slack, Zeilen, Jones, and Hale had smelled gunpowder in battle.

Twelve noncommissioned officers served in the four companies. Only one, Sgt. Thomas A. Buckley, had battle experience. Three musicians and one apprentice music boy were also assigned to the battalion. There were 324 privates. Some were enlisted as recently as July 8 and had less than a week's drill. The majority of the battalion had enlisted during May and June, but could not be considered properly trained by any stretch of the imagination. Only seven privates had been in the Corps prior to the opening guns of Fort Sumter.

Southeast Washington

The Marine Battalion marched over these streets en route to the Long Bridge, seen in the distance.

William Henry Seward Papers,
Department of Rare Books and Special Collections,
University of Rochester Library

At 2:00 P.M., commands to form the battalion into marching order rang out across the parade ground. Muskets were smartly hoisted to the left shoulder and with the fifes and drums keeping time, the Marine Battalion marched out of Marine Barracks, Washington.

The march to the Long Bridge was just short of two miles through the streets of Washington. The Marine Battalion made the journey in time to conform with McDowell's orders to be across by 3:00 P.M., despite the heavy military traffic heading toward Virginia. Numerous regiments arriving from camps within the District were crossing the bridge, most in reasonable military order. The 27th New York was a notable exception. Coming from Franklin Square,

Area of operations, July 1861

RG 94, Civil War Atlas, plate VII

the New Yorkers spared their feet by impressing every vehicle they could lay hands upon. Omnibuses, hackneys, carts, and wagons conveying the 27th gave a carnival atmosphere to the procession.[19]

Brig. Gen. David Hunter, USA, commander of the 2d Division
Massachusetts Commandery, MOLLUS Collection, USAMHI

Col. Andrew Porter, USA, commanding 1st Brigade, 2d Division
Massachusetts Commandery, MOLLUS Collection, USAMHI

After marching one mile down the road from the Long Bridge, the Marine Battalion came to Fort Runyon and swung onto the Columbia Turnpike. Another mile brought it to Fort Albany and the Toll Gate. At this point, the Marines halted in obedience to McDowell's orders and waited for the instructions that would place them into line of march. All of the regiments that were encamped along the Virginia side of the Potomac from the Aqueduct Bridge and along Arlington Heights were converging on the Toll Gate and being segregated into brigades and divisions. While the Marines waited, Major Reynolds, as he would at every halt along the march, put the battalion through the manual of arms.[20] Reynolds, well aware of the less than adequate training his men had received, was not going to allow any such breaks in the march to pass in idleness.

The Marines were assigned to the First Brigade, led by Col. Andrew Porter, Second Division, Brig. Gen. David Hunter, commanding.[21]

Other organizations attached to the brigade and joining the Marines at Fort Albany were the 8th New York State Militia; Col. George Lyons: 14th Brooklyn Chasseurs; Col. Alfred M. Wood: 27th New York

Volunteers; Col. Henry W. Slocum: Battalion of U.S. Infantry; Maj. George Sykes: Battalion of U.S. Cavalry; Maj. Innis Palmer; and Battery D, 5th U.S. Artillery, Capt. Charles Griffin.[22] Once the different units were brought together, the Second Brigade joined the line of march near the rear of the column. The Marine Battalion wheeled into line behind Griffin's Battery.

The march from Fort Albany to the Little River Turnpike was only about three miles. But frequent delays caused the column to move at a snail's pace. The thousands of feet churning up the road in front of the Marine Battalion raised clouds of choking dust that made breathing difficult at best. The day was hot and humid. Sweat ran down the faces and necks of the Marines, attracting the dust until a mask of mud adorned every marcher. Their perspiration-drenched uniforms hung like iron weights around their bodies. Welts and sores from the constant chaffing where a cross belt, waist belt, or rifle rubbed against the body added further misery, not to mention the countless blisters raised on tender feet. Marching in the rear of the artillery brought a route step not found in any Army manual as the Marines side-stepped and dodged the droppings of a hundred battery horses. And each halt saw Reynolds bringing his men into formation, dressing the lines, and executing the inevitable manual of arms. It was well past nightfall when the Marine Battalion fell out to make camp.

Reveille sounded at daybreak, July 17. As the men of the 2d Brigade ate their breakfasts and tended to their camp chores, more troops marched by. The 5th Division was, after an all-night march, still en route to its designated position. McDowell's order of movement called for the 2d Division to be at Fairfax Court House by 8:00 A.M.[23] That hour had come and gone and the troops of the 1st Brigade, assigned to take the lead, were still waiting for the Little River Pike to be cleared of men from the 2d Brigade. Finally, the 2d Division moved out. As the Marines marched, the miseries of the first day, marginally abated during the night's rest, returned with a vengeance. Fortunately, Fairfax Court House was reached shortly after noon and the day's march was at an end.

The Marine Battalion set up camp at Fairfax and spent the rest of the day drilling while the troops of other regiments investigated the abandoned defensive works in and around the town. Some of the volunteers embarked on a spree of pillage and vandalism, looting and burning private property.[24] That night, when supper was finished and camp duties concluded, the men of the U.S. Infantry Battalion were spectators to the Marines forming up once more and presenting "the novel spectacle of battalion drill by moonlight . . . much to the interest and amusement," of the regulars.[25]

That night, about midnight, a false alarm gave confusion to the 2d Brigade. Volunteers ran in every direction. Some formed a line of battle and fired three volleys at an imagined enemy in the woods. The seasoned regulars, roused by the noise, sat up, made an assessment of the situation, recognized it to be nothing more than a case of nerves and went back to sleep.[26] The Marine Battalion, not quite so unflappable, took up their arms, but retreated to their blankets before Reynolds seized the opportunity for another drill.

July 18 saw the 2d Brigade clear its camps after breakfast, march about a mile and wait in the hot sun until 3:00 P.M. before proceeding to Centerville. On the march, the sound of guns was heard coming from the direction of Blackburn's Ford, making the blood of everyone in the column race with excitement, and, in some cases, fear. Three miles to the south, elements of the 1st Division had made contact with the Confederates and were engaged in a fire fight. The enemy was in strength and prepared to give battle.

The 2d Division marched down the Little River Pike for about two sweltering miles before turning southwest onto the Warrenton Turnpike.[27] Another three miles under the blistering sun brought the brigade to Little Rocky Run, almost two miles from Centerville. McDowell's orders had directed Hunter's Division to go into camp as near to Centerville as water could be had.[28] The troops halted, spread out on both sides of the turnpike and made camp. They would gratefully remain there for two days while their bodies recovered and McDowell and his staff put together a plan to defeat the Confederates.

The Marine Battalion spent the two days performing battalion drill and otherwise attempting to perfect its discipline. Even so, the men were glad to have time away from the march, for blisters to heal and the opportunity to wash away the grime of the road from their bodies. Many took time to write letters home and let loved ones know some of the details of this first adventure of war. Lieutenant Cartter, bored with four days of marching and drilling, wove a tale of derring-do out of whole cloth to impress the folks at home.

Willow Spring Farm, Va.
Saturday, 20 (July), 1861

Dear Mother

This place is 7 miles from Manassa gap. Last night I had a skirmish and lost 4 men killed and wounded 9. We chased about 8 thousand Seccessionist troops out of Fairfax. a person feels kind of funny when he hears Bults flying around. When you write to Father let him know that I am well and a <u>Captan And that</u> I have had a fought. I will try and write from evry place of any interest. Give love to Uncle Will, Grand Father & Mother. Your Loving Son

W. H. Carter[29]

Lieutenant Hitchcock, despite the inclusion of a few rumors, wrote a more factual account of the march and what had taken place since leaving Washington:

Camp near Centerville, Virginia
Headquarters, Battalion Marines
Col. Porter's Brigade, Corps Reserve
July 20, 1861

Dear Parents:

We have been in the field nearly a week now and have not had an engagement yet. The enemy has fled before us as we approached their different positions. We expected to have a fight at Fairfax Court House but as we approached their works they fled leaving a great quantity of flour, ham, pork, spears, shovels, etc. The works at Fairfax were good and they could have held us in check for a while, but would have been routed after a while by a flank movement. The confederates made a stand at Bull Run which is between our camp and Centerville and about two miles from us.

A fight took place at Centerville day before yesterday, the result of which we cannot get at, there are so many different reports. We have been at this encampment about 36 hours waiting for Patterson's and McClellan's to come up with their columns in order to make a combined attack upon Manassa Junction where the rebels are collected in great force. We shall bring a force of nearly 129,000 men against them: how the battle will terminate I know not. At Centerville the forces engaged were the N. Y. 69th and 12th Regiments. The 12th did not stand the fire very well for awhile but they came to after a little and went in. They were in a tight spot. They were in an angle in the road which was covered by a masqued battery that opened upon them rather unexpectedly. The killed and wounded amt. to 29, six I think were killed. I do not know when we shall advance, we may take up the line of march today, and may not leave for a number of days. We are here without tents or anything of the kind, still we manage to live very well. I am well. This is rather rough life after all, in the field as we are without the usual conveniences of camp. The 23rd Regulars are next to us commanded by Maj. Stiaso, I think.[30] Just as I write, four men of the Regt. (23) are receiving 50 lashes for desertion;

rather hard I tell you.[31] I shall write as often as I can, I cannot write more today. I was on guard last night and must get rest so as to be ready for the advance. I hope you are well at home. Much love to you and the family. Give my regards to all that might inquire after me.

As ever, your aft.
son, Robt.[32]

McDowell spent the 20th formulating a plan of attack. The Confederate right appeared too strong to break by direct assault at Blackburn's Ford. The stone bridge over Bull Run on the Warrenton Turnpike was reported to be mined and defended by well-deployed batteries of artillery. His only alternative was to make a flanking march far to the rebel left. Reconnaissance had discovered two spots north of the turnpike that could be forded. The closest was reported to be defended, but the second, some three miles north of the turnpike was not. A strong column sent by that route would be able to get in the rear of the rebel positions along Bull Run. The defenders of the first ford would be forced to abandon their positions, thus allowing Colonel Heintzelman's 3rd Division to cross the river at that point, join with Hunter's troops, and drive the enemy from the field. While the 2d and 3rd Divisions were on the move, Brig. Gen. Daniel Tyler's 1st Division would demonstrate along Bull Run below the Warrenton Turnpike and hold the Confederate troops in position.[33] Satisfied that his plan was sound, McDowell drew up his orders for the morning of July 21.

General Orders, No. 22, called for Tyler's Division to advance from its camp at 2:30 A.M., sharp, take up a position at the stone bridge on the turnpike, and open fire at daybreak. Hunter's Division would take up its march at 2:00 A.M., turn right after passing Cub Run and head north to the ford above Sudley Springs, cross Bull Run and turn south, driving the enemy from the ford that Heintzelman's Division was ordered to cross. The two divisions would then force the enemy from its positions on the turnpike, allowing a junction of all the Federal forces which would then advance to destroy the railroad connecting Manassas with the western part of Virginia.[34]

The Marine Battalion spent the day preparing for the coming march. Reynolds, true to form, put the Marines through battalion drill again and again. Around 4:00 P.M., 2d Lt. Joseph F. Baker arrived in the camp. Baker was not originally assigned to the battalion when it left Washington, which had bitterly disappointed him. Late

Topography of the operations area, July 21, 1861

RG 94, Civil War Atlas, plate III, map 2

Friday, July 19, Colonel Harris asked if he would volunteer to bring a horse to Major Reynolds. Seizing the opportunity as a stroke of good luck, Baker quickly agreed.

The journey took the better part of twenty-four hours. Rear echelon security details held him up at several points, but he finally reached the battalion at Centerville. After delivering the horse to Reynolds, Baker went to see his friends of the battalion. His fellow officers were excitedly discussing the coming battle, and chided Baker for being a latecomer. During the course of the good-natured banter, Baker was given a choice of remaining in camp or being assigned to one of the companies. Not wanting to miss the chance to take part in the adventure of his young life, Baker eagerly took a company assignment.[35]

Sleep, for many of the Marines, did not come easily. Barely audible conversations passed between friends. Letters and personal belongings passed hands with requests and promises to deliver them to loved ones at home should the unthinkable happen. Anxiety over what the morrow would bring kept many awake. Hitchcock lay on his back staring at the sky. Turning to his friend 2d Lt. Frank Munroe, Hitchcock mused, "We shall have warm work tomorrow. Probably one or two of us may not survive the battle."[36]

The Marine Battalion, as well as the rest of the 2d Division, was formed and ready to move at 2:00 A.M., July 21. Brig. Gen. Ambrose P. Burnside's Brigade took the head of the column, but made no headway.[37] The Warrenton Turnpike was jammed with Tyler's Division, who should not have started out on the turnpike until the 2d Division had passed forward. They were not to leave their camps until 2:30 A.M. for that specific reason. But Tyler had put his troops on the march too early, and it took the 2d Division over two hours, and closer to three, to reach the point where it turned to the north. The distance should have been covered in less than thirty minutes.

The 2d Division did not reach the road where it was to make its turn to the north until it was nearly 6:00 A.M. As the column swung onto that dirt road, firing was heard to the south. It was Tyler opening up on the defenses at the stone bridge. Despite his tardiness in clearing the road for the 2d Division, Tyler opened the battle right on time. McDowell's plan called for the 2d Division to be past Sudley Springs and in position to move against the rebels supposedly holding the ford where the 3rd Division was intended to cross. It was not. It was still seven miles from Sudley Ford when Tyler's guns started the battle. Officers quickened the pace of the column. Sudley Ford should have been reached by 6:30 A.M. It was nearly nine o'clock when the leading elements of the division crossed the ford and wheeled left onto the Sudley-Newmarket Road.

Just south of the ford was Sudley Church, where startled churchgoers gaped in wide-eyed amazement as 3,700 Federal soldiers marched past. Just below the church, the column halted to rest before moving on. The day was already hot and hundreds of men dashed to Bull Run to fill their canteens, attempting to ease their parched throats with water mixed with insects and mud churned up by the passage of the troops.[38] Lieutenant Hitchcock and Captain Jones passed the break discussing arrangements each promised to make for the other in the event that either one was killed. Both made a solemn vow to retrieve the body of the other should he fall in the coming battle.[39]

As the 2d Division rested, 1st Lt. William W. Averell, USA, one of Colonel Porter's staff officers, saw what he thought was a cloud of dust in the direction they were headed.[40] Taking his telescope, Averell climbed to the top rail of a fence and saw quite plainly a body of troops advancing to apparently block the road to the Federal column.[41] As he leaped from the fence to report his sighting to Porter, Averell must have wondered what the rebels were doing there in front of them. Was it chance that the Confederate commander, Gen. Pierre G. T. Beauregard, decided to strengthen his left?[42] Or had something else happened to alert the enemy to their march?[43] The news was quickly passed on to Hunter, who immediately ordered the division back onto the road and forward.

The delay caused by Tyler's Division had cost Hunter's troops more than a march in the cool of the night. It cost them the element of surprise. As a result of the three-hour delay, most of the flank march was done in daylight. At 8:30, Capt. Edward Porter Alexander, General Beauregard's signal officer, spotted the reflection of the sun on one of the brass artillery pieces in Hunter's Division.[44] It was eight miles from his observation tower at Wilcoxen's Hill, but Alexander's trained eye saw not only "the brief flash of reflected sun from the cannon but also the glint of bayonets."[45]

Alexander quickly signaled Col. Nathan G. Evans, commander of a "demi-brigade" at the stone bridge, the leftmost portion of the Confederate line.[46] Evans had the 4th South Carolina and Wheat's Special Battalion, Louisiana Infantry, some cavalry, and a few field pieces opposite the stone bridge. He had been waiting for the Federals to do something more than merely exchange harassing fire since the first discharge of Tyler's guns at dawn. Then Alexander's signal was received. "Look out for your left. You are flanked." A cavalry scout rode in at almost the same time and reported that Federal troops were crossing over the ford at Sudley Springs. Taking two of the guns, the South Carolina regiment, and the Louisiana "Tigers," Evans marched to meet the threat. These were the troops that Averell saw from his perch at Sudley Church. Now that his flank march had been discovered, Hunter would have to give battle and fight, rather than maneuver the Confederate troops from their positions.

Burnside's Brigade was in the vanguard as Hunter's Division emerged from the woods to the east of the Sudley-Newmarket Road at 9:45 A.M. The 2d Rhode Island was thrown forward to Matthews Hill and into a hail of musketry from Evans' troops on Buck Hill. Hunter was wounded and command of the division passed to Porter. Evans moved his troops forward to the southern slope of Matthews Hill where they fought off successive attempts by the Rhode Islanders to dislodge them. Soon, Burnside's entire brigade was in action and hard pressed by Confederate reinforcements arriving on the field under the command of Brig. Gen. Barnard Bee, PACS.[47]

While Burnside's Brigade was being roughly handled by the Confederates, the 1st Brigade passed through the woods over an abandoned railroad grade to the west of the road and extended the Federal line beyond the Confederate left. Griffin's six-gun West Point Battery was in the lead, followed by the Marine Battalion, 27th New York, 14th Brooklyn, 8th New York State Militia, and the Battalion of U.S. Infantry. Griffin's Battery unlimbered on the crest of a ridge some six hundred yards from the intersection of the Warrenton Turnpike and the Sudley-Newmarket Road and opened fire on the rebel artillery. The Marine Battalion took a position on the far right of the line, backed up by the battalion of U.S. Cavalry.

As the battle intensified, the sound of the firing drifted to the capital, some twenty-five miles distant. The women at Marine Barracks, Washington, comforted each other with assurances that their husbands would return safely. The wife of Capt. James Jones was glad she had accepted the invitation of Mrs. Reynolds to share her quarters while their husbands were in the field.[48] Samuel H. Huntington, father of 2d Lt. Robert W. Huntington, spent the entire day in church, praying for the safety of his son. Each time the noise from the southwest grew louder, Huntington's prayers became more fervent.[49]

As the fight progressed, the numerical strength of the Federals began to tip the battle in their favor. Griffin's Battery moved forward about 200 yards to enfilade the rebel line. Capt. James B. Ricketts' Battery came forward and unlimbered near Griffin.[50] The deadly chorus of rifled cannon shots caused the Confederate line to waver. In desperation, the rebels launched an attack on the Union center, but were beaten back with heavy losses. Sykes' U.S. Infantry Battalion, detached to bolster Burnside's worn-out troops, delivered a sharp attack that forced a crack in the Confederate right. Troops from Heintzelman's Division entered the battle on the left of the Union line and pressed the Confederates back toward Buck Hill. After a stubborn defense of nearly two hours' duration, the rebels fled the field, stampeding across the Warrenton Turnpike and beyond the hill atop which stood the house of the Widow Henry. Confederate guns under the command of Capt. John Imboden kept up a strong fire, covering the retreat.[51] Soon, however, Imboden's guns were silenced by accurate counter battery fire, and also compelled to withdraw.[52] Burnside's Brigade took Buck Hill and Porter's troops swept forward to the stone house at the crossroads. A last ditch charge by the 4th Alabama to blunt the Union advance was blasted apart by the batteries of Griffin and Ricketts. The day seemed to be won and McDowell, caught up in the excitement of seeing the Confederates being driven from the field of battle, declared it so.

The Marine Battalion emerged from the fight north of the Warrenton Turnpike in reasonably good shape. The battalion had suffered very few casualties by comparison to the regiments of Burnside's Brigade. Three Marines were reported killed by cannon fire when the battalion first debouched from the woods behind Griffin's Battery.[53] Lt. Joseph Baker was close by one of them when a shell struck the man, tearing off his leg. The burst of the round knocked Baker backwards, covering his uniform with dirt and blood, fortunately for him, none of his own.[54] But there was little time to think of those who went down. Battalion officers, screaming at the top of their voices to be heard over the din of the battle, urged the men to keep up with the guns.

2d Lt. Robert W. Huntington, USMC
NHC Photograph NH 46969

Griffin's Battery raced forward, taking up a position some one thousand yards from the woods. The Marine Battalion lunged after the battery at the double time, followed by the rest of the brigade. Assuming their stations behind the battery, the Marines prepared for battle, casting off their blanket rolls and loading their muskets. Porter took notice of how well they performed on the field in spite of their inexperience. His after action report mentioned that although they were recruits, "through the constant exertions of their officers [they] had been brought to a fine military appearance."[55]

As the Marines formed in the rear of Griffin's guns, the battle north of the turnpike was reaching a crescendo. The sharp crack of the guns, the smoke, the screaming of the wounded, the explosion of bursting shells, and the rest of the battlefield noise made the hearts of veteran Marines beat faster and heavier. Captain Jones, commanding Company B, determined that this was as good a place as any to test the mettle of his solitary subaltern, 2d Lt. Robert W. Huntington. As the brigade began to attract the attention of the rebel gunners across the turnpike, Jones ordered Huntington to dress the company. Huntington went to the front, gave the command and then walked down the front rank of Company B, bringing the Marines into proper line. As he returned to his designated position, Jones smiled with approval. He would not have to worry about Huntington doing his duty.[56]

Just before 2:00 P.M., Maj. William F. Barry, McDowell's Chief of Artillery, directed the batteries of Captains Griffin and Ricketts to maintain the pressure on the retreating enemy by limbering up and advancing to the crest of the hill across the turnpike, some one thousand yards distant.[57] Griffin remonstrated against his guns going forward without infantry support. Barry assured him that the 11th New York ("The Fire Zouaves") would be ordered to support the guns. Griffin, dubious as to the soundness of the order, moved his guns forward with not a little apprehension. After advancing some distance, Griffin halted his battery and looked for the Fire Zouaves. It would be impossible to miss them with their gaudy uniforms, but the artillery captain did not see them. Taking his guns several yards further, Griffin again halted and searched in vain for his infantry support. This time he went back to Barry and demanded to know where the Zouaves were. Barry told him they were just then ready to advance. Not to worry, they would follow him to his new position at the double-quick. Griffin was skeptical. If they were ready now, why didn't they go up the hill first and take a defensive position until the two batteries had gained the hill, unlimbered, and prepared to fire. Then they could fall back to the rear of the guns. Further, Griffin added, as a position to shell the rebels, the hill across the turnpike was not so suitable as the one behind the stone house at the crossroads.

Barry was beginning to grow impatient with Griffin's reluctance to do as he was ordered. The Chief of Artillery stated the orders came from McDowell. The guns were to advance to the hill across the turnpike. The infantry support would follow, not lead, the guns to the hill. Griffin was neither cowed, pacified, nor impressed. He told Barry that the green troops he proposed to send with him would not support him. Barry again gave him assurances that the Zouaves would do their duty. At any rate, the point was moot, McDowell wanted the guns on the top of that hill and that is where they would go. Griffin wheeled his horse and left Barry with a parting and prophetic comment, "I will go. But mark my words, they will not support us."[58]

As Griffin rode to his waiting battery, he passed Lieutenant Averell, the brigade assistant adjutant general. In tones that strongly suggested the AAG should do something about it, Griffin told him that his battery was under orders to advance to the crest of the hill across the turnpike, but had no infantry support. Averell quickly scanned the area. The 14th Brooklyn was regrouping after taking a volley from the retreating rebels. The 8th New York Militia, having been stung by the same volley that disorganized the 14th, was broken up and beyond repair. Several regiments from Heintzelman's Division were available; the 5th and 11th Massachusetts, the 1st Minnesota, and the 38th and 69th New York. The Marine Battalion, the designated infantry support to Griffin's Battery, was collecting stragglers and would soon be ready to resume its assigned duty.[59] Averell discussed sending five or six regiments as Griffin's infantry support with several other officers who agreed to form the troops and send them up the hill. Griffin was quickly made aware that additional troops were on their way.[60]

Griffin's and Ricketts' Batteries moved forward, crossed the intersection of the turnpike and the Sudley-Newmarket Road, and began to ascend the hill that had previously been referred to as a nameless eminence across the turnpike. At the crest of the one-hundred-foot rise was the house owned by Judith Henry, an elderly widow who became a casualty of the battle. To the nearby residents, the height was commonly referred to as Henry Hill, a local custom, changing the name with each subsequent owner. That afternoon's bloody work would make the appellation permanent.

In the wake of Griffin's guns came the Zouaves and the Marines at double time. The battalion trotted across the turnpike, jumped down from the northern embankment of Young's Branch, splashed across the stream and clambered up the other side. The crest of Henry Hill was about 300 yards away, all uphill. Fortunately, the ground was open pasture. Unfortunately, their wet brogans and trousers did not lend themselves to marching at double time. The guns were unlimbered and firing by the time their infantry support reached them. Griffin had detached two of his guns and sent them under the command of 1st Lt. Henry Hasbrouck to a point beyond Ricketts' Battery on the far right of the line. The 11th New York took position to the rear of these guns, while the Marines moved to the left and up between Hasbrouck and Ricketts. Much fatigued from the run up the hill, the Marines had been ordered to close up and sit on the ground.[61]

2d Lt. Robert E. Hitchcock
Norwich University, 1819-1911, Her History, Her Graduates, Her Roll of Honor

2d Lt. Joseph F. Baker
Author's Collection

A few of the Marine officers went forward to the crest of the hill to observe the artillery duel. The Confederate artillery had been employing ricochet fire very effectively. In fact, this tactic had driven the 14th Brooklyn from their first position on the hill, forcing them back to the turnpike. Lieutenant Hitchcock was heard to remark, "The cannon balls are flying pretty thick."[62] Lieutenant Baker, a few paces ahead of his comrades, heard the report of a rebel cannon and saw the ricochet of the ball. He threw himself flat on the ground as the ball passed right above him.[63] Hitchcock's cheery comment regarding the artillery duel was his last. The shot that skipped over Baker struck Hitchcock squarely in the face, tearing off his head. As he collapsed, one of his Marines instinctively reached out to grab him. As he did, a second shell tore off the Samaritan's arm and severed Hitchcock's lifeless form. The two bodies fell in a bloody heap to the ground.

As the Marines looked with horror upon the grisly scene, a loud and heated exchange was taking place between two artillery officers a few yards away. Griffin had spotted a line of troops coming out of the woods to his front. As they formed their ranks, he was sure they were rebels and ordered Hasbrouck load canister and fire on them. Barry rode up and yelled, "Captain, don't fire there; those are your battery support!" Griffin yelled back, "They are Confederates; as certain as the world, they are Confederates!" Barry insisted, vociferously, "I know they are your battery support!"[64] Griffin grudgingly obeyed Barry's order to desist and pointed the guns away from the oncoming regiment. Moments later, the 33rd Virginia Infantry, only seventy yards away from the battery, lowered their muskets, took aim, and fired a withering volley. In a matter of seconds, the course of the battle was changed. The Federal troops, to this point, had the battlefield advantage. Barry's costly error in judgment ultimately tilted the scales in favor of the Confederates.

Horses and men went down as hay before a newly whetted scythe. Griffin raced to the Fire Zouaves, appealing to them to save the guns. The New Yorkers were not able to respond. Moments before, the 1st Virginia Cavalry, led by Col. James E. B. Stuart, had struck them on their flank. Although Stuart's troopers did relatively little damage before they retired, the attack left the Zouaves on the verge of panic. When Griffin again called to them from the wreckage of his guns, they stood wide-eyed at the devastation around him. They did not move. But the Virginia infantrymen advanced. Closer and closer they came, volley firing. It was more than the Zouaves could stand. They broke and ran. A few brave men fired at the rebels and were willing to stand and fight, but they were carried away in the stampede down the hill.

The Marines, already unsettled by Hitchcock's death, were plunged deeper into confusion by the carnage wreaked upon Hasbrouck's artillerists. Several raised their muskets to answer the Virginians, but most began to edge back down the slope of Henry Hill. The 33rd Virginia fired in their direction and the battalion began to take casualties. Pvt. Frank Harris, a young Irishman from Pittsburgh, staggered from the ranks and was dead before he hit the ground, his rifle unfired. Pvt. William Barrett, next to Harris in the front rank of Marines, reported his own brush with death: "We faced them on the left of the battery, and when about fifty yards from it, our men fell like hailstones." Barrett fired three rounds at the advancing rebels before he was put out of action. "I think they intended to fix me when they hit the lock of my musket . . .which put me back about three feet. As soon as I came to my ground again two men were shot down on my right and one on my left. . . . You could hear the balls playing 'Yankee Doodle' around your ears, but could not move."[65] Although Barrett was paralyzed by fear, others, not so afflicted, began to slip out of the line of fire. Officers dashed to the rear of the battalion and shouted commands to stay in ranks and waved their swords to encourage or threaten the faint-hearted. It was no use, the panicked flight of the Zouaves from the right of the line burst upon the Marines and was a catalyst no threat could deter. After delivering a sporadic fire, the Marines were swept away

Advance of the 33rd Virginia Infantry on the Federal artillery on Henry Hill

NA Photograph 127-N-527054

by the stampede. Lieutenant Baker, while trying to halt the backward surge, was struck in the mouth by an errant bayonet and knocked unconscious.[66] The race to safety did not abate until the troops reached the crossroads.

Capt. Charles Griffin, commander of Battery B, 5th U.S. Artillery
Civil War Library

The 14th Brooklyn, somewhat tardy in marching to the support of the artillery on Henry Hill, was only partway up the slope when the torrent of fleeing Zouaves, artillery men, and Marines broke upon them. The Brooklyn boys remained steady in their ranks and pushed on. Coming to within forty yards of the rebels, the 14th delivered a volley which momentarily staggered the Confederates who quickly recovered and returned fire.[67] Confederate artillery also began firing on the 14th and, caught in a crossfire, it too, had to fall back to the crossroads.

As the 14th was exchanging fire with the rebels at the crest of Henry Hill, the mighty efforts of the Marine officers stemmed the flight of the battalion and rallied it at the crossroads. Nearby, Griffin came upon Barry. With undisguised sarcasm, Griffin asked, "Major, do you think the Zouaves will support us?" Barry, the consequences of his actions weighing heavily upon him, could only say, "I was mistaken." Griffin snapped back, "Do you think *that* was our support?" All Barry could say was, "I was mistaken." And with bitter contempt punctuating every word, Griffin spat, "Yes, you were mistaken all around."[68]

After being driven from the hill, the 14th Brooklyn rallied with the Marines near the crossroads. By that time, the battalion had regained composure enough to join the 14th and try to recover the captured artillery. The Brooklyn regiment took the lead, followed by the Marine Battalion and other regiments. Gaining the crest of the hill near the wreckage of Ricketts' Battery, they took the enemy under enfilade fire, driving them back across the plateau and into the pine woods beyond. The Union line quickly advanced to within fifty yards of the position held by the Virginia brigade commanded by Brig. Gen. Thomas J. Jackson. As the swell of the attack neared a thicket of pines, the muskets of the 4th and 27th Virginia Infantry Regiments belched forth a deadly greeting. An instant before the Virginians fired, the 14th dropped to the ground and the Marines took the full effect of the volley.[69] Their line wavered for a moment, but the Marines quickly recovered and pressed forward with the Brooklyn troops, now on their feet, and plunged into the pines. The fire intensified and the Union troops began to falter. Single men, then squads, and soon whole sections of the attacking line turned and fled. Despite the efforts of their officers to steady them, the Marines were unable to hold their ground. Whatever discipline remained from Reynolds' drills along the march to the battle lost a contest with the instinct for self-preservation, and the battalion broke for the rear. Reynolds was quickly in their midst, raining expletives on all within earshot; "language more forcible than pious," recalled the Brooklyn men, but his efforts to hold the Marines went in vain.[70] For the second time, they lost all sense of order and ran down the hill to safety, intermingling with the Brooklyn boys and the broken remnants of the second assault force.

As the Confederates took up the pursuit, Surgeon Daniel M. Conrad of the 2d Virginia Infantry surveyed the bloody aftermath of the fight. "The green pines were filled with the 79th Highlanders and the red-breeched Brooklyn Zouaves, but the only men that were

Charge to retake the guns on Henry Hill

The Marine Battalion followed behind the 14th Brooklyn Chasseurs, but were unable to hold Henry Hill for the second time.

Battles and Leaders

killed and wounded twenty or thirty yards behind and in the rear of our lines were the United States Marines."[71]

The Virginia Regiments of Jackson's Brigade swept forward, driving the Federals before them. As they approached the northern end of Henry Hill, Ricketts' Battery opened fire. Still they came on, firing as they advanced. Captain Ricketts fell to the ground, desperately wounded. His first officer, 1st Lt. Douglas Ramsay, who had a reputation for being the pinnacle of sartorial splendor in the battery, had gone into battle dressed in the finest linen and silk stockings, with his mustache waxed to sharp points. Ramsay presented a fine target, but the volleys left him unscathed. As the rebels surged forward, Ramsay ducked behind a limber. He nimbly evaded the attempt of one Virginian to capture him, but as he tried to run away another raised his musket and fired. Ramsay fell dead not far from his gun .[72] Among the officers of the Marine Battalion desperately trying to arrest the flight from Henry Hill was his brother, 1st Lt. Alan Ramsay.

1st Lt. A. Douglas Ramsay, USA
MOLLUS Collection, USAMHI

The second repulse was more than some Marines could stand and they continued their flight beyond the crossroads. The majority of the battalion, however, rallied at the crossroads and pushed up the Sudley-Newmarket Road, where it took cover behind the Henry Hill side of the embankment. Several regiments from the 1st and 3rd Divisions, intermingled in the confusion, were using the embankment for cover, preparatory to a third attempt against Henry Hill.[73] The Marine Battalion and the 14th Brooklyn joined in the advance. It had scarcely begun when reinforcements, the 2d and 8th South Carolina of Brig. Gen. Milledge L. Bonham's Brigade, arrived on the Confederate left, and opened fire on the Federal flank. This was more than the Northern troops could bear. They crowded back to the protection of the roadbed and ran down the road. Most of the Marines rallied with a scattering of troops from several disorganized regiments in the pasture on the southwest corner of the crossroads, but the fire was gone out of them. Fear was rising in its place.

During the retreat to the crossroads, Lieutenant Huntington found a discarded musket on the ground and, seeing that it was loaded, vented his frustration by firing at a mounted rebel officer in the distance. He was satisfied to see his target fall. Moments later, a wounded Marine approached him holding his musket in one hand and showing the mangled and missing fingers from a rebel shot on the other. He asked Huntington to load his musket so that he could get off one more shot.[74] Others followed those who had seen enough, ran through the crossroads, past Buck Hill, and joined the growing column of demoralized troops headed up the Sudley-Newmarket Road.

To the right and forward of the area where the Marines and the other regiments were trying to regroup, Col. Oliver O. Howard's Brigade was trying to get around the left flank of the Confederate line.[75] His first line advanced straight into rebel musketry atop Chinn Ridge. To their left, elements of the 1st Brigade, 1st Division, 1st and 2d Brigades, Third Division, were still struggling for possession of the guns on Henry Hill. Confederate reinforcements reached both areas of the battlefield at approximately the same time. Col. Arnold Elzey, having succeeded the wounded Brig. Gen. Edmund Kirby Smith in command of the 4th Brigade, Army of the Shenandoah, smashed into the right flank of Howard's Brigade.[76] It folded up and the Federals fled toward the crossroads where the Marine Battalion and other forces were trying to reorganize. When these troops saw Howard's men coming at them on the fly, they turned for the road. Some Marines paid no attention to their officers who tried to hold them in position. They bolted toward the crossroads in a race with the rest of the fleeing troops, the safety beyond Sudley Ford paramount in their minds. Beauregard, seeing the collapse of the Union

Sunken bed of the Sudley-Newmarket Road looking north toward the Stone House

Federal troops, including Marines, launched their third and final assault on Henry Hill from the cover of the high embankments, and sought refuge here when the charge was broken.

Massachusetts Commandery, MOLLUS Collection, USAMHI

right, ordered a general advance. Brigades of the Army of the Potomac joined with the Brigades from the Army of the Shenandoah, and advanced across the plateau of Henry Hill, sweeping down the northern slope and driving everything before them.

As the Marines withdrew down Henry Hill for the last time, Lieutenants Huntington and Grimes asked permission to go back and try to retrieve Hitchcock's body. Permission was denied. Overcome with grief and emotion at the thought of leaving their friend's body behind, the two young officers burst into tears.[77] Captain Jones was especially grieved since he could not redeem his promise to Hitchcock to deliver his body to his parents.[78]

Baker recovered consciousness around the time of the third retreat from Henry Hill. He was so weak that he had all he could do to run down the slope of Henry Hill. Two enlisted Marines saw his condition and gave him support, one on each side. Fortuitously, as the three Marines made their way up Buck Hill, Baker caught a glimpse of his older brother John, an officer of the First Dragoons, riding his mount some distance away. The younger brother hailed the elder, and was taken aboard the horse to safety.[79]

The Sudley-Newmarket Road was the main avenue of retreat for the beaten Union forces. Some ran, but most were too played out to do more than keep one leg moving in front of the other. Pvt. William Barrett reported that 200 of the Marine Battalion were called upon to form a rear guard for a short time before being relieved by the 71st New York State Militia.[80] Then the Marines joined the retreating mass of Federal troops. Brevet Major Zeilen had been wounded in the arm during one of the advances on Henry Hill. He walked sluggishly along the road to the ford. Loss of blood and fatigue finally took their toll and Zeilen had to rest. A log at the side of the road offered a crude but welcome haven. Pvt. Daniel Quinn found Zeilen there. He took the officer by the arm and helped him along the road until a wagon took Zeilen aboard.[81]

Reynolds would not be hurried. Averell saw him walking to the rear with his sword in hand. As he passed a tall weed, he lashed at it with his sword, cursing at the same time. Averell felt sure it was the Major's way of dealing with the humiliation he felt at the way his men had behaved.[82]

Some Union troops retreated in good order down the Warrenton Turnpike, but got caught up at the bottleneck before the bridge over Cub Run. Confederate artillery fire found the range of the bridge and quickly turned it into a scrap heap of damaged vehicles. At this point, the retreat turned into a panic-stricken rout. Men fled in all directions looking frantically for a place to cross Cub Run. Wild reports of approaching cavalry fanned the flames of the panic. Discipline and order vanished as men pushed, shoved, swung fists and feet in an attempt to get to the safety of the eastern bank of

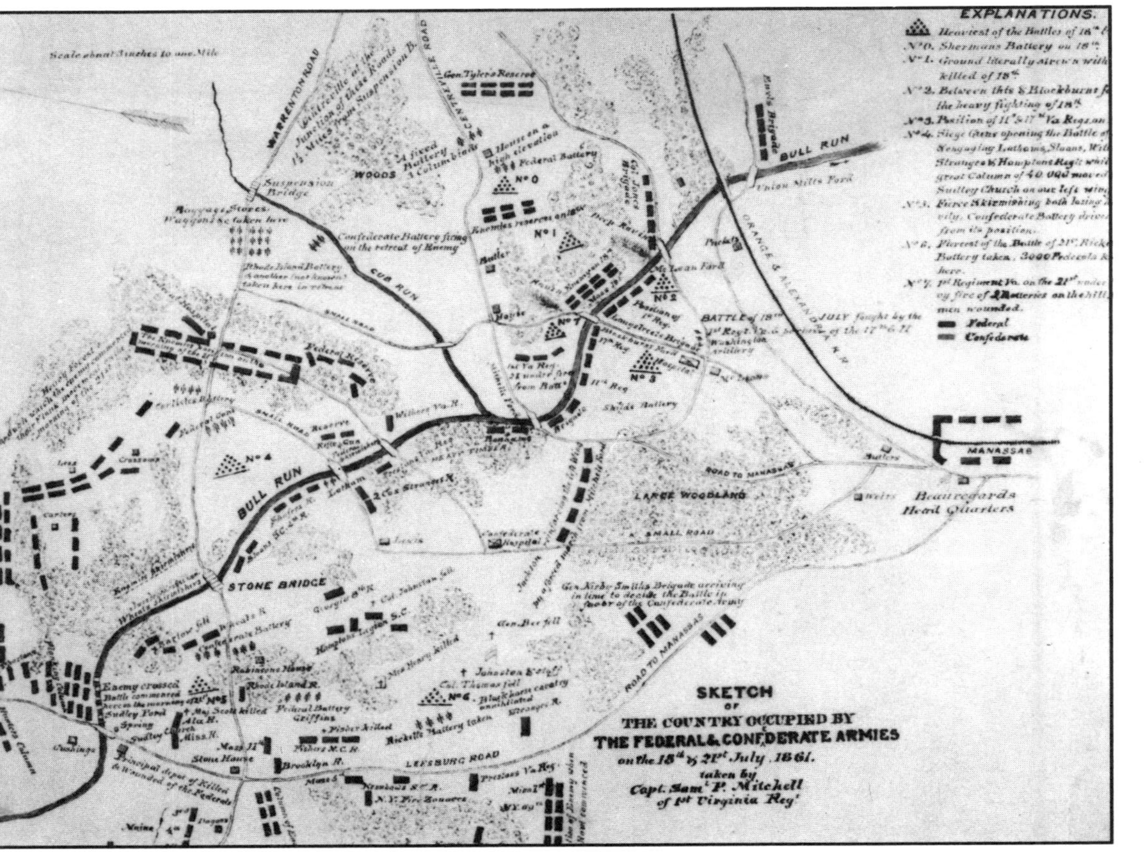

Map of the Bull Run Battlefield

Medford Historical Society

Cub Run. In the distance, beckoning the demoralized troops was the haven of Washington. All would be well again once they reached the familiar scenes of their camps around the capital. And so they pushed their way across Cub Run, thinking only of their own advantage and safety.

The Marines were no different than other troops vying for position on this escape route. Many suppressed their basic human instinct to help the afflicted and marched on, averting their eyes from the wounded. Marine Pvt. William Barrett described the retreat in a letter to a Pittsburgh friend:

> At the time of the retreat, we ran over the dead and wounded for a mile from the battery and to hear the wounded crying for help would have made the heart of stone ache. All along the road we had men, only wounded a little, who, when the long march came, had to give out and lie down and die. For ten miles this side of the field they could be seen lying here and there on the roadside.[83]

A pursuit up the Sudley Road was ordered by Beauregard, but Confederate troops became so bogged down gathering up exhausted prisoners of war that any thought of cutting off the retreating Federals had to be abandoned.

The Marines lost all semblance of organization during the retreat to, over and beyond the Sudley Ford. The entire column became nothing more than a mob, scrambling for safety. At some point along the march, Huntington became separated from his company. Totally fatigued and emotionally spent, two enlisted Marines had to help him along the roadway. Edwin S. Barrett, a civilian who accompanied the 5th Massachusetts to the battlefield, chanced upon the trio. The enlisted Marines asked his favor of giving their lieutenant a lift on his horse. Barrett readily assented and helped the exhausted officer up to the back of his saddle.

After a while, Huntington recovered somewhat, and began to speak about the battle. He told Barrett something of his personal history and about the death of Hitchcock, over which he was particularly anguished. They went on until they reached a road leading to Centerville, where they met Captain Jones, Huntington's company commander, and some other officers from the battalion. Huntington got down from the horse, and, with tears in his eyes, he took Barrett's hand and gave him his eternal gratitude.[84]

Above Centerville, the column of fugitives from the Sudley Ford met troops coming up from the blocked Warrenton Turnpike making their way across Cub Run about a thousand yards above the jammed suspension bridge over the turnpike. It was a case of every man for himself. The water at the crossing was deep, in some places over the heads of the shorter men. Non-swimmers would ordinarily have been in distress but fear is a great source of motivation. As Private Barrett wrote, "If you had seen us swimming across . . . you would have thought there was something after us then."[85]

The weary column pressed on to Washington over the roads it had so jauntily trod during the advance just a few days previously. Reynolds, having hitched a ride on a supply wagon, had hot coffee prepared and given to all the Marines that passed him. He saw very few. The procession of weary, demoralized troops wound its way through a miserable, rainy night toward Washington. When Reynolds arrived at the Long Bridge around daybreak of July 22, he saw a very large contingent of soldiers being held from crossing over the Potomac to Washington by a Provost Guard. Among them were about seventy grimy and exhausted Marines. Pride in his Corps and compassion for his men would not allow the Major to let them stand abjectly in their wet clothes, waiting to be sorted out. Reynolds' fervent appeals persuaded the Provost commander to allow the Marines to cross the river and return to Marine Barracks, Washington.[86]

The wildest sort of rumors concerning the Marine Battalion swept through Washington. It was reported that all of the officers but two had been killed. Samuel H. Huntington's colleagues at the Court of Claims, believing the rumors to be true, called to console their friend over the loss of his son. Huntington was so disturbed by the reports from Manassas that he could not sleep Sunday night and went to the Barracks early Monday morning to learn the truth. He arrived shortly after Reynolds brought his men in. When he was finally admitted to the Barracks, he found his son resting on his bed. Fatherly emotion at seeing his son safe and sound was "too overpowering to be described."[87]

Reynolds presented his after action report to Harris on July 24. It was a succinct account of the disaster, and Reynolds, in contrast to other field commanders, leveled no blame on other troops for the conduct of his men. He correctly stated they were too inexperienced for the sort of duty they were called upon to perform. It was true that they failed to hold their position on Henry Hill on three occasions on the afternoon of July 21, but they were game enough to get back into the fray after each repulse, save for the last when the entire right of the line gave way in precipitate flight. Despite their inexperience, Reynolds pointed out, the Marine Battalion received high praise from Colonel Porter in his official report of the battle. In Harris' cover letter to the Navy Department, the Commandant, with extreme mortification, wrote of the calamity to the Marine Corps as "the first instance in history where any portion of its members turned their backs to the enemy."[88] He further asked that the Marines be released from service with the Army and restored to their more legitimate duties. The request was made and granted on July 24.[89]

Over the course of the next few days, Marines of the battalion straggled in from the battlefield and reported to Marine Barracks, Washington. Letters were written home to calm the fears of loved ones whose apprehensions had been raised by the alarming accounts in the newspapers. Lieutenant Cartter, who wrote so glowingly of his prospects the day before the battle, albeit with teasingly atrocious spelling, now struck a different pose.

Washington
July 25, 1861

Dear Mother,

I returned from Bull Run on the 22nd and was so tired that I could not write before this. There is no use of my telling you about the fight for you have seen an account of it by this time. You received my letter from Spring Hill Farm. That was our last encamping place. We lost one Officer Lieut. Hitchcock and two wounded, and 30 men and got licked awfully. We have got to do better than we did at Bull Run or we will be defeated at all times. . . .

Your Loving Son
W. H. Cartter[90]

In due time, a tally of killed, wounded, and missing was made. The quiet, hardworking, and methodical Robert E. Hitchcock, who had a pre-sentiment of death before he left the barracks on July 16, was killed in action. Pvt. John E. Reily, the young Irishman who thought being a Marine was the best work he ever had in his life, was killed in action. Pvt. John Stanley, another young man from Ireland with the scars of a youthful bout with small pox on his face, was killed in action.[91] Pvt. John T. Hughes, a member of the Masonic Order, was killed in action. Also reported killed in action were: Pvts. Samuel Clegg, a nineteen-year-old machinist from Philadelphia who enlisted with his father's consent; Francis Harris, a Pittsburgh coachman; John Lane (erroneously—in fact, a prisoner of war); Martin Ward, a tall Irishman from Pittsburgh; Isaac Moore, another Irish immigrant; and Benjamin F. Perkins (erroneously—found to be a prisoner of war). Perkins' mother inquired of her son's fate a few days after the battle and received the following letter from the Commandant.

Head Quarters, Marine Corps
Washington
July 29, 1861

My dear madam;

I have just received your note inquiring for Benjamin F. Perkins and regret to reply that he was killed in the Battle of Bull's Run on Sunday, the 21st, Inst.

While I sympathize in your bereavement, it is a consolation to say he died gallantly fighting for his Country and I trust is now in a better world.

Very truly yours
Jno Harris
Col., Comdt.

To Mrs. Sarah Perkins
c/o Thomas Marshall, Esq.
Sycamore Street
South Camden, New Jersey [92]

A few days later, Mrs. Perkins received the joyous news that her son, previously reported killed in battle was, in actuality, a prisoner of war. He had been wounded during the battle and had fallen into the hands of the rebels. Private Perkins was being held at Richmond.[93]

To another worried relative, Harris wrote,

Miss Mary Barrett:

I have just rec'd. your letter asking for your brother, John Barrett, who was in the Battle of Bull's Run, on Sunday, the 21st, Inst., and, I regret to say he is one of the fourteen missing. He may be a prisoner, and, in that event, he will get back to his friends. But, in the other event, we have the consolation of knowing he was engaged in his country's cause.[94]

Pvt. George Lewis, a blacksmith who enlisted at Philadelphia on June 17, was initially reported missing. His status was subsequently changed to "supposedly dead" when reports of prisoners taken during the battle failed to list his name.

The list of wounded was headed by Bvt. Maj. Jacob Zeilen, who suffered a gunshot wound to the fleshy part of his left arm. He was back on duty on July 23, 1861. Also back on duty without missing any time were 2d Lts. John H. Grimes, who suffered a minor wound, and William H. Hale, whose leg wound was reported as serious. The wounded enlisted men were: Pvts. Joshua Etchells, gunshot wound to the right hand, crushing the ring and middle fingers; Edward H. Howell, canister wound crushing the left hand; John McGuigan, wounded in the left shoulder while advancing up Henry Hill, and George Bowers, who contracted typhoid fever while hospitalized and died on August 16, 1861. Others reported wounded were: Pvts. Allen W. Dodge, Daniel Figer, William Lang, John McKenna, Henry McCann, Michael Wheelan, John Rannahan, Thomas Potter, and John A. Cook (in actuality, a prisoner of war).[95]

Reported missing and presumed in the hands of the enemy were: Pvts. Henry Clark, a Canadian who came to the United States seeking employment and finding none, enlisted in the Marine Corps; Abel J. Wood, who had family in Massachusetts and New Jersey concerned as to his fate; Henry Beans, whose family did not know if he had been killed at Bull Run or taken prisoner, and anguished for months hoping for the latter; John Barrett, who was taken prisoner when the rebels discovered him hiding in a water-filled ditch after the last repulse of the Federal troops from Henry Hill; William Stewart, who had spent five years on the Plains with the Army before enlisting as a Marine; Michael Cannon, whose mother suffered so severe a shock, believing that her son had been killed at Bull Run, that she collapsed and was confined to her bed until he was repatriated in June of 1862; and Robert Duncanson, who was severely wounded in the leg by a shell fragment while advancing up Henry Hill with the battalion and left behind during the retreat.[96] Others reported missing were: Pvt. Frederick Otto, left behind on the battlefield with a gunshot wound to the right leg; Cpl. Garrett Steiner, gunshot wound to the right shin and left on the battlefield; Pvts. Jacob Kressler, Edward Foley, William Bradford, John Slemmons, Hugh McCoy, George Hunt, and John Lane.

Erroneously reported missing were Pvts. Edward McCristal, Jesse Dermott, and John Dempsey.[97] McCristal and Dermott straggled back to the Barracks after July 23, while Dempsey was among nine Marines posted as deserters on July 27, 1861.[98]

Some of the Bull Run prisoners of war were treated kindly following the battle. Pvt. William Stewart was taken to the General Hospital at Charlottesville where his wounded leg was treated on the evening of July 21, 1861. Pvt. Henry Clark wrote his sister from Richmond that, "We are well-treated here. We get the same rations as their own soldiers."[99] Others endured a different introduction to life as a prisoner of war. Cpl. Garrett Steiner lay on the battlefield for two days with his wounded leg before he was sent to Richmond on a livestock car.[100]

Pvt. Jacob Kressler, Bull Run prisoner of war
Courtesy of John de Leeuw and William D. Langlois

With the exception of those too badly wounded to be mobile, all those captured at Bull Run were sent to Liggon & Company's Tobacco Factory at the corner of Main and 25th Streets in Richmond, Virginia.[101] The noncommissioned officers and enlisted men were crowded into the second and top floors of the three-story, 30' x 70' building. The prison was also known as "Rocketts, No. 1," named for Richmond's waterfront slum district on the James River. Between September 1861 and February 1862, most of the prisoners of war were transferred away from Richmond to prisons at New Orleans, Louisiana; Tuscaloosa, Alabama; and Salisbury, North Carolina.[102] Those who were still incapacitated by their battlefield wounds were paroled and sent by flag of truce boat to the James River for release.[103]

Pvts. George Hunt, Hugh McCoy, John Lane, Michael Cannon, Henry Clark, Edward Foley, John Cook, Jacob Kressler, and John Slemons were sent to the Old Parish Prison at New Orleans, a disease-ridden, rat-infested, hellhole of filth. The wretched diet made scurvy a common bond of the prisoners. Tuberculosis and other diseases flourished in the close confinement and filthy conditions.[104] After many weeks of abominable confinement at Old Parish, they were rescued from the dungeon-like prison by the proximity of a Federal fleet under Capt. David G. Farragut, USN.[105] Fearing a sudden move against the Crescent City, Confederate authorities removed the prisoners on February 6, 1862, and sent them to Salisbury, North Carolina.[106]

The prison at Salisbury was an old cotton factory, a veritable palace by comparison to the black hole of New Orleans. Here they were joined by Cpl. Garrett Steiner and Pvt. William Bradford, who had been confined at Tuscaloosa since leaving Richmond. All the prisoners were finally paroled at the end of May or early part of June 1862, and sent through the lines to General Burnside's forces at New Bern, North Carolina.[107] From there they were sent by ship to the Brooklyn Navy Yard, where they reported to Maj. Addison Garland, commanding Marine Barracks, Brooklyn, between June 2–13, 1862.[108]

Garland was appalled at the condition the men were in. Their clothing could scarcely be dignified by the term. Their physical condition was deplorable. However, new uniforms would make them presentable and a return to the drill field would give them hearty appetites to recover the lost weight. Since they were restricted from taking up active service by the conditions of their paroles, Garland was instructed to keep them on duty within the confines of the barracks.[109]

There were Confederate prisoners of war taken at the battle as well. These unlucky troops were brought back to Washington with the defeated army, and kept at the headquarters of Brig. Gen. Joseph K. F. Mansfield, USA, commander of the Washington District. Later, the prisoners of war were marched to confinement at the Old Capitol Prison on First Street. One group was escorted by a detachment of Marines. As the column reached the Treasury Building, a crowd of soldiers and civilians taunted the rebels, cursed, and threw mud at them as they passed. Some were not satisfied with these simple insults and began clamoring for sterner action. Tales of atrocities committed upon the Federal dead and wounded by the victorious Confederates after the battle ended quickly spread through the gathering. Soon, the crowd was screaming for their blood, and pressed forward, shouting, "Kill them! Kill them!" The Marines quickly formed a protective ring around their charges, and lowered their bayoneted rifles. The situation nearly got out of hand, but the hard work of the Marines defeated the crowd, and the prisoners were safely moved out of danger.[110]

Some bright spots were found in the gloom of the Bull Run defeat. Several Marines had distinguished themselves on the battlefield and were promoted in recognition of their courage. Cpl. Smith Maxwell, who had been temporarily elevated to the post of quartermaster sergeant when the battalion was formed, advanced to the rank of sergeant on July 23. Pvts. John Henry Denig and Richard C. Oates were promoted to the rank of corporal on July 24.

Denig, a printer working at Indianapolis, Indiana, when the war broke out, was recommended for a commission by several prominent Indianapolis citizens in May 1861, but was disappointed in his objective when he learned there were no vacancies. He then enlisted as a private, determined to earn his commission through the ranks.[111] His promotion to the rank of corporal for battlefield service was the first step toward his goal. Denig would be heard from again.

Two other Marines who survived the battle, Pvts. Richard Binder and John Rannahan, would also leave their mark in Marine Corps history.

Canton of the National colors carried into battle at Bull Run
Marine Corps Museum. Photograph by Kate Stark

Pvt. Richard Binder
MCHC Collection

Equipment of every nature was left behind on the battlefield by the Marines during the retreat; muskets, haversacks, bayonet belts, cartridge box belts—anything that impeded flight—were cast away. Needless to say, the blankets that were removed from their shoulders and piled on the ground, as they formed behind Griffin's Battery on the morning of July 21, were not retrieved.[112] One all important item was brought safely away from the battlefield as an unknown member of the color party made sure the battle-scarred flag did not fall into the hands of the enemy.[113]

In the days following the debacle at Bull Run, the Commandant received letters from shipboard Marines who had heard that the Corps would be represented in the expedition to Virginia. They wanted a part of the action. 1st Lt. Charles G. McCawley belatedly wrote,

---

Private

U.S. S. "Macedonian"
Key West, Fla.
July 29, 1861

Dear Colonel;

I have seen by the newspapers that a battalion of Marines is serving with the Army, and I write to ask of you as a great favor to procure me orders to serve with it. As I have been so long under your command, I hardy think it is necessary to remind you of the qualifications which I hope I possess for this duty. As I am so near promotion, I venture to think that I might be there in a position to render more useful services at a time when our country must need those of every officer, and particularly those who have seen similar duty before. I cannot remain satisfied that so many of my comrades are so serving without advancing my claim upon your notice for a like favor. This ship will remain here at least two weeks more, it is thought, and as steamers are continually arriving from New York, I hope that there will be no difficulty in sending an officer to relieve me.

I have taken great pains to instruct the men under my command in their various duties and they are well instructed in Light Inf. Tactics and the drill for Skirmishers which they have practised on shore at Vera Cruz. A younger officer than myself will have no trouble in commanding them, and I most earnestly ask that you will not refuse me this opportunity of serving my country in a more useful manner than at present and in the position of a true soldier, in the field. I remain dear Colonel,

Very truly
Your Obdt. Svt.
G. McCawley

Col. John Harris
Comdt. U. S. M. C.
Washn.[114]

It must have pleased Harris to receive McCawley's request for active field service, even though it was penned and arrived long after the battalion had returned to Washington.

Another belated petition for field duty arrived from New York and likely buoyed the Colonel's sagging post-Bull Run spirits.

U. S. Steamer Richmond
New York, July 24th, 1861

Sir-

Understanding that a Marine Battalion has gone into the field, we earnestly and respectfully request that we may be allowed to join it. We are on board the Richmond, lately from the Mediterranean, are old soldiers, having been in the field before in the Mexican and Indian Wars and prefer active service. There are a number of recruits in the Barracks who would willingly take our place on board ship and do ship duty equally well. Hoping to receive a favorable answer, we remain

Very Respectfully,
James Stuart
Wm. Firth
Jas. Gurley
and others.
Privates, U. S. M.

Col. J. Harris
Commdg. Marines
Washington[115]

There were a number of privates at Marine Barracks, Washington, still shaken from their experiences at Bull Run who would have gladly let the "old soldiers" fill their brogans on the afternoon of July 21, 1861.

6

Reorganization: One Step Backward, Two Steps Forward

When Congress returned to Washington on July 4, 1861, Gideon Welles presented Colonel Harris' bill for the reorganization of the Corps (headed by a promotion for himself to the grade of brigadier general) to the Senate in his special report. It was introduced by Senator John P. Hale of New Hampshire a week later as S. 14.[1] After being read twice, it was referred to the Committee on Naval Affairs.[2] S. 14 was reported back from committee on July 16, and recommended for passage with several amendments. Due to the pressing need to act upon the naval appropriation bill, S. 14 was laid over until funding for the naval establishment was legislated.

While the Senate deliberated the appropriations for the Navy, Harris was buoyed by a letter he received from Joel Rathbone, an extremely wealthy Albany, New York, banker, political insider, and father of 1st Lt. J. Howard Rathbone, USMC. Rathbone told Harris that Congressman Charles B. Sedgewick, Chairman of the House Naval Affairs Committee, seemed favorably disposed to the idea that the Corps should be headed by a brigadier general. Senator Ira Harris told Rathbone that he would promote the matter in the Senate.[3] Rathbone promised to continue lobbying in both branches of Congress, and felt sure that Harris would see his bill made law.[4]

On July 24, Senator Hale moved to consider S. 14, and read the amendments proposed by the Committee on Naval Affairs. The first amendment, despite Rathbone's favorable inside information, struck down Harris' attempt to promote himself to brigadier general. In all, sixteen further amendments were proposed by the Naval Affairs Committee, virtually eviscerating the bill Harris submitted. One after another of his proposals were cut back or eliminated. Harris' proposal to elevate the ranks of his staff was entirely eliminated. Section 3, relative to the continuation of all previous acts concerning the Corps not inconsistent with the provisions of the new measure was stricken. An additional section to the bill was proposed by the Committee regarding the ages and qualifications of those appointed to be commissioned officers.[5]

> *And be it further enacted*, That the appointment of commissioned officers to be made under the provisions of this act shall be of persons between the ages of twenty and twenty-five years, who shall be subjected, under the direction of the Secretary of the Navy, to examination as to their qualifications for the service to which they are appointed.

This amendment was agreed to and the bill ordered to be engrossed, read the third time and passed.[6] The Senate version bore only slight resemblance to that which Harris submitted.

Bill as drawn by Colonel Harris relative to increasing the numbers of officers and enlisted men.	Final version of S. 14 in regard to increases in the numbers of officers and enlisted men.
One Brigadier General, Commandant	Two Colonels (amended by the House to One Colonel, Commandant, and One Colonel)
Two Colonels	
Two Lieutenant Colonels	Two Lieutenant Colonels
Four Majors	Four Majors
One Adjutant & Inspector	One Adjutant & Inspector
One Paymaster	One Paymaster
One Quartermaster	One Quartermaster
Two Assistant Quarter-masters	Two Assistant Quartermasters
Thirty Captains	Twenty Captains
Forty First Lieutenants	Thirty First Lieutenants
Thirty Second Lieutenants	Thirty Second Lieutenants
Two Sergeant Majors	One Sergeant Major
Two Quartermaster Sergeants	One Quartermaster Sergeant
Two Drum Majors	One Drum Major
Two Principal Musicians	One Principal Musician
240 Sergeants	200 Sergeants
270 Corporals	220 Corporals
50 Bandsmen	30 Bandsmen
90 Drummers	60 Drummers
90 Fifers	60 Fifers
3,000 Privates	2,500 Privates

The bill was then sent to the House of Representatives which took it up on July 19 as H. R. 53. The House offered two amendments to which the Senate concurred. The first was to stipulate that one of the two colonels allowed in S. 14 would be the Commandant of the Corps. The second clarified the position of officers of the Marine Corps vis-a-vis the provisions of the new act and the appointment process. It was substituted in place of the proposal set forth by Harris as Section 2.

> Sec. 2. *And be it further enacted*, That the commissions of the officers now in the Marine Corps shall not be vacated by the act, and that the President of the United States may, during the recess of the Senate, first by promotion and then by selection, appoint the officers hereby authorized, which appointments shall be submitted to the Senate at their next session for advice and consent.[7]

The Speaker of the House signed the bill on July 26, the President the next day, and the final version became "Chapter XIX, Thirty-Seventh Congress, Session 1—An Act for the better Organization of the Marine Corps."

The end result of the passage of the reorganization act froze the numbers of enlisted men at the number reached after the addition of the 932 privates authorized by President Lincoln in lieu of landsmen in the Navy. On the other end of the scale, it added thirty new positions to the hierarchy of the Marine Corps, which, once promotions were made to fill openings in the higher grades, translated into thirty vacancies for second lieutenants, a most desirable position in the military service of the United States.[8]

Because applicants for an appointment to the Marine Corps did not necessarily have to have any sort of military education or background, application was open to all who felt their credentials worthy of consideration. In theory, all that was required of an aspirant was a letter to the Secretary of the Navy expressing his desire and qualifications to enter the Corps, or one from a sponsor. If the letter registered favorably with the Secretary, the applicant would be invited to take the newly required examination before a board of Marine officers subsequent to a complete medical examination. The results of his oral presentation, written examination and general demeanor before the board would be forwarded to the Department. The Secretary of the Navy would then evaluate the reports, and make recommendations to the President for appointments. In reality, however, the process differed very little from past practice in which the sons of the politically influential gained the advantage.

Even before Congress convened in President Lincoln's special session, word of Harris' proposal to increase the Corps, and particularly the number of officers, had gained wide circulation. Letters of application and recommendation began to pour into the Navy Department. Some were addressed to the Commandant of the Marine Corps, thinking the support of Harris would weigh heavily in favor of the writer.

U. S. Flag Ship Minnesota
Hampton Roads
23d June, 1861.

Colonel
John Harris
Sir.

I have applied to my uncle Gideon Welles, Sec. of the Navy for a Lieutenancy in the Marine Corps and have since been informed that you were the proper person to apply to for that appointment. I wish very much to enter the Marine Corps and am somewhat familiar with Military Tactics. Hoping Sir, that you will take my case into your kind consideration,

I remain Very Respectfully,
Your Obedient Servant
Elias W. Hale, Junr.[9]
Commodore Stringham's Clerk
U. S. S. Minnesota[10]

A similar letter followed on July 3. Harris, to his credit, replied in complete candor.

Head Quarters, Marine Corps
Washington, D. C.
July 10, 1861

Sir:

I have received your letters of the 23rd, Ultimo, and the 3rd, instant.

I read the former to the Secy of the Navy and understand that Com. Stringham had spoken very favorably in your behalf and from the representations made to me in regard to you, I would be pleased to see you receive an appointment in the Corps. But I would remind you, success depends entirely on the amount of political influence brought to bear.

Very Resp'y +c
Jno Harris
Col., Comdt.

Mr. E. W. Hale
U. S. S. Minnesota
Fortress Monroe[11]

After the new regulations became known, applications, some renewing previous attempts to gain admittance to the Corps, began to arrive at the Navy Department. Welles directed Harris to take the necessary steps for the examinations.

Navy Department
August 15, 1861

Colonel John Harris
Com'd't., USMC

You will order a competent Board of Officers to convene at Head Quarters on the 26th, Inst., for the examination of such candidates for admission into the Marine Corps as may be permitted to present themselves by the Navy Department. The Board will consist of one captain, one first and one second Lieut. of Marines.

The Board will examine each candidate to ascertain if his mental and moral qualifications are such as fit him for the duties of a Second Lieutenant in the Marine Corps.

Candidates will, before they present themselves to the Board, be examined by a Medical Board, whose certificate will be filed with and form part of the report and will govern the Board in deciding upon the physical fitness of the candidates.

A separate report will be made in the case of each candidate and transmitted to the Department as soon as he is examined.

The record of the Board will be kept by the junior member under the direction of the presiding officer.

I am Resp'y,
Your Obt. Servt.
Gideon Welles[12]

Accordingly, Harris ordered Paymaster William W. Russell, Maj. John G. Reynolds, 1st Lt. James Wiley, and 2d Lt. Louis M. Goldsborough, Jr., to convene at Headquarters on August 26, and begin the process of examining candidates.

Regrettably, no complete record, compiled by either the examination or medical boards, is among the vast collections of the National Archives. Consequently, there is no way of knowing how many candidates were selected for examination or how many failed one or both tests. Only a handful of documents relative to that process have been located, but they present an insight to what was asked by the Board of Marine Officers in the written examination, and how a satisfactory performance by a candidate was reported to the Secretary of the Navy.

Examination of Mr. Geo. C. Reid

> I certify on honor that I was born on the 15th day of December in the year one thousand, eight hundred and (sixty lined out) forty-four, and am now twenty three years of age.[13]
>
> (signed) George C. Reid
>
> The candidate then read an extract from the "Young Officer's Companion."
>
> Suppose 2637 soldiers are formed into ranks of 3 deep. What is the number in each rank?
>
> Ans. - 879
>
> A party of soldiers at the distance of four hundred and fourteen (414) miles from Headquarters receives orders to join their corps in eighteen days. What number of miles must they march daily to reach their quarters?
>
> Ans.- 23 miles.
>
> If a certain amount of provisions must sustain a company of 799 for eighty-four days, how long would the same amount of provisions sustain 987 men?
>
> Ans. - 68 days
>
> What is geography?
>
> Ans.- A description of the earth's surface.
>
> What is the capital of South Carolina?
>
> Ans. I disremember.
>
> What is the capital of Georgia?
>
> Ans. Milledgeville.

What is the capital of Alabama?
Ans. Montgomery.
What is the capital of Austria?
Ans. I don't remember.
What is the capital of Prussia?
Ans. I don't remember.
What is the capital of China?
Ans. Peking.
What is the longest river in the world?
Ans. Amazon?
What is the next longest?
Ans. Ganges?
What is the next longest?
Ans. Nile?
What is the peculiarity of the Nile?
Ans. Its tides?
When and where was the Declaration of Independence Signed?
Ans. Philadelphia, July 4, 1776.
Who framed the Declaration of Independence?
Ans. Patrick Henry.
What was the first battle of the Revolution? When did it take place?
Ans. Lexington, 8th July, 1775.
Who was the officer that brought about the first engagement of the Revolution?
Ans. I don't remember.
Who commanded the British at Boston.
Ans. Sir William Howe.

(signed) George C. Reid[14]

A similar examination with many of the same questions may be found among the papers of the court-martial record of 2d Lt. John M. Reber.[15]

The report of Surgeon Marius Duvall certifying that candidate John C. Morgan was physically fit and a specimen of Morgan's handwriting attesting to his age accompanied the findings of the Board of Marine Officers who examined and recommended him for appointment.[16]

Head Quarters, U. S. Marine Corps
Marine Barracks, Washington, D. C.
Thursday, March 30th, 1865.

Hon. Gideon Welles
Secretary of the Navy
Sir;

In accordance with your order of the 9th March, 1865, we have carefully examined into the Mental and Moral qualifications of Mr. John C. Morgan for the duties of Second Lieut. in the United States Marine Corps, and respectfully report that in our opinion they are such as to warrant his admission into said Corps.

. . . He has the bearing and appearance of a gentleman.

Very Respectfully,
Your Obedient Servants
(signed) Thos. Y. Field
Major & Presiding Officer
C. D. Hebb
Capt. U. S. M. Corps
Francis H. Harrington
Lt. U. S. M. C. & Recorder.[17]

The Board of Marine Officers began interviewing and testing candidates promptly on August 26. Over the course of the next few weeks, thirty-one applicants were judged physically, mentally and morally competent to become officers of the Marine Corps and received appointments as second lieutenants.[18] At least four failed to pass the examination and were judged not qualified, two of them worth noting. Leonard MacKall was recommended for appointment to the Corps by President Lincoln on March 16, 1861, with the words, "Give him the first vacancy not promised."[19] MacKall was examined on August 31, and failed to pass the test. Norval L. Nokes took the examination on August 27 and failed to qualify.[20] However, his political backers persuaded Welles to give Nokes another chance.[21] He retook the examination on September 17, passed, and was appointed to the Marine Corps on November 1.

Although political influence was the yardstick by which all appointments to the Corps were measured, even the backing of the most politically powerful members of the government did not always ensure success. The examination boards were an obstacle that either tripped up appointees or persuaded them to seek a similar position with the volunteers where qualifications were not so strict. Secretary of State William H. Seward recommended three young men for appointments. When Rufus King, one of the three, was ordered to report for examination on August 26, he declined the appointment in favor of a second lieutenant's commission in the 4th U.S. Artillery. The other two did not become officers of Marines. Secretary of the Treasury Simon Cameron recommended four. One, William R. Brown, who also had a recommendation from Mrs. Mary Todd Lincoln, became a Marine officer. Harris recommended two. The application of one, his nephew John Campbell Harris was successful; Vice President Hannibal Hamlin recommended two and both were unsuccessful. Even a recommendation from the President did not guarantee an appointment. President Lincoln recommended five young men. MacKall, as noted, failed the examination. Benjamin Chambers did not make it, nor did James F. Evan, or Duncan A. Pell.[22] The one successful recommendation made by the President was on behalf of George W. Cummins, Jr., the product of a wealthy Delaware family. Cummins, remarkably, was then serving as an enlisted Marine aboard USS *Niagara*.[23]

Other enlisted Marines attempted to rise above their station in the Corps and applied for commissions, knowing there was precedent for enlisted men being commissioned from the ranks. James F. Devlin, an Irishman who enlisted soon after his emigration to this

Benjamin F. Chambers
Massachusetts Commandery, MOLLUS Collection, USAMHI

Duncan A. Pell
Massachusetts Commandery, MOLLUS Collection, USAMHI

country, had served as a private, clerk, and sergeant in the office of the Quartermaster of the Corps before being commissioned in 1839.[24] Robert Tansill enlisted as a private on March 16, 1833; promoted Corporal three months later; he was elevated to sergeant before he had served a year in the Corps. After two re-enlistments, Tansill was commissioned a second lieutenant of Marines to rank from November 3, 1840.[25]

Rufus King
Massachusetts Commandery, MOLLUS Collection, USAMHI

Encouraged by the success of those who had preceded him from the ranks, James F. Essex, orderly sergeant of the Marine Guard aboard USS *Susquehanna*, applied to Harris to be detached from his ship to pursue his hope of bettering his position in the service.[26] Essex had presented his qualifications to the Navy Department in a letter received on June 14. He now wished to make his case in person. Much to his disappointment, Essex did not receive the hoped for order detaching him from *Susquehanna*. Nevertheless, he persisted in his quest to become an officer of Marines. On September 9, the Secretary of the Navy received another letter of application from Essex. He had been in action during the recent Hatteras Expedition and had taken part in the destruction of the abandoned forts on Beacon and Portsmouth Islands. Apparently Welles was much impressed.

Essex, a native of Georgetown, District of Columbia, had been a clerk prior to enlisting in the Marine Corps. He was promoted to the rank of sergeant during his first enlistment and re-enlisted for another four years when his term expired on February 18, 1860. Welles took note of the fact that Essex was serving his second enlistment, and evidently had some concern in regard to the age of the applicant. Despite his misgivings, Welles gave a favorable reply to the sergeant.

Navy Department
Sept. 16, 1861

J. F. Essex, USM Corps

You are hereby appointed a Second Lieutenant in the U.S. Marine Corps.

It is proper to inform you that the Law for the "better organization of the Marine Corps" provides that persons appointed shall be between the ages of twenty and twenty-five years and shall also be subjected to an examination as to their qualifications for the service to which they are appointed.

Should you be found qualified under the foregoing provisions, a commission will be issued to you, otherwise this appointment to be considered as null and void.

I am Respectfully,
Gideon Welles [27]

Sergeant Essex was detached from USS *Susquehanna* on the evening of September 20, and proceeded to Hampton Roads aboard the supply steamer *Spaulding.* While he was en route to Washington, Welles requested a check of the records at Headquarters, Marine Corps. Harris replied that Essex was twenty-eight years old at the time of his last enlistment, and thus ineligible to receive a commission. Frustrated in his goal to become a Marine officer, Essex felt his experience with the Corps would win him a commission with one of the volunteer regiments. On October 3, Harris recommended that Essex, who was anxious for discharge, be granted his request. Welles agreed and Essex was discharged from the Corps on October 10, 1861.[28]

O. Sgt. Carl Wagner, noncommissioned officer in charge of the Marine Guard aboard USS *Narragansett* wrote to Harris, requesting his support for a commission as a second lieutenant in the Marine Corps. Wagner was a self-educated man whose spare time was taken up by the study of military texts. He had previously served under Harris and had known him for many years.[29] That was the only fault in Sergeant Wagner's otherwise exemplary credentials. He was too old to be considered.[30] Sgt. Charles Hancock, recommended by Major Reynolds on August 5, 1861, was turned down for the same reason.[31]

Among those who sponsored applicants were a few to whom the Navy Department and Marine Corps seemed to owe a special obligation. One was Priscilla Decatur Twiggs, niece of naval hero Capt. Stephen Decatur, USN, and widow of Maj. Levi Twiggs, USMC, killed in action at the Battle of Mexico City. However, when she wrote

Successful candidates for Marine Corps commissions,
August–September 1861

2d Lt. Henry A. Bartlett
NA Photograph 127-G-517310

2d Lt. Henry J. Bishop
NHC Photograph NH 56179

2d Lt. Charles H. Bradford
NHC Photograph NH 56225

2d Lt. William R. Brown
Author's Collection

2d Lt. Richard S. Collum
NHC Photograph NH 52769

2d Lt. George W. Cummins, Jr.
Author's Collection

2d Lt. Alfred Devereux
CWL

2d Lt. Robert O'Neil Ford
Michael J. McAfee Collection

2d Lt. Oscar B. Grant
CWL

2d Lt. John C. Harris
MCHC Collection

2d Lt. Robert S. Kidd
Courtesy of Caroline S. Chastain

2d Lt. Horatio B. Lowry
NHC Photograph, NRL (Old) 11510

2d Lt. Thomas L. McElrath
Author's Collection

2d Lt. William B. McKean
Author's Collection

2d Lt. Norval L. Nokes
Author's Collection

2d Lt. Samuel W. Powell
Dr. Ray Giron Collection

2d Lt. William B. Remey
Howard A. Hoffman Collection

2d Lt. David M. Sells
Tom MacDonald Collection

2d Lt. Eugene A. Smalley
Author's Collection

2d Lt. William J. Squires
CWL

2d Lt. Charles A. Stillman
MCHC Collection

2d Lt. Eugene B. Sturgeon
Courtesy of Mr. & Mrs. "Red" Hogan

Harris to advance the cause of Marshall Tevis, her daughter's fiancé, stating that "I think I have some claims upon the Department; every male relative I have ever known having served under the Stars and Stripes,"[32] the debt went unpaid. There is no record of Tevis being considered for a Marine Corps commission.

And so the thirty accepted applicants were appointed second lieutenants, and began the process of learning how to become officers of Marines. Those responsible for training the young gentlemen who reported to duty at Marine Barracks, Washington during the fall of 1861 would have their hands full. Of the thirty, twelve had varying types and lengths of military service. At the high end of the experience scale, two, Richard S. Collum and Eugene B. Sturgeon, had spent almost three years as midshipmen at the Naval Academy before deficiencies in studies forced their resignations. Sturgeon had also served as a third lieutenant in the United States Revenue Cutter Service for thirteen months. George W. Cummins, the applicant who had secured President Lincoln's recommendation, enlisted in the Corps on October 6, 1859, and had been a corporal since March 1860. William J. Squires had served ninety-nine days as a private of the 71st New York State Militia, one of them at the Battle of Bull Run. Eugene A. Smalley served with the three-month 19th

Ohio Militia and had fought at the Battle of Rich Mountain. The remainder had no battle or even field experience, but at least the rudiments of military drill were part of their education.[33] Four were the sons of naval officers; one, Percival C. Pope, had been a clerk on board ship to his father, Capt. John Pope, USN, for four months.[34] While strangers to the ways of the Corps, they would have some idea of military life.[35] John Campbell Harris, nephew of the Commandant, had been a clerk at Headquarters since February 1859. The rest were as green as the rawest recruit.

There was also the problem of how these thirty-one new lieutenants would be placed as far as order of seniority was concerned. Most of them shared an appointment date with at least one other lieutenant. This problem had first surfaced in regard to the eight second lieutenants who were appointed to the Corps with the same date of rank, June 5, 1861. The confusion began when the names of the eight agreed upon appointees were given, in no particular order, to an agent of the New York Associated Press. It was published the next day and the list took on a life of its own. The order in which the names were published was assumed by all, even the appointees, to be the places they held on the seniority list. The list read:

Frank Munroe
Robert W. Huntington
Jehu A. Burrough
William H. Parker
Robert E. Hitchcock
William H. Hale
John H. Grimes
Joseph F. Baker

It was rumored that Baker was dissatisfied with his position at the bottom of the list and in order to placate him, the Secretary of the Navy put the names of each lieutenant on a piece of paper, put the papers into a hat and drew them out. The order in which the names were drawn was the order in which they were assigned seniority.[36] That rumor was partially true. The names were drawn out of a hat under Welles' direction. However, Baker's complaints about his position on the list had nothing to do with the assignment of relative rank. First, the list that had appeared in the newspapers, according to Welles, had no official character. Their appointments were not official until the candidates had received their medical examinations. Once the examinations were completed, the names were indeed put into a hat and drawn by "a gentleman from New York incidentally in the Department, and in no wise interested in either of the persons appointed."[37] Second, the lottery was done in accordance with the 1857 army regulations as specified in Article 2, Section 5, which read:

> when commissions are of the same date, the rank is to be decided between officers of the same regiment or Corps by the order of appointment; between officers of different regiments or Corps; 1st, by rank in actual service when appointed; 2d, by former rank and service in the army or Marine Corps; 3d, by lottery among such as have not been in the military service of the United States.[38]

Because the first two provisions did not apply to any of the officers appointed in June, the lottery was drawn resulting in the following official list of appointments:

Frank Munroe
Robert W. Huntington
Joseph F. Baker
Jehu A. Burrough
William H. Parker
Robert E. Hitchcock
William H. Hale
John H. Grimes

The matter was thought to have been settled, but subsequent to the passage of the Act of July 26, 1861, the Senate Naval Affairs Committee questioned the lottery system. A report from that committee stated that the lottery system of fixing position by chance rather than on "moral excellence, manly courage and scientific attainment" would tend to demoralize accomplished young men planning to enter the public service.[39] On July 31, a resolution offered by Sen. John P. Hale, and unanimously agreed to by the Senate was sent to the President. Henceforth, "rank and position in the Army, Navy and Marine Corps should not be left to be decided by lot, but, all other things being equal, preference should be given to age."[40] Welles gave his opinion of the Senate resolution to the President on August 2, stating, "In this matter, the Department has no feeling, but it is desirable that it should be distinctly settled, whether hereafter the army regulations are to govern in the question of rank in the Marine Corps or whether they are to be set aside by resolution of the Senate."[41] On August 5, the final report of the Naval Affairs Committee came before the Senate. It reaffirmed the position taken by Senator Hale, but when it became known that the President stood by the Army Regulations, that position should be decided by lottery when commissions were of the same date, the resolution was rejected.[42]

Among the many applications for appointments to the Marine Corps received during the summer and fall of 1861, one stood out among the rest. It was a plea from Freeman Norvell of Michigan, asking for reinstatement to the Corps at his former position in the seniority list. His August 21 letter requesting reappointment with the rank of captain, supported by a letter of recommendation from the legislative delegation from Michigan, must have sent Navy Department clerks scurrying for records to discover why Norvell left the Corps. Norvell had been appointed second lieutenant of Marines to rank from March 3, 1847. He served with the Marine Battalion during the Mexican War and won a brevet promotion to first lieutenant for gallant and meritorious service during the assault on Chapultepec Castle. Eight years later, his Marine Corps career ended when he was tried by court-martial for drunkenness. Found guilty of the charge, Norvell was dismissed from the service on June 23, 1855.[43] Word that Norvell was seeking reinstatement made its way to Headquarters, Marine Corps. Harris, with so few experienced officers at his disposal, let it be known that he would be pleased to see Norvell back in the Corps. Eager to retrieve his reputation, Norvell sought Harris' support.

Yankton Indian Agency
Greenwood, D. T., Sept. 17, 1861

My dear Sir;

I have been much gratified to learn from Major Nicholson that you would not only not object to my reinstatement in the Marine Corps, but that you would welcome my return to it. Without this, I should not desire to again serve in it, but with it, I shall be highly delighted. You will, of course, appreciate the desire I have to obliterate my former disgrace and nothing can do this satisfactorily to myself but the opportunity to prove to my old associates that it was only temporary. I would much prefer to be indebted for this to yourself and the officers of your Corps rather than to use political influence and if you can assist me in it, I shall be very grateful.

Former Marine officer Freeman Norvell, shown here as an officer of the 1st Michigan Cavalry Regiment

Burton Historical Collection, Detroit Public Library

Under a mistaken view of the law, I have filed an application to the Sec'y. of the Navy for an appointment as Captain, but all that I wish is to again serve under your command, and, if possible, wipe out my former disgrace.

If you will assist me in this, I shall hope for an opportunity to prove my gratitude.

I am Sir, with much respect
Your Obt. Svt.
F. Norvell

Col. John Harris
Comm'dg. U.S.M. Corps [44]

Norvell sent another letter to the Department asking for reinstatement on September 22, but his attempt to rejoin the Marine Corps was not successful. While the Commandant seemed willing to give Norvell a second chance, the Secretary of the Navy was completely unforgiving.[45]

During the time that Congress considered enlarging the Corps, a fear persisted that the Confederates, victorious at Bull Run, would try to take advantage of the disorganized condition of the Federal army and make a move on the capital. To forestall any attempt of the rebels to use the Potomac as an invasion route, the battery erected

"Marine Battery," Fort Ellsworth, Alexandria, Virginia
Frank Leslie's Illustrated Newspaper

Washington Navy Yard, 1861

LC Photograph

at Alexandria in June was strengthened. Ninety seamen, seventy from the Washington Navy Yard, twenty from USS *Pawnee*, and another twenty from USS *Perry*, under their own officers were dispatched to the garrison.[46] An attack on the fort by Confederates had been a matter of concern for the Navy Department as early as July 23, since the number of sailors were not sufficient to defend their battery. On July 26, 2d Lieutenant William H. Cartter, one sergeant, three corporals, and forty privates were transferred from Marine Barracks, Washington, to the Navy Yard.[47] All but thirteen privates were sent to Fort Ellsworth to reinforce the sailors stationed there, along with 110 more sailors, three IX-inch guns and five howitzers.[48] During August, fifteen additional privates were sent from the Navy Yard to augment the Marine detachment.[49]

In addition to supplying Marines for Fort Ellsworth, Harris was obliged to transfer Marines from Headquarters as often as Capt. John A. Dahlgren, USN, Commandant of the Washington Navy Yard, requested them.[50] There had been fifty-nine Marines at the Navy Yard in June 1861, and this number had been increased to one hundred one by the end of July. To meet the needs of his expanding responsibilities of protecting the stores and equipment, Dahlgren had called for twenty Marines on July 24, fifty on July 25, and more in August.[51] Harris, hard pressed to meet the demands for Marine Guards destined for warships, complied with the orders grudgingly.

Head Quarters, Marine Corps
Washington, D. C.
August 15, 1861

Sir;

The President of the United States was at the Navy Yard last evening, and informed Captain Dahlgren that sixty army prisoners would be sent down for him to take charge of and he sent to me to aid him in that duty. For that purpose, I dispatched one sergeant, one corporal, and thirty privates to the Navy Yard. The frequent calls for men interfere very much with my efforts to prepare for the contemplated wishes of the Department and I hope the security of these prisoners will be provided for in some other way.

I also beg leave to recommend the forty-odd Marines that are stationed at the fort near Alexandria may be withdrawn, and that duty be performed by the troops stationed near it. Our men require a great deal of drill to make them good soldiers and this cannot be done while they are so constantly on guard, which they are at Alexandria.

I am Sir,
Very Respectfully +c
Jno Harris
Col., Comdt.

The Hon. Gideon Welles
Secretary of the Navy [52]

Toward the end of July, Capt. Thomas T. Craven, USN, told Welles that arms were being collected at certain points along the Maryland shore for shipment to the rebels in Virginia.[53] He asked for the services of a United States Marshal armed with a search warrant in order to find and seize the weapons.[54] Welles replied to Craven the next day, "No search warrant will be necessary. You are hereby authorized, if you are satisfied that the arms are intended for the rebels, to seize them and refer the parties to the Department. You will call upon Colonel Harris or Captain Dahlgren for assistance should any further force be necessary."[55]

Craven kept his vigil off the Maryland shore and by mid-August was satisfied that Port Tobacco, Maryland, was a hotbed of illegal arms smuggling. Eleven Marines from USS *Pawnee* had been sent ashore under the command of Henry M. Blue, Master, USN, on August 10 to arrest a man suspected of being active in smuggling

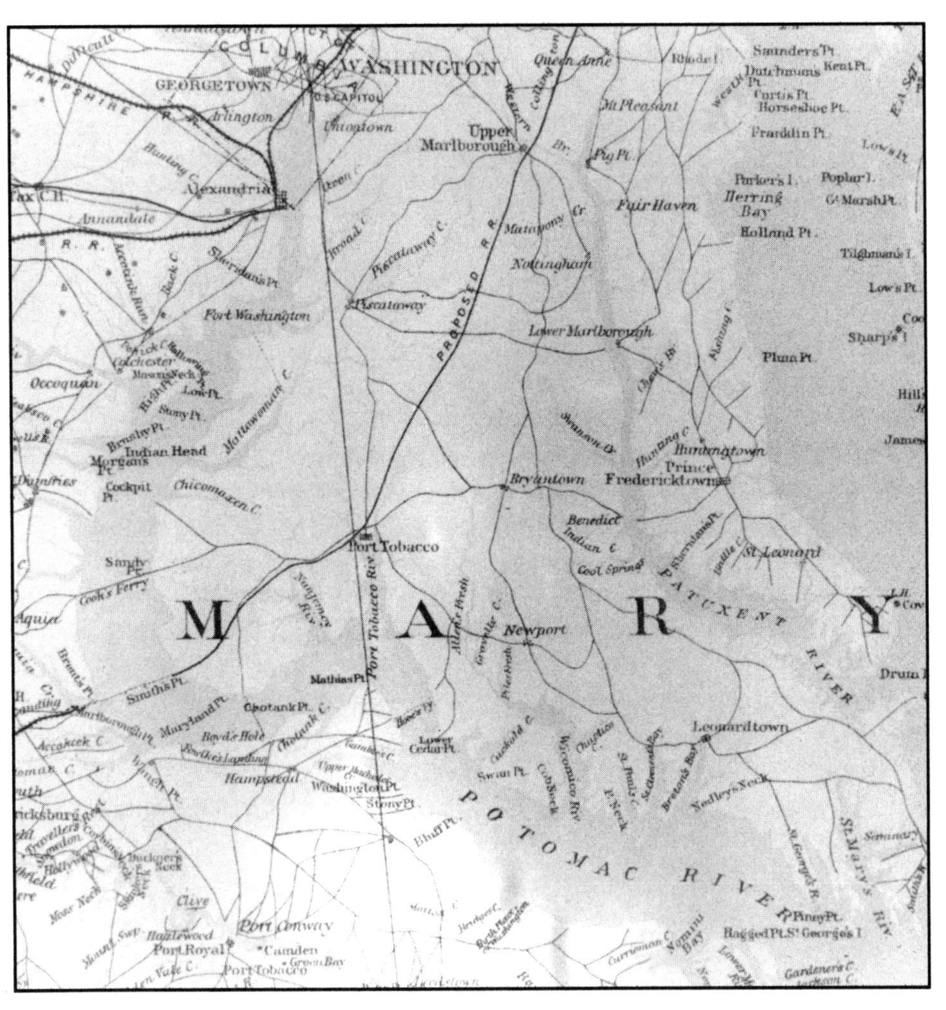

Area of operations, Potomac River

RG 94, Civil War Atlas, plate CXXXVII

operations.[56] Craven's report to the Department of the incident spurred Welles to action. On August 19, Harris was directed to detach 200 Marines (nearly three quarters of his effective force at Marine Barracks, Washington) in full marching kit, properly officered, and have them report to Captain Dahlgren at the Navy Yard by 10:00 P.M. that night.[57] Craven was instructed to search Port Tobacco and the surrounding area for the contraband arms but warned not to go beyond the effective range of the guns of his supporting vessels in case he ran into strong opposition.[58]

The expedition sortied at 11:00 P.M., and Captain Dahlgren telegraphed Fox that the steamer *Baltimore* had left the Navy Yard with the Marines and four launches full of armed sailors. 2d Lt. Louis M. Goldsborough, Jr., one of the Marine officers detached from Marine Barracks, Washington, kept this account of the expedition:

> Left Head Quarters, Washington at 10 P.M. with 200 Marines, Major Reynolds commdg, Lieuts. Goldsborough, Munroe, Huntington, Burrough, Parker and Grimes. Left Navy Yard wharf at 11 P.M. for the Potomac Flotilla which we joined at 4:30 A.M. Took on board from U.S.S. "Pawnee" a Sergeant and 17 private Marines. Left P. F. at 8 A.M. accompanied by U.S. Steamers "Freeborn" and "Resolute" (Captains

USS *Seminole* and *Pawnee* engaging Confederate batteries at Evansport, Virginia

<u>*Harper's Weekly*</u>

Harold [Harrell, Abram D.] and Budd) for Port Tobacco. Landed at 10 A.M. with all the Marines and a detachment of 25 sailors and marched for town. Searched, found nothing. Returned on board about sun down and got underway for Leonard Town. Reached L. T. at 5:30 A.M. Landed at 6:30 and marched into the town. This time the force was the same as the day before except the "Pawnee's" Guard who, in consequence of bad conduct did not join the party. Searched the town—found nothing. Just after leaving Leonard Town, the "Freeborn" ran ashore, and was, after a detention of about an hour and a half, pulled off by the "Resolute" at 9:30. Left L. T. and started for Washington.

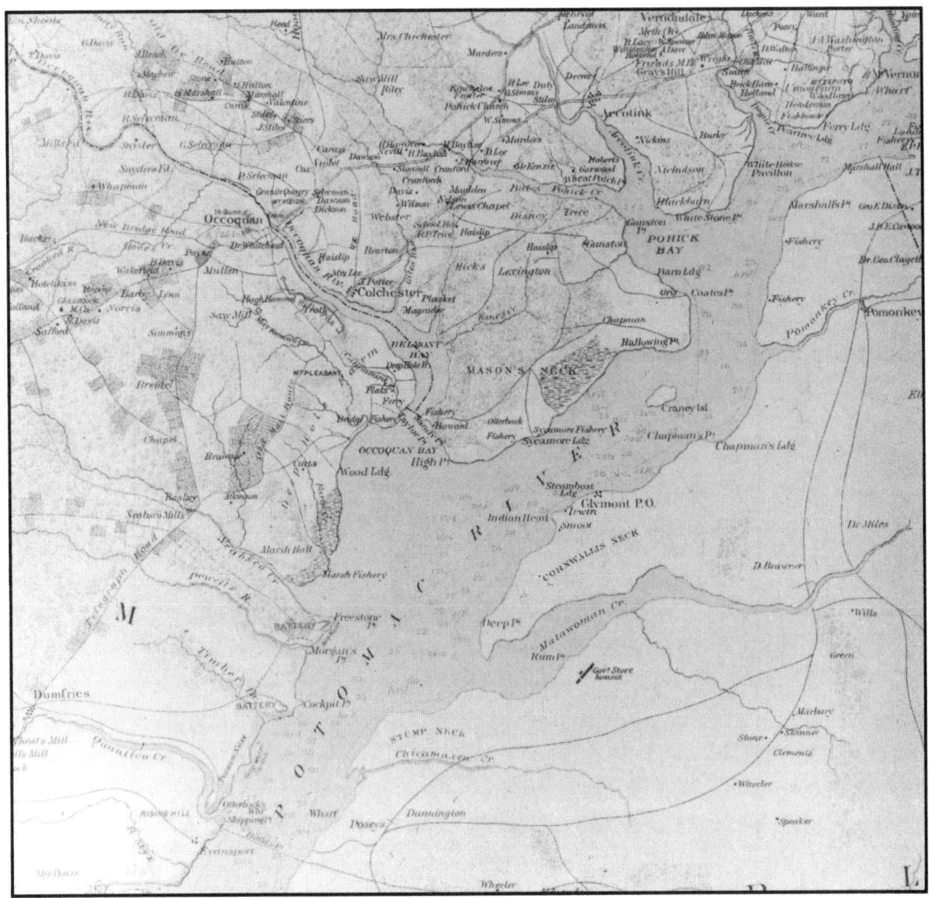

Location of Confederate batteries on the Upper Potomac River

RG 94, Civil War Atlas, plate VIII

> Stopped on the way up at the Potomac Flotilla and sent the "Pawnee's" Guard on board of her. Reached Washington at 10:30 and marched into Barracks.[59]

Goldsborough also wrote his mother of the expedition and summed up the affair by saying, "We were gone two days and had a very pleasant time of it."[60]

On August 24, based upon information supplied by two runaway slaves that the very area that Marines had searched was an active staging point for arms and men being sent across the Potomac, Fox sent another message to Craven. The information had been forwarded over the signature of Maj. Gen. George B. McClellan, USA,

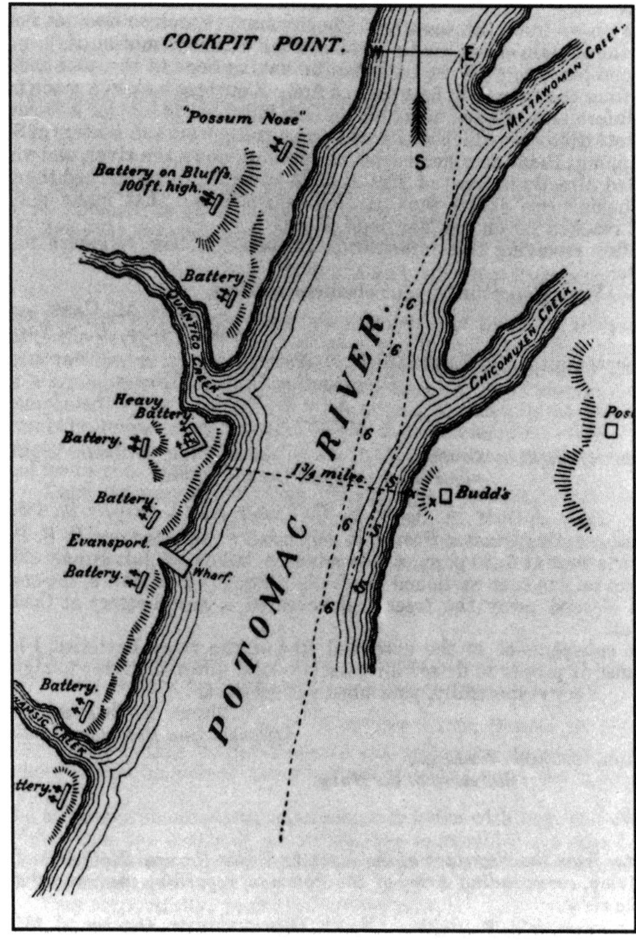

Detail of rebel batteries on the Upper Potomac River

N. O. R., 4:725

Confederate battery at Shipping Point

Frank Leslie's Illustrated Newspaper

Confederate battery at Budd's Ferry

Harper's Weekly

and being of sufficient importance, Fox authorized Craven to call upon the services of the Marines to investigate the situation.[61] Having just returned from the thorough search of the locales mentioned in the dispatch from the Department, Craven did not feel compelled to call the Marines out again and give them another "pleasant time." He so reported to the Department on September 5.[62]

The Marine Guards of three U.S. gunboats, USS *Pocahontas, Seminole*, and *Pawnee*, received a chance for both serious gunnery work and dodging enemy fire while running down the Potomac River in mid-October. On October 15, *Pocahontas* steamed past the Confederate battery at Evansport, Virginia, and fired several shots, receiving none in return, but apparently waking the gunners from a late morning nap. About an hour later, the dull boom of cannon was heard from the direction of Evansport; *Pocahontas* reversed course and steered toward the sound of the guns. A short time later, USS *Seminole* was seen coming down river at full steam. The garrison at the Evansport battery, having been shaken out their lethargy by the shelling of *Pocahontas*, took out their frustration on *Seminole*.[63]

USS *Pawnee* made the same journey the next day. As she passed the batteries at Quantico a few miles north of the Evansport battery, the rebels opened fire. After running the gauntlet for twenty-five minutes, a damage assessment found that the ship had been struck on the hull three times above the water line. One shot ripped open the splinter netting, while others passed through the rigging. Another shot struck the mizzenmast. But the fire of the enemy went unanswered.[64] *Pawnee*'s mission was not to engage the rebels, but to rendezvous with USS *Mount Vernon* above Maryland Point. The sailors and Marines gritted their teeth, ducked the shot, shells, and splinters, counting on another day to return the favor of the rebels.

Abraham Lincoln was rumored to have said, "I hope to have God on our side, but we must have Kentucky." That statement could equally have been applied to Maryland. That state controlled communications between the capital and rest of the country. Lincoln was very uneasy about Maryland's devotion to the Union, given his threatened passage through Baltimore en route to his inauguration, the street riot there when Massachusetts volunteers passed through, and the constant speeches of pro-Southern state politicians. The Maryland Legislature was scheduled to convene on September 17, and Lincoln was quite concerned that it would vote an ordinance of secession. Acting through the War Department, Lincoln made certain this would not take place.

War Department
September 11th, 1861.

General:

The passage of any act of secession by the Legislature of Maryland must be prevented. If necessary, all, or any part of the members must be arrested. Exercise your own judgment as to the time and manner, but do the work effectively.

Very Respectfully,
Your Obedient Servant
Simon Cameron
Secretary of War

Major-Gen. N. P. Banks [65]
Commanding near Darnestown, Md. [66]

The arrests of some of Maryland's leading secessionists were quickly effected and, as a consequence, no ordinance of secession was introduced. In fact, the rump legislature was so cowed by the action, that it voted a resolution repudiating the very idea of secession. Those who were taken into custody were brought to Annapolis and sent aboard the transport *Baltimore* for passage to New York, and ultimate incarceration at Fort Lafayette. Marines were sent from Marine Barracks, Washington, to secure the prisoners and accompany them to their destination. To all intents and purposes, it seemed like routine duty. However, the lure of money turned that assignment into something quite sinister.

1st Lt. Robert W. Huntington was in command of the Marine detachment guarding the "Maryland State Prisoners," and on September 23, a day into the voyage to New York, was approached by Pvt. Henry T. McGraw, who reported a most strange occurrence. McGraw told Huntington that L/Sgt. William Toombs had asked him to join in a plan to free their prisoners. Toombs, according to McGraw, said that certain of the prisoners would pay several hundred dollars to arrange an escape from the ship. Further, a life-long stipend of twenty-five or thirty dollars per month would be paid by those they helped.[67] After conducting a brief investigation, Huntington promptly placed Toombs under arrest.

After the Maryland prisoners were turned over to the authorities at Fort Lafayette and the detachment returned to Washington, Huntington made an official report of the incident to the Commandant.[68] The charges were "of so serious a character," Harris immediately requested that Welles authorize a trial by court-martial.[69]

Toombs was brought to trial on October 3, 1861, at Marine Barracks, Washington, on the charge of "Endeavoring to corrupt privates of the Marine Corps to betray their trust." His defense in the matter was, simply stated, to test the loyalty of Privates McGraw and William McMullin. There never was any plot to help the Maryland prisoners escape. McGraw and McMullin testified that Toombs was quite serious in his talk of helping the Marylanders escape. Toombs had told both that he was in the war to make as much money as he could from it. The court believed the testimony of the two Marine privates, and found Toombs guilty. He was sentenced to be confined at the District of Columbia prison until February 27, 1865, the expiration date of his enlistment, without pay or allowances.[70] Toombs' disgraceful conduct was the sole instance of a Marine who valued money more than his honor during the entire conflict.

The verdict in the trial quickly made the rounds of Marine Barracks, Washington, and, with a generous dose of rumor, was reported home. Pvt. George Riddell wrote his mother:

> That Seargeant of marines you read about that was going to go run the vessell ashore and release the prisoners, bribe the sailors by giving them a commission in the rebel navy, set fire to the magazine, he was to receive 500 Dollars and a commission of Coronal, has had his sentence read out Friday night. He is to have a ball and chain riveted around his ancle and to carry that for six months in solitary confinement, hard labor, dark cell, and be fed on bread and water and be drummed out of the service and be arrested and confined in the Penitentury for life.[71]

Captain Dahlgren's seemingly insatiable demand for Marines to garrison Fort Ellsworth continued to be a constant source of aggravation to Harris. The Commandant's appeals to the Department for relief went unanswered. Dahlgren requested fifty more Marines on September 3 (reduced to thirty by Welles), twenty on September 10, and another fifty on September 12.[72] Finally, Welles acted to secure the return of the Marines from duty at Alexandria. It was not, however, to satisfy the complaints made by Harris. Welles had other plans for the Corps,[73] and, for this reason, McClellan was requested to provide troops to garrison Fort Ellsworth, so that the Marines could be returned to Washington.[74] McClellan, although possessive regarding troops he needed for his own plans, obliged Welles, and the Marines were relieved on October 1.[75]

The anticipated return of the Marines from Fort Ellsworth and the continual arrival of recruits from the Philadelphia Rendezvous, crowded living arrangements at Marine Barracks, Washington. To accommodate the growing population of enlisted Marines, the stables at the south end of the Barracks were converted into quarters for the men.[76]

The newly appointed Marine officers found their quarters somewhat less than comfortable, and probably would have preferred the renovated stables to the quarters to which they were assigned.

Easby's House
Washington, September 19th, 1861.

Sir.

The undersigned, Second Lieutenants in the Marine Corps, temporarily quartered near the Marine Barracks in a house known as Easby's, beg leave most earnestly to represent that, in their belief & experience, the last named place is very prejudicial to the health of its occupants and therefore pray their early removal.

In this opinion they are fortified by the facts that they are all men of strong constitutions and yet each has suffered continued derangement of system since his residence at the above place; that on the adjacent lots there are several large stagnant pools of water, from which arise unhealthy "miasmas;" that the trees and undergrowth approach too near to admit of the necessary dryness in and around the house; that the ground is unfavorable to a proper drainage and (probably more detrimental than all), it has a damp, nauseous, unwholesome smell, at least intensely disagreeable to the sense.

It is also believed by the undersigned, from what they hear, that it is generally reputed an unhealthy place.

In conclusion, your petitioners again begging an early and favorable consideration of their case, subscribe themselves,

With great respect,
Your Obdt. Servants,
Rich'd S. Collum
W. Rawle Brown
Rob't O'Neill Ford
Jno. C. Harris
Wm. B. McKean
Henry A. Bartlett
David M. Sells

Col. John Harris,
Comdt. U.S. Marine Corps
Headquarters [77]

While the Corps was suffering through these bouts of growing pains at Washington, the first amphibious landing of the war took place at Hatteras Inlet, one of the main thoroughfares for blockade running traffic to North Carolina ports in Albemarle and Pamlico Sounds.

The operation to seize the forts guarding Hatteras Inlet was an outgrowth of the July 16 report submitted by the members of a "confederence for the consideration of measures for effectually blockading the South Atlantic coast." Hatteras Inlet was the main channel in North Carolina waters through which smugglers ran goods to the Confederacy. Initially, the members of the board thought that merely denying access to Hatteras Inlet and the North Carolina ports would suffice. Sinking hulks in the channel beyond the inlet would accomplish the purpose, while reserving a safe harbor for shallow draft warships patrolling the inner bar.[78] When the South fortified Hatteras Inlet, the plans changed. Rather than merely denying interior navigation to the rebels through Pamlico and Albemarle Sounds, the Navy Department suggested taking Hatteras Inlet by amphibious landing and using the area as a base for projecting Federal forces to the North Carolina coast. The War Department, eager to retrieve prestige lost on the battlefield of Bull Run, was receptive to the plan, and agreed to supply 900 troops for the operation.

The plan was simplistic by design. A squadron would proceed to Hatteras Inlet, conveying three transports filled with troops. An amphibious landing would place these troops on the beach within striking distance of the earthworks guarding the entrance to the inlet. The guns of the squadron would soften up the enemy positions with a heavy bombardment and the troops would then take the forts by direct assault.

On August 13, 1861, orders were sent to Maj. Gen. John E. Wool, USA, commanding at Fort Monroe, to prepare a detachment of troops for the expedition.[79] The force was to have a portion of regulars but the majority were to be volunteer troops.[80] Maj. Gen. Benjamin F. Butler, USV, was selected by Wool to organize the expedition.[81] His orders were to cooperate with Flag Officer Silas Stringham, USN.[82] Stringham, however, would have overall commander of the operation.[83] When Butler completed his preparations, the army contingent consisted of the 9th New York Zouaves, Col. Rush C. Hawkins; the 20th New York Volunteers, Col. Max Weber; Company A, Union Coast Guard (99th New York Volunteers), Capt. Richard Nixon; and Company B, 2d U.S. Artillery, 1st Lt. Frank H. Larned.[84]

The naval force consisted of USS *Minnesota*, *Wabash*, *Cumberland*, *Pawnee*, and *Monticello*.[85] It would also include the Revenue Steamer *Harriet Lane* and three army transports, *Adelaide*, *George*

Peabody, and *Fanny*, temporarily under the command of naval officers. Marine Guards were attached to all of the regular naval vessels except *Monticello*:

USS *Minnesota*; Capt. William L. Shuttleworth, 1st. Lt. William H. Cartter, three sergeants, four corporals, two musicians, and fifty privates.

USS *Wabash*; Capt. Isaac T. Doughty, two sergeants, three corporals, two musicians, and forty-four privates.

USS *Susquehanna*; 1st Lt. Philip R. Fendall, Jr., four sergeants, four corporals, two musicians, and forty-five privates.

USS *Cumberland*; 1st Lt. Charles Heywood, three sergeants, four corporals, two musicians, and thirty-six privates.

USS *Pawnee*; O. Sgt. Timothy O'Brien, two corporals, two musicians, and twenty privates.

The expedition got under way on August 26, departing Fort Monroe in stages between noon and 2:30 P.M. On the voyage south, gun crews got in much needed drill at the heavy guns in anticipation of the expected battle. At 4:00 the next afternoon, the squadron dropped anchor in three fathoms of water about a mile off Hatteras Inlet. Preparations to land the troops began immediately and continued throughout the evening. It was decided that Marines from the squadron would also take part in the landing.

At 6:00 A.M., August 28, the transports got under way. *Fanny* came alongside USS *Wabash*, took aboard forty-four Marines under the command of Captain Doughty, and then came up to *Cumberland* to receive twenty-seven of her guard with First Lieutenant Heywood. USS *Monticello* received Captain Shuttleworth, Lieutenant Cartter, and the Marine Guard from *Minnesota*. *Minnesota*'s Marines were sent on board *Fanny* at 11:45 A.M.[86] *Pawnee*'s Marines did not go ashore, nor did those aboard *Susquehanna*. Both detachments, however, rendered good service at their guns in the ensuing battle.

While the Marines and army troops were being ferried to shore, the fleet opened fire on the rebel forts. The embarkation of the assault force and the subsequent actions of the fleet and the troops ashore were described by Pvt. Daniel O'Connor, a member of the Marine Guard of USS *Cumberland*:

> We sent 27 Marines on board the fanny, 37 from the Minisoto 36 from the wabash numbering in all 100 Marines to land under cover of our guns with 400 & 50 of Zouaves half the compliment that came from hampton the other 400 & 50 were kept on board the

Adlade for a reinforcement we hoisted anchor at 5 oclock A.M. we were towed by the wabash she had orders not to part with us watsoever & we not to drop anchor at ¼ past 9 oclock A.M. the wabash comminced hostillitys by 1 of her buldogs barking the down fall of Jefferson Davis bang bang was the order of the day for 1 hour & ½ we fired as hard as we coúld throwing shel in to the enemys battery like showers of hail & knocked down their flag staff ¼ to 11 oclock A.M. the word, cease firing was giving at said time the enemy avacuated the fort taking a lot of wounded with them besides two boat loads of dead & wounded they carried a way during the firing the troops landed and rallied on the fort they had a hard run the Marines in front & hoisted the American colors on the battery the Suskahanna came in during the firing which added 1 more to our number we spliced the main brace & drank Uncle Sams health during the firing none of the ships came to anchor they went round & round trough and fro so as the rebles could not get our range 16 Marines were kept on board 2 was sick & 14 to complate the guns crew your humble servant was 1 we had 2 after guns in the cabin one port & 1 stabord the smoke bothered us a good deal but so we made some splinded shots the commodore stringham compliminted capt. marsden on the good firing of his crew our noble captain marsden took it as cool as if he was going to take dinner the officers & men fought brave the day was pleasant the Thermomethor at 74 the enemy opened fire from a nother battery & we comminced again & kept up a brisk fire for about 20 minutes the enemy slackened fire & we stopped a few minutes to cool our guns & comminced again we kept up our fire for 15 minutes & silenced the enemy then we got orders for sea when we got rightley under way the enemy comminced again & we put a bout at the sight of the cumberland putting a bout they ceased fireing & we were ordered a way a gain we cruised out side that night & next morning the 29th we came in a gain our noble pilot by orders of our brave Captain brought us in as close to the enemys battery as he could & right opsite it they comminced firing at ½ past 7 oclock & the cumberland got in & comminced firing at 9 oclock A.M. sending every shell in to the enemys battery & making great havock among them they had 13 thirty 2 pound guns on the 2 fort & 1 11 inch that was dismounted the first fort had 6 thirty 2 pound guns their fort was made with barrels filled with sand they made very poor shots falling short or going over us the only ship that was struck was the Suskahanna who got a shot in her stern the enemy slackened fire a $\frac{1}{4}$ to 10 oclock & all but our pivot guns knocked off at 4 minutes past 10 oclock the pivots kept fire for a bout an hour and knocked off the enemy was fairly well silenced then but not beaten we spliced the main brace & drank to the president on the evening of the 28 our troops shelled out of the avacuated fort they rallied on after they first landed by the Harriet lane & Pawney through a mistake & they slept on the beach that night about 2 oclock P.M. our pivots comminced firing a gain & the cumberlands doing some great exacution & especily the 2 last shots made some afull havock at half past 3 oclock P.M. the enemy histed the flag of truce & swarmed around the flag staf the victory was ours we gave three cheers the Army Navy & Union for ever the soldiers who lay on the beach all night got orders to take possession of the fort it was a great sight to see them coming up in double quick on the beach the word halt was given a short distance of a few yards from the fort & General Butler met the rebel leader who wanted to surrender on conditions that the officers could go home with their arms & the privates without arms but commodore stringham would not agree to such a thing as that so they had to surrender as prisoners before the troops started to go in to the fort the Zouaves wanted to go in first the Marines would not stand it & General Butler gave the words companies halt forward Marines next was a company of regular Artillery & next the Zouaves we took 600 & 50 prisoners & fifty wounded the rebel Account was 40 killed & that they burried them when the flag of truce was flying they had a lot of old flintlock muskets plenty of powder & shot and shell a great deal of provisions a good looking lot of young men but not good anough to gain the victory this is the place the south ust to have all her stores landed it is an inlet to the Elisabeth river it is 50 miles from Wilmington &—— from Richmond

Area of operations, August–September 1861

Harper's Weekly

Soldiers and Marines land from the fleet at Hatteras Inlet
National Archives Photograph 127-N-309959

Bombardment of Forts Hatteras and Clark
NHC Photograph, USN 902922

Virgina there is some more sush places but we will put a stop to them The prisoners said they received no pay since the war comminced there was 2 reble steamers with troops from norfolk on the river & could not land them it was luckey for them for if they did they would be killed or made prisoners of nor could they come to rescue their beating soldiers the Harriet lane runned aground as she was going to cut off the enemys retreat all of her guns were hove over board & they are getting her off every tide all we lost out of the whole fleet & troops was 1 man & he got drowned by falling out of a boat the prisoners are gone on to New York in the Minnisoto flag ship when the navy will get trough with the south Jef Davis will have nothing to brag of the names of the ships engaged are as follows the Minnisoto Wabash first class steam frigates Suskahanna 2 side wheel the Pawney Stars & Harriet lane gunboats the Peabody Fanney & Adlade tug boats we took the enemy by surprise

Yours
Daniel O'Connor

Mr Timothy J Hayes [87]

The actual landing of the Marines and Butler's troops was a badly managed affair. The Marines were brought close inshore by the tug *Fanny* and loaded into small boats and launches for the journey to the beach. Butler's force was packed into two dismasted schooners and towed in by *Adelaide* and *George Peabody*. The heavy and pounding surf, breaking some distance from the beach was something the planners did not take into account. The violent motion of the sea made the passage extremely difficult. Skilled, or perhaps just plain lucky oarsmen brought a portion of the landing force safely through the breakers. Other hapless boats were swamped and their human cargo had to swim to shore. Some of the boats were left to their own devices once the bombardment began, but the *Fanny*, by means of a cable, managed to pull one of the schooners to safety.

Some fifty-four Marines made it to the beach where they were organized by Doughty, Shuttleworth, and Cartter. About sixty members of the artillery and 200 soldiers from the three New York regiments landed about three miles from Fort Clark. There they remained, spectators to the bombardment, waiting for relief, reinforcement or

Forts Hatteras and Clark

Battles and Leaders

some signal from the fleet as to what they were to do. They were in a most precarious situation. They were too few to advance on the forts and certainly were in no position to make a successful defense should the Southerners decide to deal with them.

Shortly after noon, the rebels were driven out of Fort Clark, according to reports made by Butler and Stringham, or, according to Col. William F. Martin, commander of the defenses, evacuated the work after running out of ammunition. The fleet ceased fire at 12:30 P.M. The troops on the beach, having observed the garrison fleeing from Fort Clark, formed up and quickly advanced to take possession of the work. Too quickly, it seems, for the gunners aboard *Pawnee* and *Harriet Lane*, oblivious to the cease fire signal, kept up the fire on Clark. One of Hawkins' Zouaves was slightly wounded—fortunately, the only casualty of the blunder. Marine Lieutenant Cartter and Navy Asst. Surg. William M. King were covered with dirt by the explosion of a shell, but were otherwise unhurt.[88] The bewildered occupiers of Fort Clark immediately sensed the danger of becoming victims of friendly fire and abandoned the fort, beating a hasty retreat to the safety of the beach. Cartter wrote home that "The Rebels caught <u>fits</u> and so did we!"[89]

Stringham, laboring under the mistaken belief that both enemy forts had been abandoned, sent in USS *Monticello* to take possession of the works. That vessel was immediately taken under fire by Fort Hatteras and the engagement began anew. The bombardment continued until 6:15 P.M. when threatening weather conditions, more likely to do damage to the fleet than the guns of Fort Hatteras, convinced Stringham to cease fire for the day and head for the safety of deeper waters. The Marines and soldiers on the beach were left to make do as best as they could. Lt. John Sanford Barnes, USN, observed the hardy band of souls on the beach and entered his thoughts in his journal.[90]

> These men were huddled on the beach at the spot where they were tumbled ashore, and were evidently getting along badly enough. If the threatening gale should become a reality, there was not the ghost of a chance for them and we already looked upon them as the enemy's property. . . . No attempt was made to relieve or reinforce them, but they were left to the chance of the enemy's letting them alone through the night, and the weather becoming calm, than which nothing was more unlikely. Never shall I forget the disgust, amazement and chagrin experienced and expressed by everyone that night![91]

In addition to the unfortunate Marines and soldiers ashore, several boats carrying either the former or the latter had been drifting aimlessly about on the water throughout the day. Having lost their oars in the attempt to pass through the surf that morning, they helplessly rode the waves, waiting to be saved. Forty Marines and sixty soldiers from the 20th New York were rescued by boat crews from USS *Susquehanna* before she turned to the open sea to weather out the expected storm. The wretched condition of the Marines taken aboard gave rise to much apprehension among those on the ship for their brothers ashore.[92]

The Marines and the regulars of the 2d Artillery passed the night on the rain-swept beach under strict discipline. The same could not be said for the volunteers. In fact, they had a very merry time of it. Captain Doughty reported that pickets from the New York units under orders to let no one pass in or out of their lines, looked the other way as their friends were allowed to "pass and repass with plunder belonging to the inhabitants of the place consisting of ladies silk dresses, bonnets, gaiters, shoes and all manner of wearing apparel. Their conduct throughout was most disgraceful and unbecoming soldiers of the U.S. Service."[93] The actions of the New Yorkers were not unnoticed in other quarters. Lieutenant Barnes called the Union Coast Guard "a miserable, thieving set of rascals," and the 20th New York, "a promiscuous crowd of . . . Germans who were but little better than their confreres, the *Brigands*."[94]

In the morning, the troops ashore were soaked to the skin but otherwise quite safe. Stringham ordered *Monticello* to see to their needs and to take them aboard if they wished. Having endured the miserable night without shelter, the Marines and Regulars chose to see the battle through. The volunteers also opted to stay, perhaps hoping for more booty.

At 8:00 A.M., the fleet opened fire on Fort Hatteras. Private O'Connor was back at his gun, and reported the action to his brother-in-law in his inimitable style.

> My station was first loder & you never see a sweep blacker than me from powder, smoke & sweat   i had a fuss with the ordley Sargent 2 days before the battle   i came out victorious   we have made it up since   he was captain of our guns and a poor captain he was   i had to sight the guns the most of the time & do me own work to   i had nothing on but an under shirt & pants   no shoes nor cap   after the first hour & ½ firing the captain of the ship came along & looked at me & laughed at my black figure & compliminted us on our good firing   he came to me on the 10th & told me he would make me captain of the guns & promote me to the rank of Corporal but i declined the

offer & told him i was not ambitious & that i was as high as i wanted to be in the service.[95]

After three hours of constant bombardment, the Confederate flag was struck. Stringham, not wanting to suffer a repeat of the previous day's embarrassment when he thought both forts had surrendered, ordered no cessation of fire. The shells continued to fall until a white flag was raised over Fort Hatteras. The Marines and regulars, who suffered a night of privation for this moment, immediately formed up, and, carrying the Stars and Stripes at the front, marched at the double time to the works. Butler landed from the tug *Fanny*, and arranged the surrender of the Confederate troops.

Two weeks after the surrender of Hatteras Inlet, USS *Susquehanna*, and *Pawnee*, with the tugboats *Fanny* and *Tempest* cruised south to Ocracoke Inlet, the next break in the chain of islands off the North Carolina coast. The tugs took the route close to the mainland through Pamlico Sound, towing launches containing Marines and seamen from USS *Pawnee*, commanded by Lt. James Maxwell, USN, while the deep draft warships steamed beyond the islands. Confederate forts had been erected in the vicinity of Ocracoke Inlet.[96] The mission of the Union naval forces was to destroy them.

Coming up to the inlet on the morning of September 17, Marines and sailors from *Susquehanna* landed on Beacon Island and joined those the tugs had already put ashore. 1st Lt. Philip R. Fendall led the Marines. The landing party found the fort empty, its guns

Destruction of rebel battery at Beacon Island, Ocracoke Inlet
Naval History of the Civil War

spiked and everything of value taken off. To destroy the fort, the landing party pushed every bit of flammable material up against the guns. packed gunpowder in strategic places, and laid a powder trail. After igniting the trail, the landing party took to their boats and rowed out in the channel to watch the fireworks. The Beacon Island fort soon went up with a roar and a sheet of flame. The Marines and sailors then rowed to Portsmouth Island, and marched to the hamlet of Portsmouth, a few miles to the south where they found a four-gun battery, also deserted. It, too, was torched.[97] The expedition returned to their ships on the morning of September 18.[98]

The fall of Hatteras Inlet was portrayed as a glorious victory for Union arms. Despite the relatively small number of forces engaged, the press played it up as the first major triumph since the debacle of Bull Run. Public confidence in the Lincoln Administration, the Congress, and the military was restored. However, the jubilation was not shared by the Navy Department nor by many senior naval officers. Given the overwhelming Union naval force and the paltry resistance offered by the Confederates, an easy conclusion was reached. Confederate defenses on the North Carolina coast were more than vulnerable. Stringham had rushed north to display his 700 rebel prisoners, the prize among them Capt. Samuel Barron CSN, commander of the naval defenses of Virginia and North Carolina, and formerly a venerated officer of the U.S. Navy. In doing so, he had lost the opportunity to win a relatively unopposed string of victories along the North Carolina seashore. The Department felt he was derelict in his duty for not doing so, but with the public spotlight on the victor of Hatteras, Welles was forced, for the time being, to withhold criticism of Stringham.[99]

Naval Lieutenant Barnes was thoroughly disgusted by the entire affair. He felt that proper handling of the bombardment should have ended the affair on the afternoon of the first day. His outrage at the troops being left ashore without protection during the night of August 27-28 festered like an open sore. Barnes recognized the lost opportunities and he blamed those at the top for missing them. For the moment, his journal was the receptacle of the bitter characterizations he reserved for the expedition commanders.

> The affair was a success. I close with the remark that the enemy never had more faithful allies than they had in the brutal folly, supreme ignorance and want of ordinary military and naval perception of Como. Stringham and Gen. Butler, whom I am ashamed to call our leaders! Had failure been possible, we should have encountered it. I shall leave no one of my acquaintance uninformed, and shall look forward to there being such a report of the proceedings of

this day to the government as shall result in the removal of both from active service.[100]

Cartter also wrote disparagingly of Butler in a post-battle letter to his mother, saying, "Gen. Butler that the papers talk so much about had nothing to do with it. He did not even land with the landing parties. He is not fit to command a company of school children. Nobody has a very great opinion of him. Here, they think he would make a pretty good Recruiting Officer."[101]

In fairness to Stringham, it is necessary to say that it would have been easy for the fleet to bombard the North Carolina coastal towns into submission, given his superior force and the lack of defenses on shore as his critics pointed out. However, Stringham's detractors failed to recognize that these victories would not have stood for very long. It would have been extremely difficult to hold those places for any length of time with only 900 volunteers and the few Marines that could be spared from the ships.

Stringham's lackluster performance, as viewed by the Navy Department, seemed proof that too many of the senior naval officers were beyond the age for bold action. It was a clear example to justify the retirement provisions of the recently enacted law for improving the military and naval services as far as the Department was concerned. The Marine Corps had a need to apply the same measure.

Sections 15–25 of Chapter XLII, Thirty-Seventh Congress, Session 1, "An Act providing for the better Organization of the Military Establishment,"[102] passed by Congress on August 3, 1861, dealt with certain officers of the army and Marine Corps who, by virtue of having served for more than forty years, or were incapable of active service for reasons of health, were to be placed on the retired list of officers. Section 15 dealt with those officers who had served for forty consecutive years. On their own application to the President, those officers would be placed on the list with full pay and an allowance for four rations per day. Those officers who did not avail themselves of the provisions of Section 15 and were considered as candidates for retirement for reasons of age or health, were entitled to appear before a Retiring Board made up between five and nine officers, two of whom would be medical officers. The hearing before the board would be conducted in the same manner as a court-martial or court of inquiry, with a presidential right to revise any finding of the board. Seven officers of the Marine Corps were immediately selected as candidates for retirement. Five officers: Lt. Col. James Edelin, Bvt. Lt. Col. William Dulany, Maj. Thomas English, Maj. Ward Marston, and Capt. Abraham Brevoort, all had served for more than forty years; none having opted to retire on their own application. 1st Lts. Charles Henderson and John Broome were chosen for retirement for reasons of health; the former for a long-standing absence from duty caused by heart disease and the latter for reasons of mental instability.

Welles directed Harris to preside over a Retiring Board to convene in November and conduct hearings into each case. So there would be no cause for complaint, Welles drew up guidelines under which the hearings were to be held.

> The object of the Department in convening the Board of which you are appointed President is in conformity with the laws to effect 'the better organization of the Marine Corps by retiring from it, either partially or wholly,' all such officers as may be found disqualified to perform such military service as may be necessary in the existing state of public affairs.
>
> It is to be presumed that the intention of Congress in providing for the establishment of a board, was to relieve the Department from the duty of investigating the fitness of officers for active service. The board will therefore at once enter upon this discharge of its duties without awaiting the reference to it of supposed cases of incapacity or unfitness. It will, of course, before it finds an officer incapacitated for active service, obtain all and the best evidence within its' reach bearing upon the question of fitness, but it does not follow that such evidence must be as full and exact as would be necessary to convict a party accused of a criminal offense. This view of the law would render the execution of it impracticable and defeat the purpose of its' enactment. A discretion is necessarily reposed in the board for the exercise of which each member acting under the oath prescribed by the law is responsible to his conscience alone.
>
> The law secures to each officer whose fitness may be investigated, 'a fair and full hearing before the Board if upon due summons, he shall demand it.' It will be proper, therefore, that the Board before deciding on its' report in any case shall make it known to the officer, if present in person or by counsel, the grounds of objection which may occur to them as to his fitness. But it cannot be demanded that this should be done with the precision and minuteness necessary in an indictment. The object of the law is not to punish for offenses but to relieve the service from those who are disqualified.
>
> The Commandant of the Navy Yard at New York has been directed to detail upon your application, medical

Portrait of then 2d Lt. Thomas S. English done between 1826 and 1834

NA Photograph 127-N515415

officers for the purpose of holding a survey upon such officers as may be able to appear in person before the Board.[103]

The Retiring Board convened at Marine Barracks, Brooklyn, on November 7, 1861, and consisted of Harris, President, Bvt. Maj. Jacob Zeilen, Maj. William B. Slack, Surg. Solomon Sharpe, USN, Surg. Charles D. Maxwell, USN, and P. T. Woodbury, Judge Advocate.[104] The first case to be called before the Board was that of Captain Brevoort.

The proceedings opened the next day with Judge Advocate Woodbury closely questioning Brevoort regarding his ability to take command of a company for service in the field. Would the weather have any effect on his ability to perform active service? What exactly were his duties during the previous year? Brevoort answered all the inquiries in a forthright manner. He assured the Board that there was nothing that impaired his ability to perform duty of any sort. In fact, he had recently led a company of Marines in the funeral procession of an army officer and marched for six or eight miles. After ordering a medical survey on Brevoort to be conducted that afternoon, the Board adjourned for the day.

Brevoort had conducted himself very well in the first day's proceedings. However, the second day's testimony was devastating to his cause. Surgs. Lewis J. Williams, USN, and James Suddards, USN, having performed the required survey, stated that Brevoort suffered from cancer of the jawbone.[105] The disease was so far advanced that most of the upper jaw and the palate bone were destroyed. If it were not for a gutta-percha plug that Brevoort inserted into the roof of his mouth, he would not be able to articulate at all. Both physicians agreed that Brevoort was not able to perform all the duties required of an active field officer. Brevoort called Harris as a witness, who testified that the Captain performed his duties to the entire satisfaction of Headquarters. Harris mentioned that Brevoort's attention to the additional burdens he had dealt with since the war broke out was admirable. Despite Harris' encouraging testimony, Brevoort knew that his age and illness were obstacles that could not be overcome.

He gave up his fight to remain on active duty on November 14, and submitted his request to be placed on the retired list.[106] Brevoort was detached from active duty as of November 22, 1861.[107]

While Brevoort's case was being heard by the Retiring Board, Lt. Colonel Edelin and Major English submitted their requests to be placed on the retired list; Edelin on November 11, and English two days later. Edelin was retired as of November 15, and English as of November 22.[108]

First Lieutenant Henderson did not appear before the Board but his record of continued illness since late 1859 compelled the members to recommend that he be retired. Henderson's name was placed on the retired list as of December 4, 1861.[109]

Bvt. Lt. Col. William Dulany had been a cadet at West Point for less than a year when he was dismissed on April 26, 1814. Despite his dismissal from the Military Academy, he was appointed to the Marine Corps on June 10, 1817. He had forty-four years of distinguished service behind him, including two brevet promotions for gallant and meritorious service. His service record weighed heavily in his favor, but his date of birth, June 4, 1800, worked against him. Dulany appeared before the Board prepared to defend his physical condition.

The physicians who examined Dulany found him remarkably well-fit for his age, rendering a defense of his fitness and age moot. Dulany was so preoccupied with that aspect of the proceedings that he very nearly tripped himself up in answering a relatively simple question regarding his ability to put a large body of Marines through battalion drill. Caught off guard, Dulany stammered, "With some little reading and application, and looking over the tactics, I feel sure that I could, I do not feel myself as capable in going through the minutiae of the drill as some other officers of the Corps. I know I am not. I believe I could not be technical about giving orders of command without looking them over. I consider myself capable of commanding a battalion, though I might make some errors in doing so, which would be remedied by practice."[110] Despite Dulany's clumsiness in response, the Board found him fit to remain on active duty.

William A. W. Dulany as a full colonel of Marines
MCHC Photograph

1st. Lt. John L. Broome, USMC
Courtesy of Jo Clemons

First Lieutenant Broome was summoned to appear before the Board to see if he had, in fact, recovered from the effects of a nervous breakdown suffered as a consequence of his difficulties over the loyalty oath in the late spring and summer of 1861. Broome's anxiety over the matter of whether the oaths he had drawn up and forwarded to the Navy Department were acceptable had plunged him into a depressed condition. His need for reassurance caused him to corner other officers of USS *Powhatan* in the ward room, on deck and any other place he might come across them, and explain over and over the reasons for his actions. He would then solicit opinions in regard to the likelihood of the Department accepting or rejecting his written oaths. These annoyances got so bad that officers began to avoid him. Broome then began drinking to excess. During the night, he would pace his quarters, talking to himself and disturbing the sleep of those nearby. Complaints were made to Lt. David D. Porter, commander of *Powhatan*.[111] Although Porter was on the friendliest of terms with Broome, he recognized the Marine officer's steady mental and physical deterioration and ordered him to consult with the ship's doctor. Based on Surg. Joseph Wilson's findings, Porter ordered Broome to return to the North and seek treatment.[112]

Broome returned to New York and was confined at the Brooklyn Naval Hospital from September 10–October 25, 1861. Just after his discharge from the hospital, Broome had an interview with Surg. John Lockwood, USN, and received a letter attesting to the restoration of his mental and physical health.[113] Lockwood wrote, "I was clearly of the opinion as to the state of his health of both mind and body has improved since he left this hospital. In fact, I can truly say that he appears in as good health as I have ever known him."[114] Armed with his statement of restored health, Broome reported to the Navy Department on October 30, 1861, ready to return to duty. Welles instructed him to report to Headquarters, Marine Corps.

Before Broome left for New York, the Department had issued an order for a complete examination of his mental and physical condition. The examination was conducted by Surg. William Whelan, Chief of the Bureau of Medicine and Surgery, who reported, "we cannot discover that there exists in his physical or mental condition any reason to disqualify him for the ordinary duties of an officer of his Corps."[115] Thinking his problems in the past and resolved, Broome must have been astonished to receive a summons from the Retiring Board. Broome's hearing before the Retiring Board saw witnesses painting a picture of a very unstable man during the summer of 1861. Despite the accounts of how he conducted himself while aboard *Powhatan*, his appearance before the Board, plus the letters from Surgeons Lockwood and Whelan convinced the members that Broome had been restored to full health, mental and physical. He was returned to duty.

The appearance of Maj. Ward Marston before the Retiring Board presented a singular opportunity for Harris to rid himself and the Navy Department of a long-standing nuisance. Marston had been relieved from duty by the Commandant for cause in November 1860. Since then, hardly a week had gone by without at least one letter from Marston, received by either Harris, the Secretary of the Navy, or the President, complaining of the injustice done him and pleading for his return to duty.

Marston had attended the United States Military Academy, but did not graduate. He was forced to resign from the academy as a result of deficiencies in his studies on October 31, 1818. He entered the Marine Corps as second lieutenant on March 3, 1819, and his career for the next twenty-seven years was unremarkable. He was promoted to first lieutenant on October 30, 1821, brevetted captain, for ten years' service in the same grade on October 30, 1831, and to captain, ranking from July 1, 1834.

Ward Marston, shown here wearing the shoulder straps of a lieutenant colonel of Marines
Courtesy of Mrs. Manly L. Curry

During the Mexican War, Marston, then commander of the Marine Guard of the USS *Savannah* on the California coast, performed noteworthy service ashore. He commanded the Marines in several engagements in the field and accepted the surrender of a Mexican force at Mission Santa Clara on January 2, 1847. He was, however, found guilty of scandalous conduct by a court-martial on September

17, 1847, and when Congress applied the provisions of the act of March 3, 1847, that twelve officers of the Marine Corps were to be dropped, Marston was selected as one of the twelve. Political connections restored him to his rank on March 3, 1849, and he received a brevet promotion to major dating from January 2, 1847, for his Mexican War services. His promotion to full major came on December 10, 1855.

On November 8, 1860, Marston was relieved of his command of Marine Barracks, Philadelphia due to sloppiness in preparing the muster rolls of his post. He then began a campaign of letter-writing in an effort to be restored to duty. In 1860, Marston wrote a total of twenty-two letters to the Commandant or the Department. The flood of letters intensified when the war broke out, and lasted right up to the time that he was called before the Retiring Board. All of his letters claimed his efforts to be restored to his command were a matter of honor, which, no doubt, played a significant role in the affair. However, an August 1861 letter to Welles was probably more honest when Marston complained that his absence from duty was costing him a great deal of money. In fact, since being relieved, he had lost his servant, forage allotment, double rations, quarters allowance, fuel allowance and other emoluments totaling $176.00 per month.[116] As with the dozens of other letters he had written, including two to Lincoln, no satisfaction was forthcoming. Marston saw his appearance before the Board as his last chance to be restored to duty. He came to New York well-prepared.

Testimony by Surgeon Suddards achieved the desired result for Marston as far as his health was concerned. Suddards testified that Marston was extremely well-fit for a man of his years. There was no physical reason to prevent him from serving on active duty ashore or afloat.[117]

Harris was then called as a witness for the Government. He recited a long history of Marston's shortcomings and attempted to point out that even though the Major might be physically qualified for active service, his errors in judgment clearly demonstrated that his mental capacity had been diminished during the course of his long years of service.

Marston launched his own cross-examination of Harris with questions that gave pause to the idea that his mental agility was anything but diminished. Harris was barraged with names, dates, contents of letters, all of which indicated Marston seemed to have the capacity for total recall. Harris was forced to admit that he couldn't remember the many facts that Marston presented in his interrogatories (bringing the Commandant's own mental prowess into question). Marston so successfully refuted the many charges made in the testimony of Harris that his one breach of discipline, the errors on his muster rolls from Philadelphia, was reduced to insignificance. The Board, much to Harris' disgust, judged Marston fit for active duty.[118]

7

The Marine Battalion and the South Atlantic Blockading Squadron

Confidential

Marine Barracks
Washington, 9th Augt. 1861.

Dear Major,

I recd. a verbal notice yesterday from the Secretary of the Navy, that a joint expedition, (Army & Navy) was being fitted on a large scale for important operations on our coast—in which there will be two hundred & fifty to three hundred Marines—and asked me if you would not be a proper officer to comd. the Marines, to which I replied, there was none more suitable if you would admit of it. He said it would take a month or more to prepare it. In that event, I replied, I thought your wound would be well. I was afterwards told, it was the request of the Naval Comdt. that you should be ordered, which is highly complimentary, to be selected for such important duty. All of this is a profound secret, that you must not breathe to any person. Let me hear from you on the subject, and be assured, the men will be much better prepared for service than were at Bull Run.

My kindest regards to Mrs. Zeilen.

Very truly
Yours
Jno Harris

Major J. Zeilen
Com'g. Marines
Philadelphia[1]

The expedition Harris referred to had been discussed at some length during an August 3 meeting between Secretary Welles and Capt. Samuel F. DuPont, USN. The blockade implementation conference, of which DuPont was President, recommended seizing one or more areas on the South Carolina coast as a permanent base from which the blockading fleet would operate. The assets of such permanent bases were obvious. The ships could remain on blockade duty much longer, not having to return north for refit or replenishment. The three coastal areas selected were Bull's Bay, St. Helena Sound, and Port Royal.[2] This recommendation had been discussed with the War Department and the Administration, with accord being reached on the subject. A joint Army-Navy expedition would be fitted out in such a manner as to guarantee this lodgment on the Confederacy's flank. The importance of gaining that foothold was such that *carte blanche* was given to the naval officer selected to oversee the expedition. All this was explained to DuPont during the August 3 meeting where he learned that he would be that naval officer, with "full authority necessary to insure success."[3] DuPont would make all the arrangements and his every need would be supplied. All that the Navy Department asked in return was a victory.

As the meeting progressed and DuPont laid out his plans for the operations, he specifically asked for a battalion of Marines for his force. Should an amphibious landing be necessary to complete the capture of the objective, DuPont, recalling ship to shore operations during the Mexican War in which Marines excelled, registered full faith in the ability of the Marines to land from the sea in the face of hostile fire. Further, DuPont made the stipulation that the Marines were to remain under his direct control and not be transferred to the authority of the War Department.[4]

Capt. Samuel Francis DuPont
Massachusetts Commandery, MOLLUS Collection, USAMHI

Over the course of the next several weeks, DuPont perfected his plans for the expedition and awaited the final word from the Secretary of the Navy to set things in motion. On September 18, Welles told DuPont that the Atlantic Blockading Squadron had been divided into two distinct parts.

The North Atlantic Blockading Squadron, under the command of Capt. Louis M. Goldsborough, Sr., would operate as far as the border of North and South Carolina.[5] DuPont was given command of the South Atlantic Blockading Squadron, with an operational area covering the rest of the Atlantic coast south to Cape Florida. DuPont acknowledged the orders with a request for gunboats with heavy ordnance and light draft. He also reminded Welles of his pledge to provide a battalion of Marines for the expedition. Welles immediately issued orders to the Commandant of the Corps.

Confidential

Navy Department
September 19, 1861.

Sir:

You will have the battalion of Marines, which you had verbal orders to prepare, ready to move from the 1st to the 5th of October.

Very Respectfully, &c.
Gideon Welles[6]

Upon receipt of his orders, Harris was quick to turn them to his advantage. As early as May 1861, he had asked the Department to requisition a supply of the new .58 caliber rifled muskets from the War Department. However, with Harpers Ferry then in rebel hands, there was a critical shortage of the new pattern rifled musket. Available stocks were designated for the volunteer regiments. There were none to spare for the Marine Corps. Harris had to settle for 500 of the old pattern .69 caliber muskets. These were the weapons that the Marine Battalion had carried into battle at Bull Run. Harris thought them outmoded then and certainly considered these muskets totally unsuited for the intended service of the battalion he was now organizing. He used the urgency of the operation to press his case for replacements. Since Welles had promised the expedition would be supplied with whatever it took to insure victory, he asked the War Department for new rifled muskets.

Harris also requested Welles to authorize the transfer of fifteen of the "most efficient and best instructed privates" from the guards of the Receiving Ships at New York and Boston.[7] Harris ordered the commanding officers of Marine Barracks, Boston, Portsmouth, New York, and the Washington Navy Yard for the cream of their garrisons. To Lieutenant Colonel Edelin at Boston, Harris wrote,

"Let them all be of your best drilled men for immediate duty."[8] To Captain Brevoort at Brooklyn, Harris issued an identical order in regard to the experience of the men, and added, "See that the men from the Receiving Ship are equally as efficient. . . . Tell Sergeant Lilly [Orderly Sergeant Benjamin F., in charge of the Marine Guard aboard USS *North Carolina*, Receiving Ship of the Brooklyn Navy Yard] he had better send a good sergeant with them. One that will be able to rough it."[9] Further instructions were given in regard to what the Marines were to take with them. Undress uniforms were to be worn; full dress coats and caps left behind. Each Marine was to take only his overcoat, blanket, and knapsack, with only what he could carry in it. In the event that shortages appeared, Harris ordered Quartermaster Slack to have on hand a sufficient supply of clothing and accouterments to see that every Marine was completely outfitted.

With orders issued in regard to the enlisted men and noncommissioned officers, Harris turned to the problem of assigning officers to the battalion. Zeilen, first choice to command the Marine Battalion, was still not ready for field service because of the wound he received at Bull Run. Consequently, Harris placed Maj. John G. Reynolds in command of the organization. Seven first lieutenants were detailed to the battalion: James Wiley, George R. Graham, James Lewis, Louis M. Goldsborough, Frank Munroe, John H. Grimes, and Robert W. Huntington.[10] The first three had a total of thirty-four years service with the Corps, while the last three, although short-timers, were veterans of Bull Run. Nine second lieutenants were selected for duty: William H. Parker, Eugene B. Sturgeon, Henry A. Bartlett, Thomas L. McElrath, Eugene A. Smalley, Henry B. Hoff, Samuel H. Matthews, Alfred Devereux, and Charles H. Nye.[11] All but Parker were from the incoming group of appointees, and all but Smalley without any combat experience.[12]

Samuel Reynolds, Orderly Sergeant of Marine Barracks, Washington, and a veteran of the Mexican War, was detailed as battalion sergeant major. His initial duty was to select the noncommissioned officers for service, and, from all the enlisted men arriving from the different posts, 300 of the most experienced, best drilled privates. They were to be housed separately from the rest of the enlisted Marines, and, after the final selection was made, undergo extensive battalion drill.

The last appointment to the battalion caused a storm of controversy which came as something of a shock to the Commandant. Since eight of the second lieutenants were in service for little more than a month, Harris decided to send Maj. Augustus S. Nicholson, Adjutant and Inspector of the Corps, with the battalion. His fourteen years of experience would lend a steadying influence to the new men. Nicholson, upon receipt of his orders, took immediate umbrage. He fired off a letter of protest to the Secretary of the Navy, expounding theatrically, even pompously:

> I feel sir, that I would be unworthy of the office I now hold if I were to quietly submit to the official outrage cast upon me by this order without calling upon the Honorable Secretary of the Navy to rectify an injury which I feel has been unintentionally put upon me. This order . . . places me under the command of an officer whose commission as a major is junior to mine. . . .

He went on to say that he was ready to serve his country at any time, "but cannot feel wounded at the receipt of an order which deprives me of my rank, thereby inflicting a punishment which is the province of a Court-martial. . . ."[13]

Harris, in forwarding Nicholson's epistle to Welles, wrote an accompanying letter in which he pointed out that the officer whom Nicholson objected to serving under, Major Reynolds, although appointed to the rank of major twenty-four days after Nicholson's own advancement to that grade, held "a Brevet Major's commission when Major Nicholson held that of a second lieutenant but six months." Further, Nicholson had willingly served under Reynolds at the Battle of Bull Run despite the seniority issue. Harris also stated that Nicholson had openly talked about resigning his commission at the beginning of the war, but, when the position of adjutant was vacated, such talk immediately ceased. Harris hoped that the Department would, in view of Nicholson's "contrived caviling and insubordination," give him his "due reprimand and (let him) be now and henceforth checked."[14]

Much to Harris' chagrin, no reprimand was given to Nicholson. Moreover, since the Adjutant's official sensibilities were so offended by the thought of having to serve under Reynolds, Welles ordered Harris to countermand the orders assigning Nicholson to the battalion.[15] The matter was settled, at least for the present.

The next week was spent preparing the battalion for its departure, seeing that every Marine's wardrobe was complete in every respect, and making sure that the best of the enlisted men were selected for service. At 8:42 A.M., October 15, 1861, the telegraph at Headquarters clattered into action with the message, "Get the Battalion ready to embark on the 'Pawnee' this morning."[16] The telegram was followed by a letter from Welles, repeating the order to embark the Marine Battalion, and added the news that its destination was Hampton Roads.

The fleet being assembled by DuPont at Hampton Roads would develop into the largest ever assembled in the Western Hemisphere. Initially, fifty ships ranging from steam-driven warships to chartered ferry boats would form DuPont's squadron. More would be added as the squadron cruised south to its destination.[17] Twelve thousand army troops under the command of Brig. Gen. Thomas W. Sherman, USV, took passage aboard several transports.[18] Sherman's orders from Lt. Gen. Winfield Scott were very specific. No land officer could be subjected to the orders of a naval officer, and vice versa. The relationship between the land and naval forces was narrowly defined, with a strict accountability:

> Cordiality and deference on the part of our land forces toward those of our Navy, in the joint service in question, need scarcely be enjoined. Hearty reciprocity can not fail to be the result. To this end free and frequent conferences between the joint commanders are recommended. Accordingly, the President, Commander in Chief of the Army and Navy, requires and expects the most effective and cordial cooperation between the commanders of the expedition, their officers and men, and will hold all, in proportion to rank, to a strict and severe responsibility for any failure to preserve harmony and to secure all the objects of the joint expedition.[19]

Scott's orders mentioned the possibility that some of Sherman's troops might be called upon to serve as Marines aboard ship. However, there was little likelihood of that exigency arising. Marines, in addition to the 328 enlisted men and nineteen officers of the battalion, were attached to eleven warships of the squadron as Guards:

USS *Alabama*: O. Sgt. Dennis Dease, two corporals, and ten privates.

USS *Augusta*: O. Sgt. Thomas Sullivan, two corporals, and ten privates.

USS *Bienville*: O. Sgt. Charles Bradley, two corporals, and twelve privates.

USS *Florida*: O. Sgt. Morris Wassman, two corporals, and ten privates.

USS *Mohican*: O. Sgt. Francis Doyle, two corporals, and ten privates.

USS *Pawnee*: O. Sgt. Timothy O'Brien, one sergeant, two corporals, one drummer, and nineteen privates.

USS *Pocahontas*: O. Sgt. James Linus, two corporals, and ten privates.

USS *Seminole*: O. Sgt. Henry Ulian, two corporals, and ten privates.

USS *Susquehanna*: 1st Lt. Philip R. Fendall, one orderly sergeant, two sergeants, four corporals, one drummer, one fifer, and thirty-eight privates.

USS *Vandalia*: 1st Lt. John I. Schermerhorn, one orderly sergeant, one sergeant, two corporals, one drummer, one fifer, and twenty-one privates.

USS *Wabash*: Capt. Isaac T. Doughty, one orderly sergeant, two sergeants, four corporals, one drummer, one fifer, and forty-five privates.

To be attached to the squadron from her station off Georgetown, South Carolina, was:

USS *Sabine*: Capt. William Stokes Boyd, one orderly sergeant, two sergeants, four corporals, one drummer, one fifer, and forty privates.

These additional two hundred ninety-four enlisted men and three officers from the fleet could, in an emergency, form a reserve for the battalion. Their primary duty, however, would be at the secondary guns of their ships in the coming battle where sea-going Marines customarily served in combat.

USS *Pawnee* took aboard the Marine Battalion at the Washington Navy Yard on the afternoon of October 15, and prepared to steam down the Potomac River to Hampton Roads. However, Capt. Thomas T. Craven came upriver just as the *Pawnee* was getting under way. Craven announced that the new Confederate batteries along the Potomac were fully manned and prepared to oppose passage to Hampton Roads. Pawnee's deep draft would confine the ship to the channel, well within the range of the enemy guns. It was a matter for the Department to decide. Welles and Chief Clerk William Faxon came down to the yard around 6:00 P.M., and, after some deliberation among those concerned, it was decided to remove the Marines from *Pawnee*. The journey down river would be far safer aboard the steamboat *Mount Vernon*, since her draft would allow passage some two miles from the enemy guns. The transfer was made. Mount Vernon passed without incident, while *Pawnee* absorbed a half-dozen shots during her journey to Fort Monroe.[20]

While waiting for the rest of the fleet to rendezvous, the Marines became quite uncomfortable in the crowded conditions aboard

Pawnee. Most of the battalion were lodged on the main deck, squeezed into every available space. So far, all they had to complain of was the lack of room. Should the weather turn foul, the battalion was in for a rough trip. DuPont suggested to Reynolds that it might be a good idea to disperse the battalion among the fleet, at least giving them cover during inclement weather. Reynolds, demurred, wanting to keep the battalion together for the sake of discipline and familiarization between officers and men. As luck would have it, the *Governor,* a steamer, had just unloaded her shipment of guns from Boston at Hampton Roads, and was available for charter. DuPont and Reynolds had a short consultation, and hired the steamer to transport the Marine Battalion.

The next morning, Reynolds stopped by for a brief word, and DuPont learned that the Marine Battalion was not as happy aboard the steamer as he had thought they would be. Reynolds mentioned that his men were complaining about their accommodations, "Your plan, Commodore, was the best after all, to distribute us in the fleet."[21] DuPont, correctly assessing the situation, attributed the complaints to the fact that the Marines did not know how to take care of themselves aboard ship, and expected the Navy to look out for their needs. The fleet commander surmised the young officers expected to be entertained and waited on as though their transport was a cruise ship. Accordingly, DuPont directed the Marines be told that since the charter for the use of *Governor* had not been signed, the original plan to disperse the battalion could still be implemented. Understanding that distribution meant being subordinated to naval officers, all of the Marine officers agreed that the little inconveniences in being left to their own devices was better than being spread among the squadron.[22] Nevertheless, being quartered aboard a chartered vessel without the full complement of naval officers and crew presented some serious problems.

Indeed, the Marines of the battalion were quite unprepared for taking care of themselves aboard ship. No provisions had been made for the battalion to act as a self-contained unit. Consequently, no mess gear had been sent with it. There were no knives, forks, spoons, plates, or cooking pans. Nor were there any small stores such as tobacco or soap, further adding to the discomfort of the Marines. Reynolds had to ask Headquarters to send him all the basics as soon as possible. Harris, thinking he had covered every possible contingency before the battalion left Washington, was chagrined at this turn of events. Harris directed Major Slack to provide the articles from his quartermaster stores. He also promised Reynolds that he would ask the Department to send an order to DuPont authorizing the squadron paymasters to issue small stores and other necessities in the future. [23]

A few days later, DuPont related an incident to his wife which proved to his satisfaction how utterly helpless Marines were aboard ship without guidance from naval officers. Three Marines from the detachment aboard *Wabash*, DuPont wrote, "found a bottle of corrosive sublimate covered with rawheads and crossbones all over; but, it being dark, these they did not see and only smelling the alcohol drank; one will certainly die if not all three."[24] The results of the incident were not so dire as DuPont had predicted. Only two of the Marines, Pvts. Adam Russell and John Wonderly, were sick enough to be sent to the hospital on October 11.[25]

On October 24, Capt. James Lewis, commanding Company C, Marine Battalion, fell victim to a freak accident and had to be replaced. Lewis, while walking near the railroad tracks at Fort Monroe,

Capt. James Lewis
Connecticut State Library

1st Lt. John I. Schermerhorn
NHC Photograph NH 46098

was knocked down by a barrel that was struck by a passing train. The train sent the barrel flying through the air, severely injuring Lewis. Harris had to shuffle assignments, and order 2d Lt. Charles H. Nye to relieve Lieutenant Schermerhorn as commander of the Marine Guard aboard USS *Vandalia*, with Schermerhorn replacing Lewis at the head of Company C.[26] The Marine Battalion had yet to leave Hampton Roads and had already suffered one critical casualty. It did not bode well for an incident-free journey.

At 9:00 A.M., October 29, 1861, the fleet sortied from the anchorage at Hampton Roads. Its smooth departure was upset almost immediately. USS *Unadilla* broke down and had to be towed by *Governor*, much to the delight of the Marines. Once the fleet reached the open sea off Hampton Roads, the ships sought and settled into their places. The transports formed into three columns with gunboats protecting them on all sides. *Governor* assumed her position at the head of the center column of transports once *Unadilla* had been repaired.

During the evening of October 30, an incident, humorous, when viewed from hindsight, but deadly serious during its duration, took place. The commanding officer of the Coast Survey vessel *Vixen* became ill. Having no doctor aboard, he steered his ship to one of the transports where he hoped he would find a medical officer. Running the entire length of his column of ships, Lt. Robert Platt, USN, turned *Vixen* and bore down on *Governor*. In his haste to reach a doctor, Platt neglected to make the proper recognition signals. To Major Reynolds, the unidentified ship bearing down upon his transport was a privateer intent on breaking up the fleet. Reynolds quickly ordered the Marine Battalion to form and prepare for battle. Disaster was narrowly averted by the last-minute recognition of *Vixen* as a friendly vessel.[27]

During the forenoon of November 1, a gale blew in from the southeast. The fleet fought to maintain its alignment, but the elements proved too strong to master. By morning, only a handful of the fifty ships that left Hampton Roads in their tight and orderly formation was in sight of the Flagship. DuPont was worried about those ships blown off course by the storm. His men of war had been built to handle heavy seas, but the troop transports were coastal steamers, not used to battling that rough weather. Somewhere beyond the horizon were nearly three dozen storm-tossed craft with their precious cargo of humanity. At best, the storm had deprived the soldiers, crew, and Marines of a night's sleep and an uncomfortable loss of appetite. The worst was too terrible to contemplate.

Governor proved no match for the storm. The wind began to freshen about 10:00 A.M., and, within an hour, the hog braces began to buckle. Charles L. Litchfield, master of the ship, fortifying himself with liquor, was unable to handle the crisis. John Weidman, Acting Master, USN, quickly sent Litchfield below, and assumed command of the transport.[28] The sponsons were leaking, the pumps working only fitfully, the hog braces were broken in several places, and two feet of water was in the hold of the ship. Weidman called upon the chief mate and chief engineer to put their skills to fix those problems, but all he received in response were the blank stares of men paralyzed by fear. Weidman later said these two "conducted themselves as cowards and traitors," and of the civilian crew "the least I can say is that they were very, very worthless."[29]

Dismissing the merchant officers and crew from his presence with great contempt, Weidman called on the Marines, shouting for anyone with mechanical training to step forward. One private volunteered, and within seconds found himself up to his knees in water, hard at work on the balky pumps. While he manned the pumps, one hundred of his comrades formed a bucket brigade, and, after a time, began to make progress on lowering the water level in the hold. The remainder of the battalion was on deck, and, with ropes lashed around the hog braces, struggled to keep them intact. Lieutenant Huntington, who told his father that he thought the ship was unsafe before she left Hampton Roads, afterward wrote to tell him his worst fears had been realized. The ship threatened to come apart and the hog braces were perilously close to caving in, despite the valiant efforts of the Marines. Describing the chaotic situation on deck, Huntington wrote, "We had them (the hog braces) braced up by ropes, and the men hung to them for dear life for if the port beam had fallen, it would have carried away the whole side with the wheel house and the starboard would have crushed the boiler down below."[30]

About 4:00 P.M., the hog braces began to show evidence of total collapse. Marines immediately grabbed any available wood and used it to shore up the weakened timbers. Officers and men put their backs into the job and, in a short time, secured the situation. No sooner had the problem of the hog braces been overcome, when the chains supporting the smokestack snapped and all but three feet of it went over the side. Then the steam pipe burst. From then on, a head of steam could only be developed if the engine was shut down. These minutes without power gave the ship over to the vicissitudes of the storm. Without steam from the engine, the pumps were useless. The Marines on the bucket brigade could barely keep pace with the water coming into the hold. The situation went beyond being simply dangerous. It was critical. Weidman ordered the flag to be set to the position of distress, half mast, with union down.

Just about dusk, a steamer was seen in the distance towing another victim of the storm. All six distress rockets were fired. A response was seen, but no indication that the ship would come to the assistance of *Governor* was observed. Reynolds ordered several Marines to fire their muskets as a continuation of the distress signal, but it soon became apparent that the ship had all she could handle with the vessel under her tow.

During the night, the gasket blew out from the cylinder head, stopping the engine until jury-rigged repairs could be made. Shortly afterward, the rudder chain was lost overboard and the rudderhead of the engine broke, leaving the ship at the mercy of the elements.

Reynolds clearly recognized the only thing that kept the ship intact and afloat was the untiring exertions of his men, labors born of desperation. No one was sure he would live to see the morning.[31]

But the morning of November 2 did come, and *Governor* was miraculously still afloat. The seas had calmed somewhat and two vessels were seen coming in answer to its distress signals, USS *Isaac Smith* and *Young Rover*. By 10:00 A.M., *Isaac Smith* was close enough to lower a boat, attempting to pass a hawser between her and the helpless *Governor.* Litchfield tried to make fast the hawser, but his skills were overcome by nervous exhaustion, not to mention copious amounts of consumed alcohol, and the hawser slipped away. A second attempt to rig a hawser between the two ships proved as fruitless as the first. Eventually, the hawser was secured between the two ships, but the strain parted the massive rope and a pall of gloom fell over the Marines. *Young Rover* ran in close and her captain let them know that he would stand by until the last extremity. The news was passed to the Marines and a cheer rose. It was not much of a cheer, the men knowing full well what was meant by "the last extremity." What did encourage the Marines was the information that USS *Sabine*; Capt. Cadwalader Ringgold, USN, commanding, was close by.[32]

The gale that brought the Marine Battalion so close to its doom was, in effect, its salvation. When the storm blew up, *Sabine* left her position on the blockade off Georgetown, South Carolina, to ride out the gale in deeper waters. Had the ship not hauled off to sea, she would never have been in a position to see or be seen by *Young Rover.* By 3:00 P.M., *Sabine* came close enough to *Governor* to pass the message that everyone from the foundering vessel would be taken on board. The spirits of the men were immediately lifted, as a full-throated cheer burst forth from the Marines. The work to keep the *Governor* afloat was renewed with vigor.

Sabine dropped her anchor and paid out chain until she was close to the stern of *Governor.* The transport did the same and the distance between the two ships closed until a hawser could be passed from *Sabine* with relative ease. A second hawser was also secured between them.

In order to transfer the Marines from the wreck to the *Sabine*, a spar was rigged on the stern of the frigate, fastened so as to pivot between the two ships. The spar would be sent across from the frigate with a bosun's chair attached to the end. A Marine from the deck of *Governor* would secure himself in the chair, and, by way of ropes attached to the spar, be pulled back to the safety of *Sabine.* At 10:00 P.M. the transfer began. One Marine went safely across, then another, and another. For those waiting their turn to cross, the process was excruciatingly slow. The seas began to rise, adding to the anxiety of those aboard the transport, but the hawsers held fast and the spar continued to swing slowly between the two ships. The wind began to pick up after midnight, slowing the operation. By 1:00 A.M., the winds were at gale force and the pitching of the two ships strained the hawsers. Thirty Marines had passed to safety when one of the hawsers snapped, then the other. The stricken transport rose and plunged with the seas, and those aboard were seized with a fear that each time the bow of the ship sliced through the waves, she would continue her downward passage, taking all with her.

Ringgold also despaired when the hawsers gave way, but Lucius H. Beattie, Acting Master, USN, and several of his sailors leaped from the stern of *Sabine* to the deck of *Governor*.[33] Soon, the hawsers were fastened again. But the sea was relentless in its battle to claim *Governor*. The furious pitching and rolling of the waves brought the largest of the hawsers against the transport's stem. The sharp stem cut through the eleven-inch diameter of the hawser as though it were a piece of string. A heavy steel chain cable was passed across and secured. The rescue was begun anew but the fury of the storm caused the chain cable to snap, sending the foundering transport swinging away from the frigate, attached only by one remaining hawser. Beattie called across the waves to Ringgold, saying the transport was sinking.

Ringgold acted quickly. Before the last hawser succumbed to the elements, he ordered men to the heavy rope to haul the battered vessel alongside. As soon as the transport was close, Ringgold called across to the Marines to try and judge the roll of the ships and jump at the opportune moment to land safely on the deck of Sabine. Thirty or forty Marines managed to save themselves in this fashion, but one misjudged his leap and fell into the sea between the ships. A moment later, the two ships collided, crushing the unfortunate Marine between the hulls.[34] As the ships parted, Ringgold saw that another such collision would rip the transport asunder. He ordered the hawser be let out until the wreck was safely astern.

Up to this point, the discipline of the Marines had been unshakable. However, when *Governor* was passing to the stern of *Sabine*, six Marines broke ranks, and, panic-stricken, leaped over the side and tried to swim to *Sabine*. They were all drowned.[35] The hellish vision was imprinted into Ringgold's consciousness with searing permanence.

> Here succeeded a scene that beggars description; the despair felt on feeling this attempt at rescue and proved so unsuccessful, the bubbling cry of drowning men, the confusion on board the wreck, the unnatural glare of the

USS *Sabine* rescuing the Marine Battalion from the transport *Governor*

NA Photograph 127-N-522162 of a Color Lithograph in the Marine Corps Museum Collection

> sea and sky, caused by the rockets and the red and blue lights (signals for assistance to the *Isaac Smith* and *Young Rover*), presented a scene that might well have struck terror to the stoutest heart.[36]

Aboard *Governor*, Lieutenant Huntington encouraged his men to keep the buckets going. The Marines below decks had no idea what was going on above them. The sound of the waves pounding against the hull and the howl of the wind was all they heard. All they could see from the outside was the eerie glow of *Sabine*'s blue lights filtering through the portholes, and, being new to life aboard ship, were ignorant of their meaning or origin. Then came the collision of the two ships. Fearing the crash was but a preliminary to the side of the ship giving way, the men stopped work, their eyes darting about looking for the quickest way topside. Huntington told them the crash was "nothing but the gingerbread work," going over, and motioned them back to their jobs. But the men stood motionless, knee-deep in the water, transfixed by the sound of the crash still ringing in their ears and the ghostly pale of the blue lights. Suddenly, Cpl. William McMullin cried out, "It is the signal of a ship alongside!" The intensity of the moment broken by McMullin's exclamation, the men began to laugh, exhilarated by the knowledge that rescue was close at hand. The release of tension was too much for one Marine who grabbed a life preserver and made for the stairs. Huntington grabbed him. With a single motion, he tore off the life jacket and sent the man flying back to his place in the bucket line.

Sure their deliverance was close at hand, the Marines worked the buckets with a burst of enthusiasm. While his men bailed the hold, Huntington tried to shore up a breach near the gangway. Water was rushing in through the opening every time the ship rolled. Huntington knocked a cabin door from its hinges and started across the deck with a mind to wedge it against the hole. He afterward wrote his father how this simple task nearly cost his life.

> I just got there, and (put) the door down sideways when a sea struck the door, at the lower side first, of course, taking my feet right out from under me. The door with me on it sleeved around and was sailing with the wave right out the port. I had a long overcoat on and one of the corporals who always was a great friend of mine, took a rope in one hand and threw himself, caught my coat tail with the other. The door went right out from under me, and there I was—saved half way . . . out of the port.[37]

Around 3:30 A.M., November 3, the sea began to subside and the frantic bailing in the hold of *Governor* gained the upper hand in the race with the waves. The Marine turned mechanic made the pumps work again and Reynolds had reason to hope that the ship would remain afloat until sunrise. All of his Marines were completely worn out by the battle with the sea, and, hailing Captain Ringgold, Reynolds suggested everyone should take advantage of the calm water to rest in preparation for whatever awaited them at dawn. Ringgold agreed.

At dawn, Ringgold put his port quarter boat into the sea. He hailed Reynolds and told him that the last hope to save his battalion was to abandon ship. Each Marine was to tie a rope around his waist, throw the rest of the rope to the boat crew, then jump into the sea and swim or be hauled to the boat. Reynolds quickly ordered the first private over the side. The boat's crew plucked him from the waves and rowed him safely to the frigate. More boats from *Sabine* were lowered and the rescue began in earnest. Maintaining strict discipline, the Marines stayed at their posts until each company was called. Then, in regular order, each one tied the rope on and went over the side. By 8:00 A.M., the surviving Marines were safely aboard *Sabine*. Reynolds was the last to leave the ship.[38]

2d Lt. Samuel H. Matthews, USMC
NHC Photograph NH 48080

Since the wreck was still afloat, efforts were made to save the arms and equipment of the battalion. Lieutenants Huntington and Grimes volunteered to return to the transport to bring back what could be salvaged. Nearly all of the arms, half the accouterments, and half the cartridges were saved before the wreck became too dangerous to remain aboard. Almost all of the field gear, knapsacks, haversacks, and canteens went down with the ship. Huntington saved little more than the clothes on his back. Putting the matter succinctly to his father, he wrote, "I lost a bundle."[39] At 3:30 P.M., the sea finally claimed *Governor*.

Major Reynolds was intensely proud of the way his Marines had conducted themselves throughout the ordeal. He reported to DuPont:

> Too much praise can not be bestowed upon the officers

> and men under my command. All did nobly. The firmness with which they performed their duty is beyond all praise. For forty-eight hours they stood at the ropes and passed water to keep the ship afloat. Refreshments in both eating and drinking were passed to them by non-commissioned officers. It is impossible for troops to have conducted themselves better under such trying circumstances.[40]

Weidman's report, while criticizing the merchant seamen, praised Capt. James Wiley, and Lieutenants Huntington, Bartlett, and Matthews for rendering great assistance in keeping the vessel afloat.[41] DuPont told Reynolds the good conduct and moral courage displayed by the Marines during their ordeal had earned his warm appreciation. Further, the situation the battalion had overcome "was a more trying one than any encounter with our enemy could have been."[42] Regrettably, the unflagging efforts of 1st Lt. William S. Boyd, commander of *Sabine*'s Marine Guard, went unreported. He was at the center of all the rescue activities throughout the entire period and, in the process, damaged his lungs, forcing him to give up his post aboard *Sabine* and return North for treatment.[43]

When news of the rescue of the Marine Battalion reached the North, Ringgold became the man of the hour. Accolades and awards came from every quarter. A resolution passed the Common Council of the City of New York on January 20, 1862:

> tendering to Captain Ringgold, the officers and crew of the United States frigate *Sabine*, on behalf of the citizens of New York, thanks for their heroic, humane, and successful efforts in saving the lives of so many human beings from the wreck of the ill-fated steamer *Governor*, which foundered during the severe storm which overtook the United States squadron while proceeding from Fortress Monroe to the attack and capture of Port Royal.[44]

The Legislature of the State of Maryland voted an almost identical resolution of thanks to Ringgold, his officers, and crew on March 3, 1862.

The Life-Saving Benevolent Society of New York awarded Ringgold its gold medal, and he replied:

> To save life is an ever sacred duty. There were circumstances, however, that made the rescue in this instance peculiarly appropriate. The Marine Corps, as is well known, forms a very important branch of our Navy. As a body, it has no superior in point of discipline, gallantry, and devotion to duty.[45]

Capt. Cadwalader Ringgold
Author's Collection

Of all the honors received by Ringgold, the one that surely meant most to him was a sword, specially made by Tiffany & Company, purchased and presented by the men of the Marine Battalion as an expression of their eternal gratitude. The presentation ceremony took place aboard USS *Sabine* on July 1, 1862. Accompanying the sword was a poem written by Pvt. William Gould formerly of Company A, Marine Battalion.[46]

The *Governor*'s two-day battle with the elements put the Marine Battalion completely out of touch with DuPont. In fact, Reynolds had no idea of exactly where the fleet was heading. After consultation with Ringgold, Reynolds decided to open his sealed orders which confirmed the many rumors both officers had heard. The objective was Port Royal. Ringgold concluded that since the Marine Battalion was sure to spearhead any landing, he should join the fleet as quickly as possible. A course to join DuPont was laid on and the *Sabine* majestically pointed her bow toward Port Royal. The battalion, having been awake for almost forty-eight hours, turned in for some much needed sleep.

While the Marines were aboard *Sabine*, recovering from their ordeal, the vanguard of DuPont's fleet arrived off Port Royal. There DuPont found "eight or nine vessels," already at anchor, and was heartened to see "the horizon dotted with uprising sail."[47] He was relieved to hear of the rescue of the Marine Battalion from Lt. James W. A. Nicholson of USS *Isaac Smith*, and sent USS *Augusta* to tow *Sabine* to Port Royal as rapidly as possible.[48] The battalion and *Sabine*'s battery were still very much in DuPont's plan of action.

Just after noon, DuPont began sending his shallow draft transports and gunboats across the Port Royal bar, working them into position for the coming attack. As the last of the transports was being shepherded across, four Confederate warships under the command of Capt. Josiah Tattnall, CSN, CSS *Savannah*, *Resolute*, *Lady Davis*, and *Sampson*, slipped into the sound and opened fire at a distance of a mile and a half.[49] DuPont's gunboats returned the fire, closing within range of the forts. A few shots were exchanged between the forts and USS *Pawnee*, none taking effect. After a forty-minute duel, the warships withdrew without injury to either side.

The next day, November 5, the deep draft warships and transports were channeled across the bar and into position. DuPont saw the fortifications for the first time and became convinced that his ships would have to silence those batteries before the troops could be landed. Reports came in from gunboats doing picket duty that steamers ferried reinforcements to the forts all through the night. DuPont grew more and more agitated. He wanted to attack quickly, before any more reinforcements could be added to the enemy defenses, but he just did not have sufficient firepower to begin the attack. He needed the one hundred guns of the heavy frigates *Sabine* and *Savannah*, but to wait for them would give the rebels more time to strengthen their defenses, making his mission all the more difficult. DuPont finally decided that he would strike at once. The battle would have been opened at dusk, but the unfortunate groundings of the Flagship *Wabash* and *Susquehanna* canceled operations for the day. He delayed the attack until November 6.

The day of the attack, November 6, dawned with heavy winds from the southwest and a tide running as an ally of the defenders. To make the attack under these conditions ran contrary to DuPont's plan of attack. He had intended to use the moving bombardment tactic introduced at Hatteras Inlet by Commodore Stringham. However, that combination of wind and tide would slow his attack, giving the forts' gunners a few additional moments to train their guns on his ships. One or two seconds might make the difference between a near miss and disaster. DuPont decided the day would be better spent in drill and hoping for a very calm morning for November 7.

DuPont's final battle plan called for the warships to form in two columns. Upon entering the channel between Fort Walker on Hilton Head Island, and Fort Beauregard on Bay Point, the squadron would open fire on both fortifications as they passed. The main column consisted of the Flagship *Wabash* in the lead, followed by USS *Susquehanna*, *Mohican*, *Seminole*, *Pawnee*, *Unadilla*, *Ottawa*, *Pembina*, and *Vandalia*, the last under the tow of *Isaac Smith*. The flanking column was formed by USS *Bienville*, *Seneca*, *Curlew*, *Penguin*, and *Augusta*. Once the squadron had passed up the channel, beyond the range of the forts, the main column was to turn back, concentrating its fire on Fort Walker. The flanking column was to take up a position to enfilade Fort Walker, and prevent any sudden dash of Tattnall's flotilla against the transports. The main column would continue to steer an elliptical course, keeping up its fire until the Confederates surrendered.[50]

At 9:00 A.M., November 7, all the ships of the squadron beat to quarters. At 9:17, *Wabash* steered for the enemy, the columns forming on her. Ten minutes later, Fort Walker opened fire with Fort Beauregard following. DuPont held his fire until his forward pivot gun had a clear shot at Fort Walker. At 10:03, the first answering shot from the fleet sped on its way. For the next twenty-seven minutes, the starboard batteries of the flagship and the rest of the column delivered a tremendous fire to Fort Walker, ceasing only when guns could no longer bear on the enemy works. The roar of the cannonade was so great that it was heard in Fernandina, Florida, seventy miles to the south. The smoke from the guns ashore and afloat made visibility almost impossible.

As *Wabash* made her turn and prepared to fire on Fort Walker with her port battery, DuPont's well-laid battle plans went awry. Only *Susquehanna* from the main column followed. *Bienville*, after chasing Tattnall's gunboats away from the area, did not return to her post in the flanking column. Rather, she settled in behind *Susquehanna*, and, contrary to orders, proceeded to follow the two warships on the run past Fort Walker. The commanding officers of the rest of the ships lost all sense of order amid the smoke, noise, confusion, and excitement of the battle. Instead of following the plan, the rest of the squadron took up enfilading positions north of Fort Walker. Despite DuPont's repeated signals to the errant vessels to close on his Flagship, they held their positions until the end of the battle.[51]

The remnant of the main column steamed past Fort Walker, their guns delivering a withering barrage upon the enemy for several minutes. At 10:40, the starboard battery of the flagship opened fire on Fort Beauregard for fifteen minutes, *Susquehanna* and *Bienville* following suit. *Wabash* turned at 11:18, and ran in to within 600 yards of Fort Walker. Cruising past the enemy works, salvoes from the column devastated the battery.[52] Swinging around for another pass, the three vessels reopened fire at 11:50. At 12:10, the fourth circuit completed, DuPont ceased fire and hauled off to regroup his squadron and give the worn-out crews a chance to rest before resuming the battle.

Throughout the battle, the Marine Guard aboard *Wabash* was used as a reserve, "and whenever called upon, rendered prompt assistance at the guns with the good conduct which has always characterized their corps."[53] The guards aboard the other vessels of the squadron performed their duties in similar fashion.

Having done what little he could with his tiny fleet, Tattnall retreated to the safety of Skull Creek, north of Fort Walker. Observing

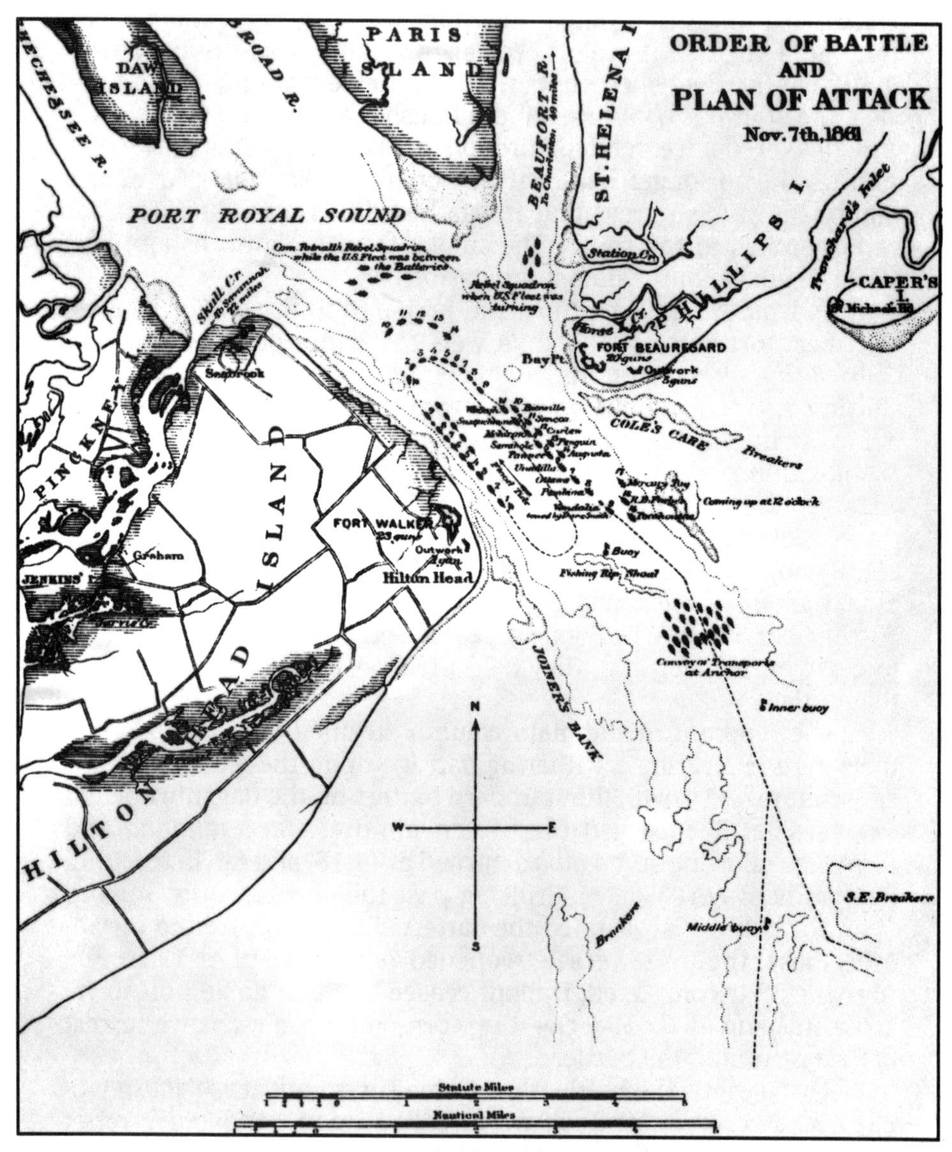

Order of Battle and Plan of Attack, November 7, 1861

NHC Photograph, NH 85538

Bombardment of Forts Walker and Beauregard, Port Royal, South Carolina
NHC Photograph NH 001099

the reduced fire from the fort, he assumed the morale and the ammunition supply at Fort Walker were running low. Running his ships into Seabrook's Landing at the rear of Hilton Head Island, Tattnall landed the Marine Guards of CSS *Savannah* and *Resolute*, sending them under Capt. George Holmes, CSMC, to reinforce the beleaguered garrison of Fort Walker. Shortly thereafter, Tattnall landed a detachment of seamen and the Marine Guard of CSS *Sampson*, and sent them to Fort Walker with a supply of naval ammunition.

While the Confederates rushed across Hilton Head Island to bolster their comrades, a signal was raised from USS *Ottawa* that Fort Walker appeared to be abandoned. A few minutes later, the same signal came from USS *Pembina*. DuPont ordered this flagship to within 500 yards of the works and opened fire. There was no response. At 2:12 P.M., Cdr. John Rodgers, USN, was ordered away with a boat's crew of sailors and Marines under a flag of truce to determine the status ashore.[54] Within a few moments after the landing, the standard of the United States was seen flying over the fort. As the National Ensign snapped in the breeze, a great roar erupted from the squadron and the transports. The cheer, echoing across the water, broke upon the heels of Fort Walker's fleeing garrison and sped them on their retreat. At 2:45, an exhilarated DuPont brought the flagship to anchor off Fort Walker and sent her Marine Guard ashore under the command of Captain Isaac T. Doughty as an occupation force.[55]

Postwar view of Marine officer Isaac T. Doughty
Courtesy of Russell Parks

The Confederate States Marines under Captain Holmes advanced to within a quarter mile of Fort Walker before the flood of refugees from the work swept past them. Holmes called a halt, and went forward to study the situation. Moments later, the second detachment came up and met the demoralized garrison of Fort Walker still in full flight to the rear. *Sampson*'s Marines, under the command of 2d Lt. David G. Raney, CSMC, quickly stopped most of them and restored order.[56] Next, the detachment moved forward under Tattnall's personal direction. Marching a few hundred yards closer to Fort Walker, the would-be reinforcements found Holmes' Marines waiting for the return of their commander. Tattnall assumed Holmes captured, and, realizing there was nothing more he could do, ordered a withdrawal.[57] Lieutenant Raney was put in charge of the Marines, forming them as a rear guard.[58] As the dispirited rebel sailors and Marines prepared to withdraw, they saw the Stars and Stripes being raised over Fort Walker, and, several minutes later, a detachment of U.S. Marines fan out to secure the abandoned fortification. They wasted no time in retracing their steps to Seabrook's Landing.

Once Fort Walker had been secured by the Marines, DuPont, well pleased that the victory belonged to the Navy, "complete and indisputable," came ashore and formally took possession.[59] A Marine aboard USS *Susquehanna* noted that it was a year to the day since South Carolina had received the news of Lincoln's election and taken the first steps toward secession. He cheerfully told his comrades, "A pleasant way this, of keeping the anniversary of South Carolina's independence!"[60] The army transports were ordered forward, and at 5:45 P.M. DuPont transferred control to Brig. Gen. Horatio G. Wright, USV.[61] The Marines from the flagship remained on picket duty, rounding up Southern stragglers, until ordered back to their ship around 7:30. Owing to the confusion of troops landing from the army transports, and some extensive hunting for souvenirs on the part of the Marines, it was not until 11:00 P.M. that all were finally reported aboard ship.[62]

USS *Seneca* was ordered up to Fort Beauregard at sunset to see if any rebels remained at Bay Point. No movement was observed. *Seneca* anchored for the night and at daybreak sent a landing party ashore. Fort Beauregard was deserted. Nothing remained but the hubris of a vanquished foe. At noon, army troops under the command of Brig. Gen. Isaac I. Stevens, USV, landed and completed the occupation.[63]

The next day, the solemn task of laying to rest those of the fleet who gave their lives for the victory at Port Royal took place. Seventeen boats from *Susquehanna*, *Pawnee*, *Mohican*, *Bienville*, and *Wabash*, escorting the remains of the dead seamen, formed in line and passed through the fleet. The ship's band from *Susquehanna* led the procession, playing funeral dirges as the boats made their way ashore. The coffins were reverently taken up and carried by the messmates of the dead sailors to a grove near the bank of a stream. The flagship's chaplain read the funeral service after which Marines from *Wabash* and *Susquehanna* fired three volleys over the graves.[64]

USS *Sabine*, carrying the Marine Battalion, arrived at Port Royal during the evening of November 7. *Sabine* was becalmed thirty-five miles from Port Royal when the action commenced. The lack of wind, which lent itself to DuPont's victory, and the failure of USS *Augusta* to locate the ship, prevented Ringgold from joining the battle. DuPont, nevertheless, was very pleased to see Ringgold arrive with his "passengers." The battalion was put ashore at Bay Point and set up camp, and quickly assumed the normal routine of garrison service. The earliest surviving report of the guard at Bay Point shows that seven Marines were punished on November 13; two for disobedience of orders, two for complaining on drill, two for talking on drill, and one, a noncommissioned officer, for striking privates.[65] The offenses clearly indicate that Major Reynolds wasted no time in working the tensions of the voyage aboard *Governor* out of his men on the drill field. As one Marine wag versified:

Our commander's name was Reynolds
On that you may depend
And out of eleven hours
It's he will drill you ten.[66]

With the Marine Battalion safely ensconced at Bay Point, Headquarters began the process of restoring the clothing and equipment lost on the *Governor*. Maj. William Russell wrote Reynolds that duplicate clothing rolls, and other paperwork necessary to implement

Marines landing at Fort Walker

NA Photograph 127-N-520461

new issues were being sent to him by steamer. He also said that 20,000 cartridges, seventy-five watch coats and 350 shirts were being dispatched by Quartermaster Slack.[67] Another letter, written by Russell to a concerned family friend of one of the privates lost from the *Governor*, provides an interesting insight into the attitude of the government at that time regarding the families of deceased servicemen.

> I regret to inform you that Lawrence Gorman is reported by the Major commanding the Battalion on board the lost steamer 'Governor,' as having been drowned on the 3rd, inst., while attempting to get on board the Frigate 'Sabine' from the sinking steamer.
>
> Gorman, having been but a few months in service, would have nothing due him on final settlement of his accounts and I am sorry to say that the Government makes no provision for the mothers of those lost in the service.[68]

An immediate consequence of establishing a base at Port Royal was the number of men reporting sick. Within two weeks of making camp on Jenkins Island, the Marines were paying an increasing number of visits to Asst. Surg. David F. Ricketts, the battalion medical officer. As of November 20, Ricketts had treated two cases of intermittent fever, one case of remittent fever, one case of typhoid fever, two cases of scurvy and twenty-eight cases of diarrhea.[69]

Another problem manifested itself on the night of November 20-21, 1861. The local plantation owners having fled at the approach of the Federal invasion fleet, their slaves were left to their own devices. After the occupation of Hilton Head and Bay Point, many Blacks moved to the perimeter of the Union encampments, seeking employment and safety. Several members of the 79th New York State Militia became confused in regard to what sort of employment the women who occupied a shack near Marine sentinel post No. 7 engaged in. There was a commotion in those quarters just around midnight, and Marines on guard apprehended those responsible. 2d Lt. Eugene B. Sturgeon, Officer of the Guard, investigated the matter, and reported, "Certain privates, accompanied by two officers of the 79 Reg. of the N. Y. S. M. had entered the building and endeavored to violate the persons of the negro women who inhabited it, and that the resistance of the women caused the disturbance."[70]

Once the base at Port Royal was established, DuPont began to reconnoiter the surrounding land. He was particularly concerned with denying blockade runners access to the port of Savannah, Georgia. Neutralization of enemy defenses on Tybee Island at the mouth of the Savannah River was the essential first step in cutting off this traffic. Because those defenses were weaker than those of Fort Pulaksi, a brick and mortar fortification on the opposite bank a few miles upriver, DuPont sent only five warships to destroy them.

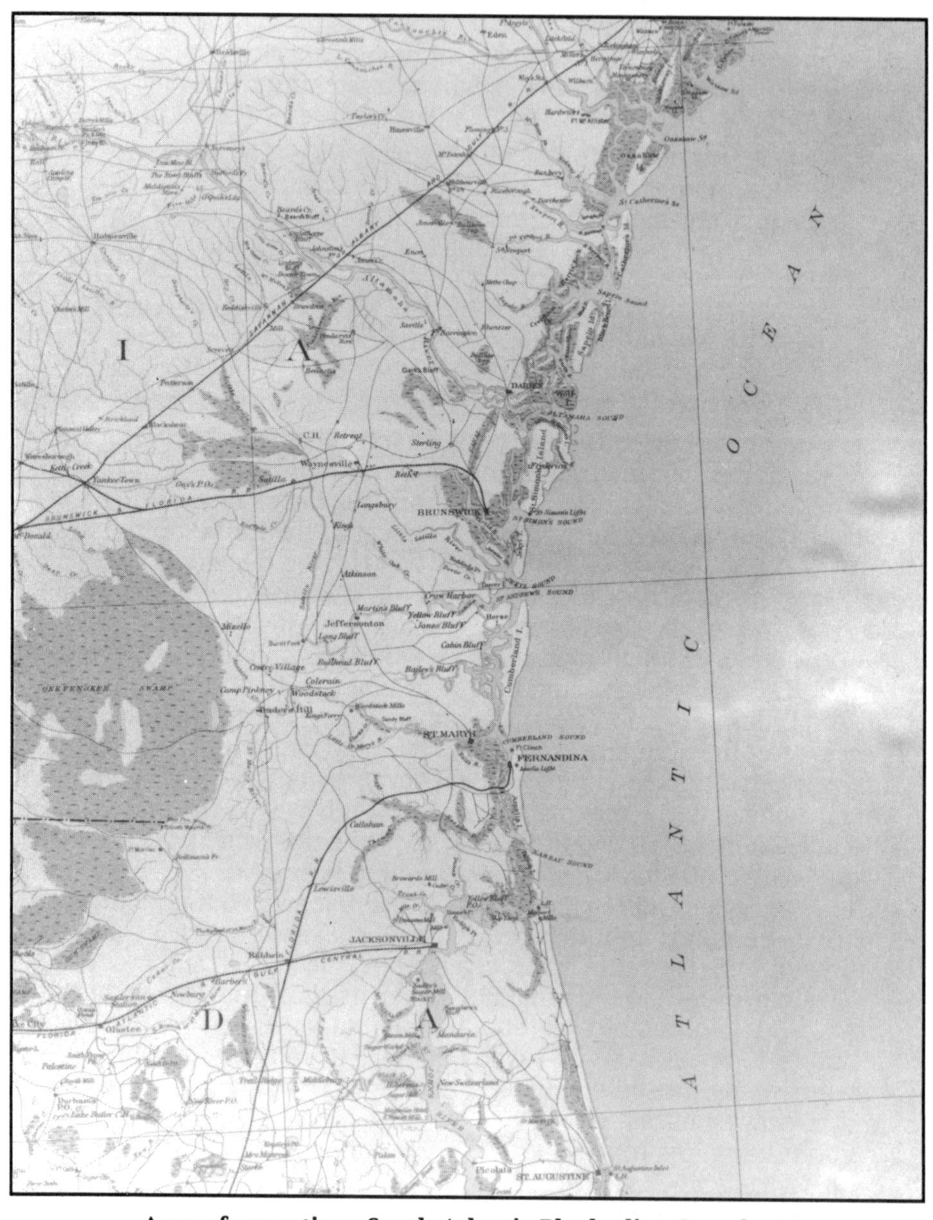

Area of operations South Atlantic Blockading Squadron, November 1861–March 1862

RG 94, Civil War Atlas, plate CXLV

The Martello Tower on Tybee Island
Massachusetts Commandery, MOLLUS Collection, USAMHI

On the morning of November 24, 1861, an expedition under the command of Cdr. John S. Missroon, USN, consisting of USS *Savannah*, *Flag*, *Seneca*, *Augusta*, and *Pocahontas*, approached Tybee Island.[71] Missroon ordered *Seneca* and *Pocahontas* to take the positions at the Martello Tower under fire. There being no reply, a landing party of sailors from *Flag*, *Seneca*, and *Pocahontas*, with the Marine Guard from the latter, went ashore under the command of Cdr. John Rodgers, USN. Finding the defenses abandoned, the landing party hoisted the U.S. flag over the lighthouse. One small portion of Georgia was thus returned to the Union. Leaving a few Marines and sailors with orders to keep the appearance that the place was occupied by a large force, Rodgers took the rest of the landing party and returned to the ship after dark.[72]

Two days later, Tattnall brought his flotilla down the Savannah River from Fort Pulaski. The rebel vessels appeared to be loaded with troops with the objective of retaking Tybee Island. The Confederates opened at long range, but their shells fell far short. *Seneca* and *Pocahontas* returned fire and drove Tattnall's ships back to the protection of Fort Pulaski. Upon hearing of the foray, DuPont decided to bring part of his squadron to Tybee Island to deter any future counterattacks.

On November 27, Tybee Island hosted: (1.) the Marine Guard of USS *Savannah*, which was landed at 8:00 and forced to retreat to the boats at 11:30 by shellfire from Fort Pulaski; (2.) DuPont, who landed with the Marine Guard and sailors from USS *Wabash* on Tybee Island, made a personal reconnaissance and left with mixed feelings regarding permanent occupation of the place; (3.) General Sherman, who also made a personal survey and, to his discomfort, found Fort Pulaski's guns would reach across the river to the island; (5.) Commander Missroon of USS *Savannah*, who recommended immediate occupation of the island by at least 500 Marines before the rebels returned and had to be forced off again. Missroon's assessment as to the importance of Tybee Island was correct. Not only did occupation of the island deter blockade runners, it provided the platform from which Fort Pulaski would be reduced.[73]

Savannah's Marine Guard under the command of 1st Lt. Philip C. Kennedy returned to Tybee Island on the twenty-eighth accompanied by thirty armed seamen, and occupied the Martello Tower. On December 5, more of *Savannah*'s crew came ashore while Cdr. Christopher R. P. Rodgers, USN, led the Marines to Little Tybee Island to verify rumors that the rebels had erected a strong battery to threaten the Martello Tower.[74] That battery turned out to be nothing more dangerous than a lookout post. Satisfied that there was no threat from Little Tybee, Rodgers and the Marines returned to their former positions.[75]

1st. Lt. Philip C. Kennedy, USMC
NA Photograph 127-N-526410

Farther north, Lt. James W. A. Nicholson, USN, made a reconnaissance of St. Helena Sound, and, with the Marine Guard of USS *Dale* aboard, steered USS *Isaac Smith* into the Ashepoo River. During a three-day journey, December 10–12, *Dale*'s Marines, under the charge of O. Sgt. Patrick Lomasney, landed and occupied a fort on Otter Island, made a survey of Fenwick's Island, and burned the headquarters of a rebel cavalry unit on Mosquito Creek. Five days later, they made another trip up the Ashepoo, traveling some sixty miles upriver without opposition.[76]

At Bay Point, DuPont had to deal with internal problems of the Marine Battalion. One concerned 1st Lt. Louis M. Goldsborough, Jr., whose abrupt transfer from USS *Pensacola* to the Marine Battalion caused his overprotective mother to pay a visit to the Commandant. Despite being forbidden to meddle further in their son's military life by her husband, Capt. Louis M. Goldsborough, Sr., USN, Mrs. Goldsborough wrote DuPont, asking him to remove her son from the Marine Battalion and bring him aboard USS *Wabash*. In a personal letter to Goldsborough, Sr., written the day after the victory at Port Royal, DuPont mentioned that as soon as young Goldsborough requested the transfer, it would be approved. However, Marine Lieutenant Goldsborough was getting along very nicely with the battalion at Bay Point and did not want the transfer. He was in command of one of the four companies of Marines and performing his duties to the entire satisfaction of the battalion commander. The situation abruptly changed when he received a severe dressing down by Reynolds after returning late from a trip to the sutler at Hilton Head. Although the tardiness was not the fault of Goldsborough, Reynolds insisted that, since he was the senior officer among the three who had permission to leave Bay Point, it was his responsibility to see to it that all returned in a timely fashion. Goldsborough remonstrated against what he perceived as grave injustice, saying that he had only been away from camp twice since the battalion landed at Bay Point, and both times with difficulty. Reynolds replied, "Yes sir, and hereafter you will meet with a great deal more difficulty."[77] Within days, Goldsborough sought and received a transfer to the Marine Guard of USS *Wabash* as second officer.[78]

DuPont's second problem was logistical. Since their camp equipage had gone down with the transport *Governor*, the battalion had survived on begged and borrowed supplies. It especially needed cooking gear and tents. Reynolds had urgently asked Headquarters to immediately send him tents, shovels, axes, hatchets, camp kettles, and mess pans to relieve him of relying on others to provide for the battalion. The Quartermaster's office finally submitted a requisition to the Navy Department for these much-needed items on December 12, but a most fortunate turn of events in South Carolina alleviated part of the problem.

On December 14, DuPont ordered Cdr. Percival Drayton, USN, to make a reconnaissance of the various inlets north of Port Royal.[79] Accordingly, USS *Pawnee*, *Seneca*, and *Vixen* ran into the North Edisto River, feeling out the defenses there. Drayton found a deserted earthwork on Edisto Island. Upon hearing that a large encampment of rebels was a short distance upriver at the hamlet of Rockville, Drayton took the Marines from *Pawnee*, and a detachment of seamen, put them aboard *Vixen* and investigated the site on the morning of December 16. At the approach of *Vixen*, the Confederates abandoned the camp, leaving all their comforts behind. Drayton landed the Marines, and, after making a careful survey of the "spoils of war," took everything of value aboard ship. Among the prizes turned over to DuPont were forty Sibley tents.[80] DuPont was delighted. He promptly gave the tents to the Marine Battalion, solving their lack of shelter.[81]

USS *St. Lawrence* dropped anchor at Port Royal in early December. The commander of her Marine Guard, 2d Lt. Richard S. Collum, sent his observations to his friend at Washington, 2d Lt. John C. Harris. With undisguised pride, he wrote, "A great number of troops are quartered in and around this place, but none of them compare with our Battalion." Collum also stated that he wished Harris "could see this country, for it is very different from our section. The rebels evince the most devilish spirit in this section, and their malignity and hatred to us can only be compared to the times of the middle ages when civil war was rampant."[82]

Headquarters, U.S. Marine Battalion at Bay Point
Massachusetts Commandery, MOLLUS Collection, USAMHI

Two days after Christmas, the Marine Guard of USS *Dale* was reconnoitering the South Edisto River when it came upon the mansion of former South Carolina Governor William Aiken. Two officers came out of the house and invited expedition commander, William Ottiwell, Acting Master, USN, to come ashore with his party.[83] Ottiwell asked, "Who are you?" With that, a dozen armed men appeared on the porch of the house. "Pickets of the Fourth South Carolina Regiment. Come on shore, I tell you," came the reply. Ottiwell declined, and the South Carolinians fired. The Marines immediately returned a volley and a sharp firefight broke out. The rebels were soon driven to the house by canister from the boat howitzer, but a few more rounds convinced them to quit the building altogether. Ottiwell sped them on their retreat with several more shots, and ceased firing only when the rebels were out of sight. This demonstration, according to *Dale*'s commanding officer, Lt. William T. Truxton, USN, would "prove to them that we are not sleeping on our watch."[84]

Two weeks later, Truxton, the Marine Guard from *Dale*, a detachment of sailors, and two companies of the 45th Pennsylvania Volunteers landed on to Bailey's Island, South Carolina. They completely scouted the island, and discovered that only slaves, abandoned by the plantation owners, remained. Truxton reported that the slaves had taken most of the furniture from the houses. During

Officers' Quarters, Bay Point
Marine Corps Research Center, Marine Corps University, Quantico, Va.

the searches of the vacant mansions, Truxton was clear that nothing be disturbed. All that was taken were "a few books, light novels, magazines and forage for the party." He commended both the volunteers and seamen for their "general good conduct." during the expedition.[85] Conspicuously absent from praise was the Marine Guard. Perhaps their "foraging" went beyond food for the mind.

While their brothers from the various ships were exploring the various inlets, rivers, and creeks in the vicinity of Port Royal, the Marines at Bay Point did little else but perform Reynolds' favorite pastime, battalion drill. Pvt. Daniel O'Neill wrote to his parents that, "Nothing of any account has transpired here since my arrival with the exception of a small battle we had the other day about 20 miles up the river. . ."[86]

2d Lt. Charles Bradford was so bored and depressed by the seemingly endless rains, that he asked his father to send him some French language books so that he might pass the monotonous days to some profit.[87] Both Bradford and O'Neill reported rumors that the Marine Battalion would be sent home by the end of February. Bradford told his father that the rumors had gained such credence, 2d Lt. Eugene Smalley, acting quartermaster for the Marine Battalion, had wagered fifty dollars, giving even odds on a departure from Bay Point in less than six weeks.[88]

2d. Lt. Charles H. Bradford
MCHC Collection

DuPont had plans that would relieve the boredom of the Marine Battalion, but before he could put them into operation, he had to secure the approaches to the Savannah River and block the passage of supplies to Fort Pulaski. On January 17, 1862, DuPont ordered Cdr. John Rodgers to undertake this mission. Rodgers organized an expedition consisting of the gunboats *Pembina*, *Ottawa*, *E. B. Hale*, and *Henry Andrew*, with two launches manned by Marines and seamen from USS *Susquehanna*. 1st Lt. Philip R. Fendall commanded the Marines.[89]

The expedition departed Port Royal at 9:00 A.M., January 25, and during the course of the next three weeks *Susquehanna*'s Marines and sailors were constantly occupied. The two launches performed picket duty, took soundings, ferried materials for the construction of two batteries, one on Venus Island, the other on Bird Island, and scouted the numerous eddies and backwaters of New River. While towing a scow loaded with heavy guns to one of the batteries being constructed, one of the launches was swept away by the current of the Savannah River, bringing it dangerously close to Fort Pulaski. Bending their backs to the oars, the Marines and sailors turned the launch and came back safely to the battery on Venus Island.[90] When the batteries on Venus and Bird Islands were completed, the 3rd Rhode Island Artillery relieved Rodgers' force.[91] The expedition returned to Port Royal on February 18.

The successful emplacement of the Venus and Bird Island batteries was the final piece of the network of defenses that DuPont fashioned to protect Port Royal. All of the inland waterways and their environs leading to Port Royal were secure. He was now prepared to launch the second stage of his plan to secure the South Atlantic coast. The Marine Battalion would finally be lifted from its doldrums.

Major Reynolds received orders to have the battalion ready to board the transport steamer *McClellan* on the afternoon of February 21. Many of the officers who had long since grown weary of the inactivity, the climate, and each other's company were delighted.[92] Lieutenant Huntington exhibited the general attitude at Bay Point when he wrote his father about some of his fellow officers. He considered Captain Wiley "brusque, bull-headed," and often "fussy as an old maid." Wiley was not well-liked by the younger officers. Further, his many mistakes while drilling the battalion did not earn him respect, particularly when he took offense at being told about them. Lieutenant Grimes was resented by some because they thought his commission was the result of nepotism. His uncle, James W. Grimes, was Chairman of the Senate Naval Affairs Committee.[93] Despite that, Huntington admired him for his ability to tell the tallest of tales with the straightest face.[94]

Preparations for active service also brought a solution to Lieutenant Goldsborough's continuing dissatisfaction. After arranging a transfer to USS *Wabash*, he was much surprised to learn that he would not have his own room as he did aboard USS *Pensacola*.[95] After a few weeks of less than comfortable quarters, Goldsborough petitioned DuPont to remove the assistant medical officer from his quarters in the wardroom. Goldsborough claimed the single bed room on grounds of seniority. DuPont pointedly refused, stating that the room in question had always been assigned to the medical staff of any warship, regardless of rank, and he was not going to disturb the arrangement.[96] Goldsborough's gaffe might have brought more unhappiness in his position aboard the flagship but for Reynolds' intervention. With the battalion making ready for embarkation, Reynolds wanted Goldsborough to resume his position as commander of Company D.[97] He was detached from *Wabash* on February 23.

Heavy fog at Port Royal prevented DuPont from leaving on schedule. Reynolds took advantage of the delay to report to Headquarters that he knew nothing of the destination or service intended for his Marines. Also, fifty Marines, by order of DuPont, were being left at Bay Point under the command of 2d Lt. Charles A. Stillman.[98] The letter was sent off to the dispatch boat, the same boat that brought two letters from Reynolds' wife.

The letters sent the major's blood boiling. The Senate had finally begun to consider the promotions following the retirements of Lieutenant Colonel Edelin, Major English, and Captain Brevoort. It was also discussing the new positions created by the Act of July 26, 1861, the second colonel, lieutenant colonel, assistant quartermaster, the yet unfilled captaincies, and the vacancies those promotions would leave. The crux of Mrs. Reynolds' letters concerned the second colonelcy. There was movement within the Senate to make staff officers eligible for the position. This contradicted all past construction of laws regarding advancement of the line within the Corps. Staff officers simply were ineligible to advance to the line. However, Paymaster Russell, said to be encouraged by his supporters in Congress and the junior officers of the Marine Corps, was rumored to be politicking for the colonelcy.[99]

This news upset Reynolds to such a degree that he felt compelled to write identical letters to the Commandant and each officer on the Marine Corps Staff expressing his outrage at Russell's attempt to displace the senior line officers, and, himself in particular.

'Not Official'

Headquarters,
Marine Battalion
Bay Point, Port Royal, S. C.
February 22, 1862

Sir:

The glove of Major John George Reynolds is at the feet of any officer who aspires to supersede him in rank for energy, activity, and endurance. If there be one, let him come forth under this challenge, and Major Reynolds will meet him with black board and chalk, as he has done under fire. Enemy rear fire is far more to be apprehended than a square, bold front.

Any advantage taken in the advance of one who may be in service, is, in the estimation of the undersigned, mean and contemptible, applicable alike to the Head, as well as the foot of the Corps.

Jno. Geo. Reynolds

Col. John Harris
Command't. Marine Corps
Washington, D. C.[100]

Before posting the four letters, Reynolds showed one to 2d Lt. Thomas L. McElrath, battalion Adjutant. McElrath advised him not to mail the letters, knowing full well that the contents would only cause trouble for Reynolds.[101] However, Reynolds, still upset, was adamant. He mailed the letters on February 23, the morning the battalion embarked aboard the transport McClellan.

Considering Reynolds' mental state, it is not surprising that the embarkation of the battalion did not proceed smoothly. In the course of marching to the point of departure, Reynolds noticed that Captain Wiley's company was not in the column and called out for him. 1st Lt. John I. Schermerhorn, commander of Company C, answered the summons by mistake. Highly agitated, Reynolds told Schermerhorn that he was looking not for him, but for Wiley. Schermerhorn replied that Wiley had taken his company in advance of the rest of the battalion and was embarking his men. This was not what Reynolds wanted to hear. General Sherman was taking passage aboard the *McClellan*, and to see the Marine Battalion embark in a disjointed fashion would be an embarrassment. Exclaiming, "My God! What can Captain Wiley be thinking of?"[102] Reynolds went off in pursuit of his errant company commander.

Wiley was moving the first section of his company into the boats that would ferry them to the *McClellan*, when Reynolds came down the beach. Coming up to Wiley, Reynolds asked what he was doing, Wiley responded that he was embarking his company in accordance with orders. "Who in the devil gave you the order?" Reynolds snapped back. Before Wiley could respond, Reynolds began giving orders in regard to the embarkation of the second, third, and fourth sections of Wiley's company. Wiley pointed out that the major was giving the orders to embark before the boats were close enough for the men to board without getting their arms and accouterments wet. Reynolds, losing what was left of his composure, replied in a loud manner, that it was "no matter . . . the men must embark" when he gave the order even "if they had to swim for it." Although Company A did not swim to their boats, the men had to wade some twenty-five or thirty yards through the surf to reach them.[103] The officers who witnessed the outbursts and peculiar contrariness of the major were certain that he was under the influence of alcohol. The embarkation of the rest of the battalion proceeded without incident, and concerns regarding the forthcoming operation overtook Reynolds' strange behavior.[104] Once aboard ship, Reynolds was able to gain control of his emotions and resumed his normal relationships with his officers. He did, however, confide to McElrath on several occasions while the battalion was at sea, that he wished he had never mailed the letters. McElrath was right. They would only lead to trouble.

Bad weather prevented the departure of DuPont's fleet until February 28. By that time, it was common knowledge that the seizure of Fernandina, Florida, was the objective of the expedition. Fernandina had an excellent harbor and rail connections to Savannah, Georgia. It had the potential for becoming a primary haven for blockade runners once the blockade had sealed Savannah. On August 5, 1861, USS *Jamestown* had chased a vessel into Fernandina Harbor which was later identified as the bark *Alvarado.* She had been captured two weeks earlier by the privateer *Jeff Davis.* A prize crew was bringing *Alvarado* to Fernandina to offload her cargo when *Jamestown* intervened. The prize hoisted more sail, but failed to reach the safety of Fernandina's seacoast batteries, grounding about a mile and a half from shore. The prize crew quickly lowered boats and abandoned ship.

Three boats were lowered from *Jamestown*, filled with armed sailors and Marines, the latter under the command of 2d Lt. George P. Houston, to try and bring off the ship, and, if unsuccessful, set her ablaze. While the boats were pulling toward the bark, Confederate artillery came down to the beach, unlimbered and opened fire. But the range was too great, and the fire of the light guns did no damage to the boat crews. They boarded *Alvarado* and prepared to haul her off the shoal when a rebel steamer was seen coming up. The boats were recalled and *Alvarado* was put to the torch.[105] The incident proved that to effectively close access to Savannah, Fernandina had to be occupied.

The ships and transports departed Bay Point under orders to rendezvous in St. Andrews Bay, Georgia, just north of Fernandina. Twenty warships made up DuPont's squadron. Two deep draft vessels, USS *Wabash* and *Susquehanna*, led the column, but if the rebel defenses in and around Fernandina had to be bombarded, the eighteen gunboats DuPont ordered south would have to do the close in work. In addition to the 289 officers and men of the Marine Battalion, there were Marine Guards within the squadron totaling 230 men that DuPont could call upon if necessary.

Marines and sailors returning to USS *Jamestown* after firing the brig *Alvarado*

Harper's Weekly

On March 1, DuPont ordered the attack on the defenses of Fernandina. The gunboats were to enter the inland passage between Cumberland Island and the mainland, followed by the troop transports. After reaching the southern tip of Amelia Island, the Marine Battalion, led by Reynolds, and the 97th Pennsylvania Infantry, under the command of Col. Henry R. Guss, were to land, and, with naval gunfire support, assault and take the enemy batteries. The heavy warships, at the same time, were to bombard the works on the northern end of Amelia Island, and, once they were silenced, the remainder of the troop transports would pass to the landing at Fernandina to occupy the town. Every effort would be made to prevent the Confederates from escaping, with particular attention paid to the railroad bridge from Amelia Island to the mainland.[106]

As the operation began on the morning of March 2, an escaped slave reported that the defenses around Fernandina were being abandoned. DuPont signaled the squadron to make speed and intercept the retreating enemy. The squadron made for the main channel between the islands but was too late to prevent the Confederates from escaping. USS *Ottawa* closed and fired a few shots at a train making for the mainland, but only one shell took effect as the train sped away to safety. Goldsborough described the action from his vantage point.

> They had a train of cars to get off in, and had all the night before been hard at work removing everything they could

put on them. When the "Ottawa" came upon them, she and the cars had a most exciting race for the bridge, which had she reached first, everything on the island would have fallen into our hands. She only had a short distance to go, while the cars had to run about five miles, and she would have beaten them had she not run on shore just at the critical moment. When this accident occurred, finding she could do no more, she gave them a dose of her tremendous shells, knocking one of the cars off the track, and killing and wounding many. We found the shattered car the next day, covered with blood and the remains of those killed.[107]

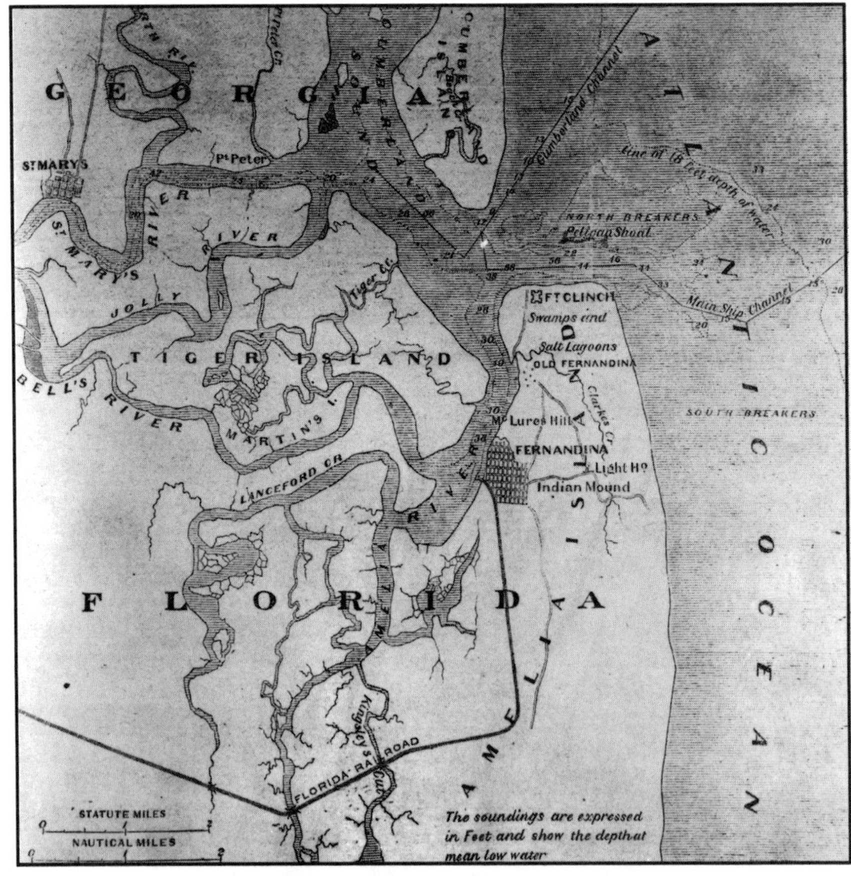

Area of operations, March 1–4, 1862

Florida State Archives

Just before noon, a column was observed marching southward on Cumberland Island. Marines from *Wabash* and *Susquehanna*, ferried into the shallows by *Keystone State*, were landed at 11:45 A.M., in the hope of intercepting them. In Cumberland Sound, those aboard the ships at anchor strained their ears to hear the sounds of battle, but they were disappointed. The Marines did not make contact with the fleeing soldiers and, at 2:00 P.M., they were recalled.[108]

The Marine Battalion landed on Cumberland Island, according to the original plan and took possession of the abandoned fortifications. Goldsborough was quite impressed with these batteries and those across the channel on Amelia Island, grateful that the fleet did not have to fight its way past them.

> I visited the fort and a line of 22 masked batteries in connection with it. If the "Wabash" and large ships had attempted to pass them, I believe that they would have been blown out of the water. The fortifications at Hilton Head are nothing to them.[109]

The fort Goldsborough referred to, Fort Clinch, was occupied by Marines and sailors from USS *Mohican* under the command of Lt. Henry W. Miller, USN, on the morning of March 4.[110] Landing at 11:05 A.M., they raised the U.S. flag over the deserted fort and waited for soldiers from the transports to relieve them. They returned aboard ship that evening.[111]

At 7:00 on the morning of March 4, Marines from the gunboats were ordered ashore to take possession of Fernandina. The Guards of USS *Wabash* and *Susquehanna* again went aboard *Keystone State*, expecting to fight their way into the town. However, they met only feeble resistance at Fernandina, a few scattered musket shots from retreating enemy pickets, and were firmly established ashore. No landing was made from *Keystone State*.[112] DuPont was pleased to report to the Secretary of the Navy that, "We captured Port Royal, but Fernandina and Fort Clinch have been given to us."[113] On March 6, the Marine Battalion was brought up from Cumberland Island to relieve the guards from the various gunboats at Fernandina.

Having secured Fernandina, DuPont ordered his gunboats to take possession of the surrounding area. USS *Ottawa* occupied St. Mary's, Georgia, on March 4, after routing its garrison with canister and grape. Marines and seamen from USS *Pocahontas* occupied St. Simon's Island, Georgia, on March 9, and, the next day, in company with Marines from USS *Mohican*, took possession of Brunswick. Later that afternoon, *Mohican*'s Marine Guard and a company of armed sailors landed on Jekyl Island. Finding the island and the fortifications abandoned, the landing party raised the Stars and Stripes over the works.[114]

Fort Clinch, Amelia Island

Harper's Weekly

After meeting only sporadic resistance, DuPont saw there was no need for the Marine Battalion for the present. He was unwilling to waste his Marines on occupation duties when the Army could easily perform that work. Accordingly, the battalion returned to Bay Point on March 8 aboard USS *Bienville*.

Once the battalion had re-established itself at Bay Point, Reynolds wrote to the Commandant in regard to pay and small stores.[115] In response to Reynolds' complaint on February 8, 1862, Harris had promised to ask the Secretary of the Navy to have the paymasters of the South Atlantic Blockading Squadron to resolve these problems, but nothing had happened. The officers were so embarrassed for lack of money that DuPont offered to advance their pay from his own funds. DuPont was most solicitous in regard to the welfare of the Marines, but there was only so much he had the authority to do. Reynolds was irritated by the attitude of the several assistant paymasters, who served everyone else their small stores first. If anything was left over, it was reserved for the Marines. It was an intolerable situation. Reynolds complained that since debarking at Bay Point, the battalion had received no small stores. Further, "We have received no pay (and) every mail brings piteous letters from the wives of our men expressing their need, &c, &c."[116]

DuPont's squadron off Fernandina, March 4, 1862

Frank Leslie's Illustrated Newspaper

Reynolds was particularly aggravated by the paymaster of the *Wabash*:

> to whom the accounts were sent with instructions to pay and otherwise attend to our wants, (but he) had such an accumulation of accounts with other ships of the squadron, that he positively declined having anything to do with the Battalion other than directing from whence provisions could be obtained. We have had a very limited supply of small stores for reason that we are not recognized by any particular Paymaster.[117]

Reynolds was convinced that a sergeant from Headquarters should be appointed sutler for the battalion. That done, "The soldier's small requirements would be met and much trouble and vexation to others avoided." As things were, the battalion commander reported, "We are at large, belonging no where and cared less for in consequence."

The problems Reynolds endured would have to be relegated to a lower priority for the time being. On March 11, Cdr. Christopher R. P. Rodgers, USN, went ashore at St. Augustine, Florida, and accepted the surrender of the city. Most of the inhabitants professed to be Unionists, treating Rodgers and his party with friendliness and courtesy. However, some 800 Confederate troops were said to have recently evacuated the town, and DuPont feared their return. To prevent them from torching the city, he put Captain Doughty and the Marine Guard of *Wabash* ashore at St. Augustine along with a company of the 7th New Hampshire Volunteers. Doughty was to be the senior officer ashore.[118]

With the Confederate threat to St. Augustine looming as a distinct possibility—such a raid had taken place at Jacksonville, Florida—DuPont thought the Marine Battalion would be an ideal force to guard the city. On March 15, Capt. James L. Lardner, commanding officer of USS *Susquehanna*, was ordered to inform Major Reynolds to have the battalion ready to embark upon the *Keystone State* for transport to St. Augustine.[119]

USS *Keystone State* stopped at St. Augustine on March 17 to send her Marine Guard ashore to augment Doughty's force. DuPont promptly sent her north to Bay Point to bring the Marine Battalion back to the city. Two days later, DuPont received a visit from General Sherman. Sherman seemed quite perturbed that the Navy had captured the entire coast, and, particularly, that Marines were holding St. Augustine. Sherman was further upset when DuPont told him that the Marine Battalion was on its way from Bay Point to garrison Fort Marion at St. Augustine. That would give the Army the opportunity to secure Jacksonville and other points. Sherman demurred, saying that

McClellan expected him to move against Charleston, South Carolina. DuPont lectured him on the need to protect Jacksonville and St. Augustine. Such protection was a matter of moral and political principle. It had to take precedence over military ideas. Confiding his thoughts regarding Sherman's pique over the success of the Navy to his wife, DuPont thought Sherman might send an officer senior in rank to Major Reynolds to St. Augustine just to spite him. If he did that, DuPont resolved to send the battalion north. "They are too well-trained men to be lost out here any longer."[120]

The battalion received its orders for St. Augustine on March 19, but since rumor that the Marines would be ordered south reached Bay Point before USS *Susquehanna* did, it came as no surprise.[121] On the afternoon of the twenty-first, the harbor at Port Royal was filled with boats from every naval vessel, all transporting the Marines and their camp equipage to USS *Bienville*. By 5:30 P.M., the last boat came alongside and off-loaded her cargo.[122]

Bienville steamed into St. Augustine Bay on the morning of March 23, and her crew wasted no time in getting the gear of the battalion on deck. By noon, all was ready to be transported ashore. The battalion and its equipment were transferred to a schooner for the run to shore, and a short time later it anchored off the bar. Before the Marines and their equipage were debarked, Capt. Charles Steedman, USN, commanding officer of *Bienville*, and Major Reynolds left the schooner to meet DuPont.[123]

Conditions at St. Augustine had significantly changed in the previous two days. DuPont's fear that Sherman would do something to spite the Navy had come to pass. Referencing Sherman's actions in a letter to his wife, DuPont wrote:

> I found he had sent a lieutenant colonel and two companies to St. Augustine, though he had my note saying I was going to place the battalion there. This, (Commander C. R. P.) Rodgers thinks, is the most unhandsome thing he has done. I will send the battalion home now—is idle to attempt to fit it in anywhere and they are a fine body of well-disciplined troops and should be employed. I will first see what Major Reynolds thinks.[124]

While DuPont waited for *Bienville* to arrive with the Marine Battalion from Bay Point, news of a tragic affair near Smyrna, Florida, came to him. Boats from USS *Henry Andrew* had gone down Mosquito Lagoon to investigate an abandoned fort near Smyrna. When the officers and men landed, they were ambushed. Thomas A. Budd, Acting Lieutenant, USN, and S. W. Mather, Acting Master, USN, were killed in action, as were four seamen. The slain officers had been warned beforehand not to venture inside Mosquito Inlet since enemy troops were reported in force around that area. They had paid for the rash act with their lives. The bodies of Budd and Mather were retrieved under flag of truce and returned to the flagship. When they were brought aboard, DuPont's passion momentarily overcame his military training. As he explained to his wife:

> I had nearly made up my mind, when I saw those two fine officers' bodies passed on board, that such an act must be punished and thought seriously of sending for the Marine Battalion—for the *Isaac Smith*, etc., and organizing a campaign and driving these fellows out—and signaled the *Penguin* to get ready for sea.

Commander Rodgers joined him later and counseled,

> however natural my desire was, it could lead to nothing. . . . Without knowledge of the country or a supply of water, the Marines could not leave the gunboats. . . . I then remembered that it was my duty to do what was right and not to act from a vindictive spirit and a personal desire to chastise.[125]

So ended that last thought of utilizing the Marine Battalion as a landing force for the South Atlantic Blockading Squadron. When DuPont went back to St. Augustine, he found *Bienville* preparing to off load the battalion. DuPont summoned Reynolds aboard *Wabash*, and, after a long consultation, the two decided that the Marines would be sent back to Washington.[126]

Before Reynolds left, DuPont wrote a letter of commendation praising both the major and the Marine Battalion.

Flagship Wabash

Off St. Augustine, Fla., March 25, 1862

Major:

I enclose an order for you to return to Washington with the battalion.

No one is aware better than myself that the battalion has had, from circumstances beyond your control and mine, many privations to endure, commencing with the loss of the transport *Governor* and continued in various ways since, but these have all been borne in the best possible spirit, which has been greatly appreciated by me.

I part with the battalion with regret, mingled with the satisfaction that more important service awaits it than could be, from the nature of things, offered on this coast.

Major, you carry with you my great regard and high admiration for you as a soldier and an officer, and I trust your long and faithful services are soon to be rewarded by promotion.

Very respectfully, etc.,

S. F. DuPont
Flag Officer

Major J. G. Reynolds, U.S. Marine Corps
Commanding Marine Battalion[127]

DuPont wrote letters to the Secretary of the Navy and the Commandant of the Marine Corps explaining his reasons for returning the Marine Battalion to Washington. He was frank in explanation and generous in praise. To Welles, DuPont wrote:

> I think it is my duty to inform the Department of the earnest zeal which has ever actuated Major Reynolds in all the duties pertaining to his command, resulting in its fine discipline and in an eager anxiety on the part of every officer and man for more active service in the field.[128]

and to Harris,

> I believe but few officers would divest themselves of such a body of men as I am now doing, but after trying in vain to find them a sphere worthy of their efficiency, I deem it my duty to the public service and to the battalion to adopt the course I have. . . .
>
> Colonel, from the time of the unfortunate accident of the *Governor* up to the present hour, the battalion has been called upon to endure many privations, and, without troubling you with any details, they seemed to be such as were beyond my control for the moment. The principal error was coming out without accounts and without a special paymaster; from this resulted all the difficulties.
>
> But it is my duty to inform you that a body of men more subordinate, devoted, loyal and accommodating to circumstances, however trying, could not be found in any service.
>
> Major Reynolds has maintained throughout his reputation as a soldier and an officer.[129]

DuPont was quite unwilling to give Sherman the satisfaction of leaving any person associated with the naval service potentially subject to the orders of the Army at St. Augustine. When Reynolds

A National Flag emblazoned with the words "U.S. Marine Corps"
The Marine Battalion serving with the South Atlantic Blockading Squadron would have carried a similar flag.

NA Photograph 127-N-A49043

received his orders to re-embark the Marine Battalion aboard the *Bienville*, Captain Doughty received instructions to quit St. Augustine, and, with his guard, report back aboard the flagship. After Doughty reported aboard *Wabash*, DuPont sent for him and gave him a copy of a most unusual letter received from the government and citizens of St. Augustine.

St. Augustine, Fla.,
March 25, 1862

Sir:

The undersigned, the mayor and city council and citizens of St. Augustine, beg leave to express their heartfelt gratification and satisfaction of the polite and urbane course of Major Isaac T. Doughty and officers of the United States Marines since their

> arrival in and occupancy of this city, and of the good conduct and discipline of the troops under their command, and also their unfeigned regret at their departure; and respectfully ask that our high appreciation of their gentlemanly demeanor be conveyed to Major Doughty and his command.[130]

The St. Augustine delegation had requested that Doughty and his Marines be replaced by the Marine Battalion, and were deeply disappointed to learn that no Marines would be available to garrison their city.

Bienville left St. Augustine for Bay Point on March 25. The detachment and all else left there when the battalion embarked for St. Augustine was brought on board, and the ship began the journey to Washington. On March 31, *Bienville* docked at the Washington Navy Yard. The Marine Battalion disembarked, formed, and marched up the yard and back to Marine Barracks, Washington.[131]

8

Coastal Operations: The Gulf Blockading Squadron July 1861–March 1862

The failure of the Confederacy to adequately fortify and defend Ship Island, Mississippi, has long been considered a key to the loss of New Orleans.[1] The island was the linchpin in the communications link between Pensacola, Mobile, and the Crescent City, but the Southerners made no serious attempt to occupy it until July 6, 1861. The Union was equally lax in the matter. Inexplicably so, since the nearest base from which the ships blockading the Gulf coast of the Confederacy could refit was Key West. With Pensacola in enemy hands, Ship Island seemed a logical choice as a base of operations. Her harbor, with its depth in excess of three fathoms, could accommodate even the largest Union warships.

The August 9, 1861, report of the conference to implement the blockade stated:

> military possession be taken of Ship Island as the depot, harbor of resort, and point d'appui of the blockading vessels, which will control the access to New Orleans through the lakes and along the east coast of the Delta. Ship Island is also the key to the blockade and possession of Mississippi Sound and control of the coasts of Mississippi and Alabama. . . . The Military possession of Ship Island is no less important to our naval operations in Mississippi Sound than to the blockade of New Orleans. . . . the entire possession of Ship Island and its substitution for Pensacola as a naval station are indispensable. . . .[2]

By the time the report reached the Secretary of the Navy, the rebels had been in occupation of Ship Island for over a month. What could have been seized, occupied, fortified, and made ready

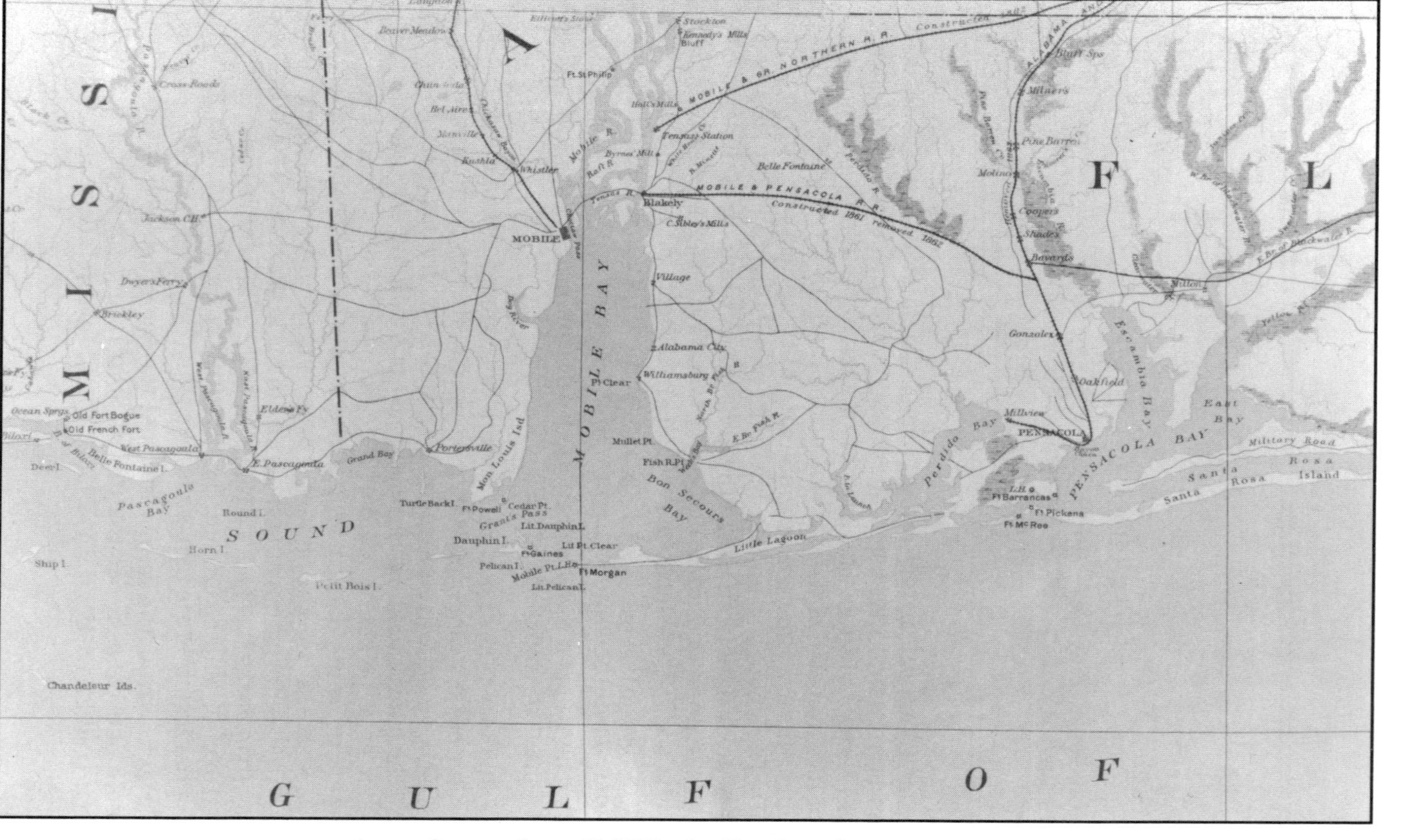

Area of operations, Gulf Blockading Squadron, 1861–1862

RG 94, Civil War Atlas, plate CXLVII

for service with minimum effort before the Confederates made their move, might now require a full-fledged military operation to secure.

The Confederate occupation of Ship Island began with all the trappings of a filibustering expedition. Capt. Edward Higgins, aide-de-camp to Maj. Gen. David E. Twiggs, Commander of Department No. 1 (Louisiana, and the Gulf coasts of Mississippi and Alabama), received permission to commandeer lake steamers for the purpose of intercepting boat expeditions from Union blockading vessels.[3] Higgins "borrowed" the side-wheelers *Cotton* and *Swain*, along with their civilian crews and then searched for fighting men.

Higgins went to the New Orleans Navy Yard and there found his old friend from the U.S. Navy, Lt. Alexander F. Warley.[4] Warley was executive officer of CSS *McRae*, a would-be commerce raider that was fitting out for a dash through the blockade. Higgins recruited Warley for his expedition, who, in turn, "volunteered" the entire crew of *McRae*, right down to the ship's boys and the surgeon. O. Sgt. John Morgan and the twenty Confederate States Marines serving as the ship's guard also went along.[5] Before launching his expedition, Higgins rounded up a sergeant's squad of the 4th Louisiana, and persuaded Capt. Reuben T. Thom, CSMC, to give a few dozen recently recruited Marines some field experience.[6]

The expedition rendezvoused at New Orleans on July 4, with Capt. A. L. Myers in command of *Oregon*, and Warley taking the helm of *Swain*.[7] The adventure started the next day with the two side-wheelers churning their way across Lake Ponchatrain and out into Mississippi Sound, anchoring at Bay St. Louis, Mississippi, for the night. The morning of July 6 found the two ships prowling Ship Island Channel in search of USS *Massachusetts*, the Union blockader known to patrol those waters. The Confederates were disappointed in their search for the blockader, and, as an afterthought, Higgins decided it would be well to land the guns, munitions, and the crews on Ship Island. The four guns mounted in a sand-bagged battery would give *Massachusetts* an unpleasant surprise when she returned to her station.

All assisted in manhandling the four guns from *Oregon* to the beach and then to their platforms. Sandbags were positioned and all was in readiness by 8:00 P.M. An eight-inch rifle and a 32-pounder mounted at each end of the battery provided the main weaponry, while two howitzers were set up between them. Higgins, in the meantime, had departed for New Orleans with the *Oregon*, promising to return with ammunition, more guns, and reinforcements. Warley had to hold the island for a couple of days with the soldiers, sailors, and Marines, about 130 men, against whatever the Federals decided to put against them.

On the afternoon of July 8, a company of the 4th Louisiana Infantry under the command of Captain Roland landed on the island, a most welcome addition to the tiny force Warley had. The infantrymen were placed in positions calculated to repel any landing that the Federals might attempt. When his dispositions were completed, Warley had the eight-inch rifled gun on one end of his sandbagged work under the command of Midn. Charles W. Read.[8] Next were two howitzers commanded by Midn. Sardine G. Stone, Jr., and William R. Dalton.[9] The 32-pounder, commanded by Midn. John H. Comstock, rounded out the battery.[10]

USS *Massachusetts* came up to Ship Island on the night of July 8, and dropped anchor a mile offshore. The customary Marine Guard, under the charge of O. Sgt. John Gottemeyer, augmented her crew. On the morning of the ninth, Warley gave the signal to open fire on the *Massachusetts.* Read, whose reputation as a crack shot with the great guns at Annapolis preceded him, sighted the 8-inch rifle, fired and missed his target by 100 yards. The *Massachusetts* returned fire and a forty-minute duel ensued. Neither side registered any hits, although the 32-pounder sent several shots through the rigging of the warship. The rebels, running short of ammunition, reportedly retrieved the spent shells from the guns of the Federal warship from the sand, and those that fit their guns were returned with dispatch.[11] *Massachusetts* hauled off to Chandeleur Island around 6:00 A.M., but returned when her skipper, Cdr. Melancton Smith, USN, saw three rebel steamers approaching the island.[12] A few shots were exchanged, again without damage to either side, and the *Massachusetts* drew off to Chandeleur Island once more.[13]

Higgins returned from New Orleans, with three full companies of the 4th Louisiana and thirteen heavy guns with ample ammunition. By nightfall, all had been put ashore. Higgins turned over command of the island to Lt. Col. Henry W. Allen of the 4th Louisiana before departing aboard *Oregon.*[14] Warley embarked his weary sailors and Marines aboard *Swain* and returned to New Orleans.[15] This was the first time, but certainly not the last, that Marines from both sides viewed each other over the sights of their weapons.

A few days later, with all the guns properly mounted in the batteries at Ship Island, the steamers *Oregon* and *Grey Cloud* attempted to engage *Massachusetts.*, and bring her within range of the shore batteries. Commander Smith, recognizing the ploy, did not take the bait and drove the enemy vessels off with a few well-placed rounds. The engagement, although insignificant, did convince Capt. William Mervine, USN, commanding officer of the Gulf Blockading Squadron, that Ship Island was a potential source of irritation to his operations, and that it should be dealt with before its defenses were solidified.[16]

Mervine asked Capt. William W. McKean, USN, to bring USS *Niagara* to Fort Pickens, and, in conjunction with USS *Colorado*, launch an attack on Ship Island. Mervine also requested Col. Harvey Brown, USA, to give him two rifled cannon from his defenses for the expedition. However, McKean heard that CSS *Sumter* was attempting to bring several of her prizes into Cuban waters, and, disregarding Mervine's orders, went in pursuit of the rebel commerce raider. Without the support of *Niagara*, Mervine was obliged to cancel his assault.[17] By the time *Niagara* returned from her fruitless attempt to intercept *Sumter*, Mervine was convinced that only a large force could overcome the island's defenses.[18]

The Navy Department was not pleased with the news from the Gulf. In a dispatch to Captain Mervine dated August 23, 1861, Welles informed him of his surprise when he learned that "so important a position as Ship Island should have been permitted to be fortified and retained by the insurgents." He went on to rebuke the Gulf Blockading Squadron commander for his lethargy, stating, "You have large ships, heavy batteries, and young and willing officers, with men sufficient to dispossess the insurgents from Ship Island. They might have been prevented entirely from intrenching themselves upon it. . . .There is a great uneasiness in the public mind, as well as anxiety in the Department, on the apparent inactivity of our squadron."[19]

The tenor of Welles' letter stung Mervine. He quickly replied that his orders when he came on station made no reference to Ship Island whatever, and were "so peremptory that I should give my whole attention to make the blockade I was sent to establish an effective one, that I did not feel justified in removing the vessels from their stations to make any side movements, however important they might appear to be." He went on to say that things were not so "inactive" within the cruising grounds of the Gulf Blockading Squadron as the Secretary had stated. In fact, one boat expedition had been sent against the Pensacola Navy Yard, and another to spike the guns at rebel-held Fort McRee had been ready to go on the night of August 5, when the Army fell victim to the lethargy Mervine had been accused of.[20]

The first operation had been launched from USS *Niagara* and *Colorado*. The rebel schooner *Judah*, fitting out at the Pensacola Navy Yard, was a tempting target for many naval officers who wanted to relieve the monotony of blockade duty. Consequently, on the night of August 3, five boats were assembled from the two ships and filled with Marines and sailors. Capt. Theodorus Bailey, USN, was in overall command.[21] At dark, the boats from *Niagara* and *Colorado* pushed off and headed for the objective.

At midnight, the expedition neared the wharf of the Pensacola Navy Yard. A sentry hailed the boats, and, hearing no reply, ran to the guardhouse and gave the alarm. The guard turned out, and soon the entire area was alive with troops forming up in answer to the long roll.[22] Six signal rockets fired off by the guard were seen from the deck of *Niagara*.[23] A fire balloon was set aloft over the navy yard and the batteries illuminated and manned. Much to the relief of the attacking force, the rockets and other illuminating devices were so poorly made that their gunners could see nothing to shoot at. The officers, sailors, and Marines in the boats slipped away in the darkness, all the while enjoying the pyrotechnic display and the excitement ashore.[24]

Given the active reaction to the abortive cutting out operation of August 3, it is not surprising that Colonel Brown, commanding at Fort Pickens, viewed the expedition planned for the night of August 5 with some apprehension. Brown was to contribute a sizable portion of the 300-man assault party from his garrison, Marines and sailors from the blockading squadron making up the balance. The plan was to blow the gate of Fort McRee open with a naval friction fuse, overcome the garrison, spike the guns, and torch everything possible on the way out of the fort. Mervine and those naval officers selected by him for the operation met with Brown on August 4. They found him reluctant to hazard his troops to an assault so soon after the abortive expedition of August 3. The Confederates were certain to be on the alert after the raid. Without regard for the opinions of the naval officers, all of whom were in favor of the raid, Brown decided to call off the operation.[25]

Despite Brown's lack of enterprise, the officers of the squadron were captivated by the possibility of attacking the Pensacola Navy Yard and destroying the schooner that the rebels were so flauntingly fitting out at the wharf. After giving the defenders time to calm down after the August 3 raid, another night operation was planned. At 11:00 P. M. on the night of September 13, a boat expedition cast off from USS *Colorado* under the command of Lt. John H. Russell, USN.[26] Among the raiders were 1st Lt. Edward McDonald Reynolds, USMC, with twenty Marines from the Guard of *Colorado*.

The expedition set out in four boats from the flagship, carrying 100 sailors, Marines and officers to the wharf where *Judah* was berthed. To distinguish friend from foe in the darkness, Marines and sailors wore their white summer headgear. Breech-loading Sharps rifles, sword bayonets, pistols, and cutlasses were issued. A twelve-pound boat howitzer was mounted in the bow of each boat. Lieutenant Russell gave instructions for the operation after the four craft reported at the rendezvous point off Fort Pickens. The boats were:

> To creep into the harbor, passing the rebel forts and batteries, and Braxton Bragg's encampment of 6,000 men; two boat's crews to surprise the schooner Judith, lying in the dock, drive the crew ashore, and set fire to her, while the crews of the other two boats were to land at one of the wharves directly under the shears, a few rods above, and capture and spike a large twelve-inch pivot gun, the most dangerous piece of ordnance they were in possession of at that time.[27]

The expedition passed the enemy positions undetected, and launched their attack from the east, the direction from which the Confederate patrol boats usually came. At 3:30 A.M., the boats closed in on the schooner and were within a few yards when a sentry gave the alarm. The night exploded into a cacophony of rebel drums beating the long roll, shouts of the sentries and the guard turning out, mixed with the curses and whoops of the attackers. A six-pounder boat howitzer, mounted at the bow of the first boat, announced the arrival of the raiding party with a blast of canister. Three Confederate States Marines on the wharf were wounded.[28] Tar balls were set afire and hurled from the boats onto the deck of the schooner. In an instant, the boats pulled alongside. Marine Pvt. John Smith was the first to board, but in his haste to clamber over her gunwale, lost his kepi. Mistaking Smith for the enemy, a sailor ran him through with a sword bayonet. Lieutenant Reynolds was wounded in the shoulder as he attempted to board the ship, and toppled back into his boat. A sniper, perched in the rigging of the ship, killed two seamen, one of whom fell heavily upon Reynolds.[29] Before the sharpshooter could fire again, he was shot down by a sailor named Fitzsimmons.[30]

The fight aboard the schooner was sharp and short. The raiders and the guard struggled on the deck in hand-to-hand combat. The night air was filled with the sharp crack of pistol shots, the deeper bark of muskets, the curses of men swinging cutlasses and thrusting bayonets, punctuated by the shrieks and groans of pain from those cut down. Within minutes, the rebels were driven off the boat to the wharf or over the side into the water. Being reinforced by a company of "regulars" rushing to the scene, the guard quickly recovered, rallied on the wharf and kept up a hot fire on the sailors and Marines as they went about their work to torch the ship.[31] Lieutenant Russell was grazed by a musket ball, as was Lt. Francis B. Blake, USN. Midn. Francis Higginson, USN, lost the tip of his thumb.

Attack on the privateer *Judah*

NHC Photograph NH 59157

Seamen Robert Clark and Edward Osbourne were dangerously wounded by buckshot. Pvt. Martin Bannon tripped over a hawser, and fell heavily on his right knee. He had to be carried from the privateer. Pvt. Terrance O'Dowd was felled by a gunshot through his right thigh. Pvt. Savillion Coburn was hit in the side. Pvt. Charles Carberry went down with a severe head wound.[32] Gunfire also felled nine more seamen.[33] In the hellish glare of the burning tar balls, the attackers returned the gunfire and struggled to remove their wounded comrades to safety. Others brought up turpentine from the boats and spread soaked wood shavings on the deck of the prize. The raiders, satisfied that their work was well-done, retired to their boats as *Judah* was quickly consumed by flames.

The sailors and Marines of the other two boats accomplished their mission as well. The single sentry at the battery was shot down as the boats pulled ashore. The gun, a ten-inch Columbiad, was spiked and its tompion carried off as a souvenir. The boats pulled away and joined the two hauling off from the flaming hulk of *Judah*. As they made for Fort Pickens, a Harbor Police boat tried to intercept them, but was driven off by two loads of canister from the boat howitzers. As the boats pulled away, they fired several more canister rounds toward the wharf.[34]

Their incendiary work done, Marines and sailors from the USS *Colorado* haul off, leaving *Judah* in flames

Harper's Weekly

Mervine sent off a lengthy account of the action to the Department, certainly intended to refute any charges of inactivity on the part of his squadron. He was generous in praising the members of the expedition and stated, "The Marines, especially, seem to have sustained the reputation borne by their branch of the service, as they receive encomiums from all sides."[35]

On the shore, however, the Confederate States Marines came in for heavy criticism from Brig. Gen. Braxton Bragg. Previously, when nine enlisted Marines failed to return from their tour of boat duty in Pensacola Harbor on the night of September 8, Bragg leveled a charge of gross neglect of duty at Lt. Col. Henry B. Tyler, CSMC, commanding officer of the Confederate States Marine Battalion, for failing to send an officer with the patrol. Bragg issued a special order, stating, "The desertion, from this service to the enemy, of a whole boat's crew of Marines on duty under the orders of a private, reflects great discredit on the discipline and management of that organization."[36] Moreover, he was certain the deserters had guided the boat attack that destroyed the *Judah*, and somehow contrived with their fellow Marines on sentry duty that night to ensure the success of the Federal attack.[37]

While Mervine studied plans to wrest Ship Island from the rebels, the Confederates were considering the need to maintain the exposed garrison. Col. Johnson K. Duncan took command of Ship

Island while Lieutenant Colonel Allen was on leave of absence.[38] Duncan, undoubtedly aware of the relatively easy capture of Forts Hatteras and Clark by naval bombardment, called the island indefensible, and so reported to General Twiggs. Twiggs, despite advice to the contrary, recommended to the War Department that the island be abandoned. On September 13, Adj. Gen. Samuel Cooper sent orders to Twiggs to evacuate Ship Island.[39]

During the period September 14–16, Colonel Duncan worked furiously to remove all the guns, stores, and other valuable property. On the sixteenth, he ordered the barracks and outbuildings set afire and took the garrison back to New Orleans. A most disconsolate Lieutenant Colonel Allen, one of those who strongly opposed evacuating the island, left a departing message at the fort, welcoming the Federals. Allen hoped that he and they would meet again and at "closer quarters," but for the time being, wished them a happy and healthy stay on the island.[40]

After the Confederates left Ship Island, boat crews of sailors and Marines from USS *Preble* and *Marion* were sent ashore and put out the fires, salvaging many of the buildings. On the morning of the seventeenth, Commander Smith sent a landing party of Marines and seamen from USS *Massachusetts* ashore to raise the Stars and

Ship Island, Mississippi

Harper's Weekly

Stripes over the fort and take possession of the place.[41] Over the next several weeks, Marines from USS *Preble*, *Marion*, *Potomac*, *Niagara*, *Rhode Island*, *Mississippi*, and *Colorado* were sent ashore to garrison the fort, now christened "Fort Massachusetts." The duty was rotated among the guards of the various ships with some coming ashore merely to take target practice and get a chance to feel the sand under their feet, a welcomed relief from the routine of shipboard duty. For two Southern-born Marines, their time at Ship Island presented an opportunity to return to their own people.

On November 17, O. Sgt. Francis S. Worth of *Mississippi*'s Marine Guard informed his commanding officer, 1st Lt. Philip H. W. Fontané, that Cpl. James R. Easton of his Guard and Pvt. David L. Dixon from the *Potomac* had discussed stealing a boat, rowing it to the mainland and deserting to the enemy.[42] This information had been reported to him by Pvt. Richard Carmen on the tenth, and the sergeant, after completing his own investigation, was sure the two intended to carry out their plans. Fontané duly reported the matter to the commanding officer at Ship Island, Lt. Thomas McKean Buchanan, USN.[43] Buchanan also delved into the matter. His investigation found that Easton repeatedly told his comrades that he would not fight against Virginia, his native state. Carmen told Buchanan that Dixon was agreeable to the plan and, further, that Dixon often made contemptuous remarks regarding the cowardice of those in command of Union warships not willing to go up against the Southern navy. Buchanan also learned that a boat had been secreted near the Ship Island lighthouse, and felt that it would be used by Easton and Dixon to make their escape.[44]

Commander Smith promptly had the two Marines arrested and brought aboard USS *Massachusetts*, where he had them confined in double irons. After reporting the case to Captain McKean, it was decided to send the two north aboard USS *Connecticut* to be dealt with at Headquarters, Marine Corps. Still in irons, Easton and Dixon were sent aboard *Connecticut* on November 26. Before the ship left for the North, it was found there was insufficient evidence to prove that Private Dixon was a party to the plan to desert, and he was restored to duty.[45]

Easton arrived at the Brooklyn Navy Yard on December 17, and was placed in confinement. He remained in his cell until February 18, when he was discharged in disgrace by order of the Secretary of the Navy.[46]

The limited manpower reserves of the Navy were quite stretched by the occupation of Ship Island. There simply weren't enough men to provide a permanent garrison for Fort Massachusetts. Therefore, news that the chartered steamer *Constitution* was preparing to bring two regiments of Army troops to Ship Island came as a great relief.[47] The steamer arrived at Ship Island on December 3, with 2,000 soldiers under the command of Brig. Gen. John W. Phelps, USV.[48] In a gradual transferal of forces, the Marines from the several vessels were returned to their original shipboard duties. At 3:00 P.M., December 26, command of Ship Island was turned over to the Army.[49]

After the evacuation of Ship Island by the rebels and its immediate occupation by Union forces, Confederate-held Pensacola became the object of attention on the Gulf coast. Possession of the harbor and facilities at Pensacola would certainly give the government an enormous advantage in planning future moves. It would also silence Colonel Brown.

In the months since the Army had taken responsibility for Fort Pickens, Brown was a constant source of irritation to the Navy. It seemed as though every time the rebels launched a dinghy at Pensacola, Brown feared it to be the prelude to a major attack across Pensacola Bay, and urgent messages to the squadron for immediate reinforcements were sure to follow. When McKean took command of the Gulf Blockading Squadron from Capt. Henry Adams, USN, Brown promptly sent the new commander a list of his demands.

> 1st. That you will place your vessels, not other wise engaged in enforcing the blockade, in such a position near your present anchorage as, in your judgment, may prevent a landing of the enemy on the island.
>
> 2d. That you will keep a small steamer, as now, at the northeast end of the island to guard that entrance.
>
> 3d. That you give me such facilities in unloading vessels as from time to time may arrive as your crew and boats can afford.
>
> 4th. That you will be pleased to send me two complete crews to man the boat left here by Captain Adams, the crews to live in the fort and be rationed by me.
>
> 5th. That you will send a quartermaster or other petty officer to reside in the fort, and who is acquainted with the signals, to take charge of mine, that, if necessary, communication by signals may be held between the fort and ships.

Brown ended his letter with an unveiled threat that it would not be his fault if the same harmony (as existed under Captain Adams' tenure) did not continue.[50]

McKean was highly indignant at the tone of Brown's letter. Knowing that Brown would not hesitate to complain to Washington if even the smallest of his wishes were not complied with, McKean acquiesced, albeit with pointed sarcasm, to all of Brown's requests.

McKean even sent Marines to Santa Rosa Island to strengthen the picket boat patrols.[51]

Although Brown had vetoed the proposed attack on Fort McRee on August 4, the success of the raid carried out by Marines and seamen on September 13-14, had encouraged him to the point that he was suggesting initiating a joint Naval and Army bombardment against Pensacola. All that was needed, according to Brown, was a wind blowing from the right direction to engulf the navy yard and the adjacent facilities, including the steamer *Fulton*, in flames.[52] On October 3, Brown enlarged upon his new-found audacity, and suggested to McKean that there was no time like the present to attack. Reliable information had come to him that the best troops from the Pensacola garrison had been withdrawn to Virginia. The enemy, therefore, was weak in terms of numbers and quality of troops. He proposed two plans. The first was to carry Fort McRee by direct assault. The Army at Fort Pickens would provide the preliminary bombardment, while the Navy supplied the bulk of the forces for the attack. The second plan called for the Navy to run in as close to the mainland as possible and, in concert with the artillerists at Fort Pickens, bombard the Confederates out of Pensacola. The bombardment would be followed by a landing at Pensacola to secure the shore installations. Brown unequivocally stated that the weakness of the enemy was evident by the fact that the garrison had "suffered him to fire into the dry dock and subsequently to burn it, and afterwards Captain Bailey to attack the navy yard, burn a vessel in the slip, and spike one of his most important guns without, in any manner, resenting these gross and palpable insults."[53] Brown would quickly come to rue his arrogance.

On the night of October 8-9, the "weakened and inferior" rebels launched a surprise attack on Santa Rosa Island, caught the troops of the 6th New York asleep in their tents, and, after scattering them, set the camp and storehouses on fire. Having caused as much damage as circumstances permitted, they withdrew to their boats. While waiting to be towed back to the mainland, their tow rope became entangled in the screw of the steamer *Neaffie*. While the propeller was being cleared, the Southerners were attacked by the 1st U.S. Artillery. In the ensuing action, the Confederates suffered 87 casualties. They did, however, manage to carry off twenty prisoners of war with them, including the commanding officer, Maj. Israel Vogdes, USA.[54] While the fighting was still ongoing, USS *Potomac* was hailed by a boat from Fort Pickens, requesting assistance in repelling the attack. The Marine Guard under the command of 1st Lt. George W. Collier was sent aboard the steamer *McClellan* to the fort, but by the time it reached the scene, the raiders were safely back to Pensacola.[55]

1st Lt. McLane Tilton, USMC
George Menegaux Collection

Brown's reaction to the raid was predictable. For the next few weeks, he thought every movement on shore was a preliminary to an all-out attack on Santa Rosa Island. 1st Lt. Alan Ramsay, commander of the Marine Guard of USS *Richmond*, wrote his Commandant that with "every little skirmish or anticipated attack on Pickens, Colonel Brown has the Marines from the vessels off Fort Pickens."[56] On the night of October 27–28, Brown sent a frantic message to the commanding officers of USS *Rhode Island* and *Colorado* that an attack was imminent. 1st Lt. McLane Tilton, second officer of the Marine Guard of USS *Colorado*, wrote his uncle:

> last night we were signaled from the fort that 'the enemy were landing' on the upper end of the Isld. It was the old cry of "Wolf," but nevertheless, the Marine Guard was ordered ashore, and passed the night in the sand and bushes, acting as the reserve for a company of skirmishers across the island. No opportunity for glory, however, offered itself, and this morning (the Marines) took their grog in which I joined, looking very disappointed.[57]

While *Colorado*'s Marines spent the night on the beach, *Rhode Island* cruised back and forth along Santa Rosa Island, ready to intercept a phantom landing force.

Two weeks later, Brown reported that an escaped slave brought him news that the rebels were prepared to assault Santa Rosa Island with a force of 4,000 during the night of November 11. However, Brown claimed, the attack was called off at the last moment due to the gathering of a dense fog bank. Now that the fog had lifted on the morning of November 12, Brown feared the attack would be launched that very night. He pleaded with Captain McKean to send *Colorado* to protect Fort Pickens from the "very great superiority of the numbers of the enemy."[58] Brown's opinion of his enemy had grown appreciably in the six weeks since his scathing criticism of their military competence.

Although Brown was eager for the Navy to reduce the rebel forts and batteries so that the chances of a repeat performance of the October 9 raid would be significantly reduced, there was not enough force at hand to accommodate him. Increased activity in the Passes of the Mississippi River and in the Ship Island and Chandeleur Island Sounds demanded Captain McKean give the situation at Fort Pickens and Pensacola a lower priority.

As early as September 20, indications of batteries being emplaced along the lower Mississippi River gave rise to concerns that the South was attempting to expand its fortifications along the several passages to the main channel of the river. If there were no Southern batteries there, sites for the erection of batteries at the Head of the Passes to forestall any hostile activity were to be selected. An on-site assessment was required and the shallow draft steamer USS *Water Witch* was selected to make a reconnaissance. Cutters from USS *Niagara* were to ascend the river from the South West Pass for the same purpose.

At 4:30 A.M., September 20, the *Niagara* party, consisting of 100 seamen and Marines cast off and rowed upriver. Finding no sign of the enemy, they returned to the ship at 12:20 P.M.[59] Later that morning, *Water Witch*, with a detachment of sailors and Marines from USS *Richmond* went upriver through Pass à l'Outre and, when some four miles from the Head of the Passes, saw the rebel gunboat CSS *Ivy* rapidly steaming up the South West Pass. *Ivy* reached the Head of the Passes before *Water Witch*. A running gun duel ensued, with both ships firing at long range, neither doing any damage to the other. The enemy being at a distance safe enough for a survey of the ground to be made, a cutter was lowered and an engineer officer made an examination of the ground on both sides of the river. The mission satisfactorily completed, *Water Witch* retraced her passage, returning to her station off Pass à l'Outre before sundown.[60]

Quite confident of securing the Head of the Passes, USS *Richmond* and *Preble* steamed up Pass à l'Outre with the intention of erecting a battery on shore. On the afternoon of October 9, their complacency was shattered when *Ivy* appeared, and, at a distance of four miles, opened fire. Capt. John Pope, commanding officer of USS *Richmond*, was astonished to see the enemy shells explode some 500 yards beyond his ship. The gun crews and Marines of both vessels raced to their stations, but *Ivy*'s single gun out-ranged anything aboard *Richmond* or *Preble*. Pope hastily sent a message to McKean, saying that his position was untenable, and that his ships were likely to be driven from their position at the Head of the Passes at any moment. From the anxiety expressed in Pope's message, it appeared likely that if *Ivy* pressed her attack, the two Union warships would have struck their colors.[61] However, the gunboat was satisfied with merely sending her calling cards and retired upriver.

Pope regained his composure after *Ivy* departed and returned to the task of erecting the battery at the Head of the Passes. *Richmond* and *Preble* were soon joined by *Water Witch* and *Vincennes* as a covering force for the construction. Despite the increased force, Captain George N. Hollins, CSN, an officer of the "Old Navy," delivered a night attack that caught Pope completely by surprise and threw Union operations on the lower Mississippi into disarray.[62]

At 3:45 A.M., October 12, the starboard watch aboard *Richmond* was taking on coal when the low silhouette of the ram CSS *Manassas* became visible in the reflected light from the ship's lanterns. Before the alarm rattles could be sprung, the ram smashed into the side of the ship, crushing the planking and tearing a hole the size of a twelve-pound round shot through the hull below the water line. The ram was making ten knots when she struck, and the impact of the collision tumbled many of the crew and Marines from their hammocks, giving them a running start to their stations when the long roll was beat. As *Manassas*, her machinery deranged by the shock, drifted into the darkness, a broadside was loosed from *Richmond*'s port battery. A second followed, joined by three broadsides from *Preble*. The ram was so low in the water that most of the shots passed harmlessly over her. Those that took effect struck the ram's two smoke stacks, collapsing both and placing her crew in peril of being suffocated by noxious fumes trapped below. For a few moments, *Manassas* was at the mercy of the Union flotilla as she lay helplessly in the water. In the time it took for *Preble*'s guns to be sponged out, Engr. William Hardy, CSN, opened the forward hatch, scrambled out on the rounded roof of *Manassas*, and, with an ax, chopped away the wreckage of the stacks, all the while under small arms fire (presumably from the Marine Guard of USS *Preble*). Her vents cleared, the ram got under way.[63] By the time *Preble*'s guns were again loaded, *Manassas* had disappeared into the night.

Pope ordered an immediate withdrawal down the South West Pass. As the ships began running down river, Hollins' squadron—CSS *Ivy*, *James L. Day*, *Tuscarora*, and *McRae*—came into view, preceded by three huge fire rafts. They took up the pursuit after the current swept the fire ashore. *Ivy* took the lead, her single rifled gun sending shells after the retreating Union vessels. The chase continued down the South West Pass until both *Richmond* and *Vincennes* grounded some distance short of the bar. *Preble* crossed the bar, taking up a position to protect two colliers, while *Water Witch* remained close to the immobile pair.

Attack by the Confederate States Navy at the head of the passes

Harper's Weekly

The Confederate gunboats dropped anchor beyond the range of the Union guns and put their own long range cannon into action. *Richmond* was the primary target, and, although not struck, several enemy shots passed through her rigging while her decks were washed with the spray of near misses. *Richmond*, having grounded broadside to the enemy squadron, her port battery and rifled gun on the poop deck had a clear field of fire upriver. Although her return fire fell short of the rebel ships, the volume was sufficient to convince Hollins not to venture any closer.

Cdr. Robert Handy of USS *Vincennes* was unconvinced that Hollins would not close with his ship.[64] Only two of his guns were able to return fire. Shortly thereafter, Handy, letting his worst fears govern his actions, sent word to Pope that he wanted to abandon ship.[65] Pope replied that *Vincennes* should be defended to the last, and only if the Confederates were in the act of boarding the ship was Handy to set her afire. Moments later, Pope ordered the signal flag "Engage the enemy" raised. A very confused Commander Handy excitedly turned to his first lieutenant and the signal quartermaster for its meaning. The first lieutenant, with the signal book in hand, replied that the blue-white-blue flag meant "Abandon ship."[66] Without signaling to the flagship for confirmation of the order, Handy ordered a slow match set to the powder magazine and everyone into the boats. 1st Lt. John H. Higbee, commander of *Vincennes*' Marine Guard, quickly had his Marines over the side and on their way to USS *Water Witch*. Shortly thereafter, Handy, with *Vincennes*' flag wrapped around his waist, presented himself to an upset Pope, who demanded an explanation. Handy stammered to his astonished Flag Officer, that he left the ship in response to the signal flag raised aboard *Richmond*. Once the confusion over the signal flag was explained, and, after waiting some time for an explosion to destroy *Vincennes*, a boat's crew returned to the ship where they found the slow match no longer burning and the ship in no danger of destruction. A mortified Handy was ordered back to his ship with his crew and Marines.[67] Adm. David D. Porter later called the matter "the most ridiculous affair that ever took place in the American Navy," and that it presented "an example unmatched in any navy in the world."[68]

The October 12 engagement at the Head of the Passes brought United States and Confederate States Marines into collision for the second time. CSS *McRae* carried a Marine Guard of some twenty men under the command of O. Sgt. John Seymour. 1st Lt. Alan Ramsay commanded forty-three Marines aboard USS *Richmond*, while twenty-nine served under Higbee on USS *Vincennes*, and another twenty-five were aboard USS *Preble* under the charge of O. Sgt. Andrew J. Gilman. Apart from the assault upon the pride of the

Vincennes detachment for having been ordered to abandon their ship, no injury was done to either force of Marines.

A week after the humiliation at the Head of the Passes, the Marine Guard of USS *Massachusetts* received another opportunity for gunnery practice when CSS *Florida* made her first sortie against the warships anchored at Ship Island.[69] *Massachusetts* quickly engaged the rebel gunboat, and a long-range battle was soon in progress. The superior range of the rifled cannon aboard *Florida* kept *Massachusetts* at bay, one of the rebel shells doing considerable damage to the ship. For the rest of the engagement, *Massachusetts* managed to keep well out of reach of the Confederate gunboat.[70]

After the Head of the Passes operation, McKean's attention could concentrate on Brown's repeated requests for a combined Army-Navy bombardment of the positions at Pensacola. Before plans were solidified, an unexpected source of information presented itself. On the night of November 13, a small boat carrying three men landed on Santa Rosa Island. One of them was 1st Lt. Adam N. Baker, CSMC. He had duped the other two into rowing him into Pensacola Bay under the guise that he was selecting a site on Deer Point to erect a battery. Once away from shore, Baker ordered them to row to Fort Pickens. Baker had resigned his commission as

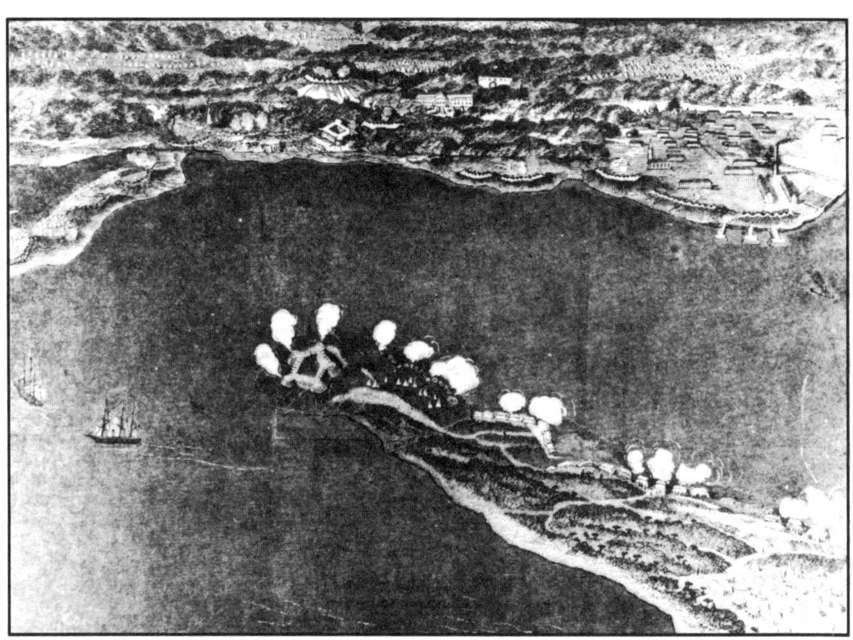

Bombardment of Pensacola

Harper's Weekly

a first lieutenant of U.S. Marines on April 20, at Norfolk, Virginia, and had offered his services, first to Virginia and a few months later, to the Confederacy. After Baker had been turned over to Capt. Thomas Selfridge, USN, commanding officer of USS *Mississippi*, he played the role of the prodigal son, and, in his efforts to redeem himself among his old comrades of the naval service, divulged all he knew of the rebel plans and dispositions.[71] Assured by the information Baker gave, Brown felt certain that, given the proper wind conditions, the rebel facilities on the mainland could be destroyed, even if only a few fires were started by the shelling. Brown gave the impression that he would not feel safe from another attack unless every structure in the vicinity of Pensacola was leveled.

Marker buoys, designating the depth of the water at opportune firing positions near Santa Rosa Island, were set out during the night of November 21. USS *Richmond* and *Niagara* were quietly brought up, anchored, and, at first light, were prepared to open on the enemy fortifications.

During the course of the day-long bombardment, *Niagara* effectively silenced the enemy guns at Fort McRee. *Richmond* took up a position nearer to the shore and assisted in the barrage until an enemy battery was moved to a position to take her under fire. After receiving a number of direct hits, *Richmond* was ordered away from the action. Despite the damage to *Richmond*, Capt. Francis B. Ellison, USN, reported the conduct of the ship's company "evinced the highest order of coolness and gallantry, and no more confusion or excitement prevailed than in ordinary target practice."[72] The firing was kept up by both sides until a sudden rain squall put an end to the contest at 9:00 P.M.

The next morning, the bombardment was resumed. *Richmond*, suffering from severe damage from the previous day's encounter, did not take part. *Niagara* attempted to close the range to the mainland, but the wind and accurate enemy fire took her out of the fray by mid-afternoon. Fort Pickens kept up the bombardment throughout the rest of the day and until 2:00 A.M. on the morning of the twenty-forth. Casualties in the squadron during the two-day duel amounted to one killed and seven wounded, none of them Marines.

On the shore, a battery mounting a ten-inch Columbiad near the navy yard was manned by Confederate States Marines under the command of Capt. Alfred C. Van Benthuysen, CSMC.[73] During the duel on the twenty-second, his battery had fired only two shots at Fort Pickens when he received orders to cease fire, lest the attention of the gunners at Fort Pickens be drawn to the nearby steamer CSS *Time*. The next day, however, Van Benthuysen's Marines were given orders to answer any shots from Fort Pickens. At 10:30 A.M., Colonel

Brown ordered his guns at Fort Pickens to open fire. The Confederate Marine battery immediately replied, the first of the rebel guns to do so. Van Benthuysen's first three shots fell short of Fort Pickens, but those that followed struck the fort, or landed inside. Three were direct hits on the embrasures. His battery fired the last shot of the two-day engagement at 4:00 A.M., November 24.[74]

A second company of Confederate States Marines, commanded by Capt. Reuben T. Thom, CSMC, was part of the reserve force kept out of the line of fire behind the north wall of the navy yard. All troops not serving the guns were placed into this reserve, standing by to repel any landing attempt. The reserve was under the command of Col. Daniel W. Adams, PACS.[75] While the Marines of Van Benthuysen's battery were in the direct line of fire from Fort Pickens, his company went unscathed. Although sheltered by the navy yard wall, two of Captain Thom's Marines were wounded by fragments of brick when a stray shot struck the wall.[76]

After the dust settled from the two-day artillery duel, no military or naval action occurred at Pensacola until January 1, 1862. The Confederates greeted the New Year by firing on a Federal ship making its way to Santa Rosa Island. Fort Pickens replied and in an off and on again affair that lasted through the day, managed to set fire to a few buildings near the navy yard. Nothing further took place at Pensacola until Confederate military disasters at Fort Donelson, Shiloh, and New Orleans compelled the government at Richmond to order all the troops and ordnance to points more critical. By May 10, 1862, everything of military value had been skillfully taken away without the knowledge of Federal forces at Fort Pickens. The first inkling that something was occurring at Pensacola was when observers at the fort saw the glow of fires set at the navy yard by the last Confederates as they departed. Everything of military value from the Pensacola Navy Yard to Fort McRee was put to the torch. When troops from Fort Pickens were ferried across Pensacola Bay by USS *Harriet Lane*, they raised the Stars and Stripes over a heap of smoldering ruins.[77]

On November 8, 1861, an incident took place about 550 miles southeast of Pensacola that brought the United States and Great Britain to the brink of war. Capt. Charles Wilkes, USN, acting on his own authority, stopped the British mail steamer *Trent* nine miles from the coast of Cuba for the singular purpose of arresting John Slidell and James M. Mason, Confederate envoys to France and Great Britain.[78] Wilkes hunted the British ship from Key West to the port of Havana, Cuba. Learning the ship was in the harbor at Havana, Wilkes ordered his ship, USS *San Jacinto*, to a position near the Paredon Grande Light and waited. At 11:40 A.M., on the morning of November 8, the mail steamer was sighted and Wilkes pounced upon his prey.[79]

At midday, Wilkes, keeping *San Jacinto* on a course to intercept, ordered a shot fired across the bows of the British steamer. When the vessel showed no signs of stopping, a second shot was fired. The mail steamer halted. Coming up to within hailing distance, Captain Wilkes dispensed with formalities and pleasantries, simply stating that he intended to board the ship, and Lt. Donald Fairfax, USN, was sent with a boat's crew to demand the surrender of the rebel party. A few moments later, two more boats were dispatched, one carrying O. Sgt. Nicholas Burke and seven enlisted Marines.[80]

Lt. Donald McN. Fairfax, USN
Connecticut State Library

Mason, Slidell, and their party refused Lieutenant Fairfax' request that they peacefully accompany

USS *San Jacinto* in pursuit of the British mail steamer *Trent*
NA Photograph 127-N-523509

him to *San Jacinto.* They insisted that they would not leave the ship unless force was applied. Fairfax immediately summoned the Marines from their boat. The arrival of the Marines caused great commotion among the passengers. Expressions of disbelief and outrage followed the Marines. "Did you ever hear of such an outrage?" "Marines on board!" "Did you ever hear of such a piratical act?"[81] The Marines paid no attention to the comments and, with bayonets fixed, reported to Fairfax outside the main deck cabin.

The show of force and the laying of hands upon their persons was sufficient to satisfy the honor of both Confederate envoys. However, after Mason had been removed from the cabin, Fairfax became involved in an altercation with one of the passengers when he attempted to bring Slidell out of his stateroom. When other passengers began jostling him, Fairfax called for the Marines. Confronted by leveled muskets bristling with bayonets, the passengers immediately drew back. Fairfax, seeing them sufficiently intimidated by the Marines, shouted for the way to be cleared.[82] One of the Marines recalled that Mason was escorted off the ship by Fairfax, who had a firm grip on his collar. Sergeant Burke and the Marines took Slidell in charge.[83]

Mason and Slidell were ultimately transported to Fort Warren in Boston Harbor. In the North Wilkes was acclaimed a hero. In Great Britain, a base villain. There was much indignation at the Court of St. James over Wilkes' violation of international law, and Great Britain rattled her saber so far as to send several thousand troops to Canada. For several weeks, it appeared that war was imminent. The South held its collective breath as they waited for an ultimatum to come from Lord Palmerston, the British Prime Minister, an ultimatum that would certainly be refused by Washington. War would follow. The blockade would be broken by the Royal Navy. The Coldstream Guards would march into battle alongside Confederate troops. British intervention meant independence for the Confederacy. But there was no ultimatum and no British intervention. Tempers cooled and passion abated. Ultimately, the Lincoln Administration gave up the prisoners and provided them transportation to Europe. However, no apology was rendered to the British Government. Wilkes' act was disavowed by the United States as being "unauthorized."

In early December, Marines were involved in another encounter with the rebel navy more than faintly reminiscent of the affair at the Head of the Passes. On December 2, Cdr. T. Darrah Shaw, commanding officer of USS *Montgomery*, was ordered to blockade Horn Island Pass, relieving USS *R. R. Cuyler*.[84] Shortly after 8:00 A.M., December 4, the steamers CSS *Florida* and *Pamlico* were observed making for *Montgomery* at a high rate of speed. The long roll was beaten, and the ship's company quickly took their posts, O. Sgt. William McGrath and the Marine Guard manning one of *Montgomery*'s four 32-pounders.

Shaw took his ship to deeper waters for maneuvering room and opened fire on the steamers at 9:30 A.M. Their guns were long-range rifles, and superior to those aboard *Montgomery*. All of Shaw's shot fell short, and he, "not wishing to expose this vessel, officers and crew to certain destruction from a force so much superior to us in every way," decided not to close with the enemy, but to haul off, steer a course to Ship Island, and see if he could persuade Cdr. Melancton Smith to bring up supporting vessels to Horn Island Pass.[85] During the exchange, Shaw's clerk tied up the signal book, log, letter book, and other documents, preparatory to tossing them over the side in the event of the ship's capture. Shaw's actions appeared to McKean as those of an officer who had been cut from the same bolt of cloth as Cdr. Robert Handy, formerly of USS *Vincennes*. McKean felt only contempt for officers who turned tail at the sight of rebel "men of war," converted merchant vessels with improvised deck mounts for guns. Shaw was relieved from duty on December 28, and followed Handy into obscurity.

Three days later, Marines aboard USS *Massachusetts* and *DeSoto* almost saw action when USS *New London* reported the gunboats CSS *Pamlico* and *Oregon* at the wharf off Mississippi City, Mississippi. The Union vessels ran in to engage them, but coming up fast on shoal water, *Massachusetts* and *DeSoto* were forced to heave to and let *New London* bring the enemy to battle. Lt. Abner Read, USN, took *New London* as close to the shore as the draft of the ship would allow, but still too far off for his guns to reach *Pamlico* and *Oregon*.[86] Read then ran up the rebel flag, union down, and issued a challenge to battle in the form of a gun fired leeward. The gunboats declined the invitation, and, sure that the Federal vessels could not get close enough to disturb them, returned to the wharf.[87] Unable to induce the Confederate gunboats to battle, the three Union warships returned to Ship Island. A. L. Myers, Acting Master, CSN, commanding CSS *Oregon*, saw the episode in a different light. He reported that the Federals declined combat and turned tail when he opened fire.[88]

McKean was pleased with the aggressiveness of Read, and a few weeks later sent orders to Commander Smith to put Read in the van of an expedition to Biloxi, Mississippi, and capture a vessel reported to be there. On December 31, USS *Massachusetts* and *New London* made steam for Biloxi. Aboard *New London* was a detachment from USS *Niagara*, including thirty Marines under the command of 1st Lt. George Butler. Joining the *Niagara*'s men aboard *New London* was the Marine Guard from USS *Massachusetts.*[89]

At 8:00 A.M., the approaches to Biloxi were sounded and the depth found to be too shallow to allow the deep draft vessels to proceed any further. The Marines and sailors scheduled to form the attacking force were transferred to USS *Henry Lewis.* In company with *Water Witch,* she steamed up to the city and anchored at 11:00 P.M.[90] The Marines landed and demanded the surrender of the city. Lt. Thomas McKean Buchanan, USN, accepted the surrender of Biloxi, and promptly ordered the dismantling of a two-gun battery near the Biloxi Lighthouse. A small schooner, unaware of the proceedings, came up, and, after a brief chase, was captured. While no Confederate steamer was located, the mission was otherwise a complete success.[91]

The morning of January 20, 1862, found USS *R. R. Cuyler* patrolling the eastern approach to the Mobile bar, when a strange schooner was seen anchored some eight or ten miles distant. Lt. Francis Winslow, USN, commanding officer of *Cuyler,* ordered a course heading to inspect the vessel.[92] When about five miles from the stranger, Winslow observed her heading for the beach. When she grounded, her crew went over the side and fled to the brush. *Cuyler* pressed forward and Winslow soon saw a group of men congregating on the beach with the apparent intent to destroy the beached schooner. He dispersed them with a few well-placed rounds from his Parrott gun.[93]

The executive officer, Lt. J. Van Ness Philip, USN, then took a boat to the vessel and secured her for towing.[94] While hauling down the schooner's sails, a volley of musketry from the beach sent the boarding party scattering for cover. Lieutenant Winslow ordered O. Sgt. Robert G. Baird to form the Marine Guard on the quarter-deck and to open fire on the rebels ashore. The fire of the Marines, accompanied by a few more shells from the Parrott gun effectively drove them away.

Winslow dispatched two more boats to secure the schooner when events began to go wrong. One boat was swamped and its crew ended up in the water. The first tow rope snapped under the strain, and the second fouled in *Cuyler*'s propeller. While he recovered from these mishaps, the Confederates returned and opened fire on the boats. Four seamen went down. This time the Parrott gun could not be brought to bear. The burden of suppressing the fire fell to Orderly Sergeant Baird and the Marines. The guard kept up a rapid fire, pinning the Confederates behind the sand dunes. Fortunately, USS *Potomac*'s commanding officer, Capt. Levin M. Powell, USN, heard the exchange of gunfire.[95] He promptly sent Actg. Midn. Charles H. Humphrey, and John J. Read with twenty sailors and seven

Marines to *Cuyler*'s assistance.[96] The *Potomac*'s boats were taken in tow by USS *Huntsville*. Coming into range, *Huntsville* opened fire, and the boats cast off their tow lines. Under covering fire from the sailors and Marines in the rescue craft, *Cuyler's* sailors were brought out. The rebels were driven off just before nightfall, and the schooner *J. W. Wilder* was hauled off the beach and taken as a prize.[97]

Three days after the incident involving the capture of the *Wilder*, O. Sgt. John H. Percival, the Marine Guard, and sailors from USS *DeSoto*, boarded and seized the blockade runner *Major Barbour* off Caillou Island, Louisiana. Her cargo was found to contain gunpowder, nitrates, sulfur, percussion caps, and pistols.[98] *DeSoto*, one of the most successful interceptors of blockade runners, added another prize to her list. Her tally of prizes would ultimately reach twenty-three.

On March 1, 1862, USS *New London* paid a return visit to Biloxi, Mississippi. There were signs that the populace of the town were not abiding by the terms of its surrender two months previously. Taking in tow a launch with Marines from USS *Hartford*, *New London* anchored off the town. About 11:00 A.M., the Marines cast off from the ship. Joined by *New London*'s cutter, the two boats made a complete search of the Biloxi area. They found the town to be nearly empty of young men, while the old men, women and children went about their business. To all appearances, the town was not engaging in any activity which could be thought to be in support of the Confederacy. The whole expedition amounted to a seven-hour excursion ashore.[99]

A landing party of sailors and Marines from USS *Mercedita* visited the town of Apalachicola, Florida, on the morning of March 24, 1862. Under orders from Cdr. Henry S. Stellwagen, USN, commanding officer of *Mercedita*, Lt. Trevett Abbot went ashore to demand the surrender of the place in the name of the government.[100] Unfortunately for Abbot, those who met him at the wharf claimed to have no authority to surrender. Abbot threatened naval bombardment, but to no avail. The delegation shrugged its collective shoulders. A frustrated Trevett recalled the landing party, returned to his ship and made his report.[101] Stellwagen was not satisfied.

On April 3, *Mercedita* again visited Apalachicola. Stellwagen, accompanied by O. Sgt. John Dwyer and the Marine Guard, went ashore to demand the surrender of Apalachicola for the second time in a week. The answer was the same. The delegation from city hall stated that they were not the military, and thus did not have the authority to surrender anything. Stellwagen then pronounced Apalachicola "captured." He then gathered the citizenry around him and lectured them not to have any dealings with the Confederacy, or the Navy would return to punish them. At the conclusion of his talk, Stellwagen ordered his landing party back to the boats and, firing a salvo into the air from his boat howitzer, bid farewell to Apalachicola.[102] The town was captured, occupied, and evacuated all in the same day. It was proving to be a most unusual war.

Wharf area of Apalachicola, Florida, where Captain Stellwagen held forth on April 3, 1862

Courtesy of Mrs. Margaret Key

Appendix

The Wreck of the Governor

by
Pvt. William Gould, U.S. Marines

Comrades, listen to my story
In life we pass through varied scenes
From Hampton Roads, on board the Governor
Sailed Reynolds' Battalion of Marines

A leaky boat not fit for sea
Nor any heavy swells
The fault was Morgan's, I believe
Or Secretary Welles

Four hundred officers and men
Embarked in good condition
Under orders of the brave DuPont
For the Port Royal Expedition

Off Hatteras coast a storm arose
Which shook our poor frail craft
Our smoke stack went, her hog beams broke
Her seams yawned for and aft

The storm is raging fiercer still
The seas are running higher
We shipped a sea on our port bow
Which quenched our engines' fire

Now lads be smart, the hog beams brace
And hold on to the ropes
Bring buckets quick and bail away
These are our only hopes

Now God in mercy hear our prayer
Stretch forth thy strong right hand
Say to the raging seas, "Be Still"
Oh save our little band

We safely passed that fearful night
The longed for day appeared
And hope, bright hope beamed from each eye
And every heart was cheered

Now keep her head well to the sea
My boys, she's yet all oak
And now our hopes are crushed again
Her rudder chains are broke

A helpless wreck tossed on the sea
The sport of every wave
Above was darkness and despair
Beneath a yawning grave

What! Ho! A sail, each eye was strained
To catch the welcome sight
And now each heart did bound again
With hope, joy and delight

It proved to be the Isaac Smith
But nothing could she do
Their efforts were all in vain
Of officers and crew

The Young Rover now with canvass spread
Came bounding o'er the tide
And like a bird with wings outspread
Soon bore up alongside

Her Captain hailed, I can't do much
My stay will be but brief
Cheer up my lads, don't be dismayed
And I'll bring you relief

Away she on her mission sped
Now bounding o'er the brine
Comes the Young Rover back again
With the good old ship Sabine

'Twas Ringgold and his gallant crew
Now to the rescue came
And ever in our grateful hearts
Shall live that cherished name

They anchored near and now to work
To save us from the wreck
Spars were rigged out o'er her stern
To hoist us on her deck

Each heart was bounding now with hope
Eyes sparkled with delight
The word went round from lip to lip
We'll all get off to night

Now raged the storm more fiercely, still
'Twere madness to remain
For should she lurch and strike our ship
We ne'er could right again

Now came a scene of wild despair
Now hushed with every breath
And hearts so brave, that knew no fear
Quailed in the face of Death

Some jumped into the raging sea
And sank beneath the waves
They shrieked for aid, and some were saved
But seven found watery graves

We'll try once more, hold—bale away
Don't let your spirits fail
As yet, my boys, we've braved the sea
Yet may outride the gale

She stood by us throughout the night
Her light was our bright star
Like desert travelers we beheld
The promised land afar

Another fearful night we passed
Still, still, my boys, she floats
Now the Sabine again draws near
And lowered are all her boats

And now with lines around our waists
We jump into the sea
Haul'd to the boats, some to the ship
And thus all saved are we

Now God be praised, all safe on board
The good old ship Sabine
Thine be the Glory, Praise and Power
Sav'd by thy hand Divine

On the Governor now all eyes are bent
At anchor safe lay we
She's waterlogged, see how she rolls
Now founders in the sea

And now our grateful thanks we give
To Ringgold and his crew
Their efforts now crowned with success.
What more could mortals do?

And never can our grateful hearts
The debt of life repay
Remembrance still shall fondly cling
When roaming far away

May peace and plenty o'er them smile
Success each one attend
If tossed on life's tempestuous sea
May they never want a friend

And you my comrades tried and true
Ye nobly played your parts
The ropes held on, the water baled
With willing hands and hearts

Bound by the dangers we have passed
A kind farewell to all
In after years such scenes as these
Fond memory will recall

My task is done, we'll drink a health
The toast be your and mine
To Ringgold and his gallant crew
And the U.S. Ship Sabine

And now brave Ringgold wears a sword
Inscribed on a Medallion
Presented by the Privates of
Reynolds' Marine Battalion.

NOTES

CHAPTER 1

1. Israel Green(e), "The Capture of John Brown," *North American Review*, vol. 141, no. 6 (December 1885): 564-569. Hereinafter referred to as Greene, "Capture of John Brown." Cf., "Capture of John Brown, Major Israel Greene's Simple Story of the Affair." *Sioux Falls, Argus Leader*, May 28, 1909, which differs slightly from the former. Hereinafter cited as "Major Greene's Story." A close comparison of the two accounts reveals the latter version of events is, in certain particulars, more reliable.
2. Earlier that evening, a demand for the surrender of the insurrectionists had been sent to the engine house by Col. Robert W. Baylor, commander of the Third Regiment of Cavalry, Virginia Militia. The written reply had been signed by John Brown. See Allan Keller, *Thunder at Harpers Ferry* (Englewood, N.J.: Prentice-Hall, 1958), 114.
3. Maryland State Senate, *Document Y, Correspondence Relating to the Insurrection at Harper's Ferry, 17th October, 1859* (Annapolis, 1860), 5. Hereinafter referred to as *Document Y.*
4. Among the "extremities" Phelps considered was informing the press of the situation. If the report was exaggerated, premature publication would certainly hurt the B&O. See Ibid., 7, Telegram, Phelps to J. B. Ford (B&O Agent at Wheeling, Va.), October 17, 1859-11:30 A.M.
5. Ibid., 6. Telegram, Quynn to Smith, Frederick, October 17, 1859-10 o'clock, A.M.
6. Ibid., 7. Telegram, A. Diffey to W. P. Smith, Martinsburg, via Wheeling, October 17, 1859.
7. Ibid., 6-7. Telegram, anonymous to the Baltimore Newspaper Press, Frederick, October 17.
8. Floyd, John Buchanan (1806-1863). Virginia politician and Secretary of War under President James Buchanan. Later served as a brigadier general in the Provisional Army of the Confederate States. Commanding at Fort Donelson during the battle of February 13-16, 1862, Floyd relinquished his command, made an ignominious escape and left his troops to their fate. Less than a month later, Jefferson Davis revoked Floyd's commission.
9. *Document Y*, 9. Telegram, Garrett to Floyd, October 17, 1859-10:20 A.M.
10. Ibid. Telegram, Garrett to Buchanan, Baltimore, October 17-10:30 A.M.

11. Steuart, George Hume (1790-1867). Maryland soldier and civic leader. Participated in the War of 1812 as an officer of the "Washington Blues." Commander of the First Light Division, Maryland Volunteer Militia, 1841-1861. Father of Confederate Brig. Gen. George Hume "Maryland" Steuart. Wise, Henry Alexander (1806-1876). Virginia lawyer, U.S. Congressman, 1832-1844, U.S. Ambassador to Brazil, 1844-1847, and Governor of Virginia,1855-1860. Served as a brigadier general in the Provisional Army of the Confederate States, 1861-1865, and promoted to major general just before the end of the war.
12. *Document Y*, 9. Telegram, Steuart to Garrett, Baltimore, October 17, 1859. The services of the First Light Division, Maryland Volunteer Militia were tendered to President Buchanan at 1:00 P.M. Telegram, G. H. Steuart to Hon. J. Buchanan, Camden Station, Baltimore, October 17, 1859. Records of the Adjutant General, Record Group 94, File 386-W-1859, "Suppression of the John Brown Raid at Harpers Ferry, Oct/59." National Archives, Washington, D.C. Hereafter, all National Archives Record Groups will be cited as RG, followed by the number of that particular Record Group.
13. *Document Y*, 10. Telegram, Wm. H. Richardson, Adjutant General (of the Commonwealth of Virginia) to Garrett, Richmond, October 17, 1859-2:40 P.M. The orders from Governor Wise arrived several hours after Dr. John D. Starry, a Harpers Ferry physician, had first sent a messenger and later slipped away, riding to Charlestown to alert the authorities of the insurrection. The Jefferson County militiamen were already engaged at Harpers Ferry by the time the orders were sent. See Allan Keller, *Thunder at Harpers Ferry* (Englewood, N.J., 1958), 54-55, 72-77.
14. *Document Y*, 12. Telegram, Smith to Thos. H. Parsons, Baltimore, 10:40 A.M., October 17, 1859.
15. Telegram, Morris to "The President," Baltimore, October 17, 1859, received at Washington at 12 o'clock. RG 94, "John Brown Raid."
16. Telegram, Floyd to " Cdr., Fort Monroe," Washington, October 17, 1859. RG 94, "John Brown Raid."
17. RG 94, "John Brown Raid."
18. Stuart had invented a device to facilitate the attachment of the cavalry saber to the waist belt, and hoped to sell the idea to the War Department. Maj. H(enry). B. McClellan, *The Life, Character and Campaigns of Major-Gen. J. E. B. Stuart* (Richmond, 1880), 11.
19. Isaac Toucey, 1792-1869. Connecticut jurist and politician. U.S. Congressman, 1835-1839, Governor of Connecticut, 1846-1847, Attorney General of the United States, 1848-1849, U.S. Senator, 1852-1857 and Secretary of the Navy, 1857-1861.
20. Greene, "Capture of John Brown," 564.
21. Muster Roll of Marine Barracks, Washington, 1st to the 31st October, 1859. Entry 101, Muster Rolls. January 1798-December 1945. Records of the United States Marine Corps, Record Group 127. Hereinafter referred to as RG 127, Muster Rolls.
22. In Greene, "Capture of John Brown," Greene states that he "instantly replied to Mr. Walsh [*sic*] that we had 90 men available." "Major Greene's Story," states that Greene told Welsh he couldn't tell how many were available. The first version of the meeting relates a discussion about the trouble and Welsh replying that "Ossawatamie Brown of Kansas, with a number of men had taken the Arsenal at Harper's Ferry," before he "returned speedily to the Navy Department Building." The second account says that Welsh simply asked where he could find Colonel Harris. At the point in time when Welsh arrived at the Marine Barracks, the leader of the insurrections was still known as "Smith." Further, it seems unlikely that Welsh would have come all the way to the Marine Barracks just to find out how many Marines were ready for service and to chat with Greene. Welsh

certainly would have handed Toucey's message to Colonel Harris before returning to his post at the Navy Department.

23. Entry 42, Historical Division, Letters Received, 1818–1915. RG 127. Hereinafter referred to as RG 127, Letters Received-HD.
24. Entry 4, Letters Sent, August 1798–June 1901; March 1804–February 1884. RG 127. Hereinafter referred to as RG 127, Letters Sent.
25. Ranks and numbers compiled from the Muster Roll for Marine Barracks, Washington, October 1859. RG 127, Muster Rolls.
26. One sergeant, two corporals, and thirty-six privates were detached to Marine Barracks, Brooklyn on the morning of October 17, 1859. RG 127, Muster Rolls.
27. Toucey to Russell, Washington, November 5, 1859. Entry 1, Letters to the Commandant and Other Officers of the Marine Corps. General Records of the Navy Department. Record Group 80. Hereinafter referred to as RG 80, Letters to Marine Officers. At the time of the Harpers Ferry incident, Greene had twelve years' experience as an officer of the line. In regard to seniority, he was five years junior to Russell. However, in terms of actual field service, Greene was the more experienced officer. Russell spent just over eight years before being appointed paymaster on the staff of the Corps. Greene may have considered the paymaster's presence an affront to his professional ability since there is no mention of Russell in either of his accounts of the affair.
28. Toucey to Greene, Navy Department, October 17, 1859. RG 80, Letters to Marine Officers.
29. Greene, "Capture of John Brown."
30. *Document Y,* 15–16. Telegrams, Smith to L. M. Cole, Stationmaster, Monocacy, 9:15 P.M., October 17, 1859, and Garrett to Smith, Baltimore, October 17, 1859.
31. Greene, "Capture of John Brown."
32. Egerton to Lee, Baltimore, Md., December 22, 1859. RG 94, "John Brown Raid."
33. Douglas S. Freeman, *R. E. Lee. A Biography* (4 vols. New York, 1934–1935), vol. 1, 395.
34. J. E. B. Stuart to "My Dear Mama," Fort Riley, K. T., January 31, 1860. Typescript copy in the Harpers Ferry File, Historical Reference Branch, Marine Corps Historical Center. The Marine Corps Historical Center will hereinafter be cited as MCHC.
35. Lee to "Honble Secty of War," Relay House, October 17, 1859, 7:45 P.M. RG 94, "John Brown Raid."
36. *Document Y,* 13. Telegram, Gilbert to Smith, Washington Junction, October 17, 1859.
37. Greene, "Capture of John Brown." See also, Keller, *Harpers Ferry,* 126, and Stuart to "My Dear Mama."
38. *Report of the Select Committee in the Senate of the United States, 36th Congress, 1st Session* (Washington, 1860), 41. "Colonel Lee to the Adjutant General."
39. *Document Y,* 22. Lee to "Hon. Secretary of War," no time or date given but probably shortly after midnight, October 18, 1859.
40. Harris to Floyd, Washington, October 18, 1859. RG 127, Letters Sent. Noting that the Marines had left Washington under urgent orders, the Commandant requested, under the provision of an 1814 Act of Congress, that the Secretary send the necessary camp equipage to the Marine detachment at Harpers Ferry from army stores. However, since the Marines returned to Washington as soon as their mission was accomplished, there was no need for the War Department to fill his requisition.
41. Stuart to "My Dear Mama." Stuart wrote that 2,000 spectators were on hand on the morning of October 18, 1859.
42. Oswald Garrison Villard, *John Brown, 1800–1859: A Biography Fifty Years After* (Boston, 1910), 452. Shriver's remarks quoted as reported by his daughter, Mrs. John A. Tompkins.

43. Keller, *Harpers Ferry,* 147. In June 1860, a court of inquiry was held in regard to the actions of Colonel Baylor during the Harpers Ferry affair. O. Jennings Wise, son of Gov. Henry Wise, wrote the court stating that Baylor was guilty of cowardice in not storming the engine house when Lee offered him the task. Wise stated that Baylor gave a "False, cowardly and insulting reason for not leading the attack on the engine house. . . . to wit, that it was a duty which belonged to the mercenaries—meaning the Marines—who were paid for it." As quoted in Villard, *John Brown,* 464. Baylor was acquitted of all charges at his court of inquiry. See *Richmond Free Press,* June 21, 1860, for an account of the trial. During the Civil War, Baylor embraced secession, raised a company in Charlestown, and was elected its captain. His company, the "Baylor Light Horse," was attached to the 7th Virginia Cavalry, commanded by Col. Turner Ashby. He later served as a company commander in the 12th Virginia Cavalry Regiment. Baylor was severely wounded through the lungs on April 27, 1862, near McGaheysville, Virginia. He was taken prisoner in December 1862, while recuperating from his wounds at Harpers Ferry. While in Union hands, Baylor was tried by court-martial for having killed a Union soldier when that man was carrying a flag of truce. The charges were ultimately dropped and Baylor subsequently exchanged in December 1864. Upon his return to duty, Baylor was appointed Provost Marshal for the Valley District. He died in 1883.
44. Villard, *John Brown*, 452. The exchange between Lee and Greene was recorded in an affidavit prepared by G. A. Schoppert, who witnessed the scene. Ibid., 642, n. 60.
45. Greene, "Capture of John Brown," 566.
46. Stuart to "My Dear Mama."
47. *Senate Select Committee Report,* "Colonel Lee to the Adjutant General," 43-44, annex A.
48. "Major Russell was a charming and cultivated man of great coolness, and then about thirty-five years old. He jumped through the door with Greene, unarmed, carrying in his hand only a little rattan switch." Statement of Col. John Tompkins, son-in-law to Colonel Shriver of the Maryland Volunteer Militia as quoted in Villard, *John Brown,* 642, n. 62, Greene, "Capture of John Brown." For a different account of the assault on the engine house, see Alexander R. Boteler, "Recollections of the John Brown Raid." *Century Magazine,* vol. 26, no. 3 (July 1883): 399-411. Boteler, U.S. Congressman, 1859-1861, C. S. Congressman, 1862-1864, and colonel on the staff of Lt. Gen. Thomas J. Jackson, wrote that the Marines made three rushes with the ladder at the engine house door. At the second attempt, a volley was fired from within, wounding Privates Quinn and Ruppert, the former mortally. The third rush knocked the right hand leaf of the door inward. Greene then leaped at the door, his weight causing it to fall to the ground, and disappeared inside the building.
49. "Major Greene's Story." In Boteler, "Recollections of the John Brown Raid," the author stated that Colonel Washington, upon being freed from the engine house, told him that Greene's sword, during its downward arc, caught on a rope. Had it not, the old gentleman was sure the blow would have cleft Brown's skull. Another eyewitness to the scene several years later claimed that Greene battered Brown to the floor with his bent sword, beating him into unconsciousness with blows to the head. See, The *New York Times,* October 13, 1929, "John Brown's Raid by One Who Saw it." Copy in the "Harpers Ferry File," Marine Corps Historical Center. See also, John E. P. Daingerfield, "The Fight at the Engine-house as Seen by One of His Prisoners." *Century Magazine,* vol. 30, no. 2 (June 1885): 267. The author stated that, "Brown fell forward with his head between his knees, and Green [*sic*] struck him several times over the head . . . holding his sword in the middle and striking with the hilt and making only scalp wounds."

50. Stuart to "My Dear Mama." Greene confided to Stuart after the affair that his sword was so dull that he could not have hurt Brown with it.
51. Greene, "Capture of John Brown." Exactly what type sword Greene was carrying at Harpers Ferry has been the subject of much speculation. One school of thought contends that he had his traditional Mameluke sword with him at Harpers Ferry. The second school, to which the author subscribes, maintains that a Mameluke sword would not have bent double upon striking the breast plate, and that Greene was carrying a non-regulation sword at the time. One adherent to the idea that Greene was carrying the traditional Marine officer's sword was invited to demonstrate the validity of his position. Playing the part of John Brown, and, wearing a period cartridge box belt, he would receive the point of a Mameluke sword on the breast plate with the approximate amount of force that Brown had received in 1859. If his theory held true, the Mameluke sword would bend. He declined the test.
52. Quinn, who enlisted on November 23, 1855, was a month and four days away from his discharge when he was mortally wounded at Harpers Ferry. RG 127, Muster Rolls.
53. The *New York Times'* eyewitness account of October 18, 1929, states that the mortally wounded Anderson was kicked and spat upon while he was being brought out of the engine house and continued to be abused until he bled to death several minutes later.
54. In a February 1931 interview, former Commandant of the Corps, Brig. Gen. George Elliott said that John Roach, Drum Major of the Marine Band, a powerfully built man, hauled John Brown out of the engine house. See Col. Harold C. Reisinger, USMC, "Andrew Mealey and the Mongoose," *Marine Corps Gazette* (February 1931): 41, 52. Although the muster roll of Marines who were detached to Harpers Ferry does not list Roach, it does not mean he was not there. The muster roll does not list Russell either. Roach, prior to taking up his post as drum major on September 24, 1859, held the rank of sergeant of Marines. Twelve of his forty-six years with the Marine Corps were spent as a noncommissioned officer.
55. Thomas Drew, *The John Brown Invasion: An Authentic History of the Harper's Ferry Tragedy. . . .* (Boston, 1860), 12.
56. Boteler, "Recollections of the Raid," 410–411.
57. Lee to "Hon. Secy of War," Harpers Ferry, October 18, 1859. RG 94, "John Brown Raid."
58. *Document Y,* 21. Smith to Garrett, Harpers Ferry, October 18, 1859-8 A.M.
59. *Document Y,* 24. Smith to Victor Smith et al., (Harpers Ferry) October 18, 1859-8:30 P.M.
60. These papers were of an incriminating nature. There were over 400 letters divulging Brown's plans, many from prominent abolitionist leaders in the North. Lee forwarded them to the War Department in the care of Major Russell, who left Harpers Ferry in the afternoon of October 18. See, Lee to "Honbl Sect of War," Harpers Ferry Arsenal, October 18, 1859. RG 94, "John Brown Raid."
61. Keller, *Harpers Ferry,* 154–157. See also, *Senate Select Committee Report,* 9–12.
62. The *New York Herald's* October 19, 1859, account of the Harpers Ferry incident, arguably the most thorough, was followed by articles, including statements given by a number of the participants, in the October 24 and 26 editions.
63. Keller, *Harpers Ferry,* 157–161. For the full text of the interview, see The *New York Herald,* October 21, 1859.
64. Passenger Department, Baltimore & Ohio Rail Road, *Book of the Royal Blue,* vol. 45, no. 5 (Baltimore, 1903), 7.
65. Keller, *Harpers Ferry,* 164–165.
66. Villard, *John Brown,* 470.
67. *Senate Select Committee Report,* Colonel Lee to the Adjutant General, 43.

68. Ibid., 43.
69. Telegram, Toucey to Greene. Navy Department, October 19, 1859. RG 80, Letters to Marine Officers. The departure of the Marines pleased Harpers Ferry Superintendent A. M. Barbour not at all. Citing a "perfect panic" at Harpers Ferry, he pleaded to the Secretary of War by telegraph for troops to replace them. To placate Barbour, Floyd requested Toucey to countermand the order for the withdrawal of the Marines from Harpers Ferry. This was done on the morning of October 20 but the Marines had long since left the place. Persistent rumors of an abolitionist plot to rescue Brown caused Barbour to press his demand for troops. On October 28, Colonel Drinkard telegraphed the Harpers Ferry Superintendent that forty Marines would be sent to protect the armory the next day "if really necessary. Is it?" Secretary Floyd was at Harpers Ferry that day and convinced Barbour that the government workers should be armed to protect the armory until a company of the 1st U.S. Artillery arrived. The Marines were not sent. RG 94, "John Brown Raid."
70. *Senate Select Committee Report,* Colonel Lee to the Adjutant General, 43.
71. Ruppert, who had been in the Corps just over a month when he was wounded at Harpers Ferry, was promoted to corporal and would have been promoted to sergeant but for his inability to read and write. See, John Harris, Col., Comdt. to Capt. A. N. Brevoort, Washington, July 13, 1861. RG 127, Letters Sent. Ruppert received an Honorable Discharge from the Marine Corps at Philadelphia on October 10, 1863.
72. Harris to Toucey, Washington, November 15, 1859. RG 127, Letters Sent.
73. Lee to "Col. S. Cooper, Adjt. Genl. U.S. Army," Harpers Ferry, October 19, 1859. RG 94, "John Brown Raid."
74. RG 80, Letters to Marine Officers.
75. RG 127, Letters Received-HD. Miller and three friends, William H. Fox, John R. McNealea, and Richard H. Wiley, enlisted in the Marine Corps in January 1860. After a tour of instruction at Marine Barracks, Washington, the four were attached to the Marine Guard of USS *Niagara.* Their first sea duty was an around the world cruise when *Niagara* transported the emissaries of the Emperor back to Tokyo, Japan in the summer of 1860.
76. *The Oxford Dictionary of Quotations,* 2d ed. (London, 1955), 85.

CHAPTER 2

1. RG 127, Letters Received-HD. Copied from the *New York Times,* November 3, 1860, p. 8, col. 3.
2. RG 127, Letters Received-HD, with a clipped copy of the item which appeared in the *New York Times,* November 5, 1860, p. 1, cols. 5–6.
3. RG 127, Letters Received-HD.
4. Read to Harris (approved and forwarded by A. N. Brevoort, Capt. Comdg.), Marine Barracks (Brooklyn, N.Y.) November 5, 1860. RG 127, Letters Received-HD.
5. Harris to Toucey, Washington, November 10, 1860. RG 80, Entry 14, "Letters from the Commandant and Other Officers of the Marine Corps." Hereinafter referred to as RG 80, Letters from Marine Officers.
6. Endorsement by the Secretary of the Navy on the reverse of Harris' letter of November 10, 1860, cited above. RG 80, Letters from Marine Officers.
7. Jones to "My Dear William," U.S. Steamer *Richmond,* "Spezia" (Genoa, Kingdom of Italy) November 22, 1860, Jones Family Papers, Historical Society of Delaware.
8. Ralph W. Donnelly, "Notes of an Old-time Marine Officer, Lt. A. J. Hays." *Military Collector and Historian,* vol. 42, no. 3 (Fall 1990): 97–98.
9. John J. Crittendon (1787–1863). Kentucky Whig-Democrat politician. U.S. Senator, 1817–1819, 1835–1841, U.S. Attorney General, 1841, U.S. Senator, 1841–1847, governor of Kentucky, 1848–1850, U.S. Attorney General, 1850–1853,

and U.S. Senator, 1853-1863. He was the father of Maj. Gen. George B. Crittendon, PACS, and Maj. Gen. Thomas L. Crittendon, USV.

10. Daniel Boyer to "Dear Mother," Marine Barracks, Washington, D.C., January 13, 1861. Daniel Locker Boyer enlisted at Marine Barracks, Philadelphia on January 3, 1861. He was promoted to the rank of corporal on June 13, 1861, and My thanks to Paul Loane of Cherry Hill, New Jersey for providing copies of Private Boyer's letters.
11. RG 127, Letters Received-HD.
12. Harris to Terrett, Headquarters, Marine Corps, January 5, 1861. RG 127, Letters Sent. Terrett took 2d Lts. Clement D. Hebb and J. Ernest Meiere with the detachment.
13. U.S. Navy Department, *Official Records of the Union and Confederate Navies in the War of the Rebellion* (30 volumes with index; Washington, D.C., 1894-1922), Series I, vol. 4, 409. Hereinafter referred to as *N. O. R.,* Series I being understood, otherwise indicated. The enlisted Marines who made up the detachments of Terrett and Hays came from the Guard at the Washington Navy Yard.
14. I. Toucey to Harris, Navy Department, January 8, 1861. RG 80, Letters to Marine Officers.
15. Harris to Hays, Headquarters, January 8, 1861. RG 127, Letters Sent. 2d Lt. Becket K. Howell accompanied Hays to Fort McHenry.
16. Hays to Harris, Marine Quarters, Fort McHenry, January 9, 1861. Entry 10, General Records, Letters Received, 1819-1903. RG 127. Hereinafter referred to as RG 127, Letters Received-GR.
17. Harvey Brown (1796-1874). U.S. Military Academy Class of 1818. Seminole War and Mexican War brevets for gallantry in action. Commanding Department of Florida, 1861-1862. Brevet brigadier general, November 23, 1861. Retired, August 1, 1863, Winfield Scott (1786-1866). Commissioned captain of artillery, 1808. War of 1812, Black Hawk War, Seminole and Mexican Wars. Brevetted lieutenant general, 1847. Commander-in-chief of the United States Army, 1841-1861. Presidential candidate of the Whig Party, 1852. Retired, November 1, 1861, Order No. 1, Headquarters, Fort McHenry, January 10, 1861. Copy in RG 127, Letters Received-HD.
18. Harris to Toucey, Headquarters, Marine Corps, Washington, January 12, 1861. RG 127, Letters Sent.
19. Harris to Toucey, Headquarters, Marine Corps, Washington, January 15, 1861. RG 127, Letters Sent.
20. Captain Taylor relieved Brevet Major Terrett at Fort Washington on January 10, 1861. See Harris to Taylor, Headquarters, Marine Corps, January 9, 1861. RG 127, Letters Sent. This Lee was the eldest son of Robert E. Lee, *N. O. R.,* 4:409-410.
21. Ibid., 4:6.
22. Ibid., 5:6.
23. James Armstrong (1817-1868). Appointed midshipman, 1809. Promoted through the grades to the rank of captain, September 8, 1841. Placed on the Retired List with the rank of commodore, April 4, 1867. Court-martialed and suspended from duty for five years for his surrender of the Pensacola Navy Yard.
24. Adam Jacoby Slemmer (1829-1868). U.S. Military Academy, Class of 1850. Promoted through the grades to the rank of brevet brigadier general of volunteers, November 29, 1862. Wounded at the Battle of Murfreesboro, December 31, 1862. Reverted to the rank of lieutenant colonel after the war.
25. Rear Adm. George E. Belknap, U.S.N., "The Home Squadron in the Winter of 1860-61." Military Historical Society of Massachusetts, *Naval Actions and History, 1799-1898* (Boston, 1902), 75-100.

26. Tennent Lomax (1820–1862). Alabama lawyer, soldier, newspaperman, and politician. Served as a captain of Alabama Volunteers during the Mexican War. Prior to the Secession Crisis, Lomax served as captain of the Montgomery True Blues, and subsequently as colonel of the 2d Regiment, Alabama State Troops. He was commanding this force when the Navy Yard at Pensacola was seized. When the 2d Regiment was disbanded, Lomax was elected lieutenant colonel of the 3rd Alabama Infantry, and was later advanced to the post of regimental commander with the rank of colonel. He was killed in action at the head of the 3rd Alabama at the Battle of Seven Pines, June 1, 1862.
27. Francis B. Renshaw (?–?). Appointed midshipman, November 1, 1828. Promoted through the grades to the rank of lieutenant, September 8, 1841. Resigned his commission, January 23, 1861. Appointed 1st lieutenant, C.S. Navy, March 26, 1861. Paroled as a lieutenant commander at Montgomery, Alabama, May 20, 1865.
28. As quoted in J. Michael Miller, "Marine's Telling of 1861 Florida Navy Yard Fall Given," *Fortitudine,* vol. 20, no. 4 (Spring 1991), 8–9. Based upon the eyewitness account of James Ivey (ca. 1835–1918), who enlisted in the Marine Corps on March 16, 1866, and served until April 20, 1896, retiring with the rank of quartermaster sergeant.
29. Conway's patriotism was rewarded in communications from the Secretary of the Navy and with a gold medal struck in his honor and subscribed to by 148 Californians. *N. O. R.,* 4:55–57.
30. Ibid., 9.
31. Henry Walke (1808–1896). Appointed midshipman, February 1, 1827. Promoted through the grades to the rank of rear admiral, July 13, 1870. Placed on the Retired List, April 26, 1871. Mexican War service at the Battles of Vera Cruz, Tuspan, and Alvarado.
32. Testimony of Cdr. Henry Walke, USN. Court of Inquiry Convened at Washington, D.C., February 8, 1861, to Investigate the Surrender of the Navy Yard at Warrington, Florida, Case 3070, Entry 294, Naval General Courts-Martial and Courts of Inquiry. Record Group 45, Naval Records Collection of the Office of Naval Records and Library. Hereinafter referred to as RG 45, Court-martial Records.
33. *N. O. R.,* 4:24–27, 40–41.
34. Deck Log of USS *Wyandotte,* January 18–20, 1861. Records of the Bureau of Naval Personnel, Record Group 24. Hereinafter referred to as RG 24, Deck Logs.
35. *N. O. R.,* 4:71–77, 212–215.
36. Victor M. Randolph (1797–?). Appointed midshipman, June 11, 1814. Promoted through the grades to the rank of captain, September 14, 1855. Resignation accepted, January 14, 1861. Appointed captain, C.S. Navy, March 26, 1861. Paroled at Montgomery, Alabama, May 30, 1865.
37. RG 80, Letters from Marine Officers.
38. *N. O. R.,* 4:27.
39. Richard S. Collum, Major, USMC, *History of the United States Marine Corps* (New York, 1902), 111.
40. *N. O. R.,* 4:73. No action was taken by the Navy Department in regard to the role of Captain Watson in the surrender of the Warrington Navy Yard.
41. Joseph Holt (1807–1894), Kentucky lawyer and politician. Postmaster General during the Buchanan Administration. Replaced John B. Floyd, who resigned under a cloud of controversy, as Secretary of War on December 31, 1860.
42. Winfield Scott Papers, Manuscripts Division, Library of Congress, Accession No. 10, 943.
43. Harris to Toucey, Washington, February 15, 1861. RG 127, Letters Sent.

44. Archibald Henderson (1783-1859). Appointed second lieutenant of U.S. Marines, June 4, 1806. Promoted through the grades and to Commandant of the Marine Corps, October 18, 1820. Died, January 6, 1859.
45. "An Act for the Better Organization of the Marine Corps," passed, June 30, 1834. For an interesting and spirited account of the struggles of the Corps during the administrations of President Andrew Jackson, see J. Robert Moskin, *The U.S. Marine Corps Story* (New York, 1977), 105-109, Allan R. Millett, *Semper Fidelis* (New York, 1980), 57-68, and Colonel Robert D. Heinl, USMC, *Soldiers of the Sea* (Annapolis, 1962), 37-40.
46. William S. Dudley, *Going South: U.S. Navy Officer Resignations & Dismissals on the Eve of the Civil War* (Washington, 1980), Table II, 16-17.
47. RG 80, Letters from Marine Officers.
48. Toucey to Sayre, Navy Department, January 15, 1861. RG 80, Letters to Marine Officers.
49. Toucey to Sayre, Navy Department, February 9, 1861. RG 80, Letters to Marine Officers.
50. Toucey to Sayre (Late Second Lieutenant, Marine Corps), Navy Department, February 14, 1861. RG 80, Letters to Marine Officers.
51. Russell to Sayre, Marine Barracks, Washington, February 14, 1861. File of Calvin L. Sayre, Major, P. A. C. S., Entry 193, Compiled Military Service Records, Part 1, Staff Officer Files, Record Group 109, War Department Collection of Confederate Records. Hereinafter referred to as Staff Officers File with the name of the officer preceding, RG 109, Confederate Records.
52. Tyler to "My dear Sir," Marine Barracks, Washington, February 14, 1861. Sayre's Staff Officer File, RG 109, Confederate Records.
53. Letter of recommendation from Harris, Head Quarters, Marine Corps, Washington, Feb. 14, 1861. Sayre's Staff Officer File, RG 109, Confederate Records.
54. Ralph W. Donnelly, *Biographical Sketches of the Commissioned Officers of the Confederate States Marine Corps* (Washington, N.C., by the author, 1973, Revised, 1983), 35.
55. Donnelly, *Biographical Sketches,* 29. The Augusta, Georgia *Chronicle and Sentinel,* February 17, 1861, issue had announced Read as ninth on a list of twenty captains appointed to the Regular Army of Georgia.
56. Ibid. See also Read's Staff Officer File, RG 109, Confederate Records. Although there is no official notice of Read's serving with the C.S. Marines, he may have done so after the Battle of Port Royal for a brief period of time.
57. Howell's sister Varina was Jefferson Davis' second wife.
58. Howell to Davis, Washington, February 27, 1861. Jefferson Davis Collection, Tulane University.
59. Letter of recommendation from Harris, Washington, March 2, 1861. RG 127, Letters Sent.
60. Letter of recommendation from Harris, Washington, March 2, 1861. RG 127, Letters Sent.
61. Staff Officer Files for Hays, Holmes, and Ingraham, RG 109, Confederate Records and Donnelly, *Biographical Sketches,* 14, 16, 18.
62. Edward McPherson, ed., *The Political History of the United States of America during the Great Rebellion* (Washington, D.C., 1865), 84, as quoted in Dudley, *Resignations,* 6.
63. Toucey to Harris, Navy Department, February 28, 1861. RG 80, Letters to Marine Officers.
64. Donald A. Craig, "Today in Washington History." Undated newspaper clipping from the *Washington Evening Star,* presumably a copy of a column in the March 1, 1861, edition of the *Star.* Francis M. Scala Collection, Music Division, Library of Congress.

65. Boyer to "Dear Mother," Marine Barracks, Washington, D.C., January 24, 1861, and to "Dear Sister," Washington, D.C., February 1, 1861.
66. Testimony of Lt. Cdr. Reigert B. Lowry, USN, in the case of Capt. Edward McDonald Reynolds, USMC. *Senate Executive Document No. 9, 40th Congress, 1st Session.* March 1867.
67. In early January, a rumor was afoot that secessionists would attempt to storm the Washington Navy Yard to get weapons to prevent the inauguration of Lincoln. In addition to other security measures, Cdr. John A. Dahlgren, USN, established day and night patrols of Marines from the Navy Yard Guard and suggested Marines from the Washington Barracks be used to patrol the streets leading to the Navy Yard at night. See *N. O. R.,* 4:411–412. On February 1, a General Order was issued in which Marines were assigned to a 12-pounder howitzer under the command of Lt. Henry H. Lewis, USN, at the main entrance to the yard. See Ibid., 413.
68. Toucey to Harris, Navy Department, March 3, 1861. RG 80, Letters to Marine Officers.
69. Toucey to Harris, Navy Department, March 3, 1861. RG 80, Letters to Marine Officers.
70. Thompson to Hoff, U.S. Rg. Ship *Princeton,* Philadelphia, April 17, 1861. Copy in RG 127, Letters Received-HD.
71. Henry Kuhn Hoff (1809–1878). Appointed midshipman, October 28, 1823. Promoted through the grades to the rank of rear admiral, April 13, 1867. Placed on the Retired List, September 19, 1868. Hoff was the father of Marine officer Henry B. Hoff.
72. Thorn to Welles, Washington, April 17, 1861, Gideon Welles Papers, Library of Congress, Box 45. Quoted fully in Dudley, *Resignations,* 10.
73. David M. Sullivan, "A Glimpse of the Virginia Marine Corps," *Military Collector and Historian,* vol. 44, no. 4 (Winter 1992), 171–174. Both Baker and Rich were summarily stricken from the rolls of the Marine Corps on May 23, 1861.
74. David M. Sullivan, "The Puzzle of Adam N. Baker," *Military Collector and Historian,* vol. 41, no. 1 (Spring 1989), 2–7.
75. David M. Sullivan, "Every Inch a Rebel of the Deepest Dye: The Strange Case of Jabez C. Rich," *Military Collector and Historian,* vol. 45. no. 3 (Fall 1993), 110–116. Rich left his post without authority a year later to visit his mother in Maine and was arrested by order of U.S. Secretary of War Edward Stanton. He was imprisoned in Maine until July 14, 1864. See also Donnelly, *Biographical Sketches,* 30–33, and Part 3, Unfiled Slips and Papers File, RG 109, Confederate Records.
76. Of the four who did not, one, Maj. Addison Garland, was put in a most embarrassing position by one of his brothers. A. B. Garland wrote to Virginia Governor John Letcher on May 1, 1861, tendering the services of his brothers, Capt. Robert R. Garland, 7th U.S. Infantry, and Capt. Addison Garland, USMC, stating he was authorized to do so. See A-L Folder, Box 427, Executive Papers, Gov. John Letcher, Virginia State Archives. Robert Garland joined the Confederate cause, rising to the rank of colonel, 6th Texas Infantry. Addison Garland was not appointed to any office in the Virginia or Confederate forces, nor did he resign his Marine Corps commission. The remaining Virginians who remained loyal to their Corps and Union were Bvt. Lt. Col. William Dulany, 1st Lt. David M. Cohen, and 2d Lt. Clement D. Hebb.
77. John D. Hayes, Rear Admiral, USN (Ret.), ed., *Samuel Francis DuPont: A Selection from his Civil War Letters* (3 vols. Ithaca, N.Y., 1969), vol. 1, 63; F to "My precious," Navy Yard, Philadelphia, April 24, 1861. Du Pont was particularly distressed over the resignations of Terrett and other Virginians. He wrote, "Can you conceive of anything like it?"

78. Terrett's Staff Officer File, RG 109, Confederate Records and Donnelly, *Biographical Sketches,* 45.
79. Tyler's Staff Officer File, RG 109, Confederate Records and Donnelly, *Biographical Sketches,* 50.
80. Harris to Welles, Headquarters, Marine Corps, Washington, May 3, 1861. RG 127, Letters Sent. Other applicants were Capt. W. L. Shuttleworth, Capt. I. T. Doughty, 1st Lt. A. S. Nicholson, 1st Lt. James Lewis, and 2d Lt. Philip R. Fendall.
81. Considering Nicholson unqualified for the position, Harris tried to block his appointment. Nicholson had an interview with Secretary Welles and dispelled any misgivings regarding his fitness for the office. See Nicholson to F. P. Blair, Washington, May 9, 1861, copy in RG 80, Letters from Marine Officers for Nicholson's version of the controversy.
82. Tansill's Staff Officer File, RG 109, Confederate Records, and Donnelly, *Biographical Sketches,* 40–42.
83. *New York Times,* June 19, 1861, p. 8, col. 3, "Arrest of a Secession Lieutenant in the Navy."
84. Tyler was commissioned a first lieutenant of Confederate States Marines on August 20, 1861, and assigned to the Marine Battalion at Pensacola. His past habits brought about his downfall as he was arrested, tried by court-martial and dismissed from the Confederate service for drunkenness and conduct unbecoming an officer. See David M. Sullivan, "Baptism of Fire," *Pensacola History Illustrated,* vol. 1, no. 2 (1984), 9–14.
85. Donnelly, *Biographical Sketches,* 49, and Sullivan, "A Glimpse of the Virginia Marine Corps, 1861."
86. Simms' Staff Officer File, RG 109, Confederate Records and Donnelly, *Biographical Sketches,* 36–37.
87. For the full text of Tansill's letter, see Donnelly, *Biographical Sketches,* 41.
88. Taylor to Harris, Winchester, Va., April 25, 1861. RG 127, Letters Received-HD.
89. Welles to Stark, Navy Department, October 17, 1861. RG 80, Letters to Marine Corps Officers. Stark's bureaucratic troubles were only beginning. Detained after his notice of dismissal arrived at San Francisco, Stark escaped and made a harrowing two-month journey to Richmond. Owing to the delay in reaching Richmond, he was unable to apply for a position in the Confederate States Marine Corps until, as Stephen R. Mallory, Secretary of the Confederate States Navy, termed it, that Corps "was organized," and an officer who was junior to him in the U.S. Marine Corps, George P. Turner, had been promoted to captain. Stark was shut out of his rightful place as an officer of Confederate Marines due to a technicality. He subsequently was commissioned in the Virginia Light Artillery and rose to the rank of lieutenant colonel. Stark's Staff Officer File, RG 109, Confederate Records.
90. Franklin Buchanan (1800–1874). Appointed midshipman, January 28, 1815. Promoted through the grades to captain, September 14, 1855. Dismissed from the service, May 22, 1861. Appointed captain, Confederate States Navy, September 5, 1861. Promoted to rear admiral, August 21, 1862. Paroled, May 17, 1865.
91. David D. Porter, *The Naval History of the Civil War* (New York, 1886), 27, and Donnelly, *Biographical Sketches,* 22.
92. Harris to Meiere, Head Quarters, Marine Corps, Washington, April 26, 1861. RG 127, Letters Sent.
93. Donnelly, *Biographical Sketches,* 22.
94. National Archives Microfilm Publication M 1091, *Subject File of the Confederate States Navy, 1861-1865.* (61 rolls. Washington, D.C.) Roll 13, Subject File H, Subfile HA, "Engagements With Enemy War Vessels, Miscellaneous." Narrative

of H. Ashton Ramsay, Chief Engineer, Confederate States Steamer *Merrimac* [*sic*].

95. Greene to "The Hon. Sec. of the Navy," Berryville, Va., May 17, 1861. Copy in RG 127, Letters Received-HD.
96. Greene's Staff Officer File, RG 109, Confederate Records, and Donnelly, *Biographical Sketches, 13.*
97. Capt. W. W. McKean to Brevoort, U.S.S. *Niagara,* Quarantine Ground, New York, April 30, 1861, RG 127, Letters Received-HD, Brevoort to Harris, Brooklyn, May 1, 1861, RG 127, Letters Received-GR, Harris to Welles, Washington, May 6, 1861, RG 80, Letters from Marine Officers, and Welles to Harris, Navy Department, May 10, 1861, RG 127, Letters Received-GR. John R. McNealea enlisted in Company C, 8th Virginia Infantry, was elected second lieutenant and subsequently captured at the Battle of Gettysburg. Paroled in May 1865. William W. Fox enlisted in Company H, 8th Virginia Infantry, on July 13, 1861, was wounded at the Battle of Antietam and discharged, February 13, 1863. Richard H. Wiley served in Company K, 6th Virginia Cavalry. He died on June 12, 1862. Information courtesy of Jane Sullivan, Branch Manager, Thomas Balch Library, Loudon, Virginia.
98. Another case of a Marine refusing to take the oath of allegiance was that of Pvt. Robert L. Morgan, who gave as a reason that he was a Southerner with all his family living in Louisiana and Virginia. Given the choice of disgracefully discharging him if he was truly a secessionist or putting him to duty if he was merely trying to evade it, Colonel Harris investigated and chose the latter option. Harris to Brevoort, Headquarters, Marine Corps, June 13, 1861. RG 127, Letters Sent. Morgan served out the rest of his four years without incident.
99. Welles to Tattnall (late 1st Lieutenant, USMC), Navy Department, November 22, 1861. RG 80, Letters to Marine Officers, acknowledging receipt of his resignation dated October 7, and informing him he had been dismissed from the service as of November 22, 1861.
100. Charles Wilkes (1798-1877). Appointed midshipman, January 1, 1818. Promoted through the grades to captain, September 14, 1855. Placed on the Retired List, December 21, 1861. Promoted to rear admiral on the Retired List, August 6, 1866.
101. Donnelly, *Biographical Sketches,* 42.
102. Ibid.
103. Ralph W. Donnelly, *The Confederate States Marine Corps: The Rebel Leathernecks* (Shippensburg, Pa., 1989), 62, 103-104, 111, 124-125, 217-219.
104. *Senate Document No. 234, 58th Congress, 2d Session, Journal of the Congress of the Confederate States of America: 1861-1865* (7 volumes, Washington, D.C., 1904-1905), vol. 1, p. 266.
105. David M. Sullivan, "Four Marines at Fort Fisher," *Military Images,* vol. 14, No. 2 (September-October 1992), 6-7.
106. Henderson to Harris, Warrenton, Fauquier County, Va., May 20, 1861. RG 127, Letters Received-GR.
107. Welles to Harris, Navy Department, July 22, 1863. RG 80, Letters to Marine Officers.
108. McCawley to "The Hon R. H. Thompson, Secretary of the Navy," Washington, August 28, 1877. RG 80, Letters from Marine Officers.
109. William Wister McKean (1800-1865). Appointed midshipman, November 30, 1814. Promoted through the grades to the rank of captain, September 14, 1855. Placed on the Retired List, December 27, 1861. Promoted to the rank of commodore on the Retired List, July 16, 1862. McKean was the father of Marine officer William B. McKean.

110. *N. O. R.*, 4:200-201.
111. Charles Henry Poor (1808-1882). Appointed midshipman, March 1, 1825. Promoted through the grades to the rank of rear admiral, September 20, 1868. Placed on the Retired List, June 9, 1870.
112. *N. O. R.*, 16:528-529.
113. David Dixon Porter (1813-1891). Midshipman, Mexican Navy, 1826. Appointed midshipman, U.S. Navy, February 2, 1829. Promoted through the grades to the rank of admiral, August 15, 1870.
114. Oath of John L. Broome, 1st Lieut., U.S. Marines, U.S. Ship *Powhatan*, Pensacola, May 25, 1861. RG 80, Letters from Marine Officers.
115. McKean to Broome, U.S. Steam Frigate *Niagara*, Off Mobile, June 6, 1861. John Lloyd Broome Papers, P.C. 50, Personal Papers Branch, Marine Corps Historical Center.
116. Welles to George Broome, Navy Department, June 28, 1861. Broome Pp.
117. Porter to Broome, On Ship *Powhatan*, Off South West Pass, Mississippi, August 2, 1861. Broome Pp.
118. Welles to Maddox, Navy Department, October 3, 1861. RG 80, Letters to Marine Officers.
119. Maddox to Welles, Philadelphia, October 5, 1861. RG 80, Letters from Marine Officers.
120. The resignation and dismissal of so many officers of the regular service caused Congress to pass a measure designed to punish those who left their positions too hastily. Section 2 of the Act of August 2, 1861, made it a crime for any officer who, after tendering his resignation, left his post prior to official notice that the resignation had been received, would be charged as a deserter and punished as such.

CHAPTER 3

1. RG 127, Muster Rolls. Muster Rolls of the various Marine Barracks and detachments for the month of April 1861.
2. Harris to Toucey, Headquarters, Marine Corps, Washington, November 5, 1860. RG 127, Letters Sent.
3. Robert Anderson (1805-1871). U.S. Military Academy, Class of 1825. Promoted through the grades to brigadier general, May 15, 1861. Retired, October 27, 1863.
4. *O. R.*, 1:9-10. In Collum, *History of the Marine Corps,* 111, the author erroneously reported that Marines were among the reinforcements intended for Fort Sumter. There were none.
5. William Henry Seward (1801-1872). New York lawyer and Whig/Republican politician. Governor of New York, 1839-1842. Twice unsuccessful candidate for the Republican presidential nomination in 1856 and 1860. Secretary of State, 1861-1869.
6. Simon Cameron (1799-1889). Pennsylvania Democratic and Republican politician. U.S. Senator, 1845-1849, 1857-1861. Secretary of War, 1861-1862. Ambassador to Russia, 1862-1863, U.S. Senator, 1867-1877.
7. *N. O. R.*, 4:227.
8. Ibid.
9. Ibid., 245-247.
10. Ibid., 229.
11. *Powhatan's* Marine Guard had been sent to Marine Barracks, Brooklyn when the ship was laid up at the Brooklyn Navy Yard on April 1. The Guard was back aboard the ship by April 5. RG 127, Muster Rolls. Muster roll for USS *Pawnee,* April 1861.
12. RG 24, Deck Logs. Log of USS *Pawnee,* April 13, 1861.

13. Porter, *Naval History of the Civil War,* 99. Porter contended that Fox' dependence on the launches of the *Powhatan* was flawed. Not having examined the vessel when it was at New York, Fox had no way of knowing the launches were entirely unseaworthy. According to Porter it was either a case of poor planning or good excuse-making on the part of Fox.
14. *N. O. R.,* 245–251.
15. John P. Gillis (?–1873). Appointed midshipman, December 12, 1825. Promoted through the grades to the rank of captain, July 16, 1862. Placed on the Retired List, September 28, 1866. Promoted to commodore on the Retired List, September 28, 1866.
16. RG 24, Deck Logs. Log of USS *Pawnee,* April 13, 1861.
17. Porter, *Naval History of the Civil War,* 101.
18. Colonel Brown was ordered to take the engineer company of Sappers and Miners, Company M, Second Artillery, Company C, Third Infantry, and Company E, Third Infantry. *O. R.,* 1:365–366.
19. Andrew Hull Foote (1806–1863). Appointed midshipman, December 4, 1822. Promoted through the grades to the rank of rear admiral, July 16, 1862.
20. *N. O. R.,* 4:235.
21. Francis Asbury Roe (1823-1901). U.S. Naval Academy, Class of 1841. Promoted through the grades to the rank of rear admiral, November 3, 1884. Placed on the Retired List, October 4, 1885.
22. Israel Vogdes (1816–1889). U.S. Military Academy, Class of 1837. Served during the Seminole and Mexican Wars. Promoted through the grades to brigadier general of volunteers, November 29, 1862. Reverted to the rank of colonel after the war. Retired, January 2, 1881. Captured during the Confederate raid on Santa Rosa Island, October 9, 1861.
23. Battery A, 1st U.S. Artillery, embarked from Fort Monroe aboard USS *Brooklyn* on January 27, 1861. The unit was transferred to USS *Sabine* on March 23, and back to *Brooklyn* on April 3. Thanks to Mr. John Slonaker, Chief Historian, Reference Branch, United States Army Military History Institute for this information.
24. *N. O. R.,* 4:114.
25. Welles to Adams, Navy Department, April 6, 1861. This order was carried by Lt. John L. Worden, USN, overland to Pensacola, a very hazardous endeavor, and safely presented to Captain Adams. Attempting to retrace his route north, Worden was arrested by the rebels and held as a prisoner of war.
26. Ibid., 115–116.
27. Francis and George Gardner Papers, Library of Congress, 1/8 Seaman, MMC.
28. *N. O. R.,* 1:376. Adams to Welles, U.S. Frigate *Sabine,* Off Pensacola, April 14, 1861.
29. Gardner Pp.
30. *New York Times.* Undated clipping found in the Historical Reference Branch, Civil War File, MCHC.
31. RG 127, Muster Rolls. Muster roll of USS *Powhatan,* April 1861.
32. Gardner Pp. Musician Gardner's account was written in 1870. The time ashore lugging sandbags no doubt seemed like a period of three months to the youth. In fact, the second time the Marine Guard of USS *Sabine* was landed at Fort Pickens it was ashore from April 23–May 27, 1861.
33. RG 127, Letters Received-GR.
34. *O. R.,* 6:463.
35. John Letcher (1813–1884). Virginia Democratic politician. Member of Congress, 1851–1859. Governor of Virginia, 1860–1863.
36. Clement A. Evans, *Confederate Military History* (Atlanta, 1899. Reprint. Wilmington, N.C., Broadfoot, 1987), 4:38.

37. Arkansas left the Union on May 6, followed by North Carolina on May 20, and Tennessee on June 8.
38. William Booth Taliaferro (1822–1898). Virginia politician and soldier. Captain and major, U.S. Army, 1847–1848. Virginia House of Delegates, 1850–1853. Major general, commanding the Virginia Militia. Appointed colonel of the 23d Virginia Infantry, May 1861. Appointed brigadier general, March 6, 1862, and major general, date unknown.
39. *N. O. R.*, 4:307–308.
40. Charles Stewart McCauley (1793–1869). Appointed midshipman, January 16, 1809. Promoted through the grades to captain, December 9, 1839. Placed on the Retired List, December 21, 1861. Promoted to commodore on the Retired List, April 4, 1867.
41. Samuel Livingston Breese (1794–1870). Appointed midshipman, December 17, 1810. Promoted through the grades to the rank of captain, September 8, 1841. Placed on the Retired List, July 16, 1862. Promoted to rear admiral on the Retired List, September 3, 1862.
42. Admiral Porter was of the opinion that the Secretary of the Navy should have sent one energetic officer, a few gunboats to provide cover, tugboats in numbers sufficient to pull the serviceable ships out and a guard of fifty Marines to cow the secessionists. Porter, *Naval History of the Civil War*, 27.
43. *N. O. R.*, 4:277–278.
44. Benjamin Franklin Isherwood (1822–1915). Appointed first assistant engineer, May 23, 1844. Promoted through the grades to engineer-in-chief, March 26, 1861. Retired, October 6, 1884.
45. Edward William Sloan, III, *Benjamin Franklin Isherwood, Naval Engineer* (Annapolis, 1965), 23.
46. Hiram Paulding (1797–1878). Appointed midshipman, September 1, 1811. Promoted through the grades to the rank of captain, February 29, 1844. Placed on the Retired List, July 16, 1862. Promoted to rear admiral on the Retired List, July 16, 1862.
47. Samuel Francis DuPont (1803–1865). Appointed midshipman, December 18, 1815. Promoted through the grades to the rank of rear admiral, July 16, 1862.
48. William Wallace Hunter, (1803–?). Appointed midshipman, May 1, 1822. Promoted through the grades to the rank of commander. Resigned, April 29, 1861. Appointed commander, C.S. Navy, March 26, 1861. Promoted captain, May 13, 1863.
49. Two officers and ninety-nine enlisted Marines were ordered to USS *Pawnee*. Harris to Lieut. A. S. Nicholson, Headquarters, Marine Corps, April 19, 1861. RG 127, Letters Sent. The Marine detachment was transported to USS *Pawnee* aboard the tug *Anacostia*. The ships rendezvoused off Gemsburry Point, near Mount Vernon and at 5:15 P.M., began transferring the Marines and incendiary materials aboard *Pawnee*. RG 24, Deck Logs. Log of USS *Pawnee*, April 19, 1861.
50. Boyer to "Dear Sister," On Board U.S. Sloop of War *Pawnee* off Norfolk, April 20, 1861.
51. 1st Lt. James Lewis, 2d Lt. Philip R. Fendall, one sergeant, four corporals, and forty-three privates. Muster Roll of *Keystone State*, April 1861. RG 127, Muster Rolls.
52. A clever deception on the part of William Mahone, President of the Norfolk & Petersburg Railroad, who ran trains back and forth loaded with civilians shouting to give the impression that trainloads of soldiers were arriving. See Alan B. Flanders, "The Night They Burned the Yard." *Civil War Times Illustrated*, vol. 18, no. 10 (February 1980), 30–39.
53. Daniel O'Connor (ca. 1833–1872) Enlisted at Marine Barracks, Washington, August 27, 1855. Re-enlisted, September 5, 1860. Re-enlisted January 11, 1865.

Promoted corporal, May 27, 1865, and sergeant, December 1, 1866. Honorably discharged, January 11, 1869.

54. Daniel O'Connor to "Dear Sister," Fort Monro April 24, 1861. Daniel O'Connor Papers, Marine Corps Historical Center, Washington, D.C.
55. *Anacostia,* with a guard of twenty Marines aboard, was removed from the Norfolk expedition on April 20, and sent to patrol Kettle Bottom Shoals, below Alexandria, *N. O. R.*, 4:415.
56. Daniel O'Connor to "Dear Sister," Fort Monro, April 24, 1861. O'Connor Pp. MCHC. Rev. John G. Gammon related a similar account of the arrival of the *Pawnee* at the navy yard in *The Third Massachusetts Regiment, Volunteer Militia in the War of the Rebellion, 1861-1863* (Providence, 1906),14. Gammon recalled that there was no recognition until the band aboard USS *Pennsylvania* began playing the "Star Spangled Banner."
57. Morgan, William James et al., eds. *Autobiography of Rear Admiral Charles Wilkes, U.S. Navy, 1798-1877,* Washington, D.C., 1978), 760. Wilkes recalled that Marine Lt. Col. James Edelin came to him in a very bewildered state, requesting that the Marine Barracks be spared the torch since one of the sergeants kept a hen near his bunk and she was setting on a dozen eggs. Edelin had further cause to be upset. His son, 1st Lt. Thomas Boyd Edelin (USMA, Class of 1855), then visiting the yard, had decided to cast his lot with the secessionists. He ultimately was appointed lieutenant colonel of the 16th North Carolina Cavalry Battalion.
58. See note 57 above.
59. John F. Mackie, "The Destruction of the Norfolk Navy Yard." *Home and Country*, vol. 4, nos. 9-12 (New York, February-May 1889), 1011-12, 1041, 1057-58, 1062-63.
60. See note 51 above.
61. RG 24, Deck Logs. Log of USS *Pawnee,* April 21, 1861.
62. Russell to Welles, Washington, November 12, 1861. RG 80, Letters from Marine Officers. Russell, by way of long association with Sergeant Myers, agreed that he was not a deserter. Both were wrong. Myers had indeed deserted. Not only was Russell mortified by Myers' desertion, he was also professionally embarrassed. Before Myers deserted, he had been Russell's disbursing agent for Marine Barracks, Norfolk. When he left, Myers absconded with $599.59, for which Russell was accountable. See "Memorial of Moses Kelly, Administrator of Major W. W. Russell," House Mis. Doc. No. 30, 37th Congress, 3d Session, referred to Committee on Naval Affairs, February 23, 1863.
63. Edward Donaldson (1816-1889). Appointed midshipman, July 21, 1835. Promoted through the grades to the rank of rear admiral, September 21, 1876. Placed on the Retired List, September 29, 1876.
64. Grogan and Charlesworth subsequently traveled to Montgomery, Alabama where they enlisted in the Confederate States Marine Corps as sergeants. Grogan served throughout the war, performing duty aboard CSS *Patrick Henry* at the Battles of Hampton Roads, and aboard CSS *Richmond.* Charlesworth served aboard CSS *Virginia* during the Battles of Hampton Roads and deserted from Drewry's Bluff shortly after the May 15, 1862, battle at that site.
65. Fifer Thomas Cushley, with Pvts. William Jones, William H. Miller, Edward Robison, and John Dean fell into the hands of the rebels. Cushley reportedly died shortly after the evacuation. The four privates were visited by 1st Lt. Adam N. Baker, VMC, who offered them inducements to join the Virginia Marine Corps, even offering Private Miller the rank of orderly sergeant of the Marine Guard aboard the receiving ship of the Virginia Navy. Miller declined and soon after made good his escape with his three comrades. They reported to duty at Philadelphia on April 26. Wm. H. Miller to Harris, U.S. Naval Hospital, Chelsea, Massachusetts, September 2, 1861. RG 127, Letters Received-GR.

66. Medicus, "Affairs at Norfolk, Va." *Memphis Commercial Appeal,* April 26, 1861, p.1, col. 1. After deserting from Marine Barracks, Norfolk, Myers offered his services to the Governor of Virginia. He was made captain of Company E, 6th Virginia Infantry, but his attachment to Marine Corps discipline proved not to the liking of his recruits. The company was soon disbanded. Donnelly, *Rebel Leathernecks,* 32-33.
67. See note 51 above.
68. Edelin to Harris, Washington, April 25, 1861. RG 127, Letters Received-GR.
69. Madeline Vinton Dahlgren, *Memoir of John A. Dahlgren, Rear-Admiral, United States Navy* (New York, 1891), 332. At this time, the defensive forces at the Washington Navy Yard amounted to 1,100 local militia, sailors, and Marines.
70. See note 51 above.
71. Porter, *Naval History of the Civil War,* 843.
72. RG 127, Letters Received-GR.
73. Lieutenant Fendall's request for sea duty on a foreign station was denied. The elder Fendall's apprehensions regarding fraternal combat nearly came to fruition. James R. Y. Fendall, after accepting a commission as a second lieutenant of Confederate States Marines, was later posted to the Guard of CSS *Jamestown,* and saw duty at Hampton Roads and on the James River. Philip R. Fendall was assigned to command the Marines aboard USS *Susquehanna,* and served in the same area at the same time. On May 8, 1862, *Jamestown* attempted to pass Sewell's Point and was forced back by Union warships, among them USS *Susquehanna.* Later, Confederate States Marine officer Fendall was transferred to the Mobile Station. *Susquehanna* was posted off Mobile during the same period.
74. Dahlgren, *Dahlgren Memoir,* 331.
75. Samuel Peter Heintzelman (1805-1880). U.S. Military Academy, Class of 1826. Promoted through the grades to major general, May 5, 1862. Served in the Mexican War, winning a brevet of major for gallantry at the Battle of Huamantla.
76. Ephraim Elmer Ellsworth (1837-1861). New York/Chicago lawyer and intimate friend of Abraham Lincoln. Organized and led the 11th New York "Fire Zouaves."
77. *O. R.,* 2:40-41.
78. Reigert B. Lowry (1826-1880). Appointed midshipman, U.S. Naval Academy, January 31, 1840. Graduated, passed midshipman, July 11, 1846. Promoted through the grades to the rank of commodore, April 1, 1880. Brother of Marine officer Horatio B. Lowry.
79. Upon receiving Rowan's report of the Alexandria expedition, Welles penned a scathing letter to the commander, stating that he had made a grievous error in allowing the rebels to escape. *N. O. R.,* 4:480-481.
80. James H. Ward (1806-1861). Appointed midshipman, March 4, 1823. Promoted through the grades to the rank of commander, September 9, 1853.
81. *N. O. R.,* 4:491-492.
82. William F. Lynch (1801-1865). Appointed midshipman, January 26, 1819. Promoted through the grades to captain, April 2, 1856. Resigned, April 21, 1861. Captain, VN, April, 1861-June 6, 1861. Captain, CSN, June 10, 1861. Paroled, May 3, 1865.
83. *N. O. R.,* 4:495-496.
84. USS *Pawnee* fired 196 shell and 155 hollow shot during the four and one-half hour battle. RG 24, Deck Logs. Log of USS *Pawnee,* June 1, 1861.
85. A little over a month later, the Marine Guard of USS *Pocahontas* was able to vent its frustration when that ship encountered CSS *George Page* fitting out in Aquia Creek on the morning of July 7, 1861. A short exchange followed with *Pocahontas* firing fourteen shots at the enemy craft. The Marine Guard was reported to have made the second best shot of the contest. *N. O. R.,* 4:565-566.

86. Henry Martin Blue (?—1866). Appointed acting midshipman, U.S. Naval Academy, September 28, 1854. Graduated, midshipman, June 11, 1858. Promoted through the grades to the rank of lieutenant commander, March 24, 1865. Died, August 22, 1866. James Crossan Chaplin (?-1866). Appointed midshipman, U.S. Naval Academy, October 4, 1850. Graduated, passed midshipman, June 20, 1856. Promoted through the grades to the rank of lieutenant commander, April 18, 1863. Died, September 23, 1866.
87. RG 24, Deck Logs. Log of USS *Pawnee,* June 5-6, 1861.
88. *N. O. R.,* 4:535. See also, RG 24, Deck Logs. Log of USS *Pawnee.*
89. Ibid., 538.
90. An escort of honor consisting of 2d Lt. Robert W. Huntington, a sergeant and six privates was detailed to accompany the remains of Commander Ward to New York. Lieutenant Huntington took the casket from New York to Hartford, where he delivered the commander's body to his family. Harris to Huntington, Headquarters, June 24, 1861. RG 127, Letters Sent.

CHAPTER 4

1. Navy Department, *Laws Relating to the Navy and Marine Corps, and the Navy Department* (Washington, 1865), 70.
2. Welles to Harris, Navy Department, April 22, 1861. RG 127, Letters Received-HD.
3. Harris to Dulany, Headquarters, February 6, 1861. RG 127, Letters Sent.
4. Harris to Brevoort and another to Reynolds, Headquarters, Marine Corps, April 29, 1861. RG 127, Letters Sent.
5. John Albion Andrew (1818-1867). Free Soil and Republican politician from Massachusetts. Governor of Massachusetts, 1861-1866.
6. Reynolds to "His Excellency Governor Andrew," Marine Barracks, Charlestown, April 27, 1861. RG 127, Letters Received-HD.
7. Reynolds to Harris, Marine Barracks, Boston, December 15, 1862. RG 127, Letters Received-GR.
8. RG 127, Muster Rolls. Enlistment totals compiled from the muster rolls of Marine Barracks, Brooklyn, Boston, Philadelphia, and Headquarters for the month of May 1861. The muster roll for May 1861, Marine Barracks, Portsmouth was not preserved.
9. Harris to Welles, Headquarters, May 18, 1861. RG 127, Letters Sent.
10. Telegram. S. A. H. Marks, Quartermaster's Clerk to Maddox, Washington, April 30, 1861, reporting a communication from Sgt. Bernard Hopper at the Philadelphia Barracks stating that he was without clothing for the Marines at that post.
11. Slack to Harris, Headquarters, Quartermaster's Office, May 20, 1861. RG 127, Letters Received-HD.
12. Slack to Harris, Quartermaster's Office, January 30, 1861. RG 127. Letters Received-HD.
13. Slack to Maddox, Washington, April 20, 1861. RG 127, Entry 125, Quartermaster's Department, 1813-1863 with gaps, Letters Sent. Hereinafter referred to as RG 127, Letters Sent-QM.
14. Slack to Noe, Washington, April 30, 1861. RG 127, Letters Sent-QM.
15. Slack to Noe Washington, May 17, 1861. RG 127, Letters Sent-QM.
16. Endorsement on the reverse of Slack to Welles, Washington, May 21, 1861. RG 127, Letters Sent-QM.
17. Slack to Noe, Washington, June 1, 1861. RG 127, Letters Sent-QM.
18. Fatigue caps were in such short supply that Brevet Major Reynolds was forced to take the caps from the yard mechanics at Boston and give them to the Marine Guard then going on board the USS *Mississippi.* Harris to Reynolds, Headquarters, May 29, 1861. RG 127, Letters Sent.

19. Slack to Reynolds, Washington, April 8, 1861, RG 127, Letters Sent-QM.
20. S. A. H. Marks, Quartermaster's Clerk to Maddox, Washington, May 2, 1861. RG 127, Letters Sent-QM.
21. Slack, to Brevoort, Washington, May 29, 1861. RG 127, Letters Sent-QM.
22. Slack to Maddox, Washington, July 6, 1861. RG 127, Letters Sent-QM.
23. RG 80. Letters to Marine Corps Officers. Welles to Slack, Navy Department, April 23 and 25, 1861.
24. Slack to Reynolds, Washington, May 1, 1861. RG 127, Letters Sent-QM.
25. Reynolds to Harris, Marine Barracks, Charlestown, April 28, 1861. RG 127, Letters Received-HD.
26. Slack to Commo. John A. Dahlgren, USN, Washington, May 16, 1861, requesting transport of eight cases of rifles to Brooklyn, New York via *Keystone State.* RG 127, Letters Sent-QM.
27. Slack to Reynolds, Quartermaster's Office, Washington, May 16, 1861. RG 127. Letters from the Quartermaster of the Corps.
28. Cameron to Welles, War Department, May 21, 1861. RG 127. Letters Received-GR.
29. The Army, in an effort to save money, had converted several thousand flintlocks to percussion muskets during the 1850's. Most had been issued to the states, but a substantial number were still on hand at the Washington Arsenal in 1861.
30. Despite the worrisome news that the President might cancel the April 22 increase, Harris urged his post commanders to "make every effort to get men and get them up as fast as possible. Don't stop recruiting until you are ordered, whether you have clothing or not." Harris to Reynolds, Headquarters, May 29, 1861. RG 127, Letters Sent.
31. When Maj. Benjamin Macomber died on May 29, 1861, Brevoort, by virtue of being the senior captain, was entitled to promotion. However, his age and infirmities caused Harris to recommend that he be passed over and the second senior captain, John G. Reynolds, be promoted. Harris to Welles, Headquarters, June 8, 1861. RG 80, Letters from Marine Officers.
32. Harris to Brevoort, Headquarters, May 28, 1861, acknowledging Brevoort's letter of May 25. RG 127, Letters Sent.
33. Orders found in RG 127, Letters to Marine Officers, indicate that Guards were directed to USS *Mississippi, Wabash, Colorado, Savannah, Roanoke, Potomac, Jamestown, R. R. Cuyler, Santee,* and *St. Lawrence* by the Secretary of the Navy during the month of May. The Navy Yard Guard had been increased by thirty Marines on April 27.
34. Although speedily appointed, not all of the six new officers reported to duty at once. Two reported almost immediately. Two more reported a month after being appointed. One reported two and a half months after his appointment. The last appointee, Louis M. Goldsborough, Jr., captain's clerk to his father, Capt. Louis M. Goldsborough, Sr., aboard USS *Congress,* did not learn of his appointment until the latter part of May. Consequently, he did not report to duty until July 28, 1861. See E. W. Goldsborough to Harris, Washington, July 19, 1861. RG 127, Letters Received-GR.
35. Hitchcock to "Dear Father," Marine Barracks, Washington, D.C., June 14, 1861. Robert E. Hitchcock Papers, MCHC. A "fuss" was made. The position by lottery caused the Senate to pass a resolution stating "that the Senate are of the opinion that rank and position in the Army, Navy or Marine Corps should not be left to be decided by lot, but, that, all other things being equal, preference should be given to age." The resolution was passed on July 31, 1861, and sent to the President. Despite the opposition of the Senate, Army regulations regarding positions of rank being decided by lottery for those with the

same date of appointment prevailed. See Welles to Lincoln, Navy Department, August 2, 1861. Copy in RG 127, Letters Received-HD.

36. Navy Department, *Register of the Commissioned and Warrant Officers of the Navy of the United States, including Officers of the Marine Corps and Others for the Year 1861.* (Washington, 1861), 76–78.
37. Harris to Dulany, Headquarters, April 25, 1861. RG 127, Letters Sent.
38. Lieutenant Reynolds was detailed to command the Marine Guard of USS *Santee* at Portsmouth on May 29. He and Bvt. Lt. Col. William Dulany argued over the latter's attempt to have Reynolds not only discipline and drill the guard intended for *Santee,* but also the Marines assigned to the barracks. Reynolds to Harris, Portsmouth, June 6, 1861. RG 127, Letters Received-GR. Harris defused the situation by sending Reynolds to the *Colorado* and Hebb to the *Santee.*
39. Wiley to Harris, New York, April 21, 1861, and Pottsville, Pennsylvania, May 1, 1861. RG 127, Letters Received-GR.
40. Harris to Reynolds, Headquarters, May 27, 1861. RG 127, Letters Sent.
41. RG 127, Muster Rolls. Muster Roll for Headquarters, June 1861.
42. Harris to Welles, Headquarters, June 13, 1861. RG 80, Letters from Marine Officers.
43. RG 127, Entry 76, Service Records of Enlisted Men. 1798–1895. Service record of Lawrence Keslar. Hereinafter referred to as RG 127, Service Records.
44. Harris to Welles, Headquarters, June 14, 1861. RG 127, Letters Sent.
45. Report of the Secretary of the Navy, July 4, 1861, "Increase of the Marine Corps." RG 45, Naval Records Collection of the Office of Naval Records and Library, Entry 464, Subject Files of the United States Navy, 1775–1910. Subject File V, Subfile VN, "Naval Policy." Hereinafter referred to as Subject Files, with the specific subheading to follow.
46. Harris to Dulany, Headquarters, Marine Corps, July 8, 1861. RG 127, Letters Sent.
47. Dulany to Welles, Washington, July 23, 1861. RG 80, Letters from Marine Officers.
48. At the time of Dulany's orders, only four years and two months of his forty-four year Marine Corps career were spent at sea. Only the second lieutenants and the most junior first lieutenants on the seniority list had less sea duty than Dulany. See *Navy Register, 1861.*

CHAPTER 5

1. Reynolds was not a graduate of the United States Military Academy. He was dismissed during his senior year.
2. Robert E. Hitchcock to "My dear Mother," U.S. Marine Barrack, July 5, 1861. Hitchcock Pp., MCHC.
3. John E. Reily to "Dear Mother and Father," Marine Barricks [*sic*], Washington D.C. July 10 (1861). Pension application of James Riely. Certificate 2821. National Archives.
4. Andrew Porter (1820–1872). Non-graduate, U.S. Military Academy. Appointed first lieutenant in 1846. Brevetted twice for gallantry during the Mexican War. Promoted through the grades to the rank of brigadier general, August 6, 1861. Resigned, April 20, 1864.
5. Ramsay's information, even to the brigade the Marine Battalion would be attached to, was accurate. Ramsay to Harris, U.S. Sloop *Richmond,* New York, July 11, 1861. RG 127, Letters Received-HD.
6. Harris to Ramsay, Headquarters, July 13, 1861. RG 127, Letters Sent.

7. Telegram. Welles to Ramsay, Navy Department, July 13, 1861. Copy in RG 127, Letters Sent.
8. Irvin McDowell (1818-1885). U.S. Military Academy, Class of 1838. Brevetted captain for gallantry during the Mexican War. Promoted through the grades to the rank of brigadier general, May 14, 1861. Promoted to major general, November 25, 1872. Retired, 1882.
9. Cameron to Welles, War Department, July 12, 1861. RG 107. "Military Books." Book No. 45, July 1, 1861- August 31, 1861.
10. Telegram. Welles to Reynolds, Navy Department, July 13, 1861. Copy in RG 127, Letters Sent. Reynolds had been ordered from Marine Barracks, Boston, on June 4, reporting for duty on June 15. However, he had returned to Boston on personal matters, and was in that city when the orders were sent from the Navy Department, Telegram. Welles to Zeilen, Navy Department, July 14, 1861. Copy in RG 127, Letters Sent.
11. Welles to Harris, Navy Department, July 15, 1861. RG 80, Letters to Marine Officers.
12. Cartter to "Dear Mother," Washington, July 14, 1861. Cartter Family Papers, Manuscripts Division, Library of Congress.
13. Hitchcock Pp, MCHC.
14. As quoted in Stephen B. Oates, *With Malice Toward None: The Life of Abraham Lincoln* (New York, 1977), 271.
15. RG 127, Letters Received-HD.
16. Telegram. Slack to Maddox, Washington, July 15, 1861. RG 127, Letters Sent-QM.
17. S. H. Huntington to "My dear Wife," Washington, July 23, 1861. Robert W. Huntington Papers, MCHC.
18. Harris to Welles, Headquarters, July 16, 1861. RG 80, Letters from Marine Officers. Pennypacker, who enlisted at Philadelphia on June 5, was discharged on July 20.
19. Edward K. Eckert and Nicholas J. Amato, eds., *Ten Years in the Saddle: The Memoir of William Woods Averell* (San Rafael, Calif., 1978), 290.
20. Ibid.
21. David Hunter (1802-1886). U.S. Military Academy, Class of 1822. Resigned, 1836. Appointed paymaster and major, March 14, 1842. Appointed colonel, May 14, 1861, brigadier general of volunteers to rank from May 17, 1861, and major general of volunteers to rank from August 13, 1861. Presided over the military trial of the Lincoln Assassination Conspirators.
22. Henry Warner Slocum (1827-1894). U.S. Military Academy, Class of 1852. Resigned, 1856. Appointed colonel, 27th New York Volunteers, May 21, 1861. Promoted brigadier general of volunteers, August 9, 1861, and major general of volunteers, July 4, 1862. Resigned, September 28, 1865. The United States Infantry Battalion consisted of Companies C and G, 2d U.S. Infantry; B, D, G, H, and K, 3rd U.S. Infantry, and G, 8th U.S. Infantry, and was commanded by Maj. George Sykes (1822-1880). U.S. Military Academy, Class of 1842. Brevetted captain for gallantry during the Mexican War. Rose through the grades to brigadier general of volunteers, September 28, 1861, and major general of volunteers, November 29, 1862. Reverted to the rank of lieutenant colonel in the regular establishment in 1866. Promoted to colonel, 1868. The United States Cavalry Battalion was made up of Companies A and E, 1st U.S. Cavalry; B, E, G, and I, 2d U.S. Cavalry, and K, 2d U.S. Dragoons, and was commanded by Maj. Innis Newton Palmer (1824-1900). U.S. Military Academy, Class of 1864. Brevetted first lieutenant and captain for gallantry during the Mexican War. Promoted through the grades to brigadier general of volunteers, September 23, 1861, and major general of volunteers later in the war. Reverted to the grade

of lieutenant colonel at the end of the war. Promoted colonel in 1868. Retired, March 20, 1879. Charles Griffin (1825-1867). U.S. Military Academy, Class of 1847. Brevetted major for gallantry at the Battle of Bull Run, July 21, 1861. Appointed brigadier general of volunteers, June 9, 1862, and major general of volunteers, April 2, 1865. Reverted to the rank of colonel after the war.

23. *O. R.,* 2:304.
24. C. B. Fairchild, comp., *History of the 27th Regiment N.Y. Vols.* (Binghamton, N.Y., 1888), 10.
25. Col. Daingerfield Parker, USA, "Personal Reminiscences: The Battalion of Regular Infantry at the First Battle of Bull Run." Military Order of the Loyal Legion of the United States, Commandery of the District of Columbia, *War Papers* (Washington, D.C., 1899), 7.
26. Capt. Robert G. Carter, USA, Ret. *Four Brothers in Blue or Sunshine and Shadows of the War of the Rebellion. A Story of the Great Civil War from Bull Run to Appomattox.* (Reprint of the 1913 edition, Austin, 1978), 11.
27. The severity of the day resulted in troops collapsing from the heat. Pvt. Robert Galbraith of Company B fell out of the line of march and lapsed into unconsciousness by the side of the road from the effects of the sun. He was revived by an Army teamster, taken to the camp of the Marine Battalion at Spring Hill Farm and recovered sufficiently to take part in the Battle of Bull Run two days later. Pension Application of Robert Galbraith, National Archives.
28. *O. R.,* 2:307.
29. Cartter Pp., LC.
30. The U.S. Infantry Battalion commanded by Major George Sykes.
31. This was the last instance of enlisted men being made to suffer the lash as punishment in the military services of the United States.
32. Hitchcock Pp., MCHC.
33. Daniel Tyler (1799-1882). U.S. Military Academy, Class of 1819. Resigned in 1834. Appointed colonel, 1st Connecticut Volunteers and brigadier general of volunteers at the outbreak of the war. Mustered out on August 11, 1861, but re-appointed brigadier general of volunteers, August 13, 1861. Resigned April 6, 1864.
34. *O. R.,* 2:326-327.
35. *Alton (Illinois) Evening Democrat*, Tuesday evening, July 30, 1861, "Two Alton Boys in the Battle of Bull's Run."
36. Quote taken from an undated clipping from an unidentified Vermont newspaper found in the Hitchcock Pp., MCHC.
37. Ambrose Everett Burnside (1824-1881). U.S. Military Academy, Class of 1847. Resigned, 1853. Appointed colonel, 1st Rhode Island Volunteers at the start of the war. Appointed brigadier general of volunteers, August 9, 1861, and major general of volunteers, March 18, 1862. Commanding general, Army of the Potomac, November 1862-March 1863. Resigned, April 15, 1865.
38. John P. Victory to "The Editor of the Brooklyn Eagle," Headquarters, 14th Reg't, N.Y.S.M. July 25, 1861. *Brooklyn Daily Eagle, Wednesday* Evening, July 31, 1861, p.1, col. 4.
39. Undated clipping from an unidentified Vermont newspaper found in the Hitchcock Pp., MCHC.
40. William Woods Averell (1832-1900). U.S. Military Academy, Class of 1855. Appointed brigadier general of volunteers, September 26, 1862. Brevetted brigadier and major general, U.S. Army, at the close of the war. Resigned, May 18, 1865.
41. Eckert and Amato, *Ten Years in the Saddle,* 295.
42. Pierre Gustave Toutant Beauregard (1818-1893). U.S. Military Academy, Class of 1838. Brevetted twice for gallantry during the Mexican War. Resigned his commission as captain of engineers, February 20, 1861. Appointed brigadier

general, PACS, March 1, 1861. Promoted to general, C.S. Army to rank from July 21, 1861. Paroled at Greensboro, North Carolina, April 26, 1865.

43. Maj. Augustus S. Nicholson, adjutant of the Marine Battalion, was convinced that a Virginian named Machen, whose house was on the line of the flank march, rode to the Confederate lines to alert General Beauregard to the danger. No evidence of Nicholson's allegation has ever been uncovered. Carter, *Four Brothers in Blue*, 27.
44. Edward Porter Alexander (1835-1910). U.S. Military Academy, Class of 1857. Resigned, May 1, 1861. Appointed captain of engineers, PACS. Promoted through the grades to brigadier general of artillery, PACS, February 26, 1864. Surrendered at Appomattox Court House, April 9, 1865.
45. Gary W. Gallegher, ed. *Fighting for the Confederacy: The Personal Recollections of General Edward Porter Alexander* (Chapel Hill, 1989), 50.
46. Nathan George Evans (1824-1868), U.S. Military Academy, Class of 1848. Resigned his commission as captain of cavalry, February 1861. Appointed colonel, 4th South Carolina. Promoted brigadier general, PACS, October 21, 1861.
47. Barnard Elliot Bee (1824-1861). U.S. Military Academy, Class of 1845. Brevetted to first lieutenant and captain for gallantry during the Mexican War. Resigned his captain's commission on March 3, 1861. Appointed lieutenant colonel, 1st South Carolina Regulars on June 1, 1861, and brigadier general, PACS, on June 17, 1861. Killed in action at Bull Run, July 21, 1861.
48. Mentioned in S. H. Huntington to "My dear Wife," Washington, July 21, 1861. Huntington Pp., MCHC.
49. S. H. Huntington to "My dear Wife," Washington, July 21, 1861. Huntington Pp., MCHC.
50. James Brewerton Ricketts (1817-1887). U.S. Military Academy, Class of 1839. Promoted through the grades to the rank of brigadier general of volunteers to rank from July 21, 1861. Brevetted major general of volunteers, August 1, 1864, and of the Regular Army, March 13, 1865. Retired, January 3, 1867.
51. John Daniel Imboden (1823-1895). Elected captain, Staunton Artillery, April 1861. Organized the 1st Virginia Partisan Rangers and appointed its colonel, summer 1862. Promoted brigadier general, PACS, January 28, 1863.
52. Imboden viewed the matter differently. He reported that he kept up the duel with Griffin and Ricketts from his position on Henry Hill until he was compelled to withdraw for lack of infantry support. In fact, Imboden claimed to have been the only opposition to the Federal advance for more than a half hour after the Confederate troops retreated from the battlefield north of the Warrenton Turnpike. John D. Imboden, Brigadier General, C.S.A., "Incidents of the First Bull Run," The Century Company, *Battles and Leaders of the Civil War* (4 vols., New York, 1887), vol. 1, 229-239.
53. *Pittsburgh Post*, July 31, 1861. "Letter from a Marine Who was at Bull's Run." The writer was identified only as W. B. at the end of the item. He was, in fact, William Barrett, who enlisted in the Marine Corps at Pittsburgh on June 13, 1861. My thanks to Mike Kane of Pittsburgh, Pennsylvania, who brought this item to my attention.
54. Baker letter, *Alton Evening Democrat.*
55. *O. R.*, 2:383.
56. S. H.. Huntington to "My dear Wife," Washington, July 25, 1861, relating a conversation with Captain Jones following the battle. Huntington Pp., MCHC.
57. William Farquhar Barry (1818-1879). U.S. Military Academy, Class of 1838. Appointed through the grades to the rank of brigadier general of volunteers, August 20, 1861, and to major general of volunteers and Regulars during the course of the war. Reverted to the rank of colonel at the end of the war.
58. "Report of the Joint Committee on the Conduct of the War: The Battle of Bull Run." *The Reports of Committees of the Senate of the United States for the*

Third Session of the Congress in Four Volumes (Washington, 1863), 2:168–169. Testimony of Capt. Charles Griffin, January 14, 1862.

59. *O. R.*, 2:383.
60. Testimony of William W. Averell, January 28, 1862. "Joint Committee on the Conduct of the War," 2:215.
61. Ibid., 216.
62. Edward S. Dana to "Dear Sir," Washington, D.C., August 1, 1861. Letter to Dr. William Hitchcock, Lieutenant Hitchcock's father, in the Hitchcock Pp., MCHC.
63. Baker Letter, *Alton Evening Democrat.*
64. Griffin's Testimony, "Joint Committee on the Conduct of the War," 2:169. Major Barry's testimony before the Committee showed evidence of selective memory. He denied ever giving Griffin orders not to fire on the regiment, although he admitted he thought the troops were the 14th Brooklyn. Ibid., 142–149.
65. Barrett Letter, *Pittsburgh Post.* Francis Harris enlisted in the Marine Corps at Pittsburgh, June 8, 1861.
66. Baker Letter, *Alton Evening Democrat.*
67. The combination of the haphazard and desultory firing of the Zouaves and Marines and the volleys of the 14th Brooklyn took a heavy toll among the 33rd Virginia. Forty-three were killed, and one hundred forty were wounded. "Colonel Cummings' Account," *Southern Historical Society Papers* (vol. 34, Richmond, 1906), 367–371.
68. Griffin's Testimony, "Joint Committee on the Conduct of the War," 2:169.
69. Charles Tevis, "Colonel Fowler's Own Story." *The History of the Fighting Fourteenth* (New York, 1911), 230. See also, Robert Hunt Rhodes, ed., *All for the Union: A History of the 2nd Rhode Island Volunteer Infantry in the War of the Great Rebellion As told by the diary and letters of Elisha Hunt Rhodes, Who enlisted as a private in '61 and rose to the command of his regiment* (Lincoln, R.I., 1985), 34. Rhodes reported leaving his regiment and going forward to see what was happening on Henry Hill. He came upon a spot where the trees were spattered with blood and the ground covered by the bodies of Marines and Louisiana Zouaves. Since the Louisiana Zouave Battalion had been severely battered during earlier fighting on Matthew's Hill, it had left the field and was not engaged on Henry Hill. To what regiment these dead Zouaves belonged is a mystery.
70. Ibid.
71. D(aniel). B. Conrad, "History of the First Battle of Manassas and the Organization of the Stonewall Brigade." *Southern Historical Society Papers* (Richmond, 1891) vol. 19:82–94. In 1883, Lt. Col. E. B. Fowler, commanding officer of the 14th Brooklyn, stated that the Marines broke and ran after receiving the volley from Jackson's troops, and were followed by the "unsupported Fourteenth." However, Conrad's personal observations of the bodies lying on the ground in and near the Confederate position cast doubt on Fowler's statement. It is possible that Fowler's comments were embellishments of the 14th's combat reputation at Bull Run, while Conrad had nothing to gain by reporting that the corpses of Marines lay beyond those from the Brooklyn regiment.
72. William Owen Miller, *In Camp and Battle with the Washington Artillery of New Orleans* (Boston, 1885), 41. Andrew Douglas Ramsay was an unsuccessful applicant for a Marine Corps commission in early March 1847 despite personal recommendations from both President James K. Polk and Secretary of the Navy John Y. Mason. He was subsequently appointed a second lieutenant of the 1st Artillery Regiment to rank from June 7, 1855, and promoted to first lieutenant on February 25, 1861. An account of Ramsay's death may be found in C. A. Fonerden, *Military History of Carpenter's Battery* (New Market, 1911), 10–11. Ramsay's corpse was stripped its fine garments, with the exception of the silk stockings, by an unknown rebel after the battle.

73. This attack may have been launched in support of the 69th New York. The New Yorkers spearheaded the last attempt to retake Henry Hill from the Sudley Road position. Pvt. William Barrett stated, "We were the first called to assist the 69th."
74. S. H. Huntington to "My dear Wife," Washington, July 25, 1861. Huntington Pp., MCHC.
75. Oliver Otis Howard (1830-1909). U.S. Military Academy, Class of 1854. Elected colonel, 5th Maine Volunteers, May 5, 1861. Resigned his Regular Army commission, June 7, 1861. Brigadier general of volunteers, September 3, 1861. Major general of volunteers, November 29, 1862. Re-appointed to the Regular Army with the rank of brigadier general, December 21, 1864. Promoted major general, 1886. Retired, 1894.
76. Arnold Elzey (1816–1871). U.S. Military Academy, Class of 1837. Brevetted for gallantry during the Mexican War. Resigned his captain's commission on April 25, 1861. Appointed colonel, 1st Maryland Infantry, April–May 1861. Appointed brigadier general, PACS, to rank from July 21, 1861. Promoted major general, December 4, 1862. Paroled at Washington, Georgia, May 9, 1865. Edmund Kirby Smith (1824-1893). U.S. Military Academy, Class of 1845. Brevetted captain for gallantry during the Mexican War. Resigned his commission as major, 2d U.S. Cavalry, April 6, 1861. Appointed lieutenant colonel, PACS. Appointed brigadier general, PACS, June 17, 1861, major general, PACS, October, 11, 1861, lieutenant general, PACS, October 9, 1862, and full general, PACS, February 19, 1864. Commanding general, Trans-Mississippi Department, January 1863-June 1865. Surrendered at Galveston, Texas, June 2, 1865.
77. S. H. Huntington to "My dear Wife, " Washington, July 25, 1861. Huntington Pp., MCHC.
78. Hitchcock's body was never recovered from the battlefield. It was undoubtedly buried in one of the mass graves dug by the Confederates in the days following the battle. A memorial service was held for Hitchcock at Shoreham, Vermont, his home town, on September 11, 1861.
79. Baker Letter, *Alton Evening Democrat.*
80. Barrett Letter, *Pittsburgh Post.*
81. Daniel Quinn to Jacob Zeilen, Charlestown, Mass., October 28, 1868. RG 127, Letters Received-HD.
82. Eckert and Amato, *Ten Years in the Saddle,* 299. Averell mistakenly identified Major Reynolds as Bvt. Maj. Jacob Zeilen in his memoirs. Since Zeilen had been wounded in the arm during the fighting, he would have been in no condition to be swinging his sword at weeds.
83. Barrett Letter, *Pittsburgh Post.*
84. Edwin S. Barrett, "Adventures at Bull Run," Frank Moore, comp., *The Civil War in Song and Story 1860-1865.* (P. F. Collier, Pub., n. p., 1889), 256–261.
85. Barrett Letter, *Pittsburgh Post.*
86. *O. R.,* 2:390–391.
87. S. H. Huntington to "My dear Wife," Washington, July 24, 1861. Huntington Pp., MCHC.
88. Harris to Welles, Headquarters, July 26, 1861. RG 80, Letters from Marine Officers.
89. Welles to Cameron, Navy Department, July 24, 1861. Copy in RG 127, Letters Received-HD.
90. Cartter Pp., LC.
91. Private Stanley was originally listed as "Missing." in Major Reynolds' after action report. See *N. O. R.,* 4:581. Stanley's family was still trying to find out what happened to him as late as April 1862. See Jonas White to "The Hon. Col. John Harris, Comm'ant. of Marine Corps at Washington City," Philadelphia, April 28, 1862. RG 127, Letters Received-GR.

92. RG 127, Letters Sent.
93. Perkins had suffered a gunshot wound through the left ankle, and had been left on the battlefield. He was exchanged on January 5, 1862, and restored to duty. He died at Camden, N.J., November 17, 1919. Pension Certificate 2378.
94. Harris to Miss Mary Barrett, Headquarters, July 29, 1861. RG 127. Letters Received-GR. It is assumed that all response letters informing loved ones that a son, husband or brother was missing or had been killed in action were very similar.
95. *N. O. R.,* 4:581, "[Subenclosure.] Report of Marine Battalion under command of Major John G. Reynolds in the recent battle before Manassas, July 21, 1861," submitted by Aug. S. Nicholson, Adjutant and Inspector, Marine Barracks, Washington, D.C., July 23, 1861. This list of killed, wounded, and missing does not appear with Reynolds' report as printed in *O. R.,* 2:391-392.
96. Henry Clark's father was employed by the Canada Powder Company of Hamilton, Ontario, Canada, and very concerned about the fate of his son. Three letters written between August 5-23, 1861, can be found in RG 127, Letters Received-HD. Jno H. P. White to "The Hon, Gideon Welles," Acton, Massachusetts, August 29, 1861, and Lewis Wood to "Hon. Gideon Welles," Winslow, New Jersey, April 4, 1862. RG 127, Letters Received-GR. Mrs. Sarah Hamm to "the Hon Col. Harris," Philadelphia, August 5, 1861, and May 28, 1862. RG 127, Letters Received-GR. Pension Certificate 560, National Archives, in the name of Honora Barrett, mother of Pvt. John Barrett. Upon his return from rebel hands, Barrett was posted to duty at Marine Barracks, Philadelphia. Surg. James M. Greene, USN, reported that Private Barrett was frequently unable to perform his duties due to chronic debility. Surgeon Greene recommended that the ailing Marine be released from the service on February 1, 1862. Barrett was discharged on Surgeon's Certificate for consumption on February 6, 1862. He died of that disease on May 5, 1862. Stewart served in Company C, 10th U.S. Infantry, April 3, 1856-April 3, 1861, and enlisted in the Marine Corps on June 17, 1861. Pension Certificate of William Stewart, 16216, National Archives. John Cannon to Harris, Philadelphia, July 29, 31 and August 2, 1861, RG 127, Letters Received-HD. Michael Cannon to Harris, Philadelphia, June 12 and July 15, 1862, RG 127, Letters Received-GR. Pension Certificate of Robert Duncanson, 19203, National Archives.
97. *N. O. R.,* 4:581 (Subenclosure).
98. RG 127, Muster Rolls. Muster roll for Headquarters, July 1861.
99. Henry Clark to "My Dear Sister Hattie," Richmond, Virginia, August 3, 1861. Copy in RG 127, Letters Received-HD.
100. Pension Certificate of Garrett Steiner, 13589, National Archives.
101. Corporal Steiner and Privates Stewart, Otto, Perkins, and Barrett joined Liggon's as soon as they were sufficiently recovered from their wounds.
102. William H. Jeffrey, *Richmond Prisons, 1861-1862* (St. Johnsbury, Vt., 1893), 8.
103. Benjamin F. Perkins joined at Headquarters, January 5, 1862, John Barrett, January 8, Robert Duncanson, January 15, William Stewart, January 19, and Frederick Otto, February 23, 1862. RG 127, Muster Rolls. Muster rolls of Headquarters, January and February 1862. It is interesting to note that when Perkins and Stewart applied for payment in lieu of the rations they were entitled to while prisoners of war, the 4th Auditor demanded proof of their captivity. See, Hobart Berrian, 4th Auditor to Major William W. Russell, Paymaster, Washington March 24, 1862. The William W. Russell and John C. Cash Papers, 1852-1898, Manuscripts Department, William R. Perkins Library, Duke University, Durham, North Carolina.
104. The Pension Applications of Jacob Kressler, Navy 4500, and Abel J. Wood, Navy 20364, both describe the miserable conditions during their confinement at New Orleans.

105. David Glasgow Farragut (1801-1870). Appointed midshipman, December 17, 1810. Promoted through the grades to the ranks of rear admiral, July 16, 1862, vice admiral, December 31, 1864, and admiral July 26, 1866.
106. Jeffrey, *Richmond Prisons,* 148.
107. Ibid., 149.
108. Garland to Harris, Brooklyn, June 3, 4, 13, and 14, 1862. RG 127, Letters Received-HD. Bradford, Cook, and Cannon reported on June 2; Lane, Clark, McCoy, Kressler, and Hunt on June 4; Steiner, Wood, and Foley on June 12, and Slemons on June 13.
109. Harris to Garland, Headquarters, June 5, 1862. RG 127, Letters Sent.
110. Margaret Leech, *Reveille in Washington, 1860-1865* (New York, 1941), 106.
111. L. H. McCauley to Harris, Chambersburg, Penna., July 16, 1861. RG 127, Letters Received-GR.
112. Reynolds requested an issue of blankets be made to the men in his report of July 24, and Colonel Harris, in a postscript to his cover letter to Secretary Welles, asked permission to make the issue. Welles gave his approval on August 10. Endorsement on the reverse of Harris to Welles, Headquarters, July 24, 1861. RG 127, Letters Sent.
113. The flag was sent to Philadelphia for repair, and replacement of the staff and tassels which were left on the battlefield during the retreat. S. H. Marks, Quartermaster's Clerk to Maddox, Washington, August 14, 1861. RG 127, QM Letters Sent.
114. RG 127, Letters Received-HD.
115. RG 127, Letters Received-GR.

CHAPTER 6

1. John Parker Hale (1806–1873). New Hampshire politician. Member of Congress, 1843–1845. U.S. Senator, 1847–1853, 1855–1865. Presidential candidate of the Free Soil Party, 1852. Ambassador to Spain, 1865–1869.
2. John C. Rives, pub., *The Congressional Globe: Containing the Debates and Proceedings of the First Session of the Thirty-Seventh Congress* (Washington, 1861), vol. 56, p. 62.
3. Ira Harris (1802–1875). New York educator and politician. U.S. Senator, 1861–1867.
4. Joel Rathbone to Col. John Harris, Washington, Monday June (July) 22/61. RG 127, Letters Received-GR.
5. Previously, there had been no age provision in regard to appointments in the Corps. Augustus S. Nicholson had been appointed at the age of 16 years, 5 months and 11 days, the youngest officer ever commissioned in the Marine Corps. Isaac T. Doughty was commissioned at the age of 36 years, 7 months and 3 days, making him the oldest. The only qualification required of an applicant to the Marine Corps was that he be a gentleman.
6. *Congressional Globe,* 56:178.
7. Ibid., 235–236.
8. In 1861, a total of 626 aspirants to become officers of Marines forwarded letters of application, most of them supported by as many as a dozen letters of recommendation from parents, civic leaders, and political friends. Of that number, forty-five were appointed to the Corps in 1861 (three declining for reasons of age or better opportunity in another service). Of those who initially applied in 1861 and persisted in their desire to enter the Corps, twelve were appointed in 1862 (one declining), one in 1863, five in 1864, and one before the end of the war in 1865. Compiled from RG 45, "Key to Office Letters."
9. Elias Hale, Jr. (?–?). Appointed mate, U.S. Navy, September 23, 1861. Resigned July 10, 1863.
10. RG 127, Letters Received-GR.

11. RG 127, Letters Sent. In addition to being the nephew of the Secretary of the Navy, Hale was a cousin to Congressman James T. Hale. In spite of his close political ties, Hale was unsuccessful in his bid to enter the Corps.

    Long after the passage of the law regulating the appointment of officers in the Corps, political favoritism still prevailed.

    25 December, 1864

    Madam;

    Your letter of the 21st, Instant, requesting me to use my influence in behalf of your son with a view of obtaining an appointment in the Marine Corps has been received.

    In reply, I regret to say that I have no influence whatever in that premises, and I would advise you to obtain the aid of some political friend, it being, in fact, the only influence which can effect the object desired by your son.

    I am Madam,
    Very Respectfully,
    J. Zeilen
    Colonel, Commd't.

    Mrs. H. Crowninshield
    Charlestown, Mass.
    (RG 127, Letters Sent.)

12. RG 80, Letters to Marine Officers. William Whelan, USN, Chief of the Bureau of Medicine and Surgery, was ordered to organize a medical review board on the same day. On August 17, Welles ordered that a major, instead of a captain, be the senior member of the examination board.
13. The mistake in his birth date gives evidence that Reid was very nervous at his examination. He was, in fact, born December 15, 1840.
14. George Croghan Reid Papers, MCHC. Despite Reid's lackluster performance on the written examination, he was recommended for appointment and was commissioned a second lieutenant to rank from July 2, 1864. He spent the next forty years as an officer of Marines, rising to the grade of brigadier general.
15. RG 45, Court-martial Records. Trial of John Musser Reber, Case # 3259, June 20, 1863.
16. Marius Duvall (?–1891). Appointed assistant surgeon, January 25, 1842. Promoted through the grades to become Medical Director, USN, June 9, 1880.
17. RG 45, Subject Files, Subfile MX, "Examinations."
18. Their commissions, however, were not prepared and transmitted until April 17, 1862. The date of rank was November 25, 1861. Twelve of the thirty-one, as a result of promotions to higher grades by their seniors, were promoted to the rank of first lieutenant to rank from November 26, 1861; two with dates of rank from November 21, 1861. RG 80, Letters to Marine Officers.
19. RG 45, "Keys."
20. RG 45, "Keys."
21. During the court-martial of Lt. Col. John George Reynolds, it was claimed that Nokes was not fairly examined due to the intoxication of Major Russell, senior officer of the examining board, thus the second meeting. See Reynolds to Welles, Washington, D.C., July 23, 1862. RG 80, Letters from Marine Officers.
22. Benjamin Chambers was subsequently elected captain of Company H, 1st Pennsylvania Cavalry. Duncan Pell was commissioned captain and aide-de-camp to Maj. Gen. Ambrose P. Burnside on April 4, 1862.

23. The recommendations, declined appointments, and failed examinations may be found in RG 45, "Keys."
24. Devlin enlisted as a private in the Marine Corps on December 15, 1823, at the age of twenty-two for five years. He re-enlisted in 1828, and in 1834 was re-enlisted as a sergeant in the Quartermaster's Department. Devlin re-enlisted at the same rank in 1837 and was discharged to accept an appointment in the Corps. At the age of thirty-eight, Devlin was commissioned a second lieutenant of Marines on February 21, 1839, promoted to the rank of first lieutenant to rank from March 3, 1847, and was cashiered by verdict of a court-martial on September 18, 1852. See, Brevet Major John G. Reynolds, USMC, *A Conclusive Exculpation of the Marine Corps in Mexico* (Washington, 1853).
25. Donnelly, *Biographical Sketches,* 40–41. Tansill was promoted to the grade of first lieutenant to rank from March 17, 1847, brevetted captain for gallant service during the Mexican War to date from November 17, 1847, and promoted captain with effective date of November 29, 1858. Tansill was dismissed from the service on August 24, 1861.
26. Essex to Harris, U.S. Steamer *Susquehanna,* Charleston Navy Yard, June 18, 1861. RG 127, Letters Received-GR.
27. RG 80, Letters to Marine Officers.
28. Welles to Harris, Navy Department, October 5, 1861. RG 127, Letters to Marine Officers.
29. Wagner to Harris, Acapulco, Mexico, August 17, 1861. RG 127, Letters Received-HD.
30. Carl Wagner, a German by birth, but a naturalized citizen, enlisted at Philadelphia on December 6, 1847. He was then twenty-one years of age. Wagner made successive re-enlistments through September 29, 1863. He died at Philadelphia on September 30, 1866.
31. Charles Hancock was twenty-four years of age when he enlisted at New York on April 28, 1854. He re-enlisted in 1859, and was discharged from the Corps on April 24, 1863.
32. P. Decatur Twiggs to "My Dear Sir," Philadelphia, July 17, 1861. RG 127, Letters Received-HD. In addition to her husband and uncle being in the service of the United States, Mrs. Twiggs' grandfather had been a captain in the Continental Navy. Her father had been killed in action as a lieutenant in the Navy. One brother was a commander on the Reserved List of the U.S. Navy, while another was on active duty as a lieutenant. Her son George was killed in action during the Mexican War while holding the rank of second lieutenant of artillery in the U.S. Army.
33. Henry A. Bartlett had served as quartermaster sergeant of the 1st Rhode Island Volunteers. Frederick H. Corrie and Robert O'Neil Ford served ninety days as a private in the 7th New York State Militia, Corrie in Company E, and Ford in Company H. George Heisler served as corporal of Company A, Trenton (New Jersey) National Guard. Samuel Powell had been a private in Company B, 4th Wisconsin Cavalry. David Sells served as corporal of Company D, 2d Iowa Infantry. Charles Stillman performed the duties of paymaster to the Connecticut Volunteers.
34. John Pope (?–1876). Appointed midshipman, May 30, 1816. Promoted through the grades to the rank of captain, September 14, 1855, Retired List, December 21, 1861. Promoted to commodore on the Retired List, July 16, 1862.
35. In addition to the Popes, Henry B. Hoff was the son of Capt. Henry K. Hoff, USN, Horatio B. Lowry the son of Capt. Francis Lowry, USN, and William B. McKean the son of Capt. William W. McKean, USN.
36. Robert E. Hitchcock to "Dear Father," Marine Barracks, Washington, June 14, 1861, Hitchcock Pp., MCHC. See also, S. H. Huntington to "My dear Wife," Washington, June 6, 1861, Huntington Pp., MCHC.

37. Welles to the Senate of the United States, Navy Department, July 29, 1861. RG 46, SEN 317B-A6, No. 148.
38. Welles to the President of the United States, Navy Department, August 2, 1861. Copy in RG 127. Letters Received-HD.
39. RG 45, Subfile NI. Report of the Senate Naval Affairs Committee, July 31, 1861.
40. *Executive Journal, U.S. Senate,* vol. 2, 1858-1861 (Washington, D.C., 1862) 493.
41. Welles to The President, August 2, 1861.
42. *Executive Journal, U.S. Senate,* 549.
43. RG 45, Court-Martial Records. Case 1630, Trial of Freeman Norvell, June 20-23, 1855.
44. RG 127, Letters Received-GR.
45. Norvell accepted a commission as captain of Company M, 1st Michigan Cavalry to date from August 22, 1861. Appointed major, 5th Michigan Cavalry, August 27, 1862. Promoted lieutenant colonel, December 1, and to colonel, December 31, 1862. Charged with drunkenness while on duty, February 16, 1863. Resigned, February 27, 1863. Appointed captain and assistant adjutant general of volunteers, May 8, 1863. Resigned, May 10, 1864.
46. Dahlgren to Welles, Washington, July, 24, 1861. *N. O. R.,* 4:585. The works at Alexandria were named Fort Ellsworth, honoring the Zouave colonel who was killed during the occupation of the city.
47. Cartter's transfer to the Navy Yard was the result of his absenting himself from Marine Barracks, Washington, without permission on July 25, 1861. Major Reynolds reported him as having left the grounds in the company of ladies. When Cartter returned that evening, he was placed under arrest. Colonel Harris received a "penitent" letter from Cartter and ordered him restored to duty. Since Major Reynolds was disinclined to accept Cartter's apology, Harris sent him to the Navy Yard. See Reynolds to Harris, Marine Barracks, Washington, July 26, 1861. RG 127, Letters Received-GR, and Harris to Reynolds, Headquarters, July 26, 1861. RG 127, Letters Sent.
48. Dahlgren, *Dahlgren Memoir,* 341.
49. RG 127, Muster Rolls. Muster rolls, Washington Navy Yard and Headquarters for July and August 1861.
50. John Adolphus Bernard Dahlgren (1809-1870). Appointed midshipman, February 1, 1826. Promoted through the grades to rear admiral, February 7, 1863.
51. Welles to Harris, Navy Department, July 24 and 25, 1861. RG 80, Letters to Marine Officers.
52. RG 80, Letters from Marine Officers.
53. Thomas Tingey Craven (1808-1887). Appointed midshipman, May 1, 1822. Promoted through the grades to the rank of rear admiral, October 10, 1866. Retired, December 30, 1869.
54. Craven to Welles, USS *Yankee,* off Piney Point (on the Potomac River, July 26, 1861. *N. O. R.,* 4:588.
55. Ibid., 589.
56. RG 24, Deck Logs. Log of USS *Pawnee,* August 10, 1861, and *N. O. R.,* 4:602.
57. G. V. Fox, Asst. Sec'y. to Colonel Harris, Navy Department, August 19, 1861. RG 127, Letters Received-HD.
58. Fox to Craven, Navy Department, August 19, 1861. *N. O. R.,* 4:626-627.
59. Goldsborough Papers, Library of Congress.
60. L. M. Goldsborough, Jr. to "My dear Mother," Headquarters, Marine Barracks, Washington, August 23, 1861. Goldsborough Pp., LC.
61. *N. O. R.,* 4:634-635.
62. Ibid., 662-663.
63. RG 24, Deck Logs. Log of USS *Pocahontas,* October 15, 1862.
64. RG 24, Deck Logs, Log of USS *Pawnee,* October 16, 1861.

65. Nathaniel Prentiss Banks (1816–1894). Massachusetts Democratic politician. Governor of Massachusetts, 1858–1861. Appointed major general of volunteers, May 16, 1861. Mustered out of service, August 24, 1865.
66. Col. J. Thomas Scharf, *The Chronicles of Baltimore; Being a Complete History of "Baltimore Town" and Baltimore City from the Earliest Period to the Present Time* (Baltimore, 1874), 655–656.
67. RG 45, Court-Martial Records, Court-Martial 3092, Trial of Cpl. William Toombs. Testimony of Pvt. Henry T. McGraw.
68. Huntington to Harris, Headquarters, September 26, 1861. RG 127, Letters received-HD.
69. Harris to Welles, Headquarters, September 17, 1861. RG 80, Letters from Marine Officers.
70. Welles to Harris, Navy Department, December 2, 1861. RG 80, Letters to Marine Officers. Toombs' sentence was later changed as to place of confinement. He was sent to Fort Jefferson in the Dry Tortugas. His health deteriorated to the point that the balance of his sentence was remitted, and he was released from confinement on August 8, 1862, and dishonorably discharged from the Corps. Toombs later surfaced at Mobile, Alabama, where he enlisted in the Confederate States Marine Corps. See, David M. Sullivan, "What Became of Corporal Toombs?" *Journal of the Company of Military Historians,* vol. 45, no. 1 (Spring 1993), 2–7.
71. George Riddell to "Dear Mother," United States Marine Barracks, Washington, D.C., October 26, 1861. George Riddell Papers, New York State Archives. George Riddell enlisted as a Marine at the Recruiting Rendezvous, Philadelphia, Pennsylvania, October 14, 1861, and was honorably discharged, October 24, 1865.
72. Welles to Harris, Navy Department, September 3, 1861, and Fox to Harris, September 10, 12, 1861. RG 80, Letters to Marine Officers.
73. Welles had promised Capt. Samuel F. DuPont a battalion of Marines for his operations on the South Atlantic coast.
74. Welles to McClellan, Navy Department, September 24, 1861. *N. O. R.,* 4:684.
75. S. Thomas, AAG to Welles, Headquarters, Army of the Potomac, September 30, 1861. Ibid., 697.
76. Harris to Welles, Headquarters, Marine Corps, September 28, 1861. RG 80, Letters from Marine Officers. The expense to convert the stables was $496.40.
77. RG 127, Letters Received-HD.
78. *N. O. R.,* 12:200–201. Report of Capt. S. F. DuPont, USN, A. D. Bache, Superintendent, U.S. Coast Survey, Maj. J. G. Barnard, Engineer Corps, USA., and Cdr. Charles Davis, USN, submitted to Gideon Welles, July 16, 1861. The conference was organized by order of the Navy Department on June 25, 1861.
79. John Ellis Wool (1784–1869). Appointed captain of infantry during the War of 1812. Promoted through the grades to the rank of major general, Regular Army, May 16, 1862. Retired, August 1, 1863.
80. E. D. Townsend, Assistant Adjutant General to Maj. Gen. John E. Wool, Headquarters of the Army, August 13, 1861. *O. R.,* 4:579.
81. Benjamin Franklin Butler (1818–1893). Massachusetts Democratic/Republican/Greenback Party politician. Appointed major general of volunteers, May 16, 1861. Resigned, November 30, 1865. Governor of Massachusetts, 1882–1884. Presidential candidate of the Greenback Party, 1884.
82. Silas Horton Stringham (1797–1876). Appointed midshipman, November 15, 1809. Promoted through the grades to the rank of captain, September 8, 1841. Retired List, December 21, 1861. Promoted to rear admiral on the Retired List, July 16, 1862.
83. Special Orders, No. 13, Hdqrs. Department of Virginia, August 25, 1861. *O. R.,* 4:580.

84. Max Weber (1824–1901). Lieutenant of infantry, Army of the Grand Duchy of Baden, 1843–1848. Appointed colonel, 20th New York Infantry, May 9, 1861. Promoted brigadier general of volunteers, April 28, 1862. Resigned, May 13, 1865. Cpl. Albert Weber, brother to Colonel Weber, was discharged from the Marine Corps on October 5, 1861, to accept a commission as a second lieutenant in the 20th New York Volunteers. RG 127, Letters Received-HD.
85. USS *Susquehanna,* designated as part of Stringham's force, was released from a seven-week overhaul at Philadelphia on August 24, and was late in arriving at Fort Monroe. She joined the squadron at 10:00 on the morning of August 28, just as the bombardment of the Confederate forts commenced. Her Marine Guard of three sergeants, four corporals, two musicians, and forty privates was commanded by 1st Lt. Philip R. Fendall, Jr.
86. RG 24, Deck Logs. Log of USS *Monticello,* August 28, 1861.
87. Daniel O'Connor to "Dear Timothy," U.S. Ship *Cumberland,* September 7, 1861. Daniel O'Connor Papers, MCHC.
88. "Action of Troops Ashore," *New York Herald,* September 3, 1861, p. 8, col. 4.
89. William H. Cartter to "Dear Mother," Hatteras Inlet, September 10, 1861. Cartter Pp., LC.
90. John Sanford Barnes (1836–1911). Appointed acting midshipman, U.S. Naval Academy, October 1, 1851. Graduated, midshipman, June 10, 1854. Promoted through the grades to the rank of master, January 22, 1858. Resigned, October 5, 1858. Appointed acting lieutenant, May 1861, and lieutenant commander, July 16, 1862. Resigned February 4, 1869.
91. John D. Hayes and Lillian O'Brien, eds., "The Early Blockade and the Capture of the Hatteras Forts, From the Journal of John Sanford Barnes, July 19 to September 1, 1861." *New York Historical Society Quarterly,* vol. 46 (January 1962): 61–85.
92. Amos Burton, *Cruise of the U.S. Ship Susquehanna during the years 1860, 1861, 1862 and 1863* (New York, 1863), 68. Burton, a Marine private, enlisted on May 9, 1860, and was Honorably Discharged on May 26, 1864. Private Burton, observing the goings on after the cessation of the bombardment, confirmed fellow Marine O'Connor's claim that the Marines were first to enter Fort Hatteras. See p. 70.
93. I. T. Doughty, Capt. Com'g. Marines to Capt. Samuel Mercer, Com'g. U.S.S. *Wabash,* At Sea, August 30, 1861. Copy in RG 127, Letters Received-HD.
94. Hayes and O'Brien, "Barnes Journal," 80.
95. Daniel O'Connor to "Dear Timothy," September 12, 1861. O'Connor Pp., MCHC.
96. James G. Maxwell (?–1867). Appointed midshipman, U.S. Naval Academy, December 15, 1847. Graduated passed midshipman, June 12, 1855. Promoted through the grades to the rank of lieutenant commander, July 16, 1862.
97. Burton, *Cruise of the Susquehanna,* 77–78.
98. RG 24, Deck Logs. Log of USS *Pawnee,* September 18, 1861.
99. Stringham, stung by the lack of official recognition for his actions at Hatteras Inlet, submitted his request to be relieved from command of the *Minnesota* and the North Atlantic Blockading Squadron on September 16. He was placed on the Retired List in 1861, but, recalled to duty in 1862, he spent the rest of the war in charge of the Boston Navy Yard.
100. Hayes and O'Brien, "Barnes Journal," 84–85.
101. William H. Cartter to "Dear Mother," U.S. Frigate *Minnesota,* September 13, 1861. Cartter Pp., LC.
102. *Congressional Globe,* vol. 60, 32–33.
103. Welles to Harris, Navy Department, November 2, 1861. RG 80, Letters to Marine Officers.

104. Solomon Sharpe (?–1870) Appointed assistant surgeon, September 15, 1829. Promoted surgeon, February 20, 1838. Placed on the Retired List, August 16, 1865. Charles D. Maxwell (?–1890). Appointed assistant surgeon, September 6, 1837. Promoted surgeon, October 18, 1849. Placed on the Retired List, October 21, 1868. Recalled to active duty and promoted Medical Director, March 3, 1871.
105. Lewis J. Williams (?–1888). Appointed assistant surgeon, January 25, 1842. Promoted surgeon, August 30, 1856. Medical Inspector, March 3, 1871. Medical Director, May 28, 1871. James Suddards (?–1888). Appointed assistant surgeon, May 17, 1849. Promoted surgeon, April 24, 1861. Medical Inspector, March 3, 1871. Medical Director, April 5, 1875.
106. Record Group G 125, Records of the Office of the Judge Advocate General (Navy). Entry 57, Records of Proceedings of Marine Retiring Boards, vol. 1, Case of Capt. Abraham N. Brevoort.
107. Brevoort was so financially distressed by the loss of active duty emoluments that he requested the assistance of Harris in obtaining the post sutlership at the Brooklyn Navy Yard to supplement his income. The request became moot when Brevoort was recalled to active duty in October 1862. RG 127, Letters Received-GR. Brevoort to Harris, Brooklyn, December 6, 1861.
108. RG 125, Marine Retiring Boards, vol. 1. Recorded with the Brevoort Case.
109. RG 125, Marine Retiring Boards, vol. 1, Case of 1st Lieutenant Charles A. Henderson.
110. RG 125, Marine Retiring Boards, vol. 1, Case of Brevet Lt. Colonel William Dulany.
111. RG 125, Marine Retiring Boards, vol. 1, Case of 1st Lieutenant John L. Broome.
112. Porter to Broome, On Ship *Powhatan*, off South West Pass, Mississippi, August 2, 1861. Broome Pp., MCHC.
113. John A. Lockwood (?–?). Appointed assistant surgeon, February 8, 1832. Promoted surgeon, October 13, 1840. Resigned March 13, 1865.
114. Statement of John Lockwood, Surgeon, USN, dated October 27, 1861. Broome Pp., MCHC.
115. William Whelan (?–1865). Appointed assistant surgeon, January 3, 1828. Promoted surgeon, February 9, 1837. Whelan to Welles, Washington, November 11, 1861. Broome Pp., MCHC.
116. Marston to Welles, Philadelphia, August 19, 1861. RG 80, Letters from Marine Officers.
117. RG 125, Marine Retiring Boards, vol. 1, Case of Major Ward Marston.
118. Marston was ordered to the command of Marine Barracks, Portsmouth, on December 6, 1861. RG 127, Letters Sent.

CHAPTER 7

1. RG 127. Letters Sent.
2. *N. O. R.,* 12:201–206.
3. Ibid., 207.
4. Harris to Reynolds, Headquarters, February 15, 1862, explaining the circumstances under which the Marine Battalion was detailed to the South Atlantic Blockading Squadron. RG 127, Letters Sent.
5. Louis Malesherbes Goldsborough, Sr. (1805–1877). Appointed midshipman, June 18, 1812. Promoted through the grades to the rank of rear admiral, July 16, 1862. Placed on the Retired List, October 6, 1873. Father of Marine officer Louis M. Goldsborough, Jr.
6. RG 127, Letters Received-HD.
7. Harris to Welles, Headquarters, September 23, 1861. RG 80, Letters from Marine Officers.

8. Harris to Edelin, Headquarters, September 24, 1861. RG 127, Letters Sent.
9. Harris to Brevoort, Headquarters, September 24, 1861. RG 127, Letters Sent.
10. The three senior first lieutenants, Wiley, Graham, and Lewis, were, by order of the President, promoted to the rank of captain, temporarily, on October 18, 1861, taking rank from October 12. 1st Lt. Charles G. McCawley, not then with the battalion, was also temporarily promoted to captain. RG 80, Letters to Marine Officers. The posting of Goldsborough to the battalion caused something of a problem for Colonel Harris. Goldsborough had been detailed to the command of the Marine Guard of USS *Pensacola* on September 15, and abruptly replaced by Harris' nephew, 2d Lt. John C. Harris on September 30. Goldsborough's mother, to celebrate the posting, purchased a full sea-going wardrobe for her son, including an impressive Smith and Wesson revolver and 500 rounds of ammunition. Upon learning that her son had been detailed to the battalion, Mrs. Goldsborough made it a point to register her objections with Colonel Harris. She desisted only when her husband, Capt. L. M. Goldsborough, Sr., ordered her to do so, lest she injure their son's reputation in the Corps. See E. W. Goldsborough to "My dear Husband," Washington, October 12, 1861. Rear Admiral Louis M. Goldsborough Papers, Manuscripts Division, Library of Congress.
11. Harris to Reynolds, Headquarters, October 1, 1861. RG 127, Letters Sent.
12. Smalley had seen action as a private of the 19th Ohio Volunteers at the Battle of Rich Mountain, July 11, 1861.
13. Nicholson to Welles, Headquarters, October 3, 1861. RG 80, Letters from Marine Officers.
14. Harris to Welles, Headquarters, October 3, 1861. RG 80, Letters from Marine Officers.
15. Harris to Nicholson, Headquarters, October 7, 1861. RG 127, Letters Sent.
16. Telegram, Welles to Harris, Navy Department, 8:42 A.M., October 15, 1861. RG 127, Letters Received-HD.
17. The actual destination of the squadron was left to the discretion of Captain DuPont by Secretary of the Navy Welles. Of the three points listed in the July 26 memorandum, Bull's Bay, St. Helena Sound and Port Royal, Welles wanted two occupied. *N. O. R.,* 12:214-215.
18. Thomas West Sherman (1813-1879). U.S. Military Academy, Class of 1836. Served in the Seminole and Mexican Wars, brevetted to major for gallantry at the Battle of Buena Vista. Appointed brigadier general of volunteers to rank from May 17, 1861. Retired with the rank of major general in the Regular Army in 1870.
19. *N. O. R.,* 12:220.
20. Dahlgren, *Dahlgren Memoir,* 346.
21. Quoted in DuPont to "My dearest Sophie," *Wabash* (Hampton Roads), October 19-20, 1861. Hayes, ed., *S. F. DuPont Letters,* 1:177.
22. Ibid.
23. Harris to Reynolds, Headquarters, October 23, 1861. RG 127, Letters Sent. The term "paymaster" (purser until 1859), in the old Navy referred to any disbursing officer.
24. Hayes, ed., *S. F. DuPont Letters,* 1:177-178. Du Pont to "My dearest Sophie," *Wabash* (Hampton Roads), October 23, 1861.
25. RG 45, Muster Rolls. Muster roll of USS *Wabash,* October 1861.
26. Harris to Nye, Headquarters, October 29, 1861, and Harris to Schermerhorn, Headquarters, October 29, 1861. RG 127, Letters Sent. The orders did not reach Schermerhorn until after the Battle of Port Royal.
27. Hayes, ed., *S. F. DuPont Letters,* 1:205. Journal Letter # 1, Du Pont to "My precious Sophie," *Wabash,* at sea, October 29-November 5, 1861.

28. John Weidman (?-1891). Appointed acting midshipman, U.S. Naval Academy, September 22, 1857. Graduated midshipman, June 1, 1861. Promoted through the grades to the rank of lieutenant commander, July 25, 1866. Placed on the Retired List, June 30, 1875.
29. *N. O. R.*, 12:237-238.
30. Robert W. Huntington to "My dear Father, U.S. Frigate *Sabine*, November 8, 1861. Huntington Pp., MCHC.
31. *N. O. R.*, 12:233-235.
32. Cadwalader Ringgold (1802-1867). Appointed midshipman, March 4, 1819. Promoted through the grades to the rank of captain, April 2, 1856. Placed on the Retired List at the grade of commodore, July 16, 1862. Promoted to rear admiral on the Retired List, July 25, 1866.
33. Lucius H. Beattie (?-?). Appointed Acting Master, August 1, 1861. Honorably discharged, May 12, 1865.
34. Pvt. Edward H. Miller. Reynolds to DuPont, nd, List of noncommissioned officers and privates drowned and injured by attempting to leave the U.S. Transport Steamer *Governor*. The exact number of Marines who saved themselves by leaping to the deck of *Sabine* could not be determined.
35. Cpl. Thomas McKeown, Pvts. Manus Brown, Timothy Lacy, Laurence Gorman, Thomas Walker, and Robert Campbell. Pvt. Laurence Gorman, a naturalized Irishman, was the sole support of his mother and three younger sisters. An application for pension was filed by his mother, Julia Gorman, in December 1862. Through bureaucratic lack of attention, the application was misdirected by the Navy Pension Office. The clerk receiving it apparently did not read the application which stated that Gorman drowned in the Atlantic Ocean. Assuming Gorman was a member of the Mississippi Marine Brigade, an Army unit cooperating with the Navy on the Mississippi River, the clerk for Navy pensions sent it to his counterpart in the Army Pension Office. Since there was no Laurence Gorman in this Army unit, the application was filed away without further action. While the application languished in the wrong office, the Gorman family was reduced to the very depths of poverty. Finally, a lawyer took Mrs. Gorman's case, and by persistence, convinced the government to locate the missing application. The pension of $8.00 per month was subsequently granted to Mrs. Gorman on December 24, 1864, retroactive to the day of her unfortunate son's death, November 3, 1861. Pension Application (Navy) 789 of Julia Gorman, National Archives.
36. *N. O. R.*, 12:239-243.
37. Huntington to "My dear Father," U.S. Frigate *Sabine*, November 8, 1861. Huntington Pp., MCHC.
38. Captain DuPont, with undisguised admiration for Reynolds' action at the end of the ordeal, wrote, "The established reputation and high standing of Major Reynolds might almost dispense with any observations of my own upon the bravery and high sense of honor which he displayed in disputing with Mr. Weidman (although not a seaman) the privilege of being the last to leave the wreck." DuPont to Welles, Port Royal Harbor, S.C., November 15, 1861, as quoted in Porter, *Naval History of the Civil War*, 396.
39. Losses of equipment and personal property belonging to the Marine Battalion amounted to $7,165.57. John C. Cash, Paymaster, Marine Corps to Gideon Welles, November 26, 1862. RG 45, "Keys." Colonel Harris recommended the loss of personal effects by the officers and men of the battalion be made good. RG 80, Letters from Marine Officers, March 31, 1862. Congress voted to compensate the officers and men of the Marine Battalion for their personal losses on July 11, 1862.
40. *N. O. R.* , 12:233-235.

41. Ibid., 237–238.
42. Ibid., 238.
43. Ibid., 247. Colonel Harris happened to be in New York when Boyd arrived. He later wrote, "Captain Boyd arrived so ill that it was a matter of doubt between his physician and myself that he would live to reach his home in Philadelphia." Harris to Welles, Headquarters, October 24, 1862. RG 127, Letters Sent. Boyd never regained his health and was placed on the Retired List, effective November 3, 1862.
44. Ibid., 250. D. T. Valentine, Clerk of the Common Council, forwarding copy of the resolution to Gideon Welles, New York, June 20, 1862.
45. Ibid., 249. The Congress of the United States ultimately recognized the heroic actions of Captain Ringgold and the crew of *Sabine* by voting a resolution of thanks on March 7, 1864.
46. The entire poem is at Appendix A.
47. Hayes, ed., *S. F. DuPont Letters,* 1:212, Journal letter 1 to "My precious Sophie," November 4, 1861.
48. James William Augustus Nicholson (1821–1887). Appointed midshipman, February 10, 1838. Promoted through the grades to the rank of rear admiral, October 1, 1881. Placed on the Retired List, March 10, 1883.
49. Josiah Tattnall (1795–1871). Appointed midshipman, January 1, 1812. Promoted through the grades to the rank of captain, February 5, 1850. Resigned, February 21, 1861. Appointed captain, CSN, March 26, 1861. Guards of Confederate States Marines were serving aboard all but one of Tattnall's gunboats: Flagship *Savannah;* Capt. George Holmes, CSS *Resolute,* 2d Lt. James Thurston, CSS *Huntress,* 2d Lt. Francis H. Cameron (unsuccessful pre-war applicant for a commission in the United States Marine Corps), and CSS *Sampson,* 2d Lt. David G. Raney.
50. Hayes, ed., *S. F. DuPont Letters,* 1:222–223, n.1.
51. Daniel Ammen, Rear Admiral, U.S.N., "DuPont and the Port Royal Expedition," *Battles and Leaders,* 1:671–691.
52. *N. O. R.,* 12:302. The bombardment had so demoralized the defenders of Fort Walker that Brigadier General Thomas F. Drayton, commanding the defenses at Port Royal ordered the gunners from Capt. (late first lieutenant of United States Marines) Jacob Read's light battery, then holding a position about two miles to the rear of the fort, to reinforce the garrison.
53. *N. O. R.,* 12:267–268.
54. John Rodgers (1812–1882). Appointed midshipman, April 18, 1828. Promoted through the grades to the rank of rear admiral, December 31, 1869.
55. RG 24, Deck Logs. Log of USS *Wabash,* November 7, 1861.
56. David Greenway Raney (1838–1903). Corporal, 1st Florida Infantry, April 4–22, 1861, Appointed second lieutenant of Confederate States Marines, April 22, 1861. Promoted to first lieutenant, November 22, 1861. Surrendered at Nanna Hubba Bluff, Alabama, May 10, 1865.
57. What became of Captain Holmes during the confused situation on Hilton Head Island has never been determined. He does not appear among the lists of prisoners taken at Fort Walker, and was back with his Company by November 22. It appears that Capt. Jacob Read, commander of Company D, 1st Georgia Regulars and also holding a commission as a captain of Confederate States Marines, may have assumed command of Holmes' Company A temporarily. Read was noted as "now of the Marine Corps," in orders dated December 24, 1861. See AIGO, Richmond, Special Orders No. 274, para. 10.
58. *N. O. R.,* 12:295–298, extract from the *Savannah Republican,* November 12, 1861. An Eyewitness, "The part the Navy took in the affray at Port Royal."
59. Hayes, Ed., *S. F. DuPont Letters,* 1:225.
60. Burton, *Cruise of the Susquehanna,* 89.

61. Horatio Gouverneur Wright (1820-1899). U.S. Military Academy, Class of 1841. Appointed brigadier general of volunteers, September 16, 1861. Promoted to major general of volunteers, May 12, 1864. Reverted to his Regular Army rank of lieutenant colonel after the war. Promoted to colonel in 1879 and retired from the service in 1884.
62. John D. Hayes, ed., "The Battle of Port Royal, S.C., from the Journal of John Sanford Barnes, October 8 to November 9, 1861," *New York Historical Society Quarterly*, vol. 45 (October 1961): 365-395. It appears that Sanford felt the Marines suffered a breakdown in discipline once the army got ashore. His journal states, "The Marines behaved disgracefully, from chief to subaltern, and gave me much trouble."
63. Isaac Ingalls Stevens (1818-1862). U.S. Military Academy, Class of 1839. Brevetted twice for gallantry during the Mexican War. Resigned in 1853. Appointed colonel, 79th New York, July 30, 1861. Appointed brigadier general of volunteers, September 28, 1861. Killed in action at the Battle of Chantilly, September 1, 1862. Posthumously promoted to major general of volunteers, March 12, 1863.
64. Burton, *Cruise of the Susquehanna,* 91-92.
65. RG 127, Entry 112, Miscellaneous Records of the Adjutant and Inspector, 1798-1880. "Report of a Guard mounted at Bay Point on the 13th November, and relieved on the 14th."
66. From Marine Pvt. William Gould's, "The Wreck of the *Governor*." Civil War Miscellaneous Collection, USAMHI.
67. Russell to Reynolds, Headquarters, November 19, 1861., RG 127, Letters Sent.
68. Russell to Mr. B. L. Fahvestock, Headquarters, Marine Corps, November 22, 1861. RG 127, Letters Sent. Pensions to survivors, including mothers of unmarried servicemen, would not be granted until the passage of the Act of July 14, 1862.
69. Ricketts to Reynolds, Bay Point, November 20, 1861. RG 127, Letters Received by the Adjutant and Inspector. 1835-49, 1851-99.
70. Sturgeon to Reynolds, Bay Point, November 21, 1861. RG 127, Letters Received, A&I. No record regarding punishment of the offenders has been located.
71. John S. Missroon (1810-1865). Appointed midshipman, June 27, 1824. Promoted through the grades to the rank of commodore, July 16, 1865.
72. RG 24. Deck Logs. Logs of USS *Flag* and *Pocahontas,* entries for July 24, 1861.
73. *N. O. R.,* 12:383.
74. Christopher Raymond Perry Rodgers (1819-1892). Appointed midshipman, October 5, 1833. Promoted through the grades to the rank of rear admiral, June 14, 1874. Placed on the Retired List, November 14, 1881.
75. The march, however, gave signs of danger in regard to the health of Marine Lieutenant Kennedy. The first symptoms of the tuberculosis that would ultimately claim his life three years later, manifested themselves during the march. Kennedy was invalided home from USS *Savannah* on December 12.
76. *N. O. R.,* 12:392-393.
77. Goldsborough to Harris, U.S. Frigate *Wabash,* January 11, 1862. RG 127, Letters Received GR.
78. DuPont to Goldsborough, Flag Ship *Wabash,* December 14, 1861. DuPont Family Papers, Hagley Museum and Library, W9-3270-162.
79. Percival Drayton (1812-1865). Appointed midshipman, December 1, 1827. Promoted through the grades to the rank of captain, July 16, 1862.
80. *N. O. R.,* 12:405-406.
81. Hayes, Ed., *S. F. DuPont Letters.* 1: 289. DuPont to "My precious Sophie," Journal Letters No. 18, *Wabash,* December 25, 1861.
82. Collum to Harris, U.S.S. *St. Lawrence,* December 12, 1861. RG 127, Letters Received-HD.

83. William Ottiwell (?–?). Appointed Acting Master, June 10, 1861. Honorably discharged, December 3, 1865.
84. William Talbot Truxton (1824–1887). U.S. Naval Academy, Class of 1841. Promoted through the grades to the rank of commodore, May 11, 1882. Placed on the Retired List, March 11, 1886. *N. O. R.*, 12:436–437.
85. Ibid., 475.
86. Paul Kallina, "Letters from a Civil War Marine," *Marine Corps Gazette* (November 1981): 47–48. The battle may refer to the joint Army-Navy attack on the rebel positions at Port Royal Ferry, December 31, 1861–January 2, 1862. There is no record of Marines taking part in the fighting. My thanks to Mr. Kallina for providing me with copies of the original material.
87. Bradford to "Dear Father," Bay Point, S.C., January 18, 1862. Pension Application 5434 (Navy), of Mrs. Freeman Bradford (mother of Charles), National Archives.
88. Bradford to "Dear Father," January 18, 1862.
89. Burton, *Cruise of the Susquehanna,* 103. The Marine detachment consisted of Lieutenant Fendall, one sergeant, and five privates.
90. Ibid., 103–104.
91. *N. O. R.,* 12:500.
92. T. L. McElrath, Adjutant, Marine Battalion to 1st Lt. L. M. Goldsborough, Bay Point, March 15, 1862. Reports of quarreling among the officers of the battalion had reached Major Reynolds, who attributed them to "malignity and selfishness." Louis M. Goldsborough Papers, Manuscript Department, William R. Perkins Library, Duke University.
93. James Wilson Grimes (1816–1872) Republican politician from Iowa. Governor of Iowa, 1854–1858. U.S. Senator, 1859–1869. Chairman of the Senate Naval Affairs Committee, 1861–1863.
94. Huntington to "Dear Father," Bay Point, February 22, 1862. Huntington Pp., MCHC.
95. L. M. Goldsborough to "My dear Father," U.S. Frigate *Wabash*, December 21, 1861. Goldsborough Pp., LC.
96. DuPont to Goldsborough, U.S. Flagship *Wabash,* February 17, 1862. Du Pont Family Papers, Hagley Museum and Library. W9-3271-374.
97. Goldsborough to "My dear Mother," Bay Point, March 10, 1862. Accession 443, Hagley Museum and Library. See also, *N. O. R.,* 12:568.
98. Reynolds to Harris, Bay Point, Port Royal, S.C., February 21, 1862. RG 127, Letters Received-HD.
99. *Proceedings of A Marine General Court Martial Convened at Washington City, May 7, 1862, for the Trial of Lieut. Col. John Geo. Reynolds, U.S. Marine Corps* (Washington, 1862), passim.
100. RG 80, Letters from Marine Officers.
101. *Reynolds Court Martial,* Testimony of 1st Lt. Thomas L. McElrath, 39.
102. Ibid., Testimony of Capt. John I. Schermerhorn, 12.
103. Ibid., Testimony of Capt. James Wiley, 44–45.
104. Reynolds reported his command, consisting of "15 officers and 273 rank and file" safely aboard the transport on February 23. *N. O. R.,* 12:568.
105. Ibid., 6:57–58.
106. Ibid., 12:572. Memorandum of instructions regarding plan of operations.
107. Goldsborough to "My dear Mother," Bay Point, March 10, 1862.
108. Burton, *Cruise of the Susquehanna,* 104, and Craig L. Symonds, ed., *Charleston Blockade: The Journals of John B. Marchand, U.S. Navy, 1861–1862* (Newport, R.I., 1976), 119.
109. Goldsborough to "My dear Mother," Bay Point, March 10, 1862.
110. Henry W. Miller (?–?). Appointed acting midshipman, U.S. Naval Academy, October 22, 1852. Graduated, midshipman, June 10, 1857. Promoted through the

grades to the rank of lieutenant commander, March 3, 1865. Resigned, April 10, 1866.

111. RG 24, Deck Logs. Log of USS *Mohican,* March 4, 1862.
112. Robert Galbraith to "Dear Mother," U.S. Steamship Frigate *Wabash,* April 15, 1862. Robert Galbraith Papers, New York State Archives.
113. *N. O. R.,* 12:575.
114. Ibid., 12:583–584, 590–592.
115. Naval parlance for non-issue items sold aboard ship such as tobacco, soap, brushes, pencils, pens, and the like.
116. Reynolds to Harris, Bay Point, February 8, 1862. RG 127, Letters Received-HD.
117. Reynolds to Harris, Bay Point, S.C., March 10, 1862. RG 127, Letters Received-HD.
118. *N. O. R.,* 12:602. Nicholson was to land the Marines and New Hampshire troops from the gunboat *Isaac Smith,* the harbor of St. Augustine being too shallow for the flagship.
119. James Lawrence Lardner (1802–1881). Appointed midshipman, May 10, 1820. Promoted through the grades to the rank of commodore, July 16, 1862. Placed on the Retired List, November 20, 1864. Promoted to rear admiral on the Retired List, July 25, 1866. *N. O. R.,* 12:603.
120. Hayes, ed., *S. F. DuPont Letters.,* 1:372–374. Journal Letter No. 40. DuPont to "My precious Sophie," *Wabash,* March 19, 1862.
121. Rumor had preceded the orders. As soon as word came that St. Augustine had been taken, the officers of the Marine Battalion felt sure it would be sent there to protect the citizens. Huntington to "My dear Father," Bay Point, March 17, 1862. Huntington Pp., MCHC. The text of the orders is in *N. O. R.,* 12:631.
122. RG 24, Deck Logs. Log of USS *Bienville,* March 21, 1862.
123. Charles Steedman (1811–1890). Appointed midshipman, April 1, 1828. Promoted through the grades to the rank of rear admiral, May 25, 1871. Placed on the Retired List, September 25, 1873.
124. Hayes, ed., *S. F. DuPont Letters,* 1:377. The officer placed at St. Augustine by General Sherman was Lt. Col. Louis Bell of the 4th New Hampshire Volunteers.
125. Ibid., 380–381.
126. *N. O. R.,* 12:659.
127. Hayes, ed., *S. F. DuPont Letters,* 1:386–387.
128. *N. O. R.,* 12:657-658.
129. Ibid., 658.
130. Ibid., 659–660. Although the citizens of St. Augustine referred to Doughty as "Major," his promotion to that rank was not confirmed by the Senate vote until March 31, 1862. See, RG 24, Records of the Bureau of Naval Personnel, Entry 159, Confirmations of Appointments of Officers. January 5, 1843–August 4, 1909. Cdr. Sylvanus W. Godon, USN, was also disappointed to hear that the Marine Battalion was being sent north. He felt the battalion should be established on St. Simon's Island with a dual role. It could assist in the blocking up of Brunswick and Darien, Georgia, and act as a protective force to a self-sustaining colony of free Blacks that Godon suggested be set up there. See *N. O. R.* 12:634.
131. The young officers who had served at Bull Run, hoped to redeem their military fortunes during their association with the South Atlantic Blockading Squadron. To their regret, the opportunity did not present itself. To their chagrin, a Congressional Resolution giving a vote of thanks to Flag Officer DuPont, the officers seamen and Marines of the squadron for the victory at Port Royal was voted on February 22, 1862. The officers and men of the battalion had suffered much, but accomplished little.

CHAPTER 8

1. Peggy Robbins, "When the Rebels Lost Ship Island," *Civil War Times Illustrated*, vol. 84, no. 9 (January 1979):4-9, 42-45.
2. *N. O. R.*, 16:628-629.
3. Edward Higgins (1821-1875). Appointed midshipman, USN, January 23, 1836, and rose to the rank of lieutenant before resigning to enter the merchant service on February 16, 1854. During the Civil War, Higgins served as captain of Company I, 1st Louisiana Heavy Artillery, captain, 1st Confederate Light Battery, lieutenant colonel and colonel, 22d Louisiana Infantry. Appointed brigadier general to rank from October 29, 1862. Relieved of his duties and placed on "waiting orders" from September 1864 through the end of the war. David Emanuel Twiggs (1790-1862). Appointed second lieutenant, United States Army. March 12, 1812. Promoted through the grades to the rank of brigadier general. Brevetted major general for his services during the Mexican War. He was dismissed from the service on March 1, 1861, for having surrendered the military forces and supplies of the Department of Texas to state troops commanded by Colonel Ben McCulloch. Twiggs was appointed major general in the Provisional Army of the Confederate States on May 22, 1861, and was placed in charge of Department No. 1 on May 27. His age and infirmities led to his being relieved of command on October 7, 1861. Twiggs was the elder brother of Maj. Levi Twiggs, USMC, who was killed in action at the Battle of Mexico City, September 13, 1847.
4. Alexander F. Warley (ca. 1820-1896). Appointed midshipman, February 17, 1840. Promoted through the grades to the rank of lieutenant. Resigned, December 24, 1860. Appointed first lieutenant, CSN, March 26, 1861. Captured and paroled at Athens, Georgia, May 8, 1865.
5. A. F. Warley, "A Trifling Reminiscence of the War," Subject Files, Subfile HJ, "Joint Military Naval Engagements."
6. Reuben Triplett Thom (1823-1873). Thom served during the Mexican War as a lieutenant and captain of the Alabama Infantry Regiment. He later served as a second lieutenant in the 13th U.S. Infantry Regiment. He held the position of Quartermaster General of Alabama prior to the outbreak of the war. Initially commissioned a captain of artillery in the Alabama state forces, Thom was shortly thereafter appointed senior captain of the Confederate States Marine Corps on March 25, 1861. He was recruiting at New Orleans at the time of the Higgins Expedition.
7. A. L. Myers was the master of the *Oregon* at the time she was commandeered for the expedition. He was later commissioned acting master in the Confederate States Navy to rank from February 27, 1863, and master in the Provisional Navy to rank from June 1, 1864.
8. Charles W. Read (1840-1892). Appointed acting midshipman, U.S. Naval Academy, September 20, 1856. Graduated, midshipman, June 15, 1860. Resigned February 4, 1861. Appointed acting midshipman, C.S. Navy, April 13, 1861. Promoted through the grades to the rank of first lieutenant, Provisional Navy, January 6, 1864. Captured near New Orleans, April 24, 1865. Paroled July 24, 1865.
9. Sardine Graham Stone, Jr. (?-?). Appointed acting midshipman, U.S. Naval Academy, September 23, 1857. Resigned, January 16, 1861. Appointed acting midshipman, C.S. Navy, April 13, 1861. Promoted through the grades to the rank of first lieutenant, Provisional Navy, January 6, 1864. Captured aboard CSS *Florida* at Bahia, Brazil, October 7, 1864. Paroled, January 26, 1865. William Robert Dalton, (?-?). Appointed acting midshipman, U.S. Naval Academy, September 20, 1859. Resigned, March 11, 1861. Appointed acting midshipman, C.S. Navy, June 12, 1861. Promoted through the grades to the rank of second lieutenant, Provisional Navy, June 2, 1864.
10. John Henry Comstock (?-1864). Appointed acting midshipman, U.S. Naval Academy, January 11, 1858. Resigned, January 30, 1861. Appointed acting

midshipman, C.S. Navy, May 4, 1861. Promoted through the grades to the rank of first lieutenant, Provisional Navy, January 6, 1864. Killed in action at the Battle of Mobile Bay, August 5, 1864. Warley to Higgins, New Orleans, July 10, 1861. RG 45, Entry 463: Area File of the Naval Records Collection, "Confederate Navy, Area 6, March 1861-June 1865."

11. *New Orleans Daily Picayune,* July 10, 1861, p. 1, col. 2.
12. Melancton Smith (1810-1883). Appointed midshipman on March 1, 1826, and reached the grade of rear admiral on July 1, 1870. Placed on the Retired List on May 24, 1871.
13. Commander Smith overestimated the rebels to number between 300 and 800 men, and their armament to consist of one rifled cannon, two guns of heavy caliber and one twelve pounder, a credit to the actual numbers and guns on Ship Island. Smith to Flag Officer Wm. Mervine, USS *Massachusetts,* Off Chandeleur Island, July 9, 1861. *N. O. R.* 16:581.
14. Henry Watkins Allen (1820-1866). Served as captain of a company of Mississippi volunteers in the Army of the Republic of Texas in 1841. Elected lieutenant colonel, 4th Louisiana Infantry, May 25, 1861. Promoted colonel, March 21, 1862. Promoted brigadier general August 19, 1863. Resigned January 10, 1864, after being elected governor of Louisiana.
15. Warley, "A Trifling Reminiscence of the War."
16. William Mervine (1791-1868). Appointed midshipman, January 16, 1819. Promoted through the grades to the rank of captain, September 8, 1841, Placed on the Retired List, July 16, 1862. Promoted to rear admiral on the Retired List, August 6, 1866.
17. *N. O. R.,* 16:589.
18. Ibid., 598.
19. Ibid., 644-645.
20. Ibid., 662-664.
21. Theodorus Bailey (1805-1877). Appointed midshipman, January 1, 1818. Promoted through the grades to the rank of rear admiral, July 25, 1866. Placed on the Retired List, October 10, 1866.
22. It is very likely the guard consisted of Confederate States Marines. The Confederate States Marine Battalion was stationed at the Pensacola Navy Yard during the time the cutting out operation took place, and there are references to Marine officers being on duty at the guardhouse in the papers of Alfred Van Benthuysen in the Special Collections Branch of the Tulane University Library at New Orleans, Louisiana.
23. RG 24, Deck Logs. Log of USS *Niagara,* August 3, 1861.
24. *N. O. R.,* 16:610-612.
25. Ibid., 664.
26. John Henry Russell (1827-1897). Appointed midshipman, U.S. Naval Academy, September 10, 1841. Graduated, passed midshipman, August 10, 1847. Promoted through the grades to the rank of rear admiral, March 4, 1886. Placed on the Retired List, August 27, 1886. Russell was the brother of Maj. William W. Russell, Paymaster, United States Marine Corps, and father of Maj. Gen. John H. Russell, 16th Commandant of the Marine Corps.
27. From an undated newspaper clipping from *The Sunday Chronicle,* place of publication unknown, found in Subject Files, Subfile HA, "Engagements With Enemy War Vessels," filed in support of John H. Russell's claim for advancement "on the list," August 2, 1869.
28. *Memphis Daily Avalanche*, September 19, 1861, p. 1, col. 2. "Letter from Pensacola."
29. Boatswain's Mate Charles Lamphere and Seaman John Herring were initially interred with Marine Pvt. John Smith near Fort Pickens. All three were later moved to Barrancas National Cemetery where they lie in adjoining plots.
30. See note 24 above. Other accounts give Asst. Eng. George H. White credit for bringing the sniper down.

31. *Daily Avalanche,* "Letter from Pensacola." It is very likely these "regulars" were Confederate States Marines. See note 34, below.
32. Private Charles Carberry, an immigrant from County Donegal, Ireland, enlisted at Philadelphia, December 3, 1860. While engaged in the hand to hand combat aboard *Judah,* Carberry was struck by a pistol bullet above the left temple, causing a skull fracture and damage to the temporal artery. Despite the severity of his injury, Carberry recovered and served out his enlistment, being discharged on December 4, 1864. Carberry's post-war years were a continuous bout with increasingly painful headaches, dizziness, and loss of memory. In 1871, no longer able to work at his house painting trade, Carberry applied for a pension and was awarded $3.00 per month, increased to $4.00 in 1886. Wandering the Pacific Coast for many years, Carberry passed away at San Francisco in early 1891. Pension Application (Navy) 1634 of Charles Carberry, National Archives.
33. *N. O. R.,* 16:672–673.
34. *Montgomery Daily Mail,* September 17, 1861, p. 1, col. 1, "Down in Alabama!" It was reported by an escaped slave from Pensacola that the majority of casualties on the Confederate side were suffered by the Confederate States Marine Battalion. See Donnelly, *The Rebel Leathernecks,* 22.
35. *N. O. R.,* 16:672.
36. RG 109, Entry 265. S. O. 227, Headquarters Troops, C.S. near Pensacola, September 9, 1861.
37. *N. O. R.,* 16:675. The nine Confederate States Marines who deserted on September 8, were all Northern men cut off at New Orleans when the war started. They all claimed to have joined the Marine Corps out of economic necessity or coercion, and as an opportunity to escape to the North. They did not assist the boat expedition. See Donnelly, *The Rebel Leathernecks,* 21.
38. Johnson Kelly Duncan (1827–1862). U.S. Military Academy, Class of 1849. Service during the Seminole War of 1849–1850. Resigned, 1855. Appointed colonel of the 1st Louisiana Artillery, 1861. Promoted brigadier general, January 7, 1862. Died of fever at Knoxville, Tennessee, December 18, 1862.
39. Robbins, "When the Rebels Lost Ship Island," 43–44.
40. Ibid., 45.
41. RG 24, Deck Logs. Log of USS *Massachusetts,* September 17, 1861.
42. Easton enlisted in the Marine Corps on March 6, 1861, after serving two enlistments with the 2d U.S. Artillery Regiment. RG 127, Service Records.
43. Thomas McKean Buchanan (?–1863). Appointed acting midshipman, U.S. Naval Academy, October 1, 1851. Graduated midshipman April 15, 1855. Promoted through the grades to lieutenant commander, August 5, 1862. Died, January 14, 1863. Nephew of Rear Adm. Franklin Buchanan, CSN.
44. Buchanan to Commander M. Smith, Ship Island, November 19, 1861. RG 127, Letters Received-GR.
45. Smith to McKean, U.S. Steamer *Massachusetts,* November 26, 1861. RG 127, Letters Received-GR.
46. Welles to Harris, Navy Department, February 11, 1862. RG 127, Letters Received-GR.
47. *N. O. R.,* 6:790. The steamer *Constitution* left Hampton Roads on November 27.
48. John Wolcott Phelps (1813–1885). U.S. Military Academy, Class of 1836. Served during the Seminole and Mexican Wars, declining a brevet commission to captain for gallant service during the latter conflict. Resigned, 1859. Appointed colonel of the 1st Vermont Infantry, May 9, 1861. Promoted brigadier general of volunteers, August 9, 1861. Resigned, August 21, 1862.
49. *N. O. R.,* 17:4.
50. Ibid., 16:552–553.
51. Ibid., 554.
52. Ibid., 694.
53. Ibid., 735–736.

54. *O. R.*, 6:460-463.
55. RG 24, Deck Logs. Log of USS *Potomac*, October 9, 1861.
56. Ramsay to Harris, U.S. Sloop *Richmond*, November 27, 1861. RG 80, Letters from Marine Officers.
57. McLane Tilton to "My dear Uncle," Off Fort Pickens, Fla., October 28, 1861. McLane Tilton Papers, MCHC.
58. *N. O. R.*, 16:766.
59. RG 24, Deck Logs. Log of USS *Niagara*, September 20, 1861.
60. *N. O. R.*, 16:683.
61. *N. O. R.*, 16:699-700.
62. George Nichols Hollins (1799-1878). Appointed midshipman, February 1, 1814. Promoted through the grades to the rank of captain, September 14, 1855. Dismissed from the service, June 6, 1861. Appointed captain, CSN, June 22, 1861.
63. "The Manassas. The Part She Played in the Naval Drama." *New Orleans Daily True Delta*, Tuesday Morning, October 15, 1861. p. 1, cols. 5-6. The rebel account of the incident erroneously named the *Preble*, rather than the *Richmond*, as the victim of *Manassas*.
64. Robert Handy (?-1884). Appointed midshipman, February 1, 1826. Promoted through the grades to the rank of commander, September 14, 1855. Placed on the Retired List, February 6, 1862. Promoted to commodore on the Retired List, April 4, 1867.
65. *N. O. R.*, 16:711
66. Ibid., 719-720. Sworn statements of Signal Quartermaster William Burrows and Seaman Nathaniel P. Allen.
67. Ibid., 710.
68. Porter, *Naval History of the Civil War*, 91. Both Pope and Handy were relieved of their commands as a result of their October 12, 1861, performances in the face of an inferior enemy force.
69. Later named CSS *Selma* and attached to the Mobile Squadron.
70. *N. O. R.*, 16:742-744.
71. Thomas Oliver Selfridge, Sr. (1804-1902). Appointed midshipman, January 1, 1818. Promoted through the grades to the rank of commodore, July 16, 1862. Placed on the Retired List, April 24, 1866. Promoted to rear admiral on the Retired List, July 25, 1866. Selfridge to McKean, USS *Mississippi*, November 16, 1861. Selfridge Family Papers, Library of Congress. Baker was transferred aboard USS *Connecticut* on November 21. He languished in prison at Fort Lafayette until his uncle, Surg. Adam N. McLaren, USA, arranged for his release on February 22, 1862. After remaining idle at his family homestead at Orange, Massachusetts for several months, Baker joined the 15th Massachusetts Infantry, and shortly after joining the regiment, was killed in action at the Battle of Antietam. See Sullivan, "The Puzzle of Adam N. Baker," *Military Collector and Historian* (Spring 1989): 4.
72. Francis Bleeker Ellison (1803-1884). Appointed midshipman May 28, 1819. Promoted through the grades to the rank of commodore on the Retired List, April 4, 1867. *N. O. R.*, 16:778.
73. Alfred Crippen Van Benthuysen (1836-1871). A soldier of fortune who fought in the Crimean War, the Taiping Rebellion in China, and the Italian Wars of Liberation. Appointed captain of Confederate States Marines on March 30, 1861. Van Benthuysen was related to the family of Jefferson Davis by marriage, his aunt being the sister-in-law to the Confederate President.
74. Report of Capt. A. C. Van Benthuysen, November 26, 1861. Van Benthuysen Pp, Tulane University.
75. Daniel Weisiger Adams (1821-1872). Appointed lieutenant colonel, 1st Louisiana Regulars, February 5, 1861. Promoted colonel, October 30, 1861. Promoted brigadier general, May 23, 1862.
76. *O. R.*, 6:495.

77. Ibid., 658–659.
78. John Slidell (1793–1871). Louisiana Democratic politician. Member of Congress, 1843–1845, and U.S. Senator, 1853–1861.
79. RG 24, Deck Logs. Log of USS *San Jacinto,* November 8, 1861.
80. *N. O. R.,* 1:133–134.
81. Ibid., 135.
82. Ibid., 163.
83. John P. Fredd, "Civil War Blockade," *Recruiter's Bulletin* (March 1916): 12.
84. Thompson Darrah Shaw (?–1874). Appointed midshipman, May 10, 1820. Promoted through the grades to the rank of commander, August 7, 1850. Placed on the Retired List February 26, 1862. Promoted to commodore on the Retired List, April 4, 1867.
85. *N. O. R.,* 16:808.
86. Abner Read (?–July 12, 1863). Appointed midshipman, March 2, 1839. Promoted through the grades to the rank of commander, September 13, 1862. Died, July 12, 1863, from wounds received in action against rebel field batteries near Donaldsonville, Louisiana, July 7, 1863.
87. *N. O. R.,* 16:810–811.
88. Ibid., 811–812.
89. RG 24, Deck Logs. Logs of USS *Massachusetts, Niagara,* and *New London,* December 31, 1861. The Marines from *Niagara* had returned to their ship from garrison duty at Ship Island on December 26.
90. Ibid., Log of USS *New London.*
91. *N. O. R.,* 17:34.
92. Francis Winslow (?–1862). Appointed midshipman, July 8, 1833. Promoted through the grades to the rank of commander, May 6, 1862. Died, August 26, 1862.
93. *N. O. R.,* 17:60.
94. John Van Ness Philip (?–1862). Acting midshipman, U.S. Naval Academy, February 25, 1856. Promoted through the grades to the rank of lieutenant, Resigned June 26, 1857. Appointed acting lieutenant May 14, 1861. Died in service September 3, 1862.
95. Levin Minn Powell (1803–1885). Appointed midshipman, March 1, 1817. Promoted through the grades to the rank of captain, September 14, 1855. Placed on the Retired List, December 21, 1861. Promoted to commodore, July 16, 1862, and rear admiral, July 25, 1866, on the Retired List.
96. Humphrey entered the Naval Academy on September 22, 1858, but would be forced to resign from the service and the Academy in October 1862 due to poor eyesight. He was, nevertheless, appointed a second lieutenant of Marines to rank from March 10, 1863. John Joseph Read (1842–1910). Appointed acting midshipman, U.S. Naval Academy, September 21, 1858. Promoted through the grades to the rank of rear admiral, November 29, 1900. Retired List, June 17, 1904.
97. *N. O. R.,* 17:58–63.
98. Ibid., 88–89.
99. RG 24, Deck Logs. Log of USS *New London,* March 1, 1862.
100. Henry S. Stellwagen (?–1866). Appointed midshipman, April 1, 1828. Promoted through the grades to the rank of captain, September 14, 1855. Retired List, December 24, 1865. Died, July 15, 1866. Trevett Abbot, U.S. Naval Academy, 1848. Promoted through the grades to the rank of commander, December 12, 1867. Died, October 27, 1869.
101. *N. O. R.,* 17:194–195.
102. Ibid., 202–203.

Bibliography

Books

Baltimore & Ohio Rail Road Company. *Book of the Royal Blue.* Baltimore, 1903.

Burton, Amos. *Cruise of the U.S. Ship Susquehanna during the years 1860, 1861, 1862 and 1863.* New York, 1863.

Carter, Robert G., Capt., U.S.A., Ret. *Four Brothers in Blue or Sunshine and Shadows of the War of the Rebellion.* Austin, 1978.

Collum, Richard S., Major, USMC. *History of the United States Marine Corps.* New York, 1902.

Dahlgren, Madeline Vinton. *Memoir of John A. Dahlgren, Rear-Admiral, United States Navy.* New York, 1891.

Donnelly, Ralph W. *Biographical Sketches of the Commissioned Officers of the Confederate States Marine Corps.* Washington, N.C., 1983.

———. *The Confederate States Marine Corps: The Rebel Leathernecks.* Shippensburg, Penna., 1989.

Drew, Thomas. *The John Brown Invasion: An Authentic History of the Harper's Ferry Tragedy. . . .* Boston, 1860.

Dudley, William S. *Going South: U.S. Navy Officer Resignations & Dismissals on the Eve of the Civil War.* Washington, 1980.

Eckert, Edward K., and Nicholas J. Amato, eds. *Ten Years in the Saddle: The Memoir of William Woods Averell.* San Rafael, Calif., 1978.

Evans, Clement A. *Confederate Military History.* 17 vols. Reprint, Wilmington, N.C., 1989.

Fairfield, C. B., comp. *History of the 27th Regiment, N.Y. Volunteers.* Binghamton, N.Y., 1888.

Fonerdon, C. A. *Military History of Carpenter's Battery.* New Market, Va., 1911.

Freeman, Douglas S. *R. E. Lee: A Biography.* 4 vols. New York, 1934-1935.

Gallegher, Gary W., ed. *Fighting for the Confederacy: The Personal Recollections of General Edward Porter Alexander.* Chapel Hill, N.C., 1989.

Gammon, Rev. John G. *The Third Massachusetts Regiment, Volunteer Militia in the War of the Rebellion, 1861–1863.* Providence, R.I., 1906.

Hayes, John S. Rear Admiral, USN (Ret.), ed. 3 vols. *Samuel Francis DuPont: A Selection from his Civil War Letters.* Ithaca, N.Y., 1969.

Jeffrey, William H. *Richmond Prisons, 1861–1862.* St. Johnsbury, Vt., 1893.

Keller, Allan. *Thunder at Harpers Ferry.* Englewood, N.J., 1958.

Leech, Margaret. *Reveille in Washington, 1860–1865.* New York, 1941.

Maryland State Senate. *Document Y, Correspondence Relating to the Insurrection at Harper's Ferry, 17th October, 1859.* Annapolis, Md., 1860.

McClellan, Maj. H. B. *The Life, Character and Campaigns of Major-Gen. J. E. B. Stuart.* Richmond, Va., 1880.

McPherson, Edward, ed. *The Political History of the United States of America during the Great Rebellion.* Washington, 1865.

Miller, William Owen. *In Campaign and Battle with the Washington Artillery of New Orleans.* Boston, Mass., 1885.

Morgan, William James et al., eds. *Autobiography of Rear Admiral Charles Wilkes, U.S. Navy, 1798-1877.* Washington, 1978.

Oates, Stephen B. *With Malice Toward None: The Life of Abraham Lincoln.* New York, 1977.

Porter, David D. *The Naval History of the Civil War.* New York, 1886.

Proceedings of a Marine General Court Martial Convened at Washington City, May 7, 1862, for the Trial of Lieut. Col. John Geo. Reynolds, U.S. Marine Corps. Washington, 1862.

Rhodes, Robert H., ed. *All for the Union.* Lincoln, R.I., 1985.

Rives, John C., pub. *The Congressional Globe: Containing the Debates and Proceedings of the First Session of the Thirty-seventh Congress.* Washington, 1861.

Scharf, Col. J. Thomas. *The Chronicles of Baltimore.* Baltimore, Md., 1874.

Sloan, Edward William, III. *Benjamin Franklin Isherwood, Naval Engineer.* Annapolis, Md., 1965.

Symonds, Craig L., ed. *Charleston Blockade: The Journals of John B. Marchand, U.S. Navy, 1861-1862.* Newport, R.I., 1976.

Tevis, Charles. *The History of the Fighting Fourteenth.* New York, 1911.

Villard, Oswald Garrison. *John Brown, 1800-1859: A Biography Fifty Years After.* Boston, 1910.

Articles

Ammen, Daniel. "DuPont and the Port Royal Expedition." *Battles and Leaders of the Civil War.* 4 vols. 1:671-691. New York, 1887.

Barrett, Edwin S. "Adventures at Bull Run." *The Civil War in Song and Story, 1860-1865.* 256-261. P. F. Collier, 1889.

Belknap, George E. "The Home Squadron in the Winter of 1860-1861." *Naval Actions and History, 1799-1898.* 75-100. Boston, 1902.

Boteler, Alexander R. "Recollections of the John Brown Raid." *Century Magazine* 26 (July 1883): 399-411.

Conrad, Daniel B. "History of the First Battle of Manassas and the Organization of the Stonewall Brigade." *Southern Historical Society Papers* 19 (January-December 1891): 82-94.

Cummings, Arthur. "Colonel Cummings' Account." *Southern Historical Society Papers* 34 (January-December 1906): 367-371.

Daingerfield, John E. P. "The Fight at the Engine-house as Seen by One of his Prisoners." *Century Magazine* 30 (June 1885): 267.

Donnelly, Ralph W. "Notes of an Old-time Marine Officer, Lt. A. J. Hays." *Military Collector and Historian* 42 (Fall 1990): 97-98.

Flanders, Alan B. "The Night They Burned the Norfolk Navy Yard." *Civil War Times Illustrated* 18 (February 1980): 30-39.

Fredd, John P. "Civil War Blockade." *Recruiter's Bulletin* (March 1916): 12.

Green(e), Israel. "The Capture of John Brown." *North American Review* 141 (December 1885): 564-569.

Hayes, John D., ed. "The Battle of Port Royal, S.C., from the Journal of John Sanford Barnes, October 8 to November 9, 1861." *New York Historical Society Quarterly* 45 (October 1961): 365-395.

——, and O'Brien, Lillian, eds. "The Early Blockade And the Capture of the Hatteras Forts, From the Journal of John Sanford

Barnes, July 19 to September 1, 1861." *New York Historical Society Quarterly* 46 (January 1962): 61-85.

Imboden, John D. "Incidents of the First Bull Run." *Battles and Leaders of the Civil War.* 4 vols. 1: 229-239. New York, 1887.

Kallina, Paul. "Letters from a Civil War Marine." *Marine Corps Gazette* (November 1981): 47-48.

Mackie, John F. "The Destruction of the Norfolk Navy Yard." *Home and Country* 4 (February-May 1889): 1011-1012, 1041, 1057-1058, 1062-1063.

Miller, J. Michael. "Marine's Telling of 1861 Florida Navy Yard Fall Given." *Fortitudine* 20 (Spring 1991): 8-9.

Parker, Daingerfield. "Personal Reminiscences: The Battalion of Regular Infantry at the First Battle of Bull Run." *Military Order of the Loyal Legion of the United States, Commandery of the District of Columbia War Papers.* Washington, 1899.

Reisinger, Harold C. "Andrew Mealy and the Mongoose." *Marine Corps Gazette* (February 1932): 41, 52.

Robbins, Peggy. "When the Rebels Lost Ship Island." *Civil War Times Illustrated* 84 (January 1979): 4-9, 42-45.

Sullivan, David M. "Baptism of Fire." *Pensacola History Illustrated* 1 (1984): 9-14.

———. "The Puzzle of Adam N. Baker." *Military Collector and Historian* 41 (Spring 1989): 2-7.

———. "A Glimpse of the Virginia Marine Corps." *Military Collector and Historian* 44 (Winter 1992): 171-174.

———. "What Became of Corporal Toombs?" *Military Collector and Historian* 45 (Spring 1993): 2-7.

———. "Every Inch a Rebel of the Deepest Dye: The Strange Case of Jabez C. Rich." *Military Collector and Historian* 45 (Fall 1993): 110-116.

Manuscripts

Historical Society of Delaware, Wilmington, Delaware

Jones Family Papers

Duke University, William R. Perkins Library, Durham, North Carolina

Louis M. Goldsborough Papers

William W. Russell and John C. Cash Papers

Hagley Museum and Library, Wilmington, Delaware

DuPont Family Papers

- Library of Congress
  - Cartter Family Papers
  - Francis and George Gardner Papers
  - Louis M. Goldsborough Papers
  - Francis M. Scala Collection
  - Winfield Scott Papers
- Marine Corps Historical Center, Washington, D.C.
  - Personal Papers Branch
    - John Lloyd Broome Papers
    - Robert E. Hitchcock Papers
    - Robert W. Huntington Papers
    - Daniel O'Connor Papers
    - George Croghan Reid Papers
    - McLane Tilton Papers
  - Historical Reference Branch
    - Harpers Ferry File
    - Civil War File
    - Biographical Files
- National Archives, Washington, D.C.
  - Record Group 24
    - Bureau of Naval Personnel, Deck Logs
  - Record Group 45
    - Naval Records Collection of the Office of Naval Records and Library
      - Area File of the Naval Records Collection
      - Key to Office Letters
      - Naval General Courts-Martial and Courts of Inquiry
      - Subject File of the United States Navy
  - Record Group 80
    - General Records of the Navy Department
  - Record Group 94
    - Records of the Adjutant General
  - Record Group 109
    - War Department Collection of Confederate Records

Record Group 125

Records of the Judge Advocate General (Navy)

Record Group 127

Records of the United States Marine Corps

New York State Archives

Robert Galbraith Papers

George Riddell Papers

Tulane University Library, New Orleans, Louisiana

Jefferson Davis Collection

United States Army Military History Institute, Carlisle Barracks, Pennsylvania

Civil War Miscellaneous Collection

U.S. Government Documents

Congress. *Report of the Joint Committee on the Conduct of the War.* Washington, 1863.

House of Representatives. *Mis. Doc. No. 30, 37th Congress, 3d Session,* February 23, 1863.

Navy Department. *Official Records of the Union and Confederate Navies in the War of the Rebellion.* 30 vols. and index. Washington, 1894-1922.

——. *Laws relating to the Navy and Marine Corps, and the Navy Department.* Washington, 1865.

——. *Register of the Commissioned and Warrant Officers of the Navy of the United States, including Officers of the Marine Corps and Others for the Year 1861.* Washington, 1861.

Senate. *Executive Document No. 9, 40th Congress, 1st Session.* Washington, 1867.

——. *Executive Journal,* vol. 2, 1858-1861. Washington, 1862.

——. *Report of the Select Committee, 36th Congress, 1st Session.* Washington, 1860.

——. *Senate Document No. 234, 58th Congress, 2d Session, Journal of the Congress of the Confederate States of America: 1861-1865.* Washington, 1904-1905.

Newspapers

Alton (Illinois) Evening Democrat

Brooklyn Daily Eagle

Memphis Commercial Appeal
Memphis Daily Avalanche
Montgomery Daily Mail
New Orleans Daily Picayune
New Orleans Daily True Delta
New York Herald
New York Times
Pittsburgh Post
Richmond Free Press
Sioux Falls (South Dakota) Argus Leader
Washington Evening Star

Index

C

I

J

T

V

W

Y

Z